Faith in Black Power

FAITH IN
BLACK POWER

RELIGION, RACE, AND RESISTANCE
IN CAIRO, ILLINOIS

KERRY PIMBLOTT

 UNIVERSITY PRESS OF KENTUCKY

Scholarly publisher for the Commonwealth,
serving Bellarmine University, Berea College, Centre College of Kentucky, Eastern
Kentucky University, The Filson Historical Society, Georgetown College, Kentucky
Historical Society, Kentucky State University, Morehead State University, Murray
State University, Northern Kentucky University, Transylvania University, University
of Kentucky, University of Louisville, and Western Kentucky University.
All rights reserved.

Editorial and Sales Offices: The University Press of Kentucky
663 South Limestone Street, Lexington, Kentucky 40508-4008
www.kentuckypress.com

Library of Congress Cataloging-in-Publication Data

Names: Pimblott, Kerry, author.
Title: Faith in black power : religion, race, and resistance in Cairo,
    Illinois / Kerry Pimblott.
Other titles: Religion, race, and resistance in Cairo, Illinois
Description: Lexington, Kentucky : University Press of Kentucky, [2017] |
    Series: Civil rights and the struggle for black equality in the twentieth
    century | Includes bibliographical references and index.
Identifiers: LCCN 2016046789| ISBN 9780813168821 (hardcover : alk. paper) |
    ISBN 9780813168913 (pdf) | ISBN 9780813168906 (epub)
Subjects: LCSH: Civil rights movements—Illinois—Cairo. | Cairo (Ill.)—Race
    relations. | African Americans—Illinois—Cairo—History. | Black power. |
    African American churches—History. | Civil rights—Religious
    aspects—Christianity. | Race relations—Religious aspects—Christianity.
    | Cairo (Ill.)—History—20th century.
Classification: LCC F549.C2 P56 2017 | DDC 323.1196073/999—dc23
LC record available at https://lccn.loc.gov/2016046789

ISBN 978-0-8131-7847-9 (pbk. : alk. paper)

In Memory of Mark H. Leff

Contents

Figures and Table

Abbreviations

AME	African Methodist Episcopal Church
BEDC	Black Economic Development Conference
BEU	Black Economic Union
BPP	Black Panther Party
CAP	Congress of African Peoples
CCA	Cairo Citizens Association
CME	Colored Methodist Episcopal
CNVFC	Cairo Nonviolent Freedom Committee
COGIC	Church of God in Christ
COINTELPRO	Counterintelligence Program
CORAR	Commission on Race and Religion (United Presbyterian Church)
CORE	Congress of Racial Equality
CRC	Cairo Recreational Committee
EEOC	Equal Employment Opportunities Commission
FBI	Federal Bureau of Investigation
GCSP	General Convention Special Program (Episcopal Church)
ICC	Illinois Conference of Churches
ICR	Illinois Central Railroad
IFCO	Interreligious Foundation for Community Organization
IIC	Illinois Interracial Commission
IMC	Illinois Migrant Council
IRS	Internal Revenue Service
NAACP	National Association for the Advancement of Colored People
NBC	National Broadcasting Company
NCBC	National Conference of Black Churchmen
NCC	National Council of Churches
NOI	Nation of Islam

NPO	Nonprofit organization
OAAU	Organization of Afro-American Unity
OEO	Office of Economic Opportunity
SCLC	Southern Christian Leadership Conference
SDOP	National Committee on the Self-Development of People (United Presbyterian Church)
SIAP	Southern Illinois Association of Priests
SICA	Southern Illinois Cooperative Association
SIU	Southern Illinois University Carbondale
SNCC	Student Nonviolent Coordinating Committee
UCC	United Church of Christ
UCC-CRJ	United Church of Christ Commission for Racial Justice
UCCA	United Citizens for Community Action
UCF	United Christian Front
UCHC	United Cairo Housing Corporation
UMC	United Methodist Church
WCC	White Citizens' Council
WPA	Works Progress Administration

Introduction

On March 13, 1971, the United Front—a nationally renowned black power organization based in Cairo, Illinois—published an article written by sixteen-year-old Oklahoman Karen Rice in its weekly paper the *United Front News*. In the article, entitled "The Movement, God and Me," Rice testified to her political "awakening" while attending a Lutheran conference in Chicago. During the conference, attendees were encouraged to "get together with others of [their] own race and discover themselves as a group of people." African American students joined together in forming a black caucus called Black Youth Unlimited and, according to Rice, were "completely de-brainwashed" and "blackenized" by the experience. However, upon returning home to Tulsa, Rice struggled to find practical outlets for her heightened sense of racial consciousness. She joined a gospel troupe called the Ghetto Choir and began performing in black communities across the country, but she continued to have doubts about her role in the movement and began increasingly to doubt the relevance of her Christian faith to the black liberation struggle. "I knew that the choir was working through the hands of Jesus Christ," she explained, "but I just was not sure if this was my role in the movement." In particular, Rice struggled to reconcile her emergent sense of black consciousness with popular conceptions of Christianity as the "white man's religion": "How can we believe in something that was taught to us by the white man?" Rice asked. "It seemed [as] though our oppressor had given us this religion called Christianity so that he could control us." This, Rice explained, is probably "why black people have been a non-violent people for so long."

However, in November 1970 Rice travelled with the Ghetto Choir to Cairo, Illinois, where her understanding of the relationship between African American Christianity and black power would be radically transformed. In Cairo, Rice experienced firsthand local activists proclaiming a reconstructed and relevant black theology centered on the black experience and committed to black liberation. "After we visited this city," Rice

1

wrote, "I finally had found the answer that I have been looking for for over a year." Far from abandoning the faith, Rice explained, black power activists in Cairo demonstrated "that the way to win this battle was by living the gospel preached in the Holy Bible."[1]

Penned at the height of the black power movement, Karen Rice's articulation of one African American girl's personal struggle to reconcile her faith with the cause of black liberation resonates with a set of broader concerns that emerged in movement circles during the course of the 1960s. At the height of the movement's "heroic" phase, national civil rights organizations expressed a predominant commitment to a radical egalitarian ideology that combined a sharp critique of American racism with a patriotic appeal for the nation to make good on its stated ideals of liberty and justice for all. This liberal-integrationist ideology was often, though not always, infused with Christian discourses regarding the redemptive power of nonviolent acts in the service of racial reconciliation and the creation of a multiracial democratic "Beloved Community." As the decade wore on, however, a growing number of civil rights liberals, disillusioned by persistent violence and the glacial pace of change, began to openly question the efficacy of the movement's integrationist aims and nonviolent strategies as well as its attendant religious discourses.[2]

Longstanding fissures within civil rights organizations burst to the surface as movement participants took sharp aim at the philosophy of racial reconciliation and redemptive suffering. "I never saw my responsibility to be the moral and spiritual reclamation of some racist thug," expressed Student Nonviolent Coordinating Committee (SNCC) leader Stokely Carmichael (Kwame Ture). "I would settle for changing his behavior period." SNCC worker Cleveland Sellers agreed: "We did not believe that we were fighting to create a morally straight America. We were essentially concerned with power. Integration was never seen as anything more than a means to an end." For those who initially embraced the logic of racial reconciliation, the steady specter of racial violence and the absence of state protection often came to undermine the Beloved Community's realization and brought into question the utility of nonviolent strategies that had presumed the existence of a moral conscience to which the sins of white America could be appealed. In the wake of the 1963 bombing of the Sixteenth Street Baptist Church in Birmingham, Alabama, Anne

Moody, who had participated in the sit-ins, recalled vowing to God that she would "never be beaten by a white man again." As she communed with the divine, Moody declared: "Nonviolence is out. . . . If you don't believe that, then I know you must be white, too. And if I ever find out you are white, then I'm through with you. And if I find out you are black, I'll try my best to kill you when I get to heaven." While civil rights workers in the Deep South were losing the faith, poet and activist Amiri Baraka (LeRoi Jones) gave voice to a new generation of African American youth growing up in the nation's urban ghettoes, a world in which civil rights' emphasis on the power of nonviolence and moral suasion simply did not register. "We younger Blacks," Baraka explained, "out of school or the service or in the factories and warehouses and docks knew being 'righteous' or 'good' had never worked, except if you could fight." Thus, he argued, "The Christian essence of 'the movement' was lost to us."[3]

By the end of the 1960s, liberal-integrationism was supplanted by a black nationalist ideology that emphasized the immutable nature of racism in American society and the corollary need for racial unity and black self-determination. A blossoming of new grassroots black power organizations advocated a range of strategies to achieve black empowerment, including the formation of independent black political organizations, the establishment of black cooperatives and business enterprises, the promotion of black education and culture, and the use of armed self-help. In this moment of ideological and strategic upheaval, youthful activists often cast aside the Christian underpinnings of earlier civil rights campaigns in favor of greater tactical flexibility and what Black Panther Party (BPP) leader Huey P. Newton called "a more concrete understanding of social conditions," rooted less in the Bible than in the works of political radicals like Karl Marx, Mao Tse-tung, Frantz Fanon, and Malcolm X.[4]

As movement participants questioned whether liberal-integrationist and nonviolent strategies rooted in Christian discourses could facilitate black liberation, others audaciously contended that Christianity was in fact the primary instrument of African Americans' oppression. Strident critiques of Christianity came from the Nation of Islam (NOI), an organization that had garnered considerable support among working-class African Americans in northern cities. The organization's leader, Elijah Muhammad, spoke directly to African Americans like Rice, who had come of age in the black church.[5] Christianity, according to Muhammad, was a religion "organized and backed by the devils [white people] for the purpose of making slaves of black mankind." Muhammad explained how Christianity enslaved blacks by offering an "otherworldly" faith that promoted love for the enemy over love and protection of self and community.[6]

During the early 1960s, Elijah Muhammad's teachings on Christianity were translated to a national audience by his best-known student, Malcolm X (el-Hajj Malik el-Shabazz). In a 1963 interview Malcolm spoke to the sea change in consciousness he saw taking place in many urban communities: "The black masses that are waking up don't believe in Christianity anymore. All it's done for black men is help to keep them slaves." He asserted, "Intelligent black men today are interested in a religious doctrine that offers a solution to their problems right now, right here on this earth, while they are alive." Although only a relative handful of African Americans would follow Malcolm X into the NOI, theologian Gayraud Wilmore contends that many "believed he spoke the truth about Christianity being a religion for White people" and turned their backs on the black church.[7]

This broader historical context has led black freedom studies scholars such as political scientist Judson Jeffries to claim that Christianity simply "did not figure as prominently in the black power movement as it did in the civil rights movement." While local black power activists may have been churchgoers, Jeffries insists that "none of the commonly known leaders of the movement manifested a positive view of Christianity."[8] Indeed, while scholarship on the modern civil rights movement's "heroic" phase emphasizes the centrality of African American religious institutions and beliefs to effective movement mobilization,[9] popular and scholarly accounts of black power depict a movement marked by a profound *de-Christianization*.[10] According to standard accounts, as the black freedom movement shifted from its origins in the US South to the streets of the urban North, from racial reconciliation to black community-focused initiatives, and from nonviolence to armed self-defense, the legitimacy of Christian discourses and the organizational significance of the black church were progressively undermined. Some have gone so far as to suggest that black power's abandonment of its spiritual moorings contributed to the movement's *declension* by "jettisoning . . . the moral and social anchors that had helped regulate relationships among activists" and alienating important coalitional allies.[11]

Black Power and the Black Church

Karen Rice's story—like those of many lesser-known black power activists—raises important questions about black power's de-Christianization and bolsters recent calls from scholars in the emergent subfield of "black power studies" to probe more deeply the relationship between the black church, African American Christianity, and the black power movement.[12] The past two decades have witnessed a veritable explosion in scholarship on black power, including national narratives, organizational histories, and community-based studies that have contributed immeasurably to our understanding of the movement's dynamics.[13] However, though local studies of black power struggles in cities like Baltimore, Detroit, and Milwaukee note the continued participation of black churches, clergy, and laypersons, there has been little sustained analysis of the character, extent, or significance of the black church's involvement or the broader influence, if any, of African American Christian discourses to movement mobilization.[14]

This neglect is particularly surprising considering that scholars in the field of African American religious studies have consistently acknowledged the transformative effect of black power on the black church and African American theological traditions. Indeed, religious studies scholars including Gayraud Wilmore, C. Eric Lincoln, and Lawrence Mamiya situate black power as a watershed moment in the development of black religious thought and institutions.[15] The widespread interest of African American clergy in black power and the ideology of black nationalism was perhaps most visible in the proliferation of autonomous black church caucuses, task forces, and ecumenical bodies, most notably the National Committee of Negro Churchmen (later renamed the National Conference of Black Churchmen [NCBC]), during the late 1960s and 1970s. Through these new organizations, African American clergy worked to make the church relevant to the struggles of black communities.[16] They leveraged denominational resources and, as potently elaborated in the writings of such theologians as James Cone and Albert Cleage, developed a systematic black theology centered on the black experience and committed to black liberation.[17] However, religious studies scholars have tended to gloss over any broader effect of these new forces on local black power struggles, presuming that emergent religious bodies lacked the necessary coordination and support and that black theology was an academic pursuit, largely confined to the seminary.[18]

Shifting the focus from the seminary to the streets, this study breaks with the preceding scholarship and calls for a broader reassessment of the relationship between the black church and the black power movement. It addresses a series of pertinent historical questions: What was the nature of the relationship between the black church, African American Christianity, and grassroots black power struggles? To what extent did urban rebellions and an ascendant "new nationalism" disrupt the dominant civil rights discourse of racial reconciliation and nonviolence, and how did they jeopardize the black church's participation in black freedom struggles? How did local black power activists in Cairo transform existing theologies and institutions to meet the changing social and political realities of their historical moment? Did local activists engage the new innovations in black theology? Were meaningful ties established between local black power organizations and emergent black church caucuses, task forces, and ecumenical bodies? Most critically, how did the black church's involvement in Cairo's black power struggles influence the movement's organizational structure, leadership, ideology, and strategies?

In the process of addressing these questions, *Faith in Black Power* makes several claims about the relationship between black power, the black church, and African American Christianity. At the broadest level this study challenges dominant conceptions of black power's de-Christianization by demonstrating the sustained and pivotal role played by the black church and African American Christian discourses to movement mobilization in Cairo. While the changing political and economic realities of the black power era were disruptive to the dominant civil rights ideology and coalition, black religious discourses and institutions continued to provide the basis for a coherent movement culture, unifying ideology, and renewed access to the black church's tremendous organizational resources.

More specifically, *Faith in Black Power* shows that in their efforts to construct a viable black power movement, activists in the Cairo United Front forged important connections with nationally prominent black theologians, urban ministers, and their affiliated organizations. Taking advantage of the political opportunity provided by the urban rebellions, the United Front partnered with black church executives in exerting pressure on predominantly white denominations to render the church relevant to black liberation by extending their tremendous organizational resources to local black power organizations. Between 1969 and 1974 these efforts were remarkably successful, resulting in the transfer of more than $500,000 in grants to the United Front as well as extensive lobbying, consultancy, and legal support. Grant-awarding bodies, including the Interreligious Foundation for Community Organization (IFCO), the Episcopal Church's General Convention Special Program (GCSP), and the Presbyterian Church's National Committee on the Self-Development of People (SDOP), extended critical resources that sustained the United Front's daily operations and political programming. In contrast to federal or corporate support, church-based grants were malleable and were extended with relatively few strings, making them particularly attractive to black power activists. As a result, churches made critical contributions to those components of the United Front's operations that a governmental or corporate agency would not support, including staff salaries, office space, travel expenses, and bail bonds. Further, church-based organizations extended seed money for the initiation of the United Front's community development programs, increasing the likelihood that such initiatives would eventually receive state and federal governmental awards. As financial support for major civil rights organizations declined during the 1960s, these new resources proved invaluable and ensured that churches would be the United Front's primary source of funding.

In a period of conservative reascendancy, however, this heavy reliance on predominantly white denominations left the United Front acutely vulnerable to shifting political sentiments. An upsurge of opposition among white lay people, the emergence of an organized conservative opposition within denominational hierarchies, and the growing popularity of evangelical and fundamentalist alternatives all contributed to a significant decline in mainline denominational support for the United Front after 1972. Internal opposition to black clergy's social justice activities was compounded by pressure from national actors including, most significantly, the Internal Revenue Service (IRS) and the Federal Bureau of Investigation (FBI), which quickly mobilized to cut off funding for black power struggles. Thus, *Faith in Black Power* demonstrates the overlooked role that churches played in both the rise and the decline of black power struggles.

In the transition from advocating for civil rights to fostering black power, local activists called on the black church not only to provide important organizational resources but also to help rework the movement's dominant ideology and strategies as well as attendant religious discourses. Far from being disconnected from the emergent black theology, United Front leaders engaged the latest theological literature, invited black theologians to speak at their weekly rallies, and sent potential local leaders for training in black theology at seminaries and universities across the country. From this dynamic interaction, local activists were able to develop a distinctive grassroots black theology that served to legitimate their turn from civil rights liberalism to black power nationalism. Popularly referred to as "soulism" or "soul power,"[19] this grassroots theology also solidified support for the United Front's strategic and tactical focus on armed self-defense and the development of autonomous parallel institutions grounded in an alternative black value system of cooperation and collectivity. The dynamic relationship between black theology and the United Front's political programming was far from unique, and that relationship challenges scholars' assumption that black theology was primarily an academic pursuit that failed to influence local black churches and communities. For a brief period at the end of the 1960s and the start of the 1970s, the interaction of local struggles with black theology produced a plurality of popular grassroots theologies that facilitated and legitimized church involvement in the black power movement while providing the ideational framework for movement mobilization. In this manner black theology in the United States may have had more in common with liberation theology, its Latin American counterpart, than has been previously assumed.

Implicit in these claims is the contention that the involvement of the black church and African American Christian discourses in movement mobilization was neither inevitable nor complete but rather was contingent on the discursive labor and organizational pressures applied by activists with feet in both the church and social movement organizations. In staking this claim, *Faith in Black Power* challenges traditional portrayals of the black church as an "otherworldly" distraction or a liberatory organic source of social protest by situating the black church as a complex and heterogeneous institution capable of sustaining multiple and divergent ideological traditions simultaneously.[20] As historian Charles Payne argues, "There is nothing inherently conservative about the Church. . . . Its message can as easily be packaged in order-threatening as in order-serving ways."[21] Accordingly, securing the participation of black churches in movement mobilization required that activists work within the parameters of these existing traditions, *repackaging* dominant ideologies or recovering subjugated ones. Acknowledging this important but often obscured labor is particularly important in light of the tendency to both exaggerate and romanticize the involvement of the black church in popular and scholarly accounts of the civil rights movement.[22] The assumption that connections between the black church and the modern civil rights movement were obvious and essential has been challenged by studies showing that the majority of African American clergy failed to participate and, in fact, often opposed the idea of black church involvement in social protest.[23] Historian Allison Calhoun-Brown offers an important corrective when she states that "the movement did not rise from the church" and "the resources and ministers of the church had to be actively recruited into the movement."[24]

At root, therefore, *Faith in Black Power* is concerned with how grassroots activists recruited and sustained black church, clerical, and lay support for black power struggles at the local, state, and national levels. In my examination of this labor, I rely heavily on approaches developed by scholars of social movement theory. Social movement theorists have demonstrated that while grievances are ever-present, they do not automatically lead to collective action. Thus, they have pointed to the importance of political opportunities and organizational resources in facilitating movement mobilization.[25] However, while expanded political opportunities and organizational strength provide the structural potential for a movement, they do not in themselves make a movement. As political scientist Doug McAdam maintains, "Mediating between opportunity and action are people and the subjective meanings they attach to their situ-ations."[26] Therefore, Calhoun-Brown argues, "Much of the work done by a social movement organization involves, literally, making meanings and communicating the appropriate mobilizing messages to its constit-uents."[27] In sociological literature this process of "making meaning" is called *framing*, and it is one of the most important jobs performed by activists working within social movement organizations. Framing, more precisely defined, is the process by which a social movement organization links individual and group grievances to a broader interpretative frame-work that helps potential participants understand their experience, recog-nize that it is unjust, and envision specific ways in which they remedy it collectively.[28] Scholars have indicated that the success of such movements often hinges on the ability of organizations to deploy frames that resonate with potential participants and coalitional bodies.[29]

During the emergent stages of the modern civil rights movement, developing frames that resounded with possible participants required engaging with widely held religious beliefs and the centrality of the black church to African American communities. According to McAdam, as expanded political opportunities and "indigenous" organizational strength converged during the post–World War II era, they brought into question dominant "otherworldly" theologies that had served to inhibit political engagement. "[Christianity] was a religion of contain-ment," sociologist Aldon Morris contends, "the opiate of the masses, a religion that soothed the pains of economic, political and social exploita-tion." The transformation of this dominant religious ideology—a process McAdam has called "cognitive liberation," was vital to the emergence of the modern civil rights movement. According to Morris, a new genera-tion of "militant" ministers, including Rev. Martin Luther King Jr., played pivotal roles in "refocusing the cultural content" of churches toward a social gospel tradition, thus rendering congregants ready for activism.[30] In turn, major civil rights organizations like the Southern Christian Lead-ership Conference (SCLC) and the SNCC capitalized on cognitive libera-tion by developing ideologies, strategies, and tactics that resonated with church people and had the capability of facilitating mass mobilization. Civil rights organizations achieved this by linking liberal-integrationist ideologies and direct-action strategies and tactics to Christian discourses of racial reconciliation and nonviolence.[31] This discursive frame would prove remarkably successful in establishing a unified movement culture and solidifying coalitional links with northern white liberals.

However, as the dominant ideology and strategies of the black freedom movement shifted during the mid-1960s this civil rights frame lost resonance, jeopardizing church-based support and access to the organizational resources that had underpinned earlier civil rights struggles. In this context, *Faith in Black Power* explores how grassroots activists looked to a changing black church and black theology for help in refashioning dominant theological worldviews. Activists then used those worldviews to frame the ideological, strategic, and tactical agendas of new social movement organizations during the black power era. Though these efforts were cut short by narrowing political opportunities and state repression, their existence offers important lessons for future struggles and reminds us that the black church's involvement in social movement activity will not come without the ardent and creative labors of activists at the local level.

Black Freedom Struggles in the Borderland

A specific focus on Cairo is timely in that it converges with a growing conversation in the field of black freedom studies about local grassroots movements outside the South. Community studies now challenge the traditional conception of the US civil rights movement as a uniquely southern struggle, enhancing our understanding of local movements in the Northeast, Midwest, Pacific West, and the spaces between.[32] Straddling the cultural and spatial boundary between North and South, Cairo exemplifies the "in-betweenness" of a region that urban historian Henry Louis Taylor Jr. has defined as "the borderland." Studies of black freedom struggles in border communities such as St. Louis, Missouri, Louisville, Kentucky, and Cambridge, Maryland cast the borderland as an *interstitial* region in which northern and southern cultures, political economies, and structures of racial oppression converged, producing a distinctive set of obstacles and opportunities.[33]

Chief among borderland communities' unique characteristics, scholars contend, are the region's distinct political economy and demography.

Racial slavery was practiced across the borderland, but the plantation system that depended on a large agrarian labor force never predominated. As a result the black population in the region was generally smaller than in the Deep South, and African Americans rarely constituted more than 30 percent of the population. These regional distinctions in political economy and demography must not be understated as they had serious ramifications for the social, economic, and political opportunities of Africans Americans and help explain the apparent contradictions historians have observed in the region. The Deep South relied on a variety of mechanisms to preserve its exploitative labor system and internal class structure, including black political disenfranchisement, legal segregation, and the use of racial violence to maintain the status quo. In contrast, the comparatively small black population in the borderland and its concentration in urban industrial and service sector employment allowed for the development of a distinct system of racial oppression that blended aspects of both North and South.[34]

Black-white relations in the borderland were also regulated through the practice of racial segregation. However, local practices were often more fluid and uneven than in the Deep South; segregation often was enforced through a combination of custom and law.[35] African Americans in border cities were also enfranchised, often resulting in the rise of a black political elite that through the Republican Party engaged in a process of racial negotiation to secure civil rights reforms as well as patronage appointments and municipal jobs. In contrast to the Solid South, where the Democratic Party maintained a form of one-party rule, in the borderland African American support for the Republican Party encouraged more competitive elections, and black voters often held the balance of power.[36] Finally, racial violence, a central tool to the maintenance of the plantation economy, was less frequent and served putatively different functions in border cities. In contrast to the Deep South, where racial violence served to discipline and subjugate a large black laboring population, in border cities race riots and lynchings tended to coincide with periods of black migration and were often directed toward the expulsion of African Americans.[37]

These important regional distinctions in patterns of racial oppression allowed white civic leaders to draw points of contrast with their Deep South counterparts by situating borderland communities as beacons of racial civility and progressivism, a discourse that African American activists would regularly use to their advantage. Historian George C. Wright captured this regional quality when he defined Louisville as practicing "racism in a polite form." City leaders, Peter Levy argues, viewed Cambridge, Maryland, as a "model city" when it came to black-white relations, while Louisville even garnered some praise from national civil rights leaders for being "exceptional among southern cities in its community efforts to solve racial problems." However, while the politics of civility ensured that borderland leaders would adopt, at least in public, less confrontational approaches to black freedom struggles, scholars also contend that these discourses justified a gradualist approach to social change that for African American activists carried the risk of cooptation and incorporation.[38] Thus, far from collapsing traditional boundaries between North and South, studies of border cities demonstrate that regional particularities not only mattered but also powerfully shaped black freedom struggles.[39]

In focusing on Cairo, Illinois, *Faith in Black Power* both contributes to and complicates our understanding of black freedom struggles in the borderland. While the emergent scholarship focuses on urban places in the five traditional Civil War border states (Delaware, Kentucky, Maryland, Missouri, and West Virginia), I adopt urban historian Taylor's more expansive conception of the borderland as encompassing states and cities positioned immediately north and south of the Mason-Dixon Line. In Taylor's analysis, the five traditional border states are defined as "southern borderland states," while Pennsylvania, Ohio, Indiana, Illinois, and New Jersey are incorporated as "northern borderland states." In this context, Taylor distinguishes borderland cities as those "lying on both sides of the borderline separating the North and South" meaning that "Cincinnati and Cairo, Illinois, would be borderland cities but not Cleveland and Chicago."[40] Taylor's expanded definition of the borderland is particularly useful, because it allows scholars to elucidate important but often overlooked regional distinctions that exist within states conventionally designated as northern and between those regions and their southern borderland counterparts. This study utilizes the borderland concept to delineate Cairo's regional particularity in Southern Illinois as well as to draw important lines of comparison and distinction between Cairo as a northern borderland city and its nearby southern counterparts.

Faith in Black Power also has relevance to trends in the field of black urban history. While earlier accounts focused on the Midwest and Northeast, this work reflects the relatively recent growth of black community studies rooted in the South and the West and at the intersections of each. "For a full understanding of how white America dealt with its 'Negro problem,'" historian George C. Wright contends, "it is extremely important to discuss the circumstances of blacks in border cities."[41] Located at the confluence of the Ohio and Mississippi Rivers, Cairo was a frontier river city founded at the peak of westward expansion and the market revolution. With access to two of the nation's largest river systems, Cairo appeared peculiarly situated to capitalize on the growing commercial and industrial opportunities of the early nineteenth century. As the Ohio Valley region emerged as a national center of commerce and industry in the 1830s and 1840s, Cairo took its place as an important transshipping hub, moving goods by steamboat east and west, north and south, and shipping internationally via the Mississippi River and the Gulf of Mexico. Like other Ohio Valley river cities, Cairo's labor force expanded during this period, incorporating skilled German mechanics and unskilled Irish laborers into its ranks. After a brief period of economic stagnation, the city's position was solidified in 1851 when the Illinois State Legislature selected it as the southern terminal for the Illinois Central Railroad—a decision that further tied Cairo with Deep South communities all the way down to Mobile, Alabama. In 1859 alone six million pounds of cotton and wool, seven thousand barrels of molasses, and fifteen thousand hogsheads of sugar were shipped through the city. Thus, Cairo, like other northern borderland cities, faced south—making its profits in light manufacturing and as a key transportation center for the southern slave economy. However, Cairo's expansion, like that of most Ohio Valley river communities, was quickly outmatched by the growth of the great industrial cities to the north. Struggling to expand its manufacturing base and experiencing a precipitous decline in river and rail traffic, Cairo experienced the ravages of corporate relocation, unemployment, and population decline decades before they occurred in larger Ohio Valley metropolises like Pittsburgh and Cincinnati, foreshadowing changes that would eventually take place across the Rust Belt.[42]

Sitting ninety latitudinal miles south of Richmond, Virginia, Cairo's southern ties solidified the community's identity as "the Deep South city of the North."[43] The city's white native-born stock trace their roots back to the Upland South states of Virginia, Kentucky, and Tennessee,[44] a fact that distinguished white Cairoites from their counterparts in upstate Illinois and profoundly shaped the cultural and political context of the region.[45] Like other parts of the northern borderland, Southern Illinois's allegiances were complicated by its recent history of bound labor. While the Northwest Ordinance of 1787 banned slavery in the territory, slaveholders in the southernmost parts of Illinois, referred to locally as "Egypt," had been permitted to retain their slaves as indentured servants until the practice was finally outlawed in 1848.[46] In fact, Cairo's first African American residents had come as bonded laborers in 1818 when William Bird, a Missouri slaveholder, moved to the area and constructed the community's first commercial properties. Therefore, a reliance on slave labor, although not widespread, was not uncommon in Southern Illinois during the early nineteenth century, and several hundred African Americans worked in domestic, agricultural, and industrial capacities mirroring practices across the northern borderland. Although not all native-born whites owned slaves or supported the practice, white Cairoites exhibited little sympathy for African Americans who crossed the Ohio River from Kentucky's slave-rich Jackson Purchase region in search of a Promised Land. They exuberantly upheld the Fugitive Slave Act of 1850 and vigorously enforced the state's Black Codes and, after 1853, its black exclusion law. Accordingly, as sectional animosities increased during the 1850s and 1860s, tensions over slavery, black migration, and southern roots were exacerbated, making decisions about Civil War allegiances in Cairo and across the northern borderland especially fraught. Fears that the fiercely Democratic partisans of Southern Illinois would defect to the Confederacy ran rampant farther north, and in April 1861 Union leaders moved to secure the area by establishing a military stronghold in Cairo that would serve as a key base in the western theater. However, Copperhead sentiment persisted and the region remained remarkably Southern in its outlook.[47]

Until the Civil War, native-born whites' vigorous enforcement of the Black Codes and exclusion laws ensured that the African American population in Southern Illinois and across the northern borderland would remain extremely small. In 1860 the total black population of Illinois sat at 7,600, and only eight towns—all located outside of Southern Illinois—had a hundred or more black residents. Cairo was home to only 23 free blacks in 1860, most of them consigned to marginal domestic and service labor. During the war, however, African Americans fled to northern borderland cities in droves, resulting in a demographic revolution as black-white population ratios shifted to mirror those of the southern borderland. Cairo, with its Union military base and growing "contraband" camp, experienced the largest proportional increase as the black population grew by 3,834 percent during the 1860s. Restricted by vehement antiblack sentiment in nearby rural counties, many of the new black migrants opted to stay in Cairo, building new lives and communities together. However, as in other northern borderland communities, their efforts would be restricted by a distinctive pattern of racial oppression.[48]

Cairo's identity as a southern city in a northern state produced patterns of racial oppression that were distinct from those in upstate Illinois and neighboring communities in the southern borderland. While segregation in southern borderland cities like Louisville and St. Louis was characterized by a fluidity and unevenness in comparison to the Deep South, the separation of blacks from whites in Cairo was almost complete by the turn of the twentieth century. African Americans were excluded from the use of certain public facilities, including the Cairo Public Library and the city's swimming pool, and they faced segregation in others, including water fountains, bus stations, and restrooms. The city's hospital, St. Mary's Infirmary, maintained separate wards for black patients. Black children, irrespective of residence, attended separate and inferior schools at the elementary and senior levels. In the private sector, white-owned lunch counters, movie theaters, and bars either refused to serve blacks or provided separate and inferior facilities. Thus, in many ways life for Cairo's black residents was comparable to that of the Deep South. Importantly, however, state laws prohibiting racial discrimination ensured that Cairo's system of social segregation would hinge on custom as opposed to law, so struggles to dismantle Jim Crow in the Land of Lincoln took an entirely different shape from the Deep South or the borderland South—a shape that both afforded and necessitated distinctive strategies and tactics. These unique political realities ensured that Cairo would become an important testing ground for legal and direct-action strategies by the National Association for the Advancement of Colored People (NAACP) in the years preceding the *Brown v. Board of Education* decision, in addition to being the site of SNCC's first integration campaign north of the Ohio River in 1962.[49]

Black Cairoites' experience of racial segregation and exclusion was compounded by the extraordinarily marginalized position of the city's black working class and the attendant underdevelopment of a black middle class that in other borderland cities provided access to separate black institutions. While African Americans across the borderland were largely confined to the lowest paid and unskilled positions in domestic and service work, the economic plight of black Cairoites was particularly precarious. As river trade declined during the late nineteenth century, Cairo was unable to secure the large industrial and manufacturing contracts that ensured the survival of other, larger river cities. As a result, the city's black workers were forced into the most marginal day labor, seasonal, and service work. Historian Darrel Bigham identifies similar trends in his study of Evansville, Indiana, and contends that the absence of significant industrial opportunities in smaller Ohio River Valley communities prevented the proletarianization of black workers and severely undercut the development of the black middle class. In Cairo, as in Evansville, a small black professional class and an even smaller black business class endeavored to provide key services and facilities to black Cairoites, but they were never able to achieve the stability of their big-city counterparts. Therefore, black Cairoites were increasingly subject to the practice of racial exclusion as opposed to racial segregation, lending a sense of urgency to struggles over discrimination in public accommodations and hiring practices. Furthermore, the absence of a well-established black middle class also ensured that when those struggles did occur, black workers would play a leading role and, in comparison to many of their borderland neighbors, would be relatively unimpeded by intraracial class struggles over goals and approaches. In this sense, Cairo provides a unique opportunity to explore black worker struggles for freedom and empowerment.[50]

In their efforts to address segregation and other racially discriminatory practices, black Cairoites, like African Americans across the borderland, were able to exercise their political rights by voting and running candidates who best represented their collective agendas. Scholars have shown that the distinctive demographic and political realities of borderland communities often afforded African Americans a significant role in local politics. In the wake of the Civil War, Cairo represented one of the most extreme examples of this, as its disproportionately large black community held the balance between the Democratic and Republican parties. After 1870 black Cairoites formed Republican clubs and forged a fragile alliance with local white Republicans, securing the party's first county majority after years of Democratic domination. For the next four decades black Cairoites exerted significant influence over the local Republican Party and secured access to government reforms, appointments, and municipal jobs. However, sensing the threat posed by a black electorate, white "progressives" passed a series of measures between 1909 and 1913 that undercut black political power until the 1980s. These reforms included tighter voter registration laws, poll taxes, and the replacement of the aldermanic form of municipal governance with a city commission model, overturning the ward-based political system that had afforded black voters so much power. Cumulatively, these reforms began to exclude African Americans from local government and forestalled the politics of patronage and interracial negotiation that characterized other borderland cities. Although this limited the risk of cooptation and incorporation, it also effectively eliminated lines of communication between the city's white civic leadership and the black community, making political reform remarkably difficult without the support of the state and federal governments.[51]

For their part, Cairo's white civic leadership emphatically rejected the discourse of racial civility that underpinned struggles across the southern borderland. While southern borderland cities cast themselves as beacons of civility and racial progress compared to the Deep South, Cairo's white elite was largely uninterested in drawing such distinctions. In fact, as black Cairoites launched concerted campaigns against segregation and discriminatory practices between 1949 and 1974, Cairo's white civic leadership increasingly aligned itself with the militant segregationist stance of the Deep South, forging alliances with white supremacist organizations like the Ku Klux Klan, the American Nazi Party, and the White Citizens' Council (WCC). Such tendencies were exacerbated by Cairo's fragile economic base and the concomitant absence of northern corporate influences that some scholars have perceived as having a liberalizing effect on race relations in southern borderland communities. Facing economic collapse and mounting pressure for racial equality, Cairo's black and white communities were completely polarized by the late 1960s as the city's white leadership sought to mobilize the full weight of the state to preserve the status quo.[52]

The religious culture of white Cairoites also distinguished them from their northern counterparts and solidified the city's place within the borderland. A 1957 study of church membership in one hundred religious bodies and denominations performed by the National Council of Churches (NCC) illuminates important regional distinctions in the religious beliefs and practices of Illinoisans. In 1957 church membership in Illinois sat at 53.6 percent of the state's total population. Of that total, Roman Catholics held a slim majority at 50.1 percent, Protestants followed with 42.1 percent, and 7.8 percent identified as Jewish. This religious diversity, fueled in no small part by Chicago's role as an industrial powerhouse and home to some of the nation's largest immigrant communities, ran even deeper in some neighborhoods. In Cook County, for example, Protestants accounted for only 22 percent of all church members, while Catholics and Jews constituted 64.9 and 13.1 percent, respectively. Furthermore, Cook County's Protestant population was remarkably heterogeneous; over fifty-nine different denominations were represented.

In comparison, the sixteen southernmost counties in Egypt were overwhelmingly Protestant, representing 86 percent of all church attenders. Moreover, the Protestant population in Southern Illinois exhibited much less heterogeneity; a total of twenty-six denominations operated in the sixteen counties and only thirteen had more than a thousand members. Fundamentalist and conservative religious traditions predominated. While the Methodist Church was the state's largest denomination, in Southern Illinois it ranked second behind the Southern Baptist Convention, which constituted a staggering 47.3 percent of all Protestant church members polled. Close to half of Illinois's Southern Baptists resided in Egypt. In contrast, the influence of liberal mainline denominations was comparatively small.[53] The prominence of a comparatively homogenous conservative Protestant theological tradition ensured that Egypt's religious culture was closer to that of the US South than the Land of Lincoln. The ratio of Protestants to Roman Catholics in Southern Illinois was comparable with border states like Kentucky and West Virginia, where Protestants constituted 79.7 and 83.8 percent, respectively, of total church membership. Moreover, the Southern Baptist Church's influence was entirely consistent with trends in states bordering Cairo to the south and west. The Southern Baptists were the largest denomination in Missouri, Kentucky, Tennessee, and all of the Deep South states. This conservative religious culture provided the backdrop for black Cairoites' engagement in black liberation theology.[54]

The exclusion of black Cairoites from conventional political structures combined with the limited range of separate black institutions afforded the black church a particularly prominent role in Cairo's African American community. Typical of Ohio River Valley communities, Methodist and Baptist churches predominated and became key institutions for leadership development, education, and the provision of much-needed social services. In the absence of black political officials and a significant black business class, black clergy also continued to operate as important community representatives and leaders alongside the small number of black professionals. Furthermore, churches played an important political role; as urban historian Joe Trotter states, they functioned "as springboards for the formation of political clubs and civil rights organizations."[55] Black political ideologies were thus intimately connected to the ideational world of black churches, and struggles for black freedom hinged intrinsically on the ability of local activists to mobilize them.

I explore the changing relationship of the black church and African American Christianity to Cairo black freedom struggles over five chapters. Chapter 1 provides a broad historical overview of African American community formation in Cairo, illuminating how the region's economic instability and distinct blend of northern and southern racial practices combined to solidify the black church's emergence as the leading institution in local community-building and protest traditions. Importantly, I argue that the black church's preeminence was not inevitable. It was instead a creative and necessary response to broader patterns of black political marginalization, and it answered a lack of alternative institutions due to the precarious economic position of Cairo's black working class.

In turn, I contend that the ability of Cairo's black churches to fill this organizational vacuum was made possible by the distinctive religious tradition harbored by African American communities across the borderland. In stark contrast to larger northeastern and midwestern metropolises, Cairo found itself bypassed by the new waves of migration and industrialization that elsewhere served to transform black faith traditions, giving rise to both religious diversification and secularization during the first half of the twentieth century. Like other borderland and southern communities, Cairo maintained a comparatively strong and homogenous religious culture rooted firmly in the evangelical Baptist and Methodist traditions.

By the mid-twentieth century this distinctive religious ethos served as an invaluable institutional and cultural foundation for grassroots black freedom struggles in Cairo and across the borderland. Chapter 2 chronicles the key battles in Cairo's civil rights movement and focuses in particular on the ways activists working with SNCC and the local branch of the NAACP mobilized black congregations behind a powerful local movement aimed at upending the edifice of Jim Crow. By adopting a religious conception of civil rights liberalism rooted in black Christian discourses of racial reconciliation and nonviolence, local activists were able to recruit intergenerational and cross-class support. However, this religiously based alliance ultimately fractured under the weight of white resistance and the growing disillusionment of Cairo's black working-class youth, whose frustrations culminated in the urban rebellion of 1967. Accordingly, chapter 3 explores how black power activists rebuilt the prerebellion coalition under the banner of a reconstructed and relevant Christianity that drew on both formal black theology and grassroots religious traditions. Chapter 4 tracks black power activists' mobilization of these new discourses to secure important organizational resources and coalitional support from local, state, and national black church organizations. Finally, chapter 5 examines the closing stages of the Cairo black power struggle, situating state repression of activist church agencies and the revival of conservative political agendas within white congregations as fundamental but overlooked causes of the movement's demise.

1

On Jordan's Banks

The Origins of Community, Faith, and Struggle in Cairo

The black church has historically served as a key staging ground for black freedom struggles in Cairo, Illinois. At crucial junctures throughout the city's history, social movement organizations have relied on black churches for their extensive organizational and ideational resources. In turn, local congregations opened their doors and extended their hands in support of struggles for rights, respect, and empowerment. By the late 1960s the city's black churches had a strong legacy of protest and occupied a position of social and cultural preeminence that grassroots activists were forced to navigate in their attempts to build effective movements for racial change and social justice. However, the black church's centrality to local protest traditions was neither inevitable nor complete but rather contingent on three interrelated factors: the distinctive social and political conditions of black life in the northern borderland; the relative homogeneity of black religious traditions; and the agency and skill of activists responsible for recruiting congregations into the movement.

In this chapter I trace the broad contours of black life and community in Cairo, Illinois, across four overlapping historical periods, showing how the city's economic instability and distinctive blend of northern and southern racial practices combined to ensure the black church's emergence as the central institution in black community building and protest traditions. More specifically, I argue that the consignment of black Cairoites to the lowest rungs of the river city's declining economy hindered the development of a proletarianized black working class and attendant black middle class capable of sustaining autonomous institutions that might have rivaled the church's role in the black community. Further, political reforms passed during the early twentieth century undercut the ward-based electoral power of black voters, putting an end to an era of black officeholding and patronage. Pushed to the margins of formal political institutions, black Cairoites increasingly looked to the church as a site of political protest and social movement activity.

In turn, I demonstrate that the rise of Cairo's black churches to a position of political and cultural preeminence was also facilitated by the specific quality of the religious tradition they harbored. In contrast to many larger cosmopolitan midwestern cities, post–Civil War Cairo was bypassed by the new waves of migration and industrial expansion that elsewhere contributed to a diversification of African American faith traditions or to secularization. In contrast, Cairo, like other borderland cities, maintained a comparatively strong and homogenous religious culture rooted firmly in the evangelical Methodist and Baptist traditions. This unifying religious culture provided an important institutional basis for racial solidarity and ecumenical organizing upon which local activists would capitalize in their efforts to build viable black freedom struggles.

Way Down in Egypt Land (1818–1861)

At the dawn of the nineteenth century, a small patch of cypress-filled swampland at the confluence of America's two great waterways—the Ohio and the Mississippi—captured the interest of the new nation, North and South. Strategically located in the newly incorporated Illinois Territory on the westernmost front of the nascent American empire, these muddy bottomlands drew expeditionary forces, fur trappers, merchants, and eventually eastern speculators seeking to profit from the river traffic central to the burgeoning market revolution of the new century. Profiteers were aided in their endeavors by the encroachment of Euro-American migrants and squatters from the Upland South. They were also abetted by treaties signed with the five tribes of the Illinois Confederacy in 1803 and 1818, which resulted in the ceding of the tribes' remaining land rights, paving the way for statehood and public land sales.[1]

Despite this convergence of waters and events, efforts to capitalize on the site's position at the confluence were punctuated by a series of failures. Virginia planter and slaveholder Abraham Bird was among the first to observe the site's potential while setting up camp at the confluence on a journey to Cape Girardeau in 1795. Though Bird departed shortly after for the sugar plantations of Louisiana, his sons William and Thompson Bird expanded the family's mercantile interests to the confluence in July 1817, purchasing 318 acres in the southernmost part of the contemporary city of Cairo. On the same day that the southern planters staked their claim, an ambitious group of eastern speculators headed by the Baltimore merchant John Comegys incorporated the City and Bank Company of Cairo and purchased a larger 1,800-acre tract just north of the Birds' holdings. Envisioning a great river metropolis, Comegys and his compatriots solicited sponsorship from European financiers. However, within a few short months the project collapsed and the land defaulted back to the territorial legislature. Accordingly, it fell to the Birds' enslaved African laborers to erect the first-known permanent structures at the confluence, consisting of a waterfront tavern and store that drew the trade of flatboat and steamer crews charged with transporting cotton, sugar, rice, and human cargo.[2]

When British novelist Charles Dickens arrived at the confluence on the steamboat *Fulton* in 1842, he was anxious to see the town "vaunted in England as a mine of Golden Hope," but he was horrified to discover what he would record in his travelogue *American Notes* (1842) as little more than "a dismal swamp," "a detestable morass," and "an ugly sepulcher . . . uncheered by any gleam of promise." Cairo, which the writer parodied as "Eden" in his subsequent novel *Martin Chuzzlewit* (1843), was to Dickens the archetypal nineteenth-century "paper town" designed to appeal to distant speculators by way of "monstrous representations" that falsely portrayed a bustling river city populated by factories, hotels, and public buildings.[3] In the five years preceding Dickens's sojourn, London-based investment bankers Wright & Company had sponsored a second attempt to develop the site. In 1837 Boston merchant Darius Holbrook secured a charter aimed at transforming Cairo into a "great commercial and manufacturing mart and emporium"; using capital from Wright & Company, the newly incorporated Cairo City and Canal Company oversaw the clearing of land and construction of levees. However, Holbrook's company failed during the depression of the late 1830s, prompting an exodus of workers and a collapse in foreign investment. When Dickens arrived just a few years later he found Cairo largely abandoned; only a score of impoverished squatters remained. Desperate to recoup their losses, several of the original speculators formed the Cairo Property Trust and in 1852 secured Cairo's bid to become the southern terminus for the Illinois Central Railroad (ICR), marking a key juncture in the community's fortunes and development.[4]

In the decade that followed, Cairo would emerge as Southern Illinois's largest city and an important midwestern transshipment hub focused on the storage, processing, and transportation of staple crops, consumer goods, and enslaved workers. In 1854 the number of boats landing in Cairo totaled 3,798, surpassing nearby St. Louis, which received 3,006 vessels that same year. After the completion of the ICR in 1854, Cairo dockworkers loaded cargo directly from riverboats onto railroad cars heading northward. The commodities that they carried—molasses, sugar, wool, and cotton—reveal Cairo's dependence on the southern plantation economy as well as its role as a gateway to northern and eastern markets.[5] This unique interstitial position afforded Cairo what one scholar of the borderland has defined as "a dual personality," reflective of both northern and southern traditions.[6] In addition to the burgeoning river and rail trade, antebellum Cairo maintained a number of small industries, including lumber mills, ironworks, brickworks, and flour mills. The city's commercial expansion resulted in renewed migration, growing the population from 242 in 1850 to 2,188 just ten years later (see table 1.1). Initially populated by rural white migrants from the Upland South, Cairo—like many other borderland communities—began to attract northeastern artisanal families as well as significant numbers of German and Irish immigrants who transformed the cultural landscape by establishing their own institutions, including foreign-language newspapers, beer gardens, sports clubs, literary societies, and churches. Initially, the city's Catholic population attended St. Patrick's Church, founded in 1838. However, in 1872 the construction of St. Joseph's Church afforded German immigrants their own edifice. Parochial schooling was also established along ethnic lines; Irish immigrants attended St. Patrick's parochial school and German immigrants St. Joseph's.[7]

In contrast, Cairo's African American population remained comparatively small due to Illinois's status as a "quasi–slave state" and rigorous

enforcement of both the Fugitive Slave Act (1850) and black exclusion laws (1853). Though the Northwest Ordinance of 1787 barred the
importation of enslaved workers into the territory, human bondage persisted in the southernmost parts of Illinois, Ohio, and Delaware in a variety of de jure and de facto guises. After statehood in 1818 more than
one thousand black Illinoisans remained enslaved under a complex legal
framework: longstanding protections of the property rights of slaveholders of French descent were combined with indentured servitude and special provisions for the leasing of enslaved workers at the United States
Saline works in Shawneetown. In contrast to their southern counterparts,
the majority of those enslaved labored in domestic or industrial capacities, not in the production of cash crops. However, even in the absence of
the plantation system of agriculture that typified the political economy of
communities farther south, support for racial slavery among Egypt's pro-
southern Democrat elite was strong, prompting a failed attempt in 1824
to secure a constitutional convention permitting the ownership of chat-
tel property. As state laws governing indenture and enslavement gradually
tightened, some Alexander County slaveholders (like the Birds) shuttled
their workers back and forth across the Mississippi River to Missouri in
an effort to secure their property rights as Missouri citizens. Others, like
Alexander County state representative Henry Livingston Webb, simply
kept their indentured servants illegally. Accordingly, the earliest black
Cairoites arrived as forced laborers or manumitted slaves and entered a
northern borderland community where their rights were ambiguously
defined and almost always unprotected.[8]

Egypt's contiguity to Missouri and Kentucky's slave-rich Jackson
Purchase region raised the specter of runaway slaves and free black refugees. White opposition to black migration constrained the growth of
the black population across the northern borderland and rendered African Americans vulnerable to acts of racial violence as well as to capture
and sale into slavery.[9] Most free blacks moved to urban areas to build
communities that could afford some degree of protection. In the decade
preceding the Civil War, black Cairoites lived in close proximity to each
other in several large augmented households reflective of what Sundiata
Cha-Jua has described as the "adaptive extended kinship networks" of
black Illinoisans during this period. Cairo's African American households

often included nuclear and extended kin as well as nonrelatives. James and Maria Renfrow, a young married couple who moved to Cairo during its ascension in the 1850s, lived alongside domestic laborers Mary Head and Agga Maddox. Similarly, Andrew and Susan Mills shared their home with washerwoman Mary Posey, steward James Gale, and housekeeper Sara Wilson. By taking in boarders, families like the Renfrows and Mills fostered a culture of mutuality designed to weather the effects of Cairo's racially stratified labor market.[10]

Consigned to the lowest paid menial positions as domestic and personal servants, black Cairoites possessed little property. The wealthiest household in 1860 was headed by twenty-five-year-old cook George Williams, who amassed a fortune of just two hundred dollars. Augmented households also reflected the distinctive cultural heritage of Cairo's black residents, many of whom had recently escaped bondage and now lived in a tenuous borderland between North and South. Some, including forty-year-old Jane Robinson, opened their homes to manumitted slaves like Jane Baker, who had recently received her freedom papers from the Cook family in Alexander County. Others, like Malinda Harville, risked their own freedom by harboring runaways fleeing across the two rivers. Harville reportedly took in a man named Joseph who in August 1855 absconded from the plantation of Thomas Rodney in Mississippi County, Missouri. Harville purchased train tickets for Joseph to Chicago, an act for which she was punished by local whites, who burned her home to the ground. However, the city's railroads and steamers continued to function as important avenues for underground railroad activity led by free blacks like Harville and George J. L. Burroughs, a Canadian sleeping car porter who claimed to have smuggled many stowaways from Cairo to Chicago in the years preceding the Civil War.[11]

The precariousness of black Cairoites' freedom no doubt solidified these bonds with their enslaved brethren just across the river. The Illinois Black Codes barred black residents from voting, assembling in large numbers, and serving on the state militia, while local customs excluded them from the city's schools and the Catholic parishes. Even worse, free blacks in Cairo lived under the ever-present threat of kidnap and sale into slavery with no recourse to the courts. In July 1857 these growing tensions erupted when kidnappers descended on the home of two free black men, beating them and forcibly transporting them across the river into Missouri to be sold into slavery. One of the men, though "horribly mangled about the head," was able to escape and swam back across the Mississippi River to Cairo.[12] A few days later a gang of Missouri slave catchers arrived in Cairo pretending to look for runaways and launched an assault on the black settlement. Free blacks took up arms against the gang, shooting one white man in the face. Fearing for their lives, Cairo's black residents fled to Mound City in neighboring Pulaski County. Such events garnered little sympathy from local whites, who frequently complained that the very presence of free blacks in the city constituted a direct violation of the state's black exclusion law, which 98 percent of Alexander County voters had supported in 1848. To stave off vigilantism, local officials formed posses in the 1850s and arrested black residents under the antisettlement law. Despite these dangers, African Americans continued to migrate to Cairo and the black population rebounded to 47 in the three years after the 1857 exodus (see table 1.1). With the limited resources they pos-

Table 1.1. Population of Cairo by Race, 1850–1970

Year	White		Black		Other		Total
	(N)	(%)	(N)	(%)	(N)	(%)	(N)
1850	234	0.97	8	0.03	0	—	242
1860	2,141	0.98	47	0.02	0	—	2,188
1870	4,418	0.70	1,849	0.30	0	—	6,267
1880	5,661	0.63	3,349	0.37	1	0.0001	9,011
1890	6,622	0.64	3,689	0.36	13	0.0013	10,324
1900	7,563	0.60	5,000	0.40	3	0.0002	12,566
1910	9,108	0.63	5,434	0.37	6	0.0038	14,548
1920	10,190	0.67	5,000	0.33	13	0.0009	15,203
1930	8,948	0.66	4,575	0.34	9	0.0006	13,532
1940	8,907	0.62	5,494	0.38	6	0.0004	14,407
1950	7,722	0.64	4,383	0.36	18	0.0015	12,123
1960	5,821	0.62	3,511	0.38	16	0.0017	9,348
1970	3,905	0.62	2,351	0.37	21	0.0033	6,277

sessed, the new migrants strove to develop their own institutions, including a small private school that charged a fee of one dollar per month to the city's wealthier black families. However, broader efforts in community and institution building would await the Civil War and the vast migration of enslaved African American men, women, and children across the Ohio River.[13]

Crossing Over to Canaan Land (1861–1890)

On the muddy banks of the Ohio River, men sit hunched over, staring out across the waters, their hands resting on their knees. Nearby, women in headscarves and cheap linen dresses pull their children close as Union soldiers mill around, perhaps taking down the names of the sundry passengers recently disembarked from a nearby steamer. These scenes depicted in Sophie Wessel's 1963 painting *Contraband on Cairo Levee* capture the great tide of humanity that descended on the river town at the height of the Civil War, fleeing from a life of bondage downriver. Fearful that the strategically located transport hub and beachhead of pro-Southern Democratic partisans might fall into Confederate hands, Union forces occupied Cairo in May 1861 and established Fort Defiance as the base of US army and naval operations on the western front (see fig. 1.1). Such fears of disunion were not misplaced. Mirroring tendencies across the borderland, Egypt was deeply divided over the war, and several hundred local men ultimately volunteered to fight for Confederate units further south.[14]

Almost immediately, the trickle of fugitives swelled to a great tide; the *Cairo City Weekly Gazette* lamented as early as July 1861 that "the woods around Cairo and Bird's Point are full of runaways." In the ensuing months thousands of enslaved men and women, further emboldened by Union victories on the western front and the passage of the confiscation acts in 1861 and 1862, cast down their tools and absconded from the plantations of slavery's heartland, believing the Day of Jubilee had come and that like the Children of Israel they were to be delivered from bondage in Egypt to freedom in Canaan land. The men and women that arrived in Cairo were likely transported aboard steamers by Union forces occupying Vicksburg and parts of northern Alabama.[15] Their exodus was evocative of what W. E. B. Du Bois would later call the "general strike"

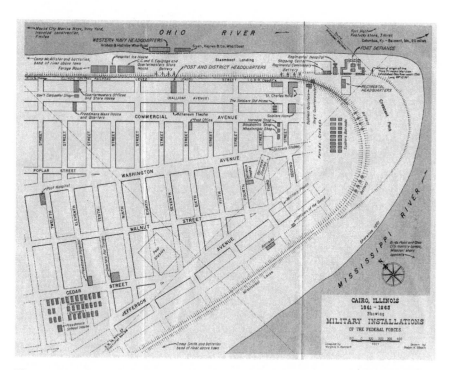

Figure 1.1. Map of military installations of the federal forces in Cairo, Illinois, 1861–1865. By permission of John Willis Allen Papers, Special Collections Research Center, Southern Illinois University Carbondale.

of the enslaved that registered a devastating blow to the Confederate war effort.[16] In a letter to abolitionist Frederick Douglass in September 1862, one writer, identified only as "H. Oscar," captured the historic transformations taking place in this most inauspicious river town at the crossroads of slavery and freedom.

> Cairo now begins to look as though the jubilee sure enough [has] come in this country. Besides what are here already, filling the old barracks, from one end to the other, still they come. Every morning, when I go down to the "Ohio Levee," I find it literally dotted over with new arrivals of contrabands. Old men and young men, old women and young women, and children here.

> The town is literally alive with them. . . . Many with whom I have talked appeared buoyant and hopefull [*sic*], and say, "God bless the Yankees." I have heard various accounts of what they thought and what they did when they heard *"dem big guns roar"*—how the men and women in the fields would prick up their ears and listen, and how they would begin to fall back upon their dignity and disregard the commands of the overseer, and rejoice and thank God that their friends had come.[17]

Here, in Cairo, thousands of formerly enslaved men and women would take their first breaths on free soil, although their fates were far from certain.

For most black refugees, Cairo was a way station on a much longer journey in search of an elusive freedom. Upon arrival the refugees were temporarily housed in the nation's only northern "contraband camp," located in an abandoned army barracks in the southwestern corner of the city on Cedar Street. At its zenith, following the passage of the Emancipation Proclamation in January 1863, the camp housed more than five thousand former slaves, predominantly women and children; hundreds more took shelter in abandoned buildings and makeshift lean-tos scattered in the marshy environs nearby. Having survived the dangerous journey out of slavery, the freedpeople now occupied filthy, overcrowded, and disease-ridden accommodations that, according to Quaker abolitionist Levi Coffin, granted "none of the comforts and few of the necessities of life."[18]

Under Coffin's supervision the Quakers operated a school for the freedpeople, while the American Missionary Association and the US Sanitary Commission combined forces to provide medical services. Fellow Quaker and nurse Laura Haviland described the "great suffering in the camp of freedmen," whose inhabitants were "almost nude" and "afraid of being returned to slavery." A distressed woman whose husband and three children had been sold away before the war begged Haviland to help her bury her last remaining child, who lay dead in a "slab hut" nearby.[19] Others registered complaints of "petty abuses and outrages" committed by local whites, including one woman who informed a camp physician that a gang of white men had sexually assaulted her two young daughters. In his letter to Douglass, H. Oscar complained that "the prejudices of the common laborers, PARTICULARLY the Irish, are raging intensely and fiercely" against the freedpeople and that he believed they "would murder every man and woman . . . if they thought they dare do it." Efforts to disperse the refugees to other counties across the state were met by a wall of white opposition. By the end of the war, many of the camp's inhabitants followed the railroads northward. However, a large number remained in Cairo, growing the river town's black community by almost four thousand percent from just 47 in 1860 to 1,849 in 1870 (see table 1.1). Together, these newly free men and women would lay the foundations of black community life in postwar Cairo.[20]

Race, Class, and Labor after the Civil War

Cairo emerged from the Civil War a larger and more robust city. The twilight of the nineteenth century witnessed an era of commercial and industrial growth unprecedented in the city's history as well as a precipitous increase in population that would not be stemmed until World War I (see table 1.1). The heart of Cairo's economy continued to be its transshipment business and the wide range of related industries that sprang from it. Cairo was the terminus for seven railroads as well as an important transfer point for packet lines conducting regular services to southern ports. Manufacturing also grew and the city functioned as an important western hub for the lumber, iron, and grain industries. While homegrown capitalists were responsible for many of these enterprises, Cairo also attracted larger national corporations like the Singer Manufacturing Company, which opened a sewing machine cabinet factory on the banks of the Ohio River in 1882.[21]

For the growing numbers of black migrants who arrived in Cairo during and immediately following the Civil War, wage-work offered a degree of economic and social independence denied by slavery and its offshoot, the sharecropping system. However, black workers were subject to a strict racial division of labor that consigned them to the lowest paid, unskilled jobs. In 1880 three-quarters of all black household heads in the workforce held unskilled positions in domestic and personal services or as common laborers. Women were employed overwhelmingly as domestics, while their male counterparts often held the most dangerous and back-breaking positions on the docks, for the railroads, and in the factories. At the Singer plant, for example, African American men worked exclusively as janitors or on the loading docks moving freight. Early postwar efforts to introduce black workers into semiskilled positions were met by violence and industrial action from Cairo's white workers. Accordingly, African Americans found themselves locked out of entire sections of the city's growing industrial and commercial economy.[22]

Despite the limited occupational opportunities available to black workers, a large number of low-paid menial jobs did exist, distinguishing this period from those that followed. Indeed, if black proletarianization ever took place in Cairo, it was in the decades immediately following the Civil War as southern blacks migrated northward, moving out of agricultural work and into wage-earning positions. Border cities were among the leading recipients of this postbellum wave of migration; the largest numbers of African Americans relocated to border south metropolises such as St. Louis, Baltimore, and Louisville. The most disproportionate increases in black migration, however, occurred in the smaller northern borderland communities of Cairo, Mound City, and Evansville, each of which had antebellum black populations of less than one hundred that ballooned during and immediately following the war by one thousand percent or more. The sheer scale of black migration to these small communities constituted a demographic revolution in which new arrivals would transform and be transformed by local conditions and practices.[23]

As a river city, Cairo's experience of black proletarianization differed from that of larger midwestern metropolises; its most potent effects took place earlier and involved nonindustrial forms of employment. With an economy centered on the commercial transshipment business as opposed to large-scale industry, Cairo did not witness the emergence of a significant black industrial proletariat that typified cities like Milwaukee, Chicago, and Detroit. Nonetheless, African Americans arriving in Cairo during the late nineteenth century transitioned from agrarian labor to wage-work, producing a substantial and politically active black working class.[24] In turn, this expansion in Cairo's black working class provided the demographic and financial basis for the formation of a small, black middle class constituted by business owners and professionals. Between

1865 and 1890 a growing number of African American entrepreneurs, including men such as William T. Scott and Thomas Freeman, established saloons, restaurants, hotels, dance halls, grocery stores, laundries, theaters, and an opera house that catered almost exclusively to a black clientele. In addition, black schoolteachers, lawyers, dentists, newspaper editors, and ministers catered to the physical, intellectual, and spiritual needs of the growing populace.[25]

African American Community Building after the Civil War

The expansion of the black working and middle classes in Cairo underpinned a new wave of community and institution building, spurred on by widespread practices of racial discrimination. In the postwar era African Americans were barred from Cairo's public schools, public library, and poorhouse. They were also subjected to an uneven system of racial segregation in railroad cars, hospitals, streetcars, steamboats, parks, churches, and white-owned businesses.[26] In response, black Cairoites mounted a vigorous campaign for full citizenship and civil rights while simultaneously forging a separate black public sphere or, as political scientist Michael Dawson terms it, a "black counterpublic," through which basic material needs could be met, culture and community preserved, and grievances openly shared.[27]

At the forefront of Cairo's black counterpublic were its churches, which were among the first institutions established by African Americans in the city. At the height of the war, refugees held their own religious services within the confines of the contraband camp while better-situated black Cairoites initiated the first wave of church planting from their homes.[28] Patterns of religious affiliation were relatively homogenous and mirrored those of other borderland communities in the Ohio River Valley, and the Baptist and African Methodist Episcopal (AME) denominations predominated.[29] By 1890 Cairo had seven black churches, including six Baptist and one AME congregation. The city's first black congregation was Ward Chapel AME Church, formed in 1863 in the home of James and Maria Renfrow. From its beginning with only eight members, Ward Chapel quickly outgrew the Renfrows' home as wartime migrants joined the congregation in seeking forms of worship independent from white control. In the following decades Ward Chapel became one of the city's largest black congregations and the institutional hub of Methodist activities in the city. The hierarchical structure of the AME Church and its insistence on an educated ministry provided Ward Chapel with institutional and financial stability. However, the denomination's strict enforcement of the itinerancy system of pastoral leadership meant that the church's clergy often lacked the deep community ties of their Baptist counterparts. In contrast, Cairo's Baptist churches exhibited greater local autonomy, allowing congregations to multiply and charismatic preachers to lead for generations. Immediately after the war, black Cairoites founded three Baptist congregations: New Hope Free Baptist Church (1867), First Missionary Baptist Church (1867), and Antioch Baptist Church (1860s). A second wave of church planting occurred during the last two decades of the nineteenth century as African Americans fled white terrorism and economic exploitation in the post-Reconstruction South. During this period, three additional Baptist congregations were established: Mt. Moriah Missionary Baptist Church (1881), Mt. Carmel Missionary Baptist Church (1880s), and Morningstar Free Will Baptist Church (1898). By the end of the century, black Cairoites had successfully built their own houses of worship and solidified a religious culture deeply rooted in both the evangelical Baptist and Methodist traditions.[30]

In a fragile and uncertain postwar context, African American congregations also served as important *springboards* for the formation of other educational, benevolent, and political institutions.[31] Prior to the creation of segregated black public schools during the 1870s, churches provided vital educational resources to their congregants, operating their own daily schools. In September 1867 Rev. Thomas J. Shores, pastor of the First Missionary Baptist Church, established the Union Free School, which served approximately three hundred students and relied on a combination of offerings from black congregants and donations from white patrons. Since African Americans were also barred from using many of the city's existing benevolent and welfare institutions, black churches also played a vital role in raising funds for the sick and needy by hosting potlucks, organizing clothing drives, and taking special offerings. Beyond these practical functions, churches were also the central social institutions in the lives of most black Cairoites, providing them with relationships, entertainment, and support. In this way churches fostered the culture of mutuality that bound community members together, lending value and meaning to their lives in the midst of racial oppression.[32]

Despite these shared traditions, black congregations also reflected nascent intraracial fissures rooted in social class, color, and region. The absence of a well-established black community prior to the Civil War meant that divisions between older and newer residents were not as potent in Cairo as in other black urban communities during this period. Still, in a city constituted almost entirely by recent migrants, origins mattered and African Americans tended to join churches that reflected their own regional and cultural backgrounds.[33] Members of Ward Chapel AME, for example, were almost exclusively from the Midwest and Upper South states of Kentucky, Tennessee, and Virginia. The Methodists' promotion of an educated ministry, more subdued forms of worship, and a theology that advocated personal frugality, temperance, and industry as keys to racial advancement provided Ward Chapel with an air of urbane respectability that attracted disproportionate numbers of black middle-class professionals, business owners, and skilled craftsmen.[34] In contrast, rural migrants from the Deep South tended to join the city's Baptist churches. Alabamians built New Hope Free Baptist Church, while families from the Louisiana and Mississippi Delta built Mt. Moriah Missionary Baptist Church after fleeing what they described as "the reign of the Ku Klux Klan" during the 1870s and 1880s. In these congregations migrants maintained the ecstatic forms of religious expression that had prevailed in the rural South, drawing criticism from segments of Cairo's black middle class. These tensions quickly extended into the political realm as Baptist ministers representing working-class southern migrant congregations blurred the boundaries between sacred and secular by running for public office, campaigning for civil rights, and leading citywide direct-action protests much to the chagrin of many of their middle-class counterparts.[35]

The Black Church at the Zenith of Black Political Power

The late nineteenth century marked the zenith of black political power in Cairo as the city underwent what one scholar has referred to as its own "social and political reconstruction."[36] The ratification of the Fifteenth Amendment in 1870 combined with the passage of other state and federal civil rights legislation situated African Americans as citizens who legally possessed all of the rights held by whites. Black Cairoites swiftly put those rights into action, fostering a dynamic political culture centered on participating in black Republican clubs, voting in local elections, and running candidates for office. In postbellum Cairo, where African Americans represented almost a third of the city's population, this newly acquired political power was by no means insignificant. Prior to the Civil War, contemporaries described Cairo's electorate as "diabolically Democratic." However, between 1870 and 1890 African Americans facilitated a political realignment that secured Republican Party dominance in local elections into the early twentieth century. Representing approximately a third of the city's electorate, black voters held the balance of power, forcing the Democrats to forgo virulently racist platforms and ensuring that white Republicans incorporated African Americans into party leadership and adopted more progressive positions on civil rights. From this tactical alliance emerged a generation of black Republican officeholders who utilized their positions within municipal and county government to advocate racial equality and the integration of public accommodations.[37]

Cairo's postwar black churches were an integral part of this vibrant political culture, functioning as key spaces for political education and mobilization. Several black congregations opened their doors to black Republican clubs, allowing them to hold their meetings in church buildings and to involve laity in debates about public policy. Baptist ministers, including Rev. Thomas Shores, Rev. Thomas Strother, and Rev. Nelson Ricks, were key leaders in the club movement and its efforts to enforce civil rights legislation in the city. Viewing the struggle for racial justice as inseparable from their Christian mission, these ministers used their pulpits to encourage black political participation and educate parishioners on local and national political affairs. Baptist ministers were peculiarly situated to take up leadership roles during this period. In contrast to their Methodist counterparts, they often served lengthy tenures, allowing them to put down roots and establish strong community ties. In turn, Baptist ministers were expected to be charismatic leaders who gave voice to the spiritual and physical yearnings of their followers. Those aligned with the radical wing of the Republican Party tended to be pastors of predominantly rural southern migrant congregations. Though their members were far from wealthy, working-class churches marshaled regular tithes and offerings to sustain their autonomy and insulate radical ministers from white control.[38]

While pastors of black working-class congregations often led the way, middle-class churches constituted by migrants from the Upper South and Midwest tended to adopt a more accommodating stance. For example, Rev. Henry Brown, pastor of Ward Chapel from 1871 to 1873, maintained a position of strict political neutrality during his tenure. Although some speculated that the Methodist minister had been influenced by recent donations made by prominent white benefactors toward the church edifice, Brown's refusal to associate with the political protest of the black working class reflected deep-seated tensions within the Methodist Church over the appropriate means of achieving equality. In the Reconstruction South, the AME Church functioned as a vital staging ground for political mobilization; its ministers and lay leaders often ran for political office. However, northern church leaders were critical of this approach and viewed frugality, temperance, and industry as the keys to racial advancement. Opposition to the involvement of clergy in political affairs was so strong at the 1872 general convention that Bishop David Payne supported a motion that, if successful, would have barred ministers from holding elected office entirely. However, despite Brown's neutrality and the occasional criticism of radical clergymen, many of Ward Chapel's members were active in Republican politics, including John Gladney, who served as Cairo's first black elected police constable, and John J. Bird, who became the city's first black police magistrate in 1873.[39] Rev. Jacob Bradley of Antioch Baptist Church was a vocal critic of the movement's radical wing, particularly Shores, whom he considered a "phoney" and criticized for trying to "excite the colored people" by convincing them that "the good people of Cairo were unwashed rebels." Bradley's political conservatism comported with his congregants, who were middle-class migrants from the Midwest and Upper South, underscoring the important political differences among black Cairoites of different class and regional backgrounds.[40]

Despite these obstacles to racial and ecumenical solidarity, black Cairoites continued to build on their growing demographic, economic, and institutional strength, achieving a number of political victories by the end of the nineteenth century. Black Cairoites came to serve in a number of elected and appointed positions: as assemblymen, county coroners, postmasters, jailors, and police constables. Moreover, by forging a tactical alliance with white Republicans, black political elites were able to broker access to patronage and municipal jobs, expanding the ranks of the middle class and upper working class. It appeared that black political power would only continue to expand, particularly in ward-based elections where black majorities could ensure the election of African American candidates. However, this optimism proved to be short-lived as the city's declining economic opportunities fueled white animosity, leading to racial violence, black disenfranchisement, and economic exclusion.[41]

A Dream Deferred (1890–1928)

The 1890s represented a watershed for Cairo, as the city struggled under the effects of a global financial crisis and its hopes of becoming a great industrial and commercial metropolis were dashed. The depression of 1893–1897 hit the river city particularly hard, resulting in business failures, a decline in river and rail traffic, escalating unemployment, and eroding expectations. In many economic sectors the effects lingered, causing disillusionment among the city's elite and prompting capital flight. While the depression certainly escalated the pace of decline, the city's economic problems were also tied to more fundamental transformations within the national economy. Cairo's heavy reliance on the transshipment business made it extremely vulnerable to the precipitous drop in river traffic caused by the surge in rail transportation. Trade on the Mississippi River plummeted during this period from 1,244,175 tons shipped in 1896 to 365,920 tons in 1908. This collapse in river trade also had a devastating impact on the small industries that had grown up around the transshipment business.[42]

As Cairo's bustling waterfronts quieted, efforts to enlarge the city's portion of rail trade were hampered by the late development of railroad bridges crossing the Mississippi River (1888) and the Ohio River (1938). Even when the Illinois Central bridge was finally opened, rail traffic tended to travel straight through, bringing little commercial advantage to the city. The biggest obstacle to economic restructuring, however, was Cairo's failure to attract large-scale industry. While larger river cities like Pittsburgh, St. Louis, and Cincinnati became hubs for heavy industries in steel, meatpacking, textiles, and chemicals, Cairo was unable to expand on its limited industrial base. Lumber and cottonseed oil remained the primary industries, and despite the best efforts of the city boosters, most corporations bypassed Cairo in favor of larger urban centers. The only perceptible signs of growth were in the underground economy of liquor and vice, which according to one scholar became "the most stable and predictable source of revenue in Cairo."[43]

Economic insecurities also served to fuel underlying racial animosities. Often the last hired and first fired, black workers bore the brunt of Cairo's financial crises but were viewed by their white counterparts as competitors rather than allies in a period of dwindling opportunities. Between 1890 and 1910 these tensions escalated as another wave of migration grew the city's black population by almost 50 percent from 3,689 to 5,434 (see table 1.1). African Americans now constituted almost 40 percent of Cairo's population, a ratio that mirrored demographic patterns in the lower Mississippi Delta more closely than the Midwest and most other border cities. White civic elites cast migrant workers as scapegoats for the city's decaying prospects, alleging that their perceived tendency toward immoral and criminal behavior deterred investment. Progressive-era reformers were particularly apt to point to the growth of black-owned taverns, brothels, and gambling houses such as the Bucket of Blood located at Thirteenth and Poplar and the Nation on Thirty-Second and Commercial as attracting a transient element to the city that fostered a culture of corruption and depravity. Politicians and law enforcement were criticized for colluding with the proprietors of these illicit establishments—some of whom, like William T. Scott and Richard Taylor (owner of a saloon called Taylor's Place on Fourth and Commercial) were also important powerbrokers in the black community. In reality, illicit businesses had been a visible presence in the city since the Civil War, receiving tacit support from politicians and law enforcement due to the revenue streams garnered from licenses, fees, and fines. However, between 1890 and 1920—a period historian Rayford Logan has described as "the nadir of American race relations"—white residents utilized these anxieties about migration, race, and criminality as a thinly veiled justification for reasserting their control over the city's social and political institutions and stripping African Americans of many of their post–Civil War gains.[44]

The Rise of Jim Crow Segregation during the Nadir

As migration and antiblack sentiment increased, local whites took steps to shore up practices of racial segregation and exclusion in a city where the ratio between black and white residents seemed to be quickly approaching parity. Segregation persisted in the school system and was extended into other public accommodations such as streetcars, restrooms, water fountains, cemeteries, and hospital wards. The new leisure and mass entertainment venues of the early twentieth century also imposed color bars. White-owned movie theaters consigned African Americans to the balcony; the city's parks designated separate areas for the races; lunch counters served black patrons through a hatch or a back door; and the Rotary Club swimming pool and municipal sports leagues excluded blacks entirely. The city's two Catholic parishes—St. Joseph's and St. Patrick's— also reinforced their strict color line. In 1889 the Sisters of Loretto began offering segregated classes to African American boys in St. Patrick's Parish. Two years later, however, even these separate and unequal services had been abandoned.[45]

Importantly, though segregation in Cairo was increasingly rigid and all-encompassing, these entrenched local customs violated state laws prohibiting segregation in schooling and other public accommodations. This flagrant disregard for antidiscrimination laws was perhaps most clear in the arena of education, where local officials openly employed racial assignment policies, placing students in separate schools expressly on account of the color of their skin. From the 1860s onward, Cairo—a town that never surpassed twenty thousand people—operated a costly dual school system that by the mid-twentieth century included two high schools, two junior high schools, and seven elementary schools. Moreover, since many smaller rural communities could not afford to maintain a separate black high school, African American children from across the county were bused lengthy distances into Cairo to attend Sumner High. Students from Sumner were not permitted to compete against white students in sports but rather competed in the Southern Illinois Conference of Colored High Schools against segregated schools from across the state line in Missouri and Kentucky.[46] This race-based assignment policy—widely adopted across southern Illinois, New Jersey, Ohio, and Pennsylvania—distinguished northern borderland communities from the de jure segregation of many parts of the border and Deep South as well as from cities further north where de facto school segregation was often attributed to underlying patterns of residential segregation. As one scholar has argued, segregation practices in the northern borderland were "far more deliberate" and "in clear violation of state law prohibiting racial separation."[47]

Residential patterns mirrored this shift toward a more rigidly segregated community. As late as 1880 African Americans had been relatively evenly distributed across all five wards in the city (see fig. 1.2). However, as housing development gradually caught up with population growth, residential segregation hardened: wealthier whites purchased homes in more desirable communities "uptown," while discriminatory rental practices forced African Americans to occupy slum accommodations close to vice districts or low-lying, flood-prone areas. One of the latter communities was Future City, a large unincorporated black enclave located in a floodplain just north of the city. Here African Americans lived without access to municipal services such as running water, emergency services, and power. In the city proper residential segregation also intensified; in 1915 only one in ten white households lived next door to a black household compared to one in three in 1880. This growing pattern of racial segregation was matched by the city's enforcement of vagrancy laws that criminalized the migrant population, put them to work on public infrastructure projects, or drove them out of the city completely.[48]

Racial Terror and the Destruction of Formal Black Political Power during the Nadir

The growing black population accompanied by white fears of racial disorder fueled an upsurge of racial violence and terrorism during the nadir. Writing in June 1910, Chicago-based antilynching activist Ida B. Wells-Barnett pointed to the seeming paradox that no other northern state had "more frequently offended in this crime" than the Land of Lincoln.

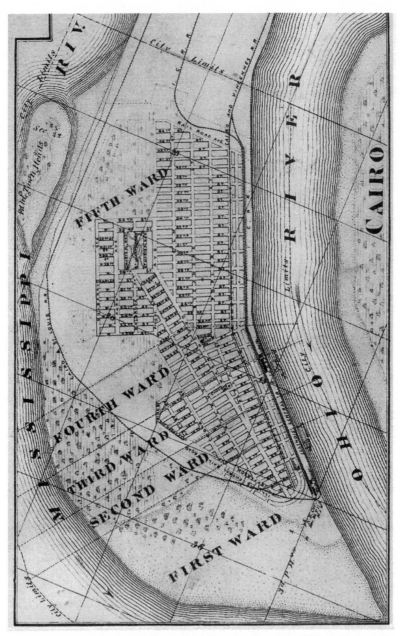

Figure 1.2. Ward map of Cairo, 1876. Reprint from the *Illinois State Atlas 1876.*

Spurred by the stifling climate of racial terror, Wells-Barnett and other influential black Chicagoans had mobilized behind the 1904 election of African American Republican Edward D. Green to the state legislature; he successfully sponsored a law aimed at suppressing mob violence the following year. The key provision of Green's law established that the seizure and lynching of individuals held in police custody would be taken as prima facie evidence of a breakdown in law and order, necessitating the immediate vacation of the sheriff's office. It was on this basis that Wells-Barnett traveled to Cairo in November 1909 after the brutal lynching of migrant worker William James, an act she would subsequently describe as "one of the most inhuman spectacles ever witnessed in this country."[49]

The threat of racial violence and mob law hung like a pall over Egypt during the nadir. Between 1880 and 1920 at least twenty-five lynchings took place across the state; the majority occurred in downstate communities, where violence was directed most frequently toward African Americans. Nowhere was the threat of mob rule more palpable than in Alexander County, where five lynchings and innumerable failed attempts kept black residents on constant guard.[50] Wells-Barnett had devoted much of her career to discrediting what she called "the old threadbare lie" that lynching was necessary to defend white womanhood from the insatiable sexual desires of black men. Rather, she insisted that rape was an *excuse* that obscured the real purpose of lynching: to promote racial deference and preserve white supremacy in economic, political, and social affairs. This rationale proved especially true in nadir-era Cairo, where acts of white on black racial violence, though overtly aimed at punishing perceived black criminality, often reflected deeper white anxieties about the expanded civic and political influence of African Americans.[51]

Since the Civil War, Cairo, like other borderland communities, had undergone its own radical reconstruction whereby African Americans, once formally excluded from civic affairs, now exerted considerable electoral power that they leveraged to secure key municipal offices and patronage appointments. What was perhaps unique in Cairo's case was the city's racial demography. By 1900 African Americans constituted 40 percent of Cairo's population, contrasting starkly with Chicago (5 percent) and other borderland cities such as Evansville (13 percent), St. Louis (15 percent), Louisville (19 percent), and Baltimore (16 percent).[52] In fact, Cairo's racial demography was more akin to communities in the Deep South, where white civic elites employed a combination of literacy tests, poll taxes, and the grandfather clause to disenfranchise black residents. The comparatively small size of the black electorate in most border cities made such measures unnecessary; in Cairo, however, blacks represented a larger, potentially independent political force that all parties with ambitions for power had to navigate. As black Cairoites rose to positions of influence within local and state government, white anxieties about the willingness of local officials to protect their own property, power, and privilege intensified. Perhaps no aspect of this shifting political landscape was more disturbing to local whites than the expanded role of black Cairoites in enforcing and prosecuting the law. The visible and active presence of African Americans on county and city juries, in police departments, and on the judicial bench sparked considerable consternation among whites who, in many cases, were principally opposed to the participation of black citizens in the arrest and prosecution of their white counterparts. Further, most whites believed that the city's interracial juries and police department were unwilling and incapable of prosecuting black defendants with the speed and severity they expected. As a result whites in Alexander County increasingly employed extralegal violence to reassert their control over the racial order, maintaining, as historian Manfred Berg states, that lynch mobs were righteous "agents of communal self-defense necessitated by a weak system of official criminal justice."[53]

In this context, the spectacle lynching of William James was not an anomaly but rather the culmination of a broader pattern of unchecked racial terrorism aimed at nullifying Cairo's reconstructed interracial polity. Accused of the rape and murder of local white shop worker Mary Pelley, James—a laborer and recent migrant from the South—was quickly picked up on circumstantial evidence and taken into police custody along with five suspected accomplices, all African American. Although the first night passed without violence, tensions mounted after Pelley's funeral the following day in which hundreds of white Cairoites converged on St. Patrick's Church, bringing the city to a virtual standstill. In a symbolic display of civic mourning, the mayor and other honorary pallbearers appointed from among Cairo's elite carried Pelley's white casket to the church. In his eulogy Father Downey of St. Patrick's Church cast Pelley's death as symptomatic of a broader breakdown in law and order in the city, singling out judges and juries for allowing "a series of abominable crimes" to go unpunished. Later that day, as mobs reassembled and rumors of a lynching spread, Sheriff Frank Davis and his deputy Thomas A. Fuller decided to flee the city with their suspect in tow.[54]

The decision to flee the city was a fateful one that cost James his life, according to Wells-Barnett. Rather than seek additional support from deputies or state officials, Sheriff Davis loaded James into a patrol vehicle and drove him to the Fourteenth Street station where they boarded a northbound train. Upon discovering the sheriff's scheme, several hundred armed whites seized a freight train, filling it to capacity and forcing the conductor to transport them northward to Karnak where sightings of the fugitives had been reported. At each station across this part of Egypt white residents armed with shotguns congregated, forcing the sheriff and his prisoner off the railroad and into hiding. In the muddy woodlands outside Karnak they were finally spotted, and members of the mob stripped the sheriff of his weapon, seized James, and transported the pair back to Cairo where "an immense crowd" stood waiting at Union Station. As the doors swung open, a man threw a rope around James's neck and dragged him from the train and down Washington Avenue. According to eyewitness accounts, the street "was filled from side to side . . . [with] men, women and children." At Eighth Street this "solid mass of humanity" swept eastwards to Commercial Avenue, where a giant steel arch stood illuminated by electric lights. A member of the crowd threw the rope over the arch and hauled James into the air to the sound of loud shouts and jeers before the rope abruptly snapped, jerking James's body back to the ground. Within an instant, members of the now ten-thousand-strong crowd began firing hundreds of rounds into James's body. His lifeless body was subsequently dragged to the scene of Pelley's death, where the mob burned him in coal oil and dismembered him, wrapping the heart and other organs in newspaper for distribution among the crowd as souvenirs. James's head was severed from his body and impaled on a nearby fencepost, a symbol of the unchecked power of white terror.[55]

Unsatisfied by the murder of James, the mob now turned its fury toward white Cairoite Henry Salzner, who was in jail accused of murdering his wife. When a man rushed to his defense, he was beaten and knocked to the ground by the mob, which proceeded to hang Salzner from a telephone pole in the courtyard of the jail. As dawn broke and the smoke settled, local officials finally called in the National Guard to disperse the crowds and regain control of the city. Salzner's father pushed his way through the swarming crowds to retrieve his son's body while William James's charred remains were reportedly transported to the city landfill.[56]

In the subsequent days white civic elites would often point to Salzner's lynching as dubious evidence that the mob's actions were not racially motivated but rather driven by a sense of general outrage at the failure of the legal system to adequately prosecute crime. Mayor George Parsons, for example, attributed the mob violence to frustration with the failure of juries to "convict in homicide cases" and of judges to employ the death penalty. "Murder in Cairo," he argued, "has, I regret to say, been tolerably safe."[57] While the mayor utilized race-neutral language in his assessment of the mob's motivations, others drew more explicit connections between the lynching and racialized anxieties of black criminality and corruption. In their statements civic elites repeatedly cautioned whites from outside the city against delivering quick judgments without understanding the city's peculiar "race problem." Central to this perceived race problem, they argued, was Cairo's distinctive racial demography, which mirrored parts of the Deep South absent the region's distinctive modes of racial control—namely legal segregation and political disenfranchisement. In a November 19 letter to the *New York Times,* W. L. Clanahan, former editor of the *Cairo Evening Citizen,* expressed his agreement with a recent editorial on the lynching in which Cairo had been described as having "a considerable colored population, including many negroes of bad character." Clanahan agreed, stating: "Out of a population of 13,000 in 1900, 5,000 of the inhabitants of Cairo were negroes. Of the 100,000 negroes in the State of Illinois 5 percent are massed in this one little town." To make matters worse, Clanahan argued, white civic elites, unlike their southern counterparts, had "dealt indulgently with the negro" by extending undeserved citizenship rights and patronage appointments: "For years it has been the policy to keep two negroes on the small police force and there have been negro Justices of Peace. A negro physician once came near being elected a member of the Board of Education." In statements like these, Clanahan and other white Cairoites drew direct linkages between expanded black citizenship rights, political power, and acts of white racial terror.[58]

In response to rampant racial violence against blacks, African American leaders picked their battles carefully, writing letters, passing resolutions, and at times employing armed self-help in defense of their friends and family. In 1904, five years before James's murder, black working-class residents had staged an armed vigil outside the courthouse in defense of A. S. Mason, a forty-year-old housepainter and popular resident of Future City accused of sexually assaulting an eleven-year-old white girl called Lillie White. Despite this display of strength, Mason was convicted and in the nights that followed police performed regular inspections of black working-class neighborhoods, arresting dozens of African Americans on manufactured and petty charges ranging from curfew violations to disturbing the peace.[59]

This climate of surveillance and legal harassment no doubt shaped subsequent responses to the mass lynching of William James, a relatively recent migrant who lacked Mason's community ties. When Wells-Barnett arrived in Cairo to investigate the lynchings and mobilize support for the dismissal of Sheriff Davis, she confronted a black ministerial elite that expressed little sympathy for either James or her cause. Wells-Barnett was scheduled to stay in the home of Rev. Samuel Hardison of Ward Chapel AME, but shortly after their introduction the fifty-three-year-old minister explained that most of Cairo's black ministers and professionals, believing James "a worthless sort of fellow," had written letters to the governor supporting the sheriff and petitioning for his reinstatement. Horrified, Wells-Barnett left Hardison's home and solicited the local pharmacist Will Taylor to aid her in investigating the lynchings as well as organizing a mass meeting of black citizens the following day. Despite reports of intimidation, turnout to the meeting was good, and Wells-Barnett used the opportunity to assuage anxieties. The seasoned activist informed the men and women present that she understood their fears in assisting the investigation publicly and that she and other black Chicagoans were willing to speak on their behalf, but she stressed that it was vital that she learn the facts of the case and secure their support. Wells-Barnett asked a number of probing questions about the sheriff's conduct, including whether he had sworn in deputies to protect James, if the National Guard had been contacted in a timely manner, and most importantly, whether removing the prisoner from the jail had made him more vulnerable to mob assault. Further, she challenged Cairo's black civic elite to look beyond James's low reputation and recognize that if "they condoned the lynching of one man, the time might come when they would have to condone that of other men higher up, providing they were black." The following day she made a similar plea to an assembly of the city's black Baptist ministers, culminating in their tearful repentance. By the end of her visit, Wells-Barnett had succeeded in convincing Cairo's leading black citizens of their error and secured a resolution demanding the permanent dismissal of Sheriff Davis.[60]

Wells-Barnett presented her findings in Springfield at a hearing on Sheriff Davis's reappointment and, much to the surprise of almost everyone involved, secured Gov. Charles S. Deneen's support for the sheriff's permanent dismissal. In his statements, Governor Deneen, a Republican, criticized the sheriff for his failure to enlist special deputies or seek the aid of the National Guard in the hours leading up to the lynching. Historians have correctly identified the ruling as a "terrific success" and an "outstanding victory" for Wells-Barnett that "all but ended lynching in Illinois." After the governor's ruling, sheriffs across the state increasingly recruited the support of deputies and national guardsmen in protecting prisoners when the threat of mob violence resurged.[61] However, proclamations of victory also served to obscure the ubiquitous nature of racial terror in Egypt even after James's lynching. In the first six months following the lynching, the National Guard was deployed to the region on at least three separate occasions to put down mob violence, including in Cairo where in February 1910 an armed mob attempted to remove two African American prisoners—Lincoln Wilson and John Pratt—from the city jail and kill them for the crime of stealing a white woman's purse. The imprisoned men were only saved by the quick reactions of eight black deputies who utilized deadly force to disperse the mob, killing its leader John Halliday, son of the city's former mayor and nephew of its leading businessman, and arresting twelve other participants. The new Republican sheriff, Fred Nellis, expressed reticence in their enlistment but faced a flat refusal by white deputies to come to the imprisoned men's aid. In the days that followed, the sheriff was taken into the National Guard's protective custody as indignant whites threatened to kill his family, bomb the courthouse, and "lynch enough to scare the rest of the negroes out of town." Despite eyewitness testimony, none of the twelve men charged with mob activity were prosecuted. In the subsequent election Sheriff Nellis was soundly defeated by his Democratic opponent, and calls for more radical reforms threatened to undercut African Americans' limited political and legal power.[62]

The tragic events of 1909–1910 represented a watershed in Cairo's history. Afterward white citizens would join hands across the political aisle to limit black citizenship, ushering in a new racial regime that would define the experience of black Cairoites until the rise of the modern black freedom movement. The tactical alliance between black and white Republicans had always been a fragile one. Black Republicans frequently questioned the commitment of their white counterparts to racial equality and mistrusted their willingness to appoint black candidates to key positions of party leadership. In turn, many white Republicans resented outspoken black political leaders and their increasing demands on the party machine. These tensions had escalated during the 1890s as heightened residential segregation led to the consolidation of black voting power, particularly in the Third and Fifth Wards (see fig. 1.2), further expanding the influence of black political elites. After witnessing black politicians secure a series of landmark victories in the 1895 and 1897 elections, white Republicans refused to support African American candidates for county office in 1898. In response, black politicians encouraged voters to protest by supporting the Democrats or the Negro Protective Party, producing a defeat for the Republicans and marking the end of a long-standing political alliance.

Over the next decade, white Republicans worked to shift the balance of power in the city by building bipartisan support for a series of electoral reforms that would effectively strip African Americans of their political power. Led by Mayor John Lansden, a Republican who viewed "the elective franchise in their [African Americans] hands" as a political "travesty," white political elites passed a new voter registration act in 1909 that required extensive proof of length and place of residency. In 1913 they replaced the ward-based system that had afforded black politicians their recent victories and substituted in its stead an at-large city commission form of government.

The enactment of the latter coincided with the Illinois State Legislature's passage of women's suffrage in 1913, a decision that transformed Cairo's electorate by enfranchising thousands of new black women voters. Taken collectively, these reforms undercut black women's new political power, disenfranchised several hundred black voters in the unincorporated suburb of Future City, actively discouraged black voting within the city proper, and practically eliminated the possibility of black candidates securing election in at-large city commission races. Between 1885 and 1901 the city had always had at least one black city council member. After 1913, however, no blacks were elected to city office for almost seventy years. Further, black Cairoites were cut off from channels of party patronage that had previously afforded them access to municipal jobs.[63]

African American Community Building during the Nadir

On the eve of World War I, black Cairoites found themselves in a declining river city that was increasingly hostile to their presence. The cumulative effect of diminishing economic opportunities, social segregation, racial violence, and political marginalization proved devastating, and between 1910 and 1920 the black population fell by 4 percent while the white population increased by 4 percent (see table 1.1). Among those leaving the city were a number of prominent community leaders, including the pastors of the two largest black Baptist congregations—Rev. Nelson Ricks of the New Hope Free Baptist Church and Rev. J. R. Bennett of the First Missionary Baptist Church. Having served their congregations for several decades, both men decided to leave the city in the immediate aftermath of William James's lynching. With the outbreak of World War I the exodus continued as hundreds of black and white workers relocated to larger urban communities in search of better-paying jobs in wartime industries. Meanwhile, Cairo's economy continued to stagnate as civic leaders failed to attract federal war contracts; several large businesses closed in rapid succession, including the Singer factory in 1916.[64]

In the context of declining opportunities, black Cairoites struggled to build on the limited economic gains they had made during the late nineteenth century. The vast majority continued to occupy a small number of tenuous positions in domestic and personal service, or they worked as unskilled laborers on the railroads, on the waterfront, and in factories. Cairo's black middle class, constituted primarily of professionals and business owners, remained comparatively small and fragile. However, the consolidation of Jim Crow segregation did contribute to a small expansion in the city's black-owned businesses. African American entrepreneurs responded to discrimination by establishing the first black-owned undertaking parlor (1901), movie theater (1905), drugstore (1909), shoe store, and baseball team. African Americans also maintained a number of grocery stores during this period, and black barbers and beauty shops continued to proliferate. However, the growing instability of Cairo's black working class ensured that most black-owned businesses relied heavily on credit sales and were vulnerable to bankruptcy and closure, a problem that would have devastating effects during the Great Depression.[65]

Black Cairoites responded to worsening social and economic conditions by deepening their community-building activities, particularly through their churches. Renewed migration spurred the formation of several new Baptist congregations, including St. Paul Missionary Baptist Church (1915), Everdale Missionary Baptist Church (1919), and First Central Baptist Church (1919). In turn, Cairo witnessed a small growth in Pentecostalism, marked by the formation in 1912 of the Cairo Church of God in Christ (COGIC). These new Baptist and Pentecostal congregations were often populated by black migrant workers, many of whom traveled to Cairo each autumn to pick cotton in the farming areas surrounding the city.[66] This growth in migration also attracted the attention of the Belleville diocese of the Roman Catholic Church, which in 1928 partnered with the Society of African Missions to found St. Columba's Catholic Mission. Since St. Patrick's and St. Joseph's parishes were rigidly segregated, the diocese purchased a disused church and a two-story school building and began offering pastoral and educational services to African American residents. Within four years of St. Columba's formation, the local black Catholic population grew from six to over one hundred.[67]

Despite the emergence of new religious traditions, the influence of Cairo's leading Baptist and Methodist congregations remained unmatched. By 1925 Ward Chapel AME boasted a membership of four hundred and the church's imposing new edifice on Seventeenth Street continued to welcome leading members of the city's professional and business classes. Rivaling Ward Chapel in size and influence were First Missionary Baptist and Mt. Moriah Baptist Churches, both of which drew hundreds of members, some from the city's small black middle class and the majority from the working class of skilled and unskilled laborers. After the formation of the National Baptist Convention of the United States of America in 1895 and the Baptist General State Convention of Illinois in 1902, Cairo's Baptist clergy began to exert their influence within the denomination at both the state and national level. In 1919 Cairo's First Missionary Baptist Church hosted the annual conference of the Illinois Baptist Convention, and four years later the congregation's minister, Rev. J. J. Olive, was elected as the organization's president. Reverend Olive forged strong ties with other local Baptist ministers, particularly Reverend Hockenhull and Rev. J. T. Brown of Mt. Moriah Missionary Baptist Church, with whom he comanaged the Baptist publication *Illinois Messenger* from 1925 to 1933. Reverend Brown also served as editor in chief of the publishing house of the National Baptist Convention USA, located in Nashville, Tennessee. In total, Cairo was home to three major black church publications during this period—the *Baptist Truth* (1899–1926); the *Illinois Messenger* (1925–1933); and the *International Evangelical Herald* (1919–1934), the official organ of the International Evangelical Bureau.[68] The preeminence of the city's black Baptist and Methodist churches continued unchallenged during the decades of migration that followed. While the processes of industrialization and urbanization in larger northern cities resulted in an exponential growth in storefront Holiness and Spiritualist congregations as well as other, non-Christian traditions, religious affiliations in Cairo would remain relatively static. A 1957 study of the city's religious patterns identified more than three-quarters of black respondents as church members, and of those indicating a denominational preference, 70.4 percent identified as Baptist and 13.5 percent as Methodist.[69]

The Black Church in the Aftermath of Political Reform

Cairo's black congregations also stepped into the political vacuum created by the electoral reforms of 1909 and 1913. While nadir-era black churches often refocused political energy inward toward building denomi-national power, black congregations in Cairo also exhibited the capacity to reach outward, providing the leadership and resources necessary to sustain campaigns for racial uplift and civil rights in a broader context of political marginalization.[70] Black middle-class churchwomen, including Florence Sprague Fields and Alice Titus Beatty, were particularly prominent; they blurred the boundary between secular and sacred work through their active participation in the national club movement and through the formation in 1905 of the Yates Woman's Club, an affiliate of the Cairo City Federation of Colored Women's Clubs. The fundraising efforts of clubwomen culmi-nated in December 1916 with the opening of Yates Memorial Hospital, the city's first black-owned and black-operated hospital. Four years later, Fields and Beatty joined other middle- and working-class churchgoers in founding the Cairo branch of the NAACP. Under the leadership of Rev. C. C. Wilson, pastor of the First Missionary Baptist Church and publisher of the *Baptist Truth*, the NAACP mounted an unsuccessful legal campaign aimed at integrating the Cairo Public Library and fought for better educa-tional and employment opportunities. During the 1920s, ministers from the city's leading congregations became active members in the NAACP, using their pulpits to decry the immorality of Jim Crow and to propagate the organization's message of liberal integration.[71]

Babylon's Falling (1929–1945)

Cairo was already experiencing a period of prolonged economic decline when the stock market crashed in the autumn of 1929. Just two years prior, rising river levels had threatened the city once again, prompting a renewed outmigration. Between 1920 and 1930 Cairo's population plummeted by 11 percent, from 15,203 to 13,532 (see table 1.1). In this context, the Great Depression was the last in a series of ongoing crises for the city, forcing many already struggling businesses to close, banks to fail, and large numbers of workers into unemployment. The city's long-standing economic problems ensured that the effects of the Depression would be more potent and enduring in Cairo than elsewhere. As late as May 1934 the *Chicago Tribune* reported that 50.4 percent of Alexander County's residents were still on the relief rolls compared to 14 percent statewide. Because of this, public emergency work programs sponsored by Franklin Roosevelt's New Deal administrations were essential to the city's survival, providing jobs and facilitating extensive municipal projects. In 1940 almost a quarter of Cairo's workforce (21.6 percent) held temporary jobs on these federal works projects, while another 8.4 percent remained unemployed, figures that vastly exceeded state averages. Entrenched practices of employment discrimination ensured that black workers were disproportionately affected; 37.8 percent hired on for federal public works projects and an additional 12.2 percent were unemployed.[72]

Despite Cairo's economic woes, black migration to the city increased during the Depression as landlords throughout the Mississippi Delta pushed sharecroppers off their farms. Between 1930 and 1940 Cairo's black population grew by 4 percent while the white population dropped by 4 percent (see table 1.1). Lewis Jones and his family arrived in Cairo in 1938 by way of Mississippi and Missouri, where they had worked as sharecroppers and day laborers in the cotton fields. Jones recalled few job opportunities in the city, though he eventually found low-paying work as a handyman at the Cairo Hotel. Such poor prospects ensured that many migrants simply passed through Cairo on their way to larger cities like Chicago and St. Louis.[73] Blues composer W. C. Handy captured Cairo's transitional identity for a new generation of seemingly rootless wanderers in his "St. Louis Blues" (1914), singing, "Help me to Cairo, make St. Louis by myself." Indeed, for many of those who stayed behind, Cairo would come to epitomize the spirit of the blues—a dying city that offered little in the way of hope or opportunity. A vast network of blues performers, including Cairo native Henry Townsend, Sonny Boy Williamson, Robert Nighthawk, Lonnie Johnson, Pinetop Perkins, Kansas City Red, Eddie Snow, and Earl Hooker, as well as popular songs like Cannon Jug Stomper's "Cairo Rag" (1928) and Henry Spaulding's "Cairo Blues" (1929), solidified Cairo's reputation as a hard but entertaining river town that understood what it meant to be both black and blue.[74]

Race, Class, and Labor during the Long Depression

After the Great Depression, Cairo's economy never recovered and demand for black labor declined. The city's black working class transformed into a permanently expendable surplus labor force. The river, rail, and factory jobs that had laid the foundation for black proletarianization during the late nineteenth century evaporated, forcing a large segment of the black population into unstable forms of day labor, seasonal work, and unemployment. Black workers fought back, organizing unions in key industries and initiating a series of strikes and protests at the Federal Barge Lines in 1933; on the docks and at the Alexander County Relief Office in 1937; and at the Valley Steel Company, Roberts Cotton Oil Company, and Cairo Meal and Cake Company in 1939. However, in a pattern that would become all too familiar over the coming decades, city leaders repressed black protests, calling in the National Guard and deputizing local white citizens.[75] During the 1937 demonstrations, African American workers protested the failure of the relief office to distribute wages to men who had been enlisted under a New Deal program to sandbag the city. When renowned artist Wendell C. Jones came to Cairo as part of the New Deal's US Treasury Department's Section of Fine Arts program, he selected these workers, responsible for heroically saving the city from floodwaters, as the subject of *Sandbagging the Bulkheads* (1942), a mural for display in the Cairo federal courthouse and post office. However, before the mural could be installed, city leaders balked at Jones's populist study of black and white workers laboring in unison to save Cairo, a decision indicative of the prejudice and obstinacy of white civic elites.[76]

World War II brought little relief, as city officials were once again unable to secure federal defense contracts. Capital flight continued apace, resulting in a series of plant closures: the Federal Barge Lines (1940), the Big Four Railroad (1941), and the Mississippi Valley Barge Line (1947), all of which had been major employers of black workers. Most of these jobs did not return after the war, and when combined with the end of federal job creation programs, the impact was devastating on the black working class. During a period of so-called national prosperity, Cairo witnessed its black unemployment rate skyrocket from 12.2 percent in 1940 to 22.7 percent by 1950. That same year, only 15.1 percent of Cairo's workforce held positions in manufacturing jobs compared to 32 percent in the rest of the state, reflecting the migration of capital to northern cities and, increasingly, to the south and west. By 1952 Cairo could claim only three establishments hiring more than a hundred workers and none exceeding two hundred. Thus, Cairo experienced the ravages of corporate relocation, deindustrialization, and deproletarianization decades before their full effects were felt in larger midwestern and Rust Belt cities.[77]

Everyone in the city felt the effect of economic restructuring, but because of ongoing practices of discrimination black workers were disproportionately impacted. A 1948 study performed by the newly established Illinois Interracial Commission (IIC) found that black Cairoites employed in the private sector were now almost universally consigned to "unskilled and service jobs with low wage scales" and that their prospects for advancement were "blocked pretty effectively by the discriminatory practices of employing concerns." The report failed to mention the contributions of local trade unions, which almost universally excluded black workers from membership. Conditions in the public sector were even worse according to the commission, which found widespread discrimination in both municipal and federal employment. African Americans went unrepresented on all city commissions, councils, and boards. They were excluded from the ranks of the fire and police departments, with the exception of a single black police officer charged with patrolling African American neighborhoods. Black doctors and nurses were barred from serving in St. Mary's Hospital and the tuberculosis sanitarium, even in the segregated wards and annexes. While some of these discriminatory employment practices had been implemented during the nadir, others were more recent. The post office, for example, had hired a number of African Americans as mail carriers throughout the early twentieth century. However, as job prospects declined in the private sector, mail carrier jobs were increasingly reserved for whites while African Americans were relegated to janitorial positions. Fearing competition for jobs, white Cairoites closed ranks further, delimiting black employment opportunities.[78]

The instability of black working-class employment had a corollary effect on Cairo's small black middle class. Reliant almost exclusively on a black clientele, African American business owners were particularly vulnerable to the effect that deproletarianization had on consumer spending. During the city's long depression, a large number of black-owned businesses failed, particularly those that had relied heavily on credit-based sales. By the 1950s businesses that provided anything but the most essential and personal services, such as funeral parlors and barbershops, simply could not survive. The age of black movie theaters, grocery stores, and opera houses had passed, and black proprietors numbered no more than twenty by the decade's end. Tightening restrictions in public and private employment also prevented African Americans from securing jobs in the clerical sector. By 1960 only 1.3 percent of black workers in Alexander County held clerical jobs, a number that compared poorly with other Illinois counties with large black urban populations, such as Champaign County (7.6 percent) and Cook County (12.9 percent). Black professionals were the largest group within the black middle class, constituting 8 percent of the city's black workers by 1960. The devastating impact of deproletarianization on black-owned businesses during the long depression prompted large numbers of middle-class African Americans to leave the city, along with many of the political and economic institutions they had forged, including the NAACP, which fell into inactivity during the 1930s. This outmigration of the black middle class was further compounded by the tendency of black high school students to leave the city following graduation. In the decade following World War II, close to 90 percent of black high school graduates left Cairo in search of jobs elsewhere.[79]

Black Churches and "Union Spirit" during the Long Depression

The impact of the long depression was also felt by the city's black churches, which were charged with the unenviable task of meeting both the spiritual and material needs of their congregants in a time of financial drought. While a number of black-owned businesses and community organizations failed during the thirties, black churches remained vital hubs of black political and social activity. A number of congregations maintained large memberships during the depression despite facing enormous financial challenges. At the peak of the crisis, First Central Baptist Church had over 300 members and 250 regular attendees, many of them migrant workers. By the early 1940s First Missionary Baptist Church maintained a membership of 650 and a regular attendance of nearly 300. Mirroring the union spirit that pervaded black working-class politics during this period, Cairo's black congregations insisted that the best way to survive the effects of the depression was to organize collectively. Rather than continue their work separately, church leaders fostered "a city-wide union spirit" by encouraging church choirs, boards, and clubs to consolidate their resources and energies. According to investigators employed by the Works Progress Administration (WPA), "the Usher boards of the city were first to unionize, then followed the gospel Choruses, the Pastors Aids, and Missionary [Society], which meets once per month from church to church." Congregations also worked together to plan "union revivals" featuring outside speakers and choirs.[80]

On one level the ecumenical activities of the long depression were motivated by practical necessity. By pooling limited resources, struggling churches ensured that their basic functions continued unimpeded and that the needs of black community members were met. However, the strengthening of ecumenical bonds also transformed church cultures and ultimately served to harmonize black religious traditions in the city. The push for unionized boards and committees, for example, encouraged more congregations to adopt the kind of administrative structures supported by larger middle-class churches. By the 1940s even the smallest congregations maintained a variety of clubs and societies, allowing for greater lay participation and institutional uniformity. Moreover, the rise of "union revivals" fostered a blending of worship styles and rituals that served to erode longstanding differences rooted in denominational affiliation and social class.[81]

This homogenization of worship styles was most apparent in the broad appeal of gospel music—a tradition that blended secular and sacred traditions, including the blues sound that was sweeping the city's bars and taverns. Initially performed by working-class Pentecostal and Baptist congregations, in larger cities gospel music was often vehemently opposed by black middle-class congregations who preferred a more conventional liturgical model that incorporated European hymns and spirituals. In Cairo, however, black congregations universally embraced the new musical style during the 1930s, forming their own gospel choirs and choruses. Increasingly, Cairo's black churches—irrespective of denomination, class, or migratory origins—embraced a shared religious culture that centered on gospel music, call-and-response oratory, communal prayer, and charismatic sermonizing.[82]

The emergence of a popular black religious culture in Cairo during this period also reflected the declining status and influence of the black middle class. As large segments of the black bourgeoisie left the city in search of opportunities elsewhere, the Methodist and Baptist congregations that had traditionally served as bastions of middle-class respectability were forced to become more inclusive of working-class participation and cultural practices. According to Hattie Kendrick, services at Ward Chapel underwent a significant transformation during the long depression, moving from very formal liturgies that featured classical recitals, hymns, and spirituals to the formation of a gospel choir and junior gospel chorus by the decade's end. The changing demographics of Ward Chapel also produced frustration with ministers like Rev. A. Attaway, whose Oxford training and scholarly manner alienated him from the majority of church members; he was forced to resign in 1933 after a single year. In contrast, Rev. John A. Randolph, who joined the congregation the following year, was widely praised for his inclusive approach to ministry. "Whatever else can be said of Rev. Randolph, he pastored," Kendrick recalled. "The affluent, the poor, the young, the old, the influential, the unknown, the sick, the well were all sheep of his fold and he was loved." While Ward Chapel remained a hub for middle-class Methodists like Kendrick, these changes in ministerial and worship styles reflected the growing influence of the black working class during the Depression years.[83]

After World War II the shared religious culture and ecumenical networks between Cairo's black congregations would function as both the backdrop and glue for the initiation of broad-based civil rights struggles. During the 1930s, black workers had fought their own battles to improve conditions through labor unions and unemployed workers' associations. However, as factories closed and companies relocated to new sites across the country, the workplace moved with them. As a result the power of local unions was broken, and black workers were stripped of the conventional tools for addressing injustice and inequality. Beyond the shop floor, black Cairoites continued to face Jim Crow practices in all areas of community life, provoking many soldiers to ask why they were fighting for freedom abroad if they could not achieve it at home. This paradox was cast into further relief in 1943 when the city began moving working-class residents from private slums into two federally funded public housing projects—Elmwood Courts for whites and Pyramid Courts for blacks. While the brick homes of Elmwood Courts were located in the more prosperous uptown district, the wood-frame dwellings of the Pyramid Courts were located on the same low-lying spot on which the Civil War contraband camp had been constructed eighty years prior. While Jim Crow was being established in public housing, the mass exodus of black proprietors and professionals ensured that the experience of racial segregation was being supplanted by one of outright exclusion. The escalation of racial segregation and exclusion in the midst of the war against fascism fueled black political protests. Although the war itself failed to reverse Cairo's declining economic fortunes, black veterans returned home determined to make lasting changes to the city's racial order.[84]

2

Redemptive Love, Vigilante Terror, and Rebellion

Cairo in the Civil Rights Cauldron

By the mid-twentieth century the social and cultural power of black churches in Cairo was unrivaled. In this rigidly segregated borderland community, black sacred edifices served both religious and worldly purposes, functioning as primary sites of black worship, welfare intervention, community building, and protest. However, the black church had arrived at this lofty position by default, its power gained as a paradoxical consequence of a broader decline in black economic and political opportunities that hindered the development and survival of alternative institutions. Filling the vacuum that remained was an unenviable task that some argued detracted from the church's primary mission of ministering to the spiritual needs of congregants. Despite these divisions, churches emerged as a primary locus for black freedom struggles during and immediately following World War II. Emboldened by the contradiction presented by a global war against fascism and racial discrimination at home, church-based activists reinvigorated the local NAACP and mounted a series of punctuated battles aimed at overturning Jim Crow.

This chapter traces the contours of Cairo's early civil rights struggles with a focus on the contested but invaluable contributions of black churches and their leading members. Beginning with the NAACP's postwar campaign to eliminate school segregation, this chapter demonstrates the centrality of black congregations and activist church leaders to mass direct action and explores the role of white violence in its derailment. In a preview of the "massive resistance" that would follow the *Brown* decision, white opposition forced the NAACP underground, frightening away supporters and compelling activists to shift to legal gradualism and accommodation, largely as a matter of survival. In this context longstanding divisions over the black church's involvement in protest activities resurfaced, contributing to a decline in church support and the marginalization of activist clergy. The eventual resurgence of mass direct action during the early 1960s coincided with the southern movement's "heroic" phase and the decision of higher authorities in the Illinois Conference of the AME Church to appoint a young militant clergyman, Rev. Blaine Ramsey Jr., to serve in Cairo. Ramsey's tenure at Ward Chapel provided the backdrop for the rise of a new generation of black student activists to join with SNCC in mounting the organization's first integration campaign north of the Ohio River. Under the influence of SNCC leaders from Nashville, student activists in Cairo adopted a distinctly religious conception of civil rights rooted in black Christian discourses of racial reconciliation and a Gandhian philosophy of nonviolence. By mobilizing this religious tradition, black youths were able to recruit intergenerational and cross-class support through the city's black congregations, and they ultimately succeeded in toppling segregation in public accommodations in the borderland community. However, in the concluding section I show how this religiously motivated alliance fractured once again in 1967 as persistent barriers to economic advancement and allegations of police brutality combined to produce a potent urban rebellion.

Hattie Kendrick and the Wartime Revival of the Cairo NAACP

On a wintery evening in January 1942, forty-eight-year-old Hattie Kendrick walked down the block from her family home on Seventeenth Street to her church, Ward Chapel, where local NAACP leaders were holding an emergency meeting. Earlier that week the nation had learned of the brutal lynching of Cleo Wright in nearby Sikeston, Missouri. Wright, accused of assaulting two white women and subsequently stabbing a night marshal, was seized from the city jail by a mob of several hundred, tied to the back of a car, and dragged through Sikeston's historically black community in broad daylight. As the authorities closed in, the mob converged on a railroad easement, doused Wright's body with gasoline, and set him alight just a few hundred yards from two black congregations in the midst of their Sabbath services.[1]

News of the lynching quickly spread to Cairo, where auto mechanic Henry Dyson and schoolteacher Omitress Sparks were already busy planning an organizing meeting to revitalize the local branch of the NAACP. Kendrick, a fellow teacher at the segregated Washington Junior High, attended the meeting at the behest of her aging mother, Charlotte Swan-Kendrick, who had been active in the Mississippi NAACP prior to moving with her daughter to Cairo two decades earlier. When Kendrick arrived at Ward Chapel that evening, the church was already "packed" with outraged residents. She slipped into one of the familiar pews and joined the others in listening to George Cross—a leading member of Graham Chapel AME Church of neighboring Mounds, Illinois—deliver a blistering speech on the paradox of fighting a war against foreign aggression when acts of terror persisted so close to home. "No, we shall not forget Pearl Harbor. Nor shall we forget Sikeston, Missouri," he bellowed to rapturous applause. As the meeting drew to a close, Dyson and Sparks moved through the crowd signing up enough new NAACP members to secure the branch's charter. Among them was Hattie Kendrick.[2]

Over the coming months Kendrick was drawn increasingly into the NAACP's orbit, motivated by the strictures of life in the borderland as well as a longer family history of racial violence and resistance. Sitting around the fire in their family home, Kendrick listened closely as her mother recited tales of her ancestors' experiences under slavery in the lower Mississippi Delta. Kendrick's grandparents on both sides had spent their early years enslaved on cotton plantations before the coming of the Civil War. Her father, Samuel Reuben Kendrick—founder of New Africa, an independent black farming community in rural Mississippi—died in 1909 at the age of fifty-six after a violent assault at the hands of white planters. The stories Swan-Kendrick told her daughter portrayed multiple generations of the Kendrick clan bound together by lives of hard labor and brutal treatment but also by great hopes and fierce resistance. Kendrick's favorite stories were those about family members who gave no quarter to their white oppressors. Among them were her maternal grandmother, Harriet Smith-Swan, who Kendrick claimed "refused to be whipped by a white woman," and her paternal grandfather, Madison Kendrick, affectionately known as "Bumpaw," who threw "pine knots at the white men who attempted to whip him." Kendrick also took great pride in recounting stories of her maternal great-grandmother, who she believed "came from Africa." While notions of African origins conjured shame among many of her peers, Kendrick embraced her heritage, imagining that she came from a lineage of greatness and that her forebears were African kings. Collectively, these storytelling traditions cast Kendrick as the heir of a long family tradition of self-determination and race pride that, ultimately, propelled her into a lifelong struggle for black freedom.[3]

Kendrick's entrée into the NAACP was also fueled by her bitter disappointment with life in the Land of Lincoln. "All has not been too well since I came up north—up north to Cairo, Illinois," she declared. Like many southern migrants, Kendrick was initially taken aback by the rigidity of segregation in a supposedly northern city as well as by the toll, both economic and psychological, it exacted on its black residents. As a schoolteacher Kendrick bore these costs every day, working in a dilapidated and overcrowded one-room schoolhouse for which she received a meager salary of eighty-six dollars per month, less than half that of her white counterparts. By paying black educators so little, school administrators were able to subsidize the exorbitant costs associated with maintaining a dual school system. For this reason, in the late 1930s and early 1940s the NAACP targeted such wage inequalities as an indirect method for achieving its broader goal of toppling Jim Crow education.[4] As historians August Meier and John Bracey explain, "The rationale for this indirect approach was to make segregated public schooling so expensive that the choice would be desegregation or economic ruin." In a move that would come to typify the organization's strategy at the national level, NAACP executives selected the borderland as a "legal laboratory" for its earliest campaigns for salary equalization, assuming easier victories in the region would set a precedent for tougher campaigns further south. By the early 1940s the NAACP had achieved landmark legal victories in these areas, including *Mills v. Board of Education* (1939) in Maryland and *Alston v. School Board of Norfolk* (1940) in Virginia, prompting branch leaders in Cairo to consider a salary equalization suit as the first step in their own campaign to overturn Jim Crow.[5]

The campaign kicked off with a mass meeting at Ward Chapel in the second week of February 1944 amid an atmosphere of excitement and trepidation. "We had thrown every thing [*sic*] . . . toward the success of the meeting," Kendrick explained. "Everybody who had any influence [or] new [*sic*] anything was on [the] program." For the keynote address branch member J. C. Lewis, a former principal of Sumner High, had invited newly elected Democratic state legislator Corneal Davis to speak. After the Depression, Chicago's growing black populace underwrote a political realignment and the election of a new generation of Democratic black legislators. Davis, Charles Wimbush, and Charles Jenkins, among others, championed progressive legislation aimed at toppling a range of discriminatory practices across the state. In Cairo, where the avenues to black political power were effectively blocked, Davis's reputation as an outspoken race leader preceded him. "A black man in the legislature . . . talking back to white folks," Kendrick recalled, "whoever heard of such [a thing]. This must be the millennium." Kendrick's respect for the politician only grew upon learning that he was an ordained minister and assistant pastor of Ward Chapel's sister congregation, Quinn Chapel AME, in Chicago (see fig. 2.1). That night Davis delivered a traditional stump speech on his election platform and as the meeting drew to a close found himself quickly cornered by a group of schoolteachers led by Kendrick and Sparks. "They was waiting for me when the services was over," Davis laughed. "They said, 'We're so glad you came except that . . . we have wanted somebody . . . to talk with the county superintendent or do something about our salaries.'" After listening to the women's stories, Davis agreed to remain in Cairo overnight and discuss the situation with the county superintendent, Leo Schultz, the following day.[6]

When Davis, Kendrick, and Dyson arrived at Cairo High School the following morning, Schultz was already standing outside. "He was out there waiting for me," Davis recalled. Before the congressman could introduce himself, Schultz bellowed, "Oh I know who you are. . . . You that nigger that came down here and got these people all stirred up?" A stunned Davis retorted, "I don't know what you're talking about. I didn't stir up anybody. I came down to make a speech for the NAACP." "Oh yes you did," Schultz fired back. "You came down here about all these niggers." Davis strove to remain calm, explaining that he had come to the county superintendent's office to locate copies of the schedule of

Figure 2.1. Rep. Corneal Davis (third from right) with Hattie Kendrick (middle) and other members of the Cairo branch of the NAACP, ca. 1940s. Courtesy of the Manuscript Division of the Library of Congress.

salaries for teachers in Alexander County. Schultz refused the request and proceeded to berate the esteemed politician. "If you know what's good for you," he threatened, "you'll get on back up there to Chicago. . . . These niggers down here are all satisfied. They get along fine." Angered and surprised by the encounter with Schultz, Davis made a commitment to Kendrick and the rest of the teachers that he would fight to obtain the records and pursue the case on their behalf. Upon returning to his office at the state capitol in Springfield, Davis reached out to rising star Thurgood Marshall, the NAACP's legal director, who encouraged the congressman to collaborate with African American attorney Z. Alexander Looby, who was fighting a similar case in Nashville. Over the coming months the two exchanged information, and Davis began building the case that would secure equal pay for the city's black teachers.[7]

The filing of the legal suit represented an important landmark in Cairo's black freedom struggle. "[It was] the first time in the history of Cairo [that] a group of Negroes presented a sound united front," Kendrick declared. As Davis's work became public knowledge, white Cairoites responded angrily by sending the congressman hate mail filled with racial epithets. "I never got so many unsigned threatening letters in all my life," Davis recalled. "One time they sent me a coffin right here in Springfield." Undeterred, Davis returned to Cairo later in the year to file suit at the courthouse, using Kendrick as the plaintiff. Upon his arrival Davis learned from community members that more threats had been made on his life. "Hell has broke loose down here," one man warned. "These white folks say they going to kill you down here. They going to lynch you!" News about Kendrick's involvement had already spread, and Davis now feared that her life might be in jeopardy. "She had already been identified. . . . Somebody had already told them that Hattie Kendricks [*sic*] got me down there, that she was the one." Accordingly, Davis committed to file the suit but insisted that local people not go with him to the courthouse for fear that their identities would be exposed.

The filing of the lawsuit was met by a media blackout in Cairo, prompting local NAACP leaders to purchase an advertisement in the *Cairo Evening Citizen* explaining the grounds for the complaint, which charged the Cairo school board with paying black teachers lower wages than their white counterparts—in direct violation of federal and state law.

"This is not only undemocratic but un-Christian," the advertisement stated. "Negroes are dying on foreign fronts for democracy, why not give them a chance to live for and with democracy at home."[8] In April 1945 *Negro City Teachers Association of Cairo vs. Vernon L. Nickell, Superintendent of Public Instruction, et al.* was finally heard before the Federal District Court for the Eastern District of Illinois with Thurgood Marshall representing the teachers alongside David Lansden, grandson of former mayor John Lansden and chairman of the Cairo NAACP branch's Legal Redress Committee. State's Attorney Peyton Berbling and local attorney D. B. Reed were present on behalf of the city. Marshall successfully petitioned the court to release local records revealing the full extent of the city's discriminatory pay scale and forcing Judge Fred Wham of Centralia to find on behalf of the plaintiffs. In a landmark victory the judge ordered a consent decree imposed on the city of Cairo mandating equal pay for black teachers. Inspired by the victory, members of the NAACP began to shift the battle to a direct assault on Jim Crow in the city's schools.[9]

Postwar Battles for School Desegregation

Shortly after winning the Cairo salary equalization suit, Thurgood Marshall announced that the NAACP was embarking on a new campaign to overturn school segregation across the northern borderland. In the southernmost parts of Illinois, Indiana, Ohio, Pennsylvania, and New Jersey, racial practices tended to mirror those of the Deep South, including the maintenance of dual school systems and the open usage of racial assignment policies by school administrators. However, as Marshall noted, important legal differences distinguished the two regions. While Deep South states tended to codify segregation through law, Jim Crow practices in much of the northern borderland operated "in spite of state statutes designed to prevent discrimination or segregation of the races in its school systems."[10] As Marshall explained in a 1948 letter to NAACP executive secretary Roy Wilkins, "The segregated schools in Southern Illinois are not only illegal but they have been declared illegal by Illinois cases. They are a disgrace to the state and even more so a disgrace to the NAACP and especially the Illinois State Conference of Branches."[11] During the late 1940s, black legislators, led by Democratic representatives

Corneal Davis and Charles Jenkins, launched their own assault on down-state school segregation, strengthening existing nondiscrimination laws and amending appropriation bills to allow for the withholding of funds from school districts that permitted such practices to go unchecked. With these new weapons in their arsenal, NAACP executives sent in Director of Branches and Field Administration Gloster Current to assist local branches across Southern Illinois in testing the laws.[12]

In Cairo, Kendrick and other activists watched closely as branches across the region mobilized black parents to attempt to enroll their children in all-white schools. In city after city these efforts were greeted by intransigence from local school authorities, prompting the NAACP to file lawsuits that ultimately forced desegregation in East St. Louis, Alton, and Edwardsville in 1950 and in Harrisburg in 1951.[13] Developments in Cairo, however, moved much slower. Representatives Davis and Jenkins visited the city in 1951 as part of a special legislative committee to investigate the reasons behind the school district's failure to comply with state mandates. In their final report the committee concluded that Superintendent Leo Schultz constituted "the main obstacle to the elimination of school segregation in Alexander County" and that black parents feared bodily violence against their children seeking to attend the school nearest their residence. Counteracting such fears was essential to desegregation campaigns, because in contrast to salary equalization suits, success hinged on the mass participation of black parents. Recognizing the need for outside support, Thurgood Marshall sent fieldworkers June Shagaloff and Lester P. Bailey to Cairo in January 1952 to negotiate with city officials and assist the local branch in registering children for transfer into white schools.[14]

Cairo's black churches were ground zero for the NAACP's desegregation campaign. Mass meetings educating parents about the benefit of integrated schools and encouraging them to submit applications for transfer requests were held at the city's two largest black congregations, Mt. Moriah Baptist Church and Ward Chapel. The NAACP's ability to access these churches hinged on the support of their members, particularly clergy and lay leaders. Since the resolution of the salary equalization suit, a number of prominent church leaders had joined Kendrick in the NAACP, including branch president Dr. W. A. Fingal and Dr. James

Carroll Wallace Jr., who served as chair of both the branch publicity and finance committees. Both men held leadership positions in their respective congregations: Fingal as a trustee at Ward Chapel and Wallace as a steward at Martin Temple. At the height of the campaign, Ward Chapel's itinerant pastor, Rev. Arthur Jelks, replaced Fingal as branch president, further cementing ties between the church and civil rights activities.[15]

However, as the spiritual home of Cairo's dwindling black middle class, Ward Chapel was fiercely divided over the church's involvement in the desegregation campaign. Kendrick, an active lay leader, quickly found herself caught in the middle of a congregational dispute about the appropriate use of the church's meeting space and resources. "A part of the church congregation was proud of the firm stand which was being made in civil rights," she explained. "The other part seemed humiliated."[16] While many of the branch's leaders were themselves middle-class professionals, Kendrick's personal writings reveal a sense of growing frustration with the conservatism of what she disparagingly referred to as the "upper tens" of her own congregation. The majority, she argued, were busy imitating "white mores" and distancing themselves from the working-class parents galvanized by the school desegregation campaign. "No self respecting member of the black bourgeoisie would done belong to that mess," she caustically declared.[17] While class pretensions certainly shaped some of the resistance, many others opposed the use of church facilities out of fear. "Some thought that such meetings were dangerous for the church," Kendrick explained. "Other members felt if we could not have Civil Rights meetings in our own churches then our Civil Rights was a farce and needed strengthening." Despite these underlying tensions, the support of Ward Chapel's lay leaders and minister ensured that it would play an integral role in the NAACP's effort to integrate the city's schools. By the start of spring semester 1952, branch leaders had recruited an unprecedented two hundred new members and filed eighty-seven transfer requests with the local school board.[18]

As word spread that black parents were planning to transfer their children on the first day of classes, white citizens mounted an organized campaign of violence and intimidation. Parents who had signed transfer requests received menacing letters from anonymous senders; white drivers issued threats to young children playing in the streets; and on the night before the first day of the semester, three crosses burned in areas with the heaviest concentration of transfer requests. Field secretary June Shagaloff, who was subjected to near continual harassment, hired two bodyguards and began carrying a weapon. While seeking to dispel parents' fears, Shagaloff also had to address the opposition of leading members of Cairo's black middle class, particularly schoolteachers, who justifiably feared that desegregation would cost them their jobs. Before classes started principal Willie Mathews of Sumner High School visited every student who had applied for a transfer and falsely informed them that all of the other applicants had withdrawn their requests. Others were visited by Rev. Mitchell Fisher of the Cairo COGIC congregation, who warned parents that they would lose welfare payments and bank credit privileges if they pursued integration. Some parents withdrew their transfer requests out of fear of reprisals. However, a larger group of undeterred parents prepared to enroll their children on the first day of classes.[19]

On January 28 the parents—with children in tow—walked to the city's historically white schools. Upon their arrival school officials determined to halt the integration drive informed the parents that their transfer requests had not been processed. Shortly after, violence broke out across the city. Armed vigilantes fired multiple shotgun blasts into the home of Dr. James Carroll Wallace; unexploded dynamite was discovered at the tire shop owned by branch vice president Henry Dyson; and Dr. W. A. Fingal received threats warning him to leave the city or "suffer the consequences." Not all of those targeted were prominent civil rights activists. Dr. Urbane Bass, a local physician who admitted that he had refused to participate in the transfer plan, narrowly averted death when vigilantes threw dynamite onto his back porch. While other downstate communities had desegregated relatively peacefully, Cairo witnessed yet another upsurge in racial violence, prompting the deployment of the National Guard and foreshadowing events that would take place in the Deep South after the *Brown* decision.[20]

Over the coming weeks state and federal investigators arrived in Cairo to ensure that the perpetrators of the bombings and cross burnings were prosecuted. Though many, including bombing victim Urbane Bass, attributed the violence to a "small minority group of hoodlums,"[21] subsequent arrests revealed that the accused included some of Cairo's most prominent business owners and trade union leaders. Among the more than twenty white men arrested were auto dealer Robert Hogan; Jack and Earl Bauer of the Bauer Bros. Oil Company; Elmer Cummings of the Cairo City Coal Company; Kenneth Sullivan of the Sullivan Electric Company; and Connell Smith, leader of the Cairo local of the American Federation of Labor's Hod Carriers, Building and Common Laborers Union.[22] Angered by the arrests, fellow merchants William Lebo and Clifford Jones pressed for charges of disorderly conduct and endangering the life of a child to be brought against the NAACP's leadership. The merchants accused the NAACP of jeopardizing the safety of black students by forcing them to enroll in all-white schools. Cairo city police officers proceeded to Ward Chapel where they arrested David Lansden, Reverend Jelks, Dr. Fingal, Dr. Wallace, Dr. S. W. Madison, June Shagaloff, and Lester Bailey. Eager to appease white citizens, State's Attorney Michael O'Shea upheld the charges and moved the case forward for prosecution.[23] When the grand jury returned in February they found no grounds for indictment, but in a lengthy statement foreman John Clarke chastised NAACP leaders for disrupting the "safety and moral conditions" of local schoolchildren and acting with an "arrogance, abusiveness and utter lack of cooperation, which could have very easily led to violence and upheaval." Shortly after, in a move that outraged not only activists but also state officials, an all-white grand jury threw out all charges against the men accused of participating in the bombing of Dr. Bass's home.[24]

As experienced civil rights activists, Shagaloff and Bailey were not entirely surprised by such acts of vigilante violence. They were, however, taken aback by the open hostility of Cairo's white civic elites to desegregation. "It was the official white reaction to this move," they argued in the April 1952 issue of *The Crisis*, "that put Cairo in the hall of infamy."[25] Shagaloff and Bailey, like many civil rights activists, had entered the borderland believing that the region represented a perfect testing ground as much for the legal contradictions it presented as for the assumed liberality of its civic elites when compared to the Deep South. As scholars of black freedom struggles in cities such as Louisville, Cambridge (Maryland), and St. Louis have argued, borderland elites tended to practice "polite racism," touting their communities as beacons of racial civility and progressivism. Believing that this politics of racial civility might be employed to their advantage, national civil rights organizations had fought and won many of their earliest campaigns in the borderland, including the desegregation of graduate and professional schools (e.g., the 1938 *Gaines v. Canada* supreme court ruling in Missouri) and the toppling of discriminatory housing practices (e.g., the 1948 *Shelley v. Kramer* ruling against racial covenants in Missouri). Accordingly, civil rights struggles often came earlier to the borderland and, as Clarence Lang assesses, "prefigured shifts in race relations for the rest of the nation."[26]

Earlier battles for school desegregation in Southern Illinois served to reinforce such assumptions about borderland elites. In East St. Louis, for example, members of the board of education, chamber of commerce, law enforcement, and the local press engaged in behind-the-scenes negotiations with NAACP members to resolve the desegregation battle peaceably.[27] Civic leaders in Cairo, however, exhibited little interest in dialogue. In what would become a hallmark of race relations in the city, Cairo's white civic elites rejected the politics of civility in favor of their own brand of "massive resistance." Shagaloff and Bailey's offer to collaborate on developing a desegregation plan was met with "stony silence" from the city council. School authorities, led by Schultz and a school board that included representation from some of the city's largest commercial and industrial interests, actively obstructed efforts to transfer black students into white schools. In fact, NAACP leaders alleged that Schultz and the school board were the only ones with the requisite information to leak the names and addresses of transfer applicants to known vigilantes.[28] Schultz did little to deter such claims, insisting in a confidential memo to the state superintendent of schools that white citizens should be commended for "their recent action," which he contended had "called [the NAACP's] hand." "It is hoped," Schultz stated bluntly, "that many of [the NAACP's] tactics will be halted as a result of this action—not only checked in Cairo, but throughout the Nation."[29] The use of vigilante violence was also tacitly endorsed by law enforcement, which the NAACP accused of much foot-dragging prior to the arrival of state and federal agents. All of this took place unchecked by the last watchdog of democratic governance: the editorial board at the *Cairo Evening Citizen* maintained a media blackout on the school desegregation campaign, refusing to publish NAACP press releases that might have dispelled rumors and lessened tensions in the city. Taken collectively, the actions of city officials presented a solid wall of opposition that distinguished Cairo from many other borderland communities facing desegregation campaigns during this period.[30]

By early March twenty-one black students had been successfully enrolled in the city's formerly all-white schools. However, continued obstructionism prompted NAACP leaders to conclude that local authorities were permitting token enrollment to deflect criticism and stall integration. Accordingly, local activists filed suit against the school district and began working with black legislators to cut off state funding. Under intense pressure the county superintendent of schools, Lucy Twente McPherson, withheld state funds for several months during the spring semester, and by the fall the total number of black students enrolled in formerly all-white schools had increased to sixty.[31] The impact of the desegregation battle was also felt in the city's parochial schools. In the spring of 1952 administrators at St. Joseph's parochial high school reported that the NAACP's "unfortunate agitation" had prompted a flood of inquiries from white citizens as to whether black children would be admitted and if the school would consider enrolling white Protestants if they "did not care to sit in the classroom with the Negroes in the public schools." Fearing the consequences of a desegregation campaign at St. Joseph's, administrators decided to temporarily close the school during the summer of 1952, publicly citing financial difficulties.[32]

Encouraged by these strides, Shagaloff and Bailey were reassigned to more troublesome areas, and journalists began to tout Cairo as a sign that even the most hostile communities could be redeemed. "Jim Crow education is on its ways [sic] out," jubilant editors at the Chicago Defender proclaimed in September.[33] Local realities, however, offered little ground for optimism, and complete integration would not be achieved until 1969 when the city's schools were finally consolidated. Until then, a "freedom of choice" model was followed by which a small number of African Americans elected to fill limited spots in the city's historically white schools while the majority continued to attend all-black schools.[34]

In September 1953 W. A. Fingal, president of the Cairo branch of the NAACP, wrote a desperate plea to Thurgood Marshall asking for field secretary June Shagaloff to be returned to Cairo immediately. The Cairo branch, Fingal explained, was caught in the middle of "a life and death struggle." The year following the desegregation campaign witnessed an upsurge in harassment and violence, forcing the Cairo branch underground. In June 1952 white Cairoites, led by a group of small-business owners, formed the Cairo Citizens Association (CCA), a forerunner to the White Citizens' Councils that would spring up across the South in the wake of the *Brown* decision.[35] The NAACP's only white member, attorney David Lansden, was targeted by the organization for his role in the pending legal suit against local school authorities. Garbage was strewn across Lansden's property, his front steps were smeared with oil, and rocks were thrown through his windows. The prominent attorney also had the misfortune of living next door to a member of the CCA, trade union leader Connell Smith, who erected what author Langston Hughes would describe as a four-foot "red arrow of bigotry" on his garage pointing toward his neighbor's property.[36] When asked by reporters from *Life* magazine to explain the purpose of the sign, Smith stated bluntly, "so I can see where the dynamite is going off." Fearful of bodily harm to his daughter, Lansden removed her from the public schools and sent her to St. Louis to complete her education.[37]

City officials also engaged in economic reprisals against Kendrick and other black activists who had supported the desegregation campaign. Members of the Interdenominational Ministerial Alliance were denied parade permits, and black entrepreneurs were prevented from obtaining the appropriate licenses to conduct business. As one of the few black schoolteachers to support the desegregation campaign, Kendrick was particularly vulnerable, and shortly after the protests she was dismissed from her position at Washington Junior High by the school board. For a single black woman with the responsibility of caring for her elderly mother, Kendrick despaired for the future: "A Negro with no job is dead [in all] . . . the ways you can die except eternal damnation." For the rest of her life, Kendrick would cobble together employment outside of the classroom as a domestic, babysitter, and tutor.[38]

In his letter to NAACP executives, Dr. Fingal stressed the chilling effect of this unchecked campaign of terror on the branch's efforts to organize black Cairoites. "Negroes are 99.9 percent scared at all times of the white folks and NAACPers," he explained. "Any local Negro who dares defy the boundaries imposed by the white brethren is in danger of hell's fire and damnation administered by his Negro fellowman." In the face of strident opposition and pressure to accommodate, the NAACP's membership plummeted from eight hundred to fifty, and branch leaders were forced to alter their strategies. NAACP member Rev. J. I. Cobb recalls branch members conducting meetings secretly out of their homes and encouraging concerned citizens to meet with them face-to-face due to fears that the organization's mail was being tampered with. Accordingly, the organization's focus shifted away from direct-action strategies to the filing of legal suits targeted at integrating the city's movie theaters and protecting its members from economic reprisals.[39] In turn, growing repression contributed to the departure of many of the branch's male officeholders, creating a leadership vacuum. In an ironic twist, black women were increasingly elected to officer positions, growing their ranks from just one in 1952 to a majority of eight two years later. Women officers such as Carrie Dunn Jones (secretary); Carmel Fowler (membership committee); Juanita Gholson (education committee); Josephine Brown (junior work committee); and Hattie Kendrick (entertainment committee and press and publicity committee) played a critical role in sustaining the organization during the doldrums of the late 1950s.[40]

Concern about the declining involvement of the city's black churches was also prominent in Fingal's report. In the summer of 1952, as fear of reprisals escalated, longstanding disagreements regarding the appropriate role of black churches in the civil rights struggle reemerged at Ward Chapel, threatening to divide the congregation. According to Kendrick, "Rev. Jelks, our pastor, called on trustee Dr. W. A. Fingal and asked him to go to Bishop Baber and asked him to replace him at the end of the conference year." Kendrick described the years immediately following Reverend Jelks's departure as "a time of problems and stagnation for the church," during which a majority of the membership refocused their energies inward. As Fingal crafted his letter to NAACP executives in September 1953, a sense of fear gripped the city's black congregations, promoting a culture of widespread accommodation. "[Eighty] percent of the Negroes dare not attend an NAACP meeting or any other meeting setting forth their rights as citizens," Fingal wrote. "They are taught through the pulpits and schools that this is just stirring up something." Out of the nearly twenty black churches in the city "only two," according to Fingal, were "available for mass assemblage" and local pastors were "afraid to come out to such meetings." Not all ministers opposed the NAACP's work, but their involvement was often constrained by the sentiments of their congregants. According to Fingal, activist ministers risked alienating their own members, who in some cases threatened to halt financial contributions if they disagreed with the church's activities. Baptist and Pentecostal ministers were particularly vulnerable to local economic pressures because they lacked the financial independence that the Methodist's hierarchical structure offered. However, as Reverend Jelks's resignation illustrates, even the Methodist itinerancy system could not insulate activist ministers from the impact of lay opposition. In this context, Jelks's resignation represented a significant loss for Kendrick and Ward Chapel's other activist lay leaders. According to Kendrick, it was for this reason she was jubilant when the bishop of the Illinois conference took what many "older and more conservative churchmen considered a long chance" by sending a youthful Blaine Ramsey Jr. to serve as Ward Chapel's pastor in 1959.[41]

Blaine Ramsey, Charles Koen, and Operation Open City

Ramsey's youth and inexperience made him a surprising choice for the pastorate of Ward Chapel. Since graduating from the University of Illinois just two years earlier, Ramsey had pastored only one congregation, a resume that hardly prepared him to lead an established congregation plagued by internal conflict. However, with the civil rights movement in full swing and a new generation of militant ministers taking the lead in cities across the South, executives in the Illinois AME conference opted to appoint the young and enthusiastic minister, who was well versed in the latest social action approaches. In the highly centralized AME Church, this denominational support afforded Ramsey a strong mandate, and his sharp intellect and charismatic persona quickly inspired the support of many of his congregants, setting the stage for Ward Chapel's reemergence at the forefront of civil rights struggles.[42]

Ramsey initially concentrated on the church's institutional needs, performing repairs, establishing a financial plan, and providing pastoral care. However, as the first year of his tenure drew to a close, the young minister began to refocus his congregation outward to conditions beyond the church walls. Like other so-called "militant ministers" of his generation, Ramsey preached a social gospel that emphasized Christ's ministry to the poor and oppressed and the church's responsibility to meet the needs of the whole person. In his weekly sermons Ramsey taught the importance of charity and mutual aid as well as issuing more direct challenges to the unjust systems of racial segregation and discrimination that kept so many of Cairo's black residents in poverty. In Kendrick's recollection Ramsey seamlessly integrated scripture and protest, carving out space for civil rights activities at the heart of understandings of Christian mission. In the process the young minister worked hard to bridge the very real theological divisions that existed between Ward Chapel's members. "In Blaine Ramsey's church," Kendrick recalled "there were two [schools of thought] on community involvement. Number one, preach Christ in him crucified—that will settle everything. The other school cried preach us a practical gospel." Ramsey's skill, Kendrick argued, was in his ability to marshal scripture to challenge this bifurcation. As Kendrick wrote in her private journals: "Blain[e] Ramsey heard both of them and understood what they were saying better than themselves. Did not they say with him every Sunday morning, [thou] shall love the Lord they God with all they heart and they neighbor as thyself. Blain looked around. He saw his people. God's black children, sick of poverty and deprivation; hungry for knowledge; thirsty for opportunity; imprisoned within walls of segregation and discrimination. Blain Ramsey heard their cry and Elijah answered, here I am Lord, send me, send me [sic]." By grounding the call for political protest in a "this-world" social gospel, Ramsey legitimized the church's involvement in civil rights work and encouraged his congregants to participate as part of their Christian duty.[43]

Ramsey's distinctive approach resonated with Ward Chapel's long-standing activist lay leaders, particularly Kendrick, who like Ramsey viewed her own activism as an extension of deep religious convictions. Like other "race women" of her generation, Kendrick viewed the black church as a foundational space for her own social justice work and its many clubs, auxiliaries, and missionary societies as natural vehicles in the battle against racial discrimination.[44] In addition to her responsibilities at the NAACP, Kendrick now served as chair of the Social Action Commission of the Fourth Episcopal District's Women's Missionary Society. In this capacity Kendrick took Matthew 25:35–36 as her mandate for an active social ministry: "For I was an hungred, and ye gave me meat: I was thirsty, and ye gave me drink: I was a stranger, and ye took me in: Naked, and ye clothed me: I was sick, and ye visited me: I was in prison, and ye came unto me." This mandate, Kendrick argued, would not be achieved "merely by sermons from the pulpit" but through the active contributions of black churchwomen to their communities. In a set of guidelines distributed to missionary societies across the district, Kendrick proposed that churchwomen serve their communities by tutoring schoolchildren, coordinating meals and clothing drives, and providing basic medical care in places where facilities were not provided. At Ward Chapel, Kendrick diligently worked to institutionalize this vision through her work as a Sunday school teacher, member of the steward board, and founder and president of the Charles A. Bolar Lyceum. Through the latter, Kendrick also educated congregants—young and old—on black history and culture as well as the responsibilities of Christian mission, service, and racial uplift.[45]

Recognizing the parallels in their work, Ramsey joined Kendrick on the executive board of the Cairo NAACP and began reaching out to the city's black ministers in an effort to reenergize the ecumenical relationships that had underpinned earlier struggles. He quickly gained the confidence of his peers in the Interdenominational Ministerial Alliance, forming strong ties with Rev. E. G. Mayes of the First Missionary Baptist Church and Rev. J. I. Cobb of the Cairo COGIC congregation, both of whom were also members of the NAACP. He also partnered with Kendrick in establishing the Ward Chapel Social Action Commission, a body charged with "coordinating activities in the areas of social, race, and economic relations as well as community cooperation." Through the Social Action Commission, Ramsey and Kendrick were able to recruit and train a new generation of church-based activists that helped reignite the civil rights struggle in Cairo.[46]

Foremost among this group was sixteen-year-old Charles Koen, a student at Sumner High who lived with his mother, Naomi Mallory (née Bondurant), in the segregated Pyramid Courts housing project. Koen's family had deep ties to Ward Chapel. His great-grandfather, George Bon-durant, had helped build the Seventeenth Street edifice; his grandmother, Christine Bondurant, served as the church organist for more than twenty years; and several of his aunts and uncles sang in the choir. As a teen-ager, however, Koen was much less involved, believing that "the church wasn't doing enough to help the poor and the struggling people." Koen's critique was not abstract but a direct response to what he described as the "humiliation and poverty" of his own childhood. Abandoned by his father before birth, Koen was raised by his teenage mother in a city that by the early 1960s had earned the title "Little Mississippi" for its depressed economy and "crazy-quilt pattern of rigid segregation." Determined to provide her son with a more stable home life, Naomi Bondurant labored as a domestic and remarried twice but was never able to escape the pov-erty of her youth. "We always had that constant hunger threat," Koen recalled. "One month my mother would go to the grocery store and buy food on credit; the next month she would pay the grocery bill and buy some food with the extra cash and the next month scuffle to pay the bill." From a young age Koen contributed to the family economy, collecting bottles and delivering papers during the school year and chopping cot-ton in the fields outside Cairo each summer. When hard times returned, Koen recalled waiting for hours with his mother in the commodity line for "white men . . . [to] fill our sacks full of dry goods, canned goods and potatoes," an experience that fostered feelings of intense bitterness and shame.[47]

While Koen felt the sting of poverty and racial inequality from a young age, he struggled to comprehend its cause. As he states in his auto-biography, "I grew up recognizing the symptoms of racism in Cairo and yet not fully understanding what the sickness was all about." This con-fusion was compounded during his teenage years as Koen made his first forays into public space alone only to run up against a rigid color line. Koen vividly recalls walking past the whites-only Mark Twain Restaurant on a warm summer evening and "longing to go in . . . and enjoy what the whites were enjoying—all the fine food, fine music, with the comfort of air conditioning." For Koen these tangible differences in rights and wealth seemed to extend into all areas of life in Cairo. "It was the same with their nice homes and fine cars," he explained. "You see blacks living in shacks while whites relax in their two-story homes surrounded by rose bushes." As the eldest son, Koen felt a tremendous responsibility to be "the father of the house" and provide a similar standard of living to those closest to him. "I wanted all that for my family too, and of course, I had no way of knowing then that their [whites] high economic status perpetuated my poverty."[48]

However, at the age of sixteen—shortly before meeting Ramsey—Koen describes an "awakening period" in which his vision of racial and class inequalities sharpened. "I still didn't really know what was going on, but from my observation I deduced that the oppression and racism we experience as blacks in Cairo controlled us psychologically." To a teenage Koen this psychological control was most visible in black Cairoites' accommodation to practices of racial exclusion in public accommodations. "The only way they could get away with stuff like that," Koen reasoned, "was because they controlled our minds." Perceiving the role that fear and accommodation played in upholding the status quo, Koen confessed to feeling even "more ashamed" and downtrodden. "My whole attitude on life changed at this point," he explained. "I guess I was seeking some kind of identity at the time, trying to be *somebody* as they so often say, struggling and feeling depressed, rejected, trying to break through all the experiences. . . . In addition to the wretched reality of my mother struggling hard, trying to provide for the family and finding it hard to do. It got the best of me." After lashing out and breaking a storefront window, Koen was sentenced to reformatory school. In desperation his mother reached out to Reverend Ramsey, who met with the judge and arranged to cover the fine and cost of repairs on his behalf. In return Koen agreed to work for the pastor, sparking a close relationship between the two. Koen recalls, "Rev. Ramsey was very instrumental in putting me on the proper track and giving me guidance which was very helpful for me on one hand and keeping me out of reform school and trouble on the other. . . . Meeting him was probably the best thing that happened to me at that point of my life." Koen's relationship with Ramsey and other activist lay leaders at Ward Chapel were transformative in that they legitimized previously unarticulated feelings of shame and frustration and provided an organizational context through which these sentiments could be directed toward constructive forms of protest. "Around about then,"

Koen states, "I started voicing my opinions on many injustices I saw." Ramsey also became a spiritual mentor whose model of an activist ministry Koen described as an "inspiration" that prepared him for his own "calling into the ministry."[49]

By the time Ramsey and Koen met in 1961, the young pastor was already testing racial barriers and contemplating a broader campaign to overturn Jim Crow in the city. Echoing the philosophy of his southern contemporary Rev. Martin Luther King Jr. as well as that of earlier black religious intellectuals like Benjamin Mays and Howard Thurman, Ramsey defined segregation not merely as an unjust social policy but as an immoral and sinful act that divided the human family and denied the sacredness of black people.[50] He visited with the all-white city council and unsuccessfully petitioned for the formation of an interracial human relations council to address widespread practices of discrimination in employment, housing, and public accommodations. Kendrick also recalled Ramsey's audacious efforts to integrate the city's exclusively white ministerial association. "He invaded their presence one morning while they were [meeting] at Glenn's—white only—Restaurant," she laughed. Stunned to see a black minister so brazenly violating the racial order, the diners fell silent as Ramsey "chided them for allowing racial segregation to exist in the [C]hristian family." When such petitions fell on deaf ears, Ramsey and other local activists, inspired by recent campaigns led by the Congress of Racial Equality (CORE) and SNCC, began to consider the use of nonviolent direct action as an alternative strategy for challenging Jim Crow. In 1961 CORE had mounted a number of struggles in borderland cities, including nearby East St. Louis and St. Louis, aimed at integrating recreational facilities. In Nashville the SNCC activists responsible for leading sit-ins at downtown restaurants were preparing to embark on the Freedom Rides to test federal rulings banning segregation on interstate travel. With these campaigns in mind, Ramsey reached out in the spring of 1962 to Nashville SNCC organizers, inviting them to come to Cairo to aid in a citywide campaign against segregation. SNCC leaders agreed, making Cairo the site of the organization's first integration campaign north of the Ohio River.[51]

Prior to their arrival, Ramsey and Cobb approached Koen to ask him to take the lead in mobilizing students from local high schools in preparation for possible direct-action campaigns. Koen embraced the role, organizing black youth and forming the Cairo Nonviolent Freedom Committee (CNVFC), using Ward Chapel as their headquarters. When SNCC fieldworkers John Lewis, Mary McCollum, James Peake, and Joy Reagon arrived from Nashville in June, they found that Koen had already organized more than seventy high school students and had additional support from John O'Neal and other students from Southern Illinois University Carbondale who had recently formed a SNCC chapter in solidarity. The fieldworkers quickly accepted their role as advisors, helping local students plan the campaign and providing training in nonviolent direct action (fig. 2.2).[52]

Many of the SNCC fieldworkers from Nashville had trained under Rev. James Lawson and subscribed to a Tolstoyan or Gandhian philosophy of nonviolence that resonated with Cairo's church-based organizing traditions.[53] The CNVFC's first newsletter reprinted SNCC's 1960 "Statement of Purpose," which affirmed the redemptive quality of nonviolence to transform hate through love in the service of forging a reconciled community.[54] The CNVFC's subsequent publications, private correspondence, and oral statements reveal that this ideology was internalized by many of the group's members, becoming "a personal philosophy" as opposed to a pragmatic strategy. In contrast to the NAACP, which focused on legal suits to force integration, SNCC and the CNVFC understood segregation to be symptomatic of what John O'Neal defined as a deeper "moral sickness" that needed to be confronted at the individual level with redemptive love. "Through the demonstration," O'Neal explained, "we confront each man—the restaurant owner, hotel owner and the people in the street who support the businessman—with his responsibility." SNCC and CNVFC leaders claimed that through this "creative interchange . . . the dignity of both white and Negro becomes reinforced," leaving open the prospect of a deeper reconciliation. Thus, while integration was an important practical goal, many local students expressed their support for nonviolence as part of a deeper spiritual mission to banish hate and forge what they described as "a truly Christian city . . . [where] law, real democracy, and Christian brotherhood will prevail." SNCC photographer Danny Lyon captured this sense of shared spiritual mission in his photograph of John Lewis kneeling in prayer alongside two

Figure 2.2. SNCC organizer John Lewis with local schoolchildren in Cairo, 1962. Danny Lyon/Magnum Photos.

come let us build a new world together

STUDENT NONVIOLENT COORDINATING COMMITTEE 8½ RAYMOND STREET, N.W. ATLANTA 14, GEORGIA

Figure 2.3. "Come Let Us Build a New World Together," SNCC Poster, 1962. Danny Lyon/Magnum Photos.

youthful CNVFC activists, an image that SNCC mass-produced and cir-culated nationwide (fig. 2.3).[55]

On June 17, 1962, Reverend Ramsey and the students from SNCC and CNVFC began their campaign by testing a small number of res-taurants and hotels. "We went to the Mark Twain Restaurant on 9th and Washington Streets," Koen recalled. "We walked in, sat down and ordered a hamburger. The lady looked down at us and said, 'What do you niggers want here?'" Koen calmly repeated the group's order and asked if she was aware that they were entitled to service under the Illinois pub-lic accommodations law. Angered, the waitress fired back, "Naw, I ain't familiar with no law, what I'm familiar with is you niggers can't eat here and if you don't get your asses out, I'm going to call the police." Shortly afterward, another interracial group was also denied service at the Cairo

Hotel, but on a return visit they were served without incident. Within ten days of these initial protests television news reporters and cameramen had descended on the city, prompting many business owners to comply with the protestors' demands. However, some proprietors refused to bend to the growing pressure and media attention. James Cox, owner of Mack's Barbecue on Sycamore Street, adamantly refused to serve interracial groups, even turning a water hose on schoolchildren seeking admission. As an angry white mob began to assemble in Mack's parking lot, waitresses locked the children out of the restaurant and watched through the windows as a melee unfolded. The students, now surrounded by a group of about sixty whites, some of whom were intoxicated, began to search for a safe way out. "As we were leaving," SNCC field secretary Mary McCollum recalled, "a man who had threatened me earlier reached out and swung at one of the boys." McCollum, trained in nonviolent methods, quickly moved in between the two and was violently slashed across the thigh. McCollum declined to press charges, stating that her purpose was to "change his [the perpetrator's] attitude rather than threaten him" and that she was "willing to suffer for that change." Koen agreed, stating: "No matter what they do or say, we will be able to accept it and forgive them for their cruelness. After they treat us cruel for so long, maybe it will get on their conscience and they'll finally realize what they're doing. I feel sorry for them in a way." Over the coming days, Cox continued to lock the restaurant doors to student groups, eventually filing trespassing charges against Koen and other student protestors.[56]

Over the next two months, the protests spread as the CNVFC launched "Operation Open City," a campaign modeled on earlier efforts in Nashville to overturn segregation in all areas of civic life.[57] Also included in Operation Open City's eleven-point plan were other goals, including the creation of a human relations council, de facto integration of the city's schools, decent housing for all, fair treatment by the police, and better employment opportunities. Despite the wide-ranging nature of the CNVFC's demands, the majority of the group's protests continued to center on the integration of public accommodations, changing focus from restaurants to recreational facilities, barbershops, and churches. While students staged sit-ins, elders affiliated with the Interdenominational Ministerial Alliance and the NAACP often worked behind the scenes to negotiate settlements with proprietors and city officials.[58]

The responses of business owners varied, though few elected to integrate voluntarily. Typical methods of obstructionism included overcharging patrons, providing poor service, or closing temporarily. However, as the protests continued many white citizens once again turned to the police and extralegal violence. By the end of the second week of protests more than forty demonstrators, some as young as thirteen, had been arrested on charges ranging from trespassing to breach of the peace and mob action. Among those arrested were CNVFC president Charles Koen, vice president Frank Hollis, and SNCC fieldworker John Lewis, who all refused bail, declaring that they would "stand witness in jail to the evil" of the city's actions. Inside the segregated jail protestors held Bible studies, sang freedom songs, and staged a spontaneous hunger strike designed to protest their conditions and, according to Koen, "to purify their souls." On July 18 Justice of the Peace Robert Williams, to the astonishment of a packed courtroom, handed down seventeen guilty verdicts on charges ranging from disorderly conduct to mob violence. Outside, more than two hundred protestors rallied, singing "The Truth Will Set Us Free," "God Is on Our Side," and "Black and White Together." Speaking before the crowd, Reverend Ramsey declared, "We are fighting against an evil system, and we shall continue until that system is defeated." Shortly after, the CNVFC received a telegram from Martin Luther King Jr.—who was leading the campaign in Albany, Georgia—extending prayers and support on behalf of the SCLC.[59]

The arrests and prosecution of young protestors sparked outrage in the black community and served as an important catalyst for the recruitment of adults, many of whom had previously chosen to stay on the sidelines. The density of black communal networks in Cairo ensured that news of the children's arrests traveled quickly, directly affecting a large cross-section of the populace. Churches became the central hubs for the mobilization of this new support and sites for the development of important intergenerational alliances that would hold the movement together in the weeks that followed. Regular mass meetings were held at Ward Chapel and the First Missionary Baptist Church featuring speakers from the Interdenominational Ministerial Alliance, the NAACP, SNCC, and the CNVFC. Student leaders used these meetings to appeal to their elders for support: "We need your financial support, but we need much more. . . . We need you with us on the picket lines and in the demonstrations. . . . We need you at the mass meetings. . . . We need your hands, your hearts, and your prayers." The students' reliance on Christian discourses of racial reconciliation and nonviolence provided a unifying basis for these cross-generational dialogues capable of generating support for tactics that elders might otherwise have opposed as too militant. Indeed, many older residents were provoked by the youths' commitment to nonviolence in the face of threats and violence. Appeals to religious discourses also served as the foundation for limited interracial cooperation. However, with the exception of Rev. P. J. Fitzsimons of St. Columba's parish, white support continued to come almost exclusively from the organizations' out-of-town allies.[60]

By August the students had successfully integrated all of the city's restaurants and had made recreational facilities the movement's primary focus. The local swimming pool, established by the Rotary Club during the twenties, was now under the ownership of the Cairo Natatorium and Recreation Club, whose management invoked the organization's status as a private, members-only club in denying black patrons admission. When sit-ins resulted in arrests, the NAACP filed suit, claiming that the swimming pool's owners had refused to admit African Americans in defiance of state and federal law (fig. 2.4). A similar suit was filed against William Thistlewood, owner of the Roller Bowl, for denying black patrons admission to the skating rink. Illinois attorney general William Clark addressed the charges, issuing a legal opinion that both facilities were public places of accommodation or amusement and therefore subject to Section 13-1 of the Civil Rights Act. Empowered by the decision, Koen led a group of thirty-eight students to the Roller Bowl on August 17 to test the ruling. Upon their arrival the group was viciously attacked by a mob of white men. "All hell broke loose," Kendrick recalled. "They were knocked down and beaten like dogs. They were beaten over the heads with iron rods wrapped in . . . [barbed] wire." Kendrick also vividly remembered how local police stood passively by, some even laughing as "our children were being attacked." Some of the children tried to flee to a nearby parking lot for protection but were confronted by a man pursuing them with

Figure 2.4. Demonstrators try to enter a "whites only" swimming pool, 1962.
Danny Lyon/Magnum Photos.

a bicycle chain. Twelve-year-old Deborah Flowers was struck about the
legs and fell to the ground. Others were chased by passing vehicles and
threatened at gunpoint before they were able to return to Ward Chapel
for safety. Koen, Flowers, and several other activists were hospitalized
with lacerations about the head, face, and arms.[61]

In the aftermath of the violence, civil rights leaders from across the
state demanded that Gov. Otto Kerner act to restore law and order in
the embattled downstate community. Leaders from the Illinois NAACP
spearheaded a demonstration in Springfield calling on state officials to
deploy the National Guard to Cairo, appoint a special attorney general
to investigate all criminal cases pertaining to the recent violence, and
prosecute any proprietors that continued to discriminate against black
patrons. Shocked and embarrassed by the violence, Governor Kerner
agreed, assigning two special attorney generals to investigate the charges
and prosecute any cases of unlawful segregation in the city. The governor's decision angered Cairo city council members, who refused to form

a human relations commission and rather shifted their attention to the passage of a new parade ordinance designed to allow local police to crack down on black protestors.[62]

Despite the city council's efforts, the violence and subsequent outcry signaled a turning point for SNCC and the CNVFC's campaign just as it had in the Freedom Rides the previous year. Facing legal suits and mounting pressure from state officials, Cairo's proprietors, including the owner of the Roller Bowl, finally relented, admitting black patrons for the first time in September 1962. That same month the Belleville diocese sought to preempt protests by admitting eleven African American students to St. Joseph's parochial school. The following year the segregated St. Columba's school and church were closed, and the sitting city council was replaced by a new slate of council members committed to restoring calm to the city. Under Mayor Thomas Beadle's leadership, the council revoked the repressive parade ordinance and encouraged businesses to comply with state and federal law on racial integration.[63]

Reverend Ramsey's efforts to break down racial barriers among the city's clergy also began to bear fruit. In the fall of 1962 two white Methodist ministers—Rev. Boyd Wagner of the First Methodist Church and Rev. William Fester of Tigert Memorial Methodist Church—resigned from the all-white ministerial association after the organization's members refused to admit black clergymen. Inspired by the recent integration campaign, particularly "kneel-ins" held by CNVFC activists at Cairo's white congregations, the two ministers organized an interracial ministerial association under a new constitution and celebrated its founding at a service attended by both black and white congregants at the First Methodist Church on Good Friday 1964. Wagner and Fester also worked behind the scenes to pressure recently elected city council members to form a human relations commission in June 1963. In this context of conciliation and reform, local protests subsided and several key leaders left the city, including Reverend Ramsey, who was reassigned to Bethel AME in Champaign, Illinois, in the fall of 1963, and Koen, who began his ministerial training at McKendree College in Lebanon, Illinois, that same year.[64]

Despite these promising signs, lasting change proved elusive. By the end of 1964 both the human relations commission and the interracial ministerial association were inactive. Liberal clergymen found themselves ostracized by hostile white congregants and left the city. As with the earlier campaign to desegregate public schools, popular resistance to integration in Cairo continued by simply taking on new forms. When the Cairo Natatorium and Recreation Club reopened on an integrated basis during the summer of 1963, the majority of its white members refused to use the facility, forcing the club to close for the season. Determined to see the pool in operation, the Beadle administration leased it from the club the following summer but chose to close the pool permanently after just two weeks in the face of ongoing opposition. After the closure the property was sold to a third party who filled the pool with cement, a powerful symbol of the intractability of local white residents to racial change.[65]

As the nation witnessed the passage of the landmark Civil Rights Act of 1964 and Voting Rights Act of 1965, three generations of grassroots activists, represented by Kendrick, Ramsey, and Koen, took stock of Cairo's own halting progress. Through their collective efforts they had succeeded in eroding the edifice of Jim Crow. Still, other problems remained. "Once we integrated all over town . . . everything ended right there," Koen recalled. The young leader was particularly worried about the movement's failure to make real headway on job opportunities and hiring discrimination. "When it came to employment, everything just dropped. It was like the struggle swept in like a cyclone, picked up the door and windows but left the house intact." Though Operation Open City had identified eliminating job discrimination as part of its eleven-point plan, local activists had struggled to shift tactics midstream. "It was ironic," Koen recalled, "but nobody wanted to move on employment; for them it was a horse of a different color. . . . When it came to finding jobs for blacks, the struggle ended and though we could eat, swim and skate with whites, we didn't enjoy the luxury. With no job, we were back where we started. Poor."[66]

As the energy of the mass movement dissipated, seventy-two-year-old Kendrick took the reins at the NAACP, serving as the branch's first female president and, once again, shepherding the organization through the doldrums. As a result of her petitions, in June 1966 the Illinois State Advisory Committee to the US Commission on Civil Rights held a public meeting in Cairo to investigate allegations of ongoing civil rights violations. The committee discovered much to substantiate local activists' worst fears, including ongoing segregation in the city's public schools and public housing as well as widespread discrimination in federal contracts, employment, and social programs. Indeed, some of the committee's most damning findings pertained to the treatment of African American welfare recipients by white social workers. In an act that many viewed as tantamount to "racial peonage," local residents testified to being routinely thrown off welfare rolls during harvest season when low-paying agricultural work was abundant in the fields surrounding the city. Local growers were accused of conspiring with the Illinois Public Aid Commission and the Illinois State Employment Service to ensure access to a cheap and dependent surplus labor force. City officials allegedly made similar arrangements for periodic flood control and road construction projects.[67]

Koen, having experienced these exploitative labor practices firsthand, returned to Cairo in the winter of 1966 determined to make a difference. The now twenty-year-old college graduate and ordained Baptist minister arrived with his new wife, Cairo native Clydia Koen (née Watson) to care for his aging mother. In turn he accepted a position as area coordinator of the Illinois Migrant Council (IMC), a nonprofit organization founded by some of the state's leading religious agencies to address the needs of migrant and seasonal workers. Shortly after its formation in March 1966, the IMC secured federal funding under the auspices of Title III-B of the Economic Opportunity Act for the purpose of establishing schools that would provide adult education classes to migrant and seasonal farm workers. On January 2, 1967, Illinois Migrant School No. 8 opened in Cairo, providing classes in basic literacy, prevocational training, and community engagement to more than 150 mostly African American seasonal farm workers. As part of their mandatory prevocational training, students were expected to survey the types of jobs available in their community and make visits to local employers to gain job experience. These requirements forced students to confront the reality of discriminatory hiring practices and succeeded in elevating the issue to a position of prominence among local activists. With Koen at the IMC's helm and Kendrick back in the classroom for the first time in more than a decade, the migrant school—and, notably, not black churches—would soon emerge as the central hub for black protest in the transition from civil rights to black power.[68]

From Civil Rights to Rebellion

Joining Koen and the IMC students in this emergent campaign against job discrimination was one of the NAACP's youngest members and Kendrick's protégée, Preston Ewing Jr. Born in Cairo in 1934, Ewing's family had moved to the city from Arkansas during the Great Depression. His father, Preston Ewing Sr., secured work as a Pullman porter, taking him on the road for long stretches but also allowing his wife Nancy the financial security to be a stay-at-home mother to their six children. Ewing's mother was an active member of Ward Chapel, serving on the willing workers committee and alongside Kendrick in the missionary society. In the quiet years that followed the SNCC campaign, Kendrick recruited the younger Ewing into the NAACP, introducing him to the legal strategies that constituted the foundation of the branch's work and preparing him for future leadership. "Hattie talked me into becoming president of the NAACP," Ewing recalled. "She said . . . , 'I'm getting up in age and we need some young people and you'd be a good person.' . . . And I said, 'Well, okay, we'll do that.'" An organized and meticulous worker, Ewing proved to be an excellent choice and quickly expanded the branch's activities around hiring discrimination.[69]

By the spring of 1967 the combined energies of Cairo's civil rights activists were aimed at addressing the jobs crisis. Members of the NAACP and Interdenominational Ministerial Alliance repeatedly approached the city council, appealing for the creation of permanent positions and an end to discriminatory hiring practices. When these efforts fell on deaf ears, Koen and Ewing launched their own historic, though unsuccessful, bids for city council seats in an election clouded by allegations of voter fraud. Subsequently, Ewing began urging the NAACP to stage a boycott of local stores that refused to hire black workers. He quickly secured the support of Koen and the IMC staff as well as members of the Interdenominational Ministerial Alliance frustrated by the city's inactivity. The group soon began planning a trip to Tougaloo College to meet with NAACP field secretary Charles Evers, who had recently reached a settlement in a ten-month-long boycott in Port Gibson, Mississippi, resulting in the appointment of a black police officer, the integration of public accommodations, and the hiring of fifteen black store clerks.[70] However, before the boycott could get under way the nation entered another "long, hot summer" in which potent rebellions erupted in more than 150 urban communities, including Cairo.[71]

At around 2 a.m. on the morning of July 16, 1967, Ewing awoke to the sound of his phone ringing. On the other end of the line was a black physician who informed Ewing that he had been called by the sheriff to examine the body of Robert Hunt Jr., a nineteen-year-old African American soldier from Urbana, Illinois, who had been found dead in his cell at the police station. Hunt, who was in Cairo to visit his aunt, had been arrested on charges of disorderly conduct after a routine traffic stop. Less than an hour after entering police custody, officers alleged that Hunt had committed suicide by hanging himself from the ceiling of his cell with his own t-shirt. Ewing proceeded to the jail, where he observed a number of inconsistencies with the police's story. Upon examining Hunt's body, Ewing noticed several bruises suggestive of a struggle. He also observed that the ceiling of the cell was constructed out of a flimsy wire mesh incapable of sustaining Hunt's body weight. As rumors trickled out regarding the suspicious circumstances surrounding Hunt's death, many black Cairoites concluded that officers had murdered the soldier, an analysis bolstered by rampant allegations of police brutality in Cairo and other urban communities during the summer of 1967. Only a week prior, accusations of police violence against an African American taxi driver sparked racial unrest in Plainfield and Newark, New Jersey, resulting in the deployment of the National Guard. Earlier in the summer violence had also flared in Omaha, Nashville, Cincinnati, Atlanta, Buffalo, and the Roxbury neighborhood of Boston. Within hours of hearing the news of Hunt's death, black working-class teens and young adults in Cairo also took to the streets in anger, pelting buildings with rocks and homemade bombs.[72]

Despite city officials' characterization of the subsequent rebellion as an act of unrestrained and indiscriminate violence, participants were highly selective in their choice of targets, focusing narrowly on the property of Cairo's small commercial and industrial elite. While Hunt's death had clearly sparked the rebellion, the participants, including large numbers from the Pyramid Courts housing project, were striking back at what they perceived as a broader pattern of violence and exploitation. On the first night of the uprising, Molotov cocktails were thrown into several

Figure 2.5. National guardsman stands with fixed bayonet at the Pyramid Court housing project in Cairo, 1967.

white-owned businesses adjacent to the Pyramid Courts, including Rink's Grocery, Elias Dollar Warehouse, and Boalbey's Market. The following night rebels targeted the White-Coleman Lumber Company on the Mississippi River levee as well as the home of the company's white foreman, John Riggs. The insurgents then made their first encroachments uptown, smashing windows at the Hanna Grocery at Thirty-Second and Poplar. When local and state police proved unable to stem the tide, the National Guard was deployed and the Pyramid Courts quickly cordoned off by a perimeter of soldiers armed with fixed bayonet rifles (see fig. 2.5).[73]

In the days that followed, black working-class youths and young adults insisted on the political nature of their acts, identifying discriminatory hiring practices as their primary grievance. "We are fighting this discrimination—this economic thing," declared John Brantley, a thirty-year-old unemployed laborer. Twenty-seven-year-old Willie Bingham agreed: "We need jobs, we got a right to live, same as you people." When asked by reporters how many jobs they were demanding, Brantley replied, "No less than half of what we rightly deserve. If you've got 20 people working in a department store, we want 10 to be Negro and 10 something else. . . . We goin' to keep fighting until we get something around here." While Brantley and Bingham refused to address whether they had been personally involved in the recent disturbances, their statements indicated support for the strategic use of property damage. For Brantley, who had participated in the CNVFC's earlier integration campaigns, white intransigence had undermined nonviolent attempts to create a just and reconciled community. In his statements to reporters, Brantley represented the rebellion not as a radical break with these earlier civil rights struggles but as simply a new weapon in the battle for racial equality. Revealingly, when asked by a reporter if he was an advocate of black power, Brantley replied, "This is not Black Power but Negro strategy." Far from rejecting the liberal-integrationist aims of earlier struggles, Brantley and many of the other rebels viewed force as the only means capable of challenging a conscienceless people who maintained their power through threats and violence.[74]

In addition to repudiating the nonviolent approach of earlier struggles, the rebels had acted independently of the city's established civil rights leadership; in so doing they shifted the movement's organizational center from the unique cross-class and intergenerational milieu of the black church to the exclusively working-class setting of the Pyramid Courts. In the midst of the hostilities, civil rights leaders held clandestine meetings with youths at the housing project in an effort to calm tempers and channel their energy back into conventional forms of political protest. Ewing pleaded with the militants to stay off the streets and refrain from further acts of arson and vandalism. However, speaking with reporters from the *St. Louis Post-Dispatch*, the young NAACP president confessed that he had been unable to control the men, whom he described as mostly unemployed "school drop-outs with nothing to do." Ewing's initial inability to secure the confidence and support of the rebels hinted at the gulf that had opened up between established civil rights leaders and the black working-class youths who bore the brunt of the city's economic hardships. In an attempt to convey the situation to local officials, Ewing explained, "I'm a radical to you, but I'm an Uncle Tom to these youths."[75]

In many ways the barrier between the two factions had more to do with class and ideology than generation. At thirty-four, Ewing was close in age to some of the rebels, but his middle-class parentage and commitment to the NAACP's time-honored strategy of legal gradualism set him apart. In contrast, Koen had grown up in the Pyramid Courts and knew many of the current residents from his work at the IMC. Like Brantley, Koen had also come to question the utility of nonviolent direct action in the face of white civic elites' intransigence: "My feeling about the whole thing was [that] the youth were tired and non-violent demonstrations had passed away in 1962. They sought to change the system peacefully back then; it didn't work." Once the National Guard had been deployed, Koen quickly emerged as a spokesperson for the youth, encouraging them to call a truce and make formal demands to city leaders. On July 20 Koen joined Ewing and other community leaders in a meeting with city officials at the Pyramid Courts. During the meeting, he presented a list of demands on behalf of the rebels. At the top of the list was the hiring of black workers by all public and private employers. Further demands included the complete desegregation of the city's schools, the reopening of the swimming pool, the appointment of a black cochief of police, and the formation of an interracial city youth commission to determine the validity of the charges against those that were arrested during the uprising. Brantley warned that if the demands were not met within seventy-two hours, "Cairo will look like Rome burning down." Another young spokesperson, James Whitfield, echoed Brantley's threat, asserting that if city leaders failed to take action within three days the cease-fire would be broken. "We want to get across that we are human beings—nothing else," Brantley explained. "We have been treated as mules." In closing, Koen reinforced these statements, explaining that the youth were seeking "harmony in the community," but if city officials failed to act, "violence will explode." After facing decades of obstructionism and violent resistance to their appeals for rights and protection, black youths determined that their demands would be met by any means necessary.[76]

Over the next three days, Cairo's white civic elite did something it had long refused to do—negotiated with Cairo's black residents. Raised in East St. Louis, where he witnessed the devastating race riot of 1917, Mayor Lee Stenzel cautioned white residents against retaliation. "I saw the slaughter and destruction," he explained. "East St. Louis hasn't amounted to a damned thing since. If it happens here like it happened there, we won't have industry for 25 years." As an expression of his commitment to avert further violence, Stenzel worked with the city council to hire one African American to both the fire and police departments as well as appointing a black officer to the position of special assistant to the chief of police. Further, the city council agreed to train a member of the police department in the field of human relations. Movement on private-sector hiring was more difficult, with both the chamber of commerce and the retail merchant's association giving verbal assurances that jobs would be opened up in the near future. Despite these limitations, youth leaders accepted the concessions as "a token of good faith," and Koen commended city leaders for taking "positive steps in the right direction." The rebels' actions had helped to secure some tangible gains for the city's black residents and increased pressure on employers to begin hiring black workers.[77]

Despite the rebels' success, the uprising and subsequent negotiations also inflamed underlying tensions within both the white and black communities. Viewing the youths' demands as extortion, many white Cairoites felt angered and betrayed by the capitulation of city officials. As in earlier moments of racial division, white merchants took the lead in organizing these latent sentiments into action. On July 21 more than four hundred white residents assembled at St. Mary's Park to call on city leaders to strictly uphold law and order. Handbills circulated by the rally's planners described the event as "an organizational meeting" of the "White Citizens Committee," and invited residents to attend and "protect your life and property."[78] By the end of July, these efforts culminated in the formation of the Committee of Ten Million, popularly known as the White Hats, an all-white civil defense organization capable of supporting local law enforcement in moments of crisis. Led by former Alexander County State's Attorney Peyton Berbling, the White Hats began staging paramilitary drills and street patrols that summer. By the spring of 1969, the organization boasted six hundred members, representing a broad cross-section of the city's white population who were ready to be deputized at a moment's notice. Notable members included youthful Baptist minister Larry Potts, warehouse owner Tom Madra, and businessmen Allen Moss and James Dale.[79]

As white opposition grew, black leaders came under increasing pressure to condemn the violence and distance themselves from so-called militants. This pressure intensified on July 23 with the outbreak of the Detroit rebellion, an uprising that eclipsed its predecessors in both loss of life and property damage.[80] The following day a group of fifteen African Americans, representing some of the city's leading religious and civic organizations, met with city officials to express their condemnation of the uprising. Led by former Cairo police officer J. R. Stokes, the group chastised black youth for engaging in acts that had "endangered the lives of innocent citizens and placed them in deadly fear of their lives." While the leaders insisted that segregation and job discrimination were realities that needed to be addressed, they strenuously objected to the use of arson and vandalism as methods for achieving these goals. The participation of Stokes, a former police officer, and Ed Wade, a county probation officer, was not entirely surprising. The NAACP had filed complaints against Stokes for his rough treatment of black citizens while on the force. However, the participation of respected civil rights leaders such as Rev. J. I. Cobb was troubling and illustrated the profound divisions that the rebellion had provoked within the black community. An active member of the NAACP and pastor of a predominantly working-class congregation, Cobb was one of the city's strongest advocates for the expansion of job opportunities, having served as the county director of the Green Finger Project, an Office of Economic Opportunity (OEO) sponsored job-training program. As a Pentecostal minister, however, Cobb's theology centered on his principled opposition to "all violence, either physical or psychological," and his commitment to interracial cooperation as not just a strategy but a goal of the civil rights struggle. While not all black Cairoites shared in Cobb's pacifism or his prioritization of racial reconciliation over black advancement, many shared in his moral condemnation of the uprising, provoking important intraracial fissures rooted in class, generation, and theology.[81]

Nonetheless, the urban rebellion represented a watershed in the Cairo black freedom struggle, marking a key transition in the movement's leadership, aims, and approaches. In one fell swoop a new generation of black working-class youth had shifted the terrain of struggle, injecting a much-needed sense of urgency and elevating their interests to the forefront. In the months that followed, Koen and Ewing renewed their efforts to reach out to black working-class youth and plug them into existing institutions and organizations. The NAACP continued its legal campaign for full integration and the elimination of discriminatory practices, filing complaints against governmental agencies and private employers. However, Ewing increasingly refocused the organization toward the plight of the black working class by holding the organization's meetings in the Pyramid Courts and mobilizing around issues such as discrimination in blue-collar employment, public housing, welfare, and the criminal justice system. Ewing also actively recruited black youth into the organization and in December his brother, Van Ewing, established the NAACP Youth Council aimed at channeling "the unused creative energies of youth into constructive creative behavior." At the migrant school, Koen also redoubled his efforts to involve unemployed young adults in the organization's programming. However, the initiatives these young men and women would develop through the NAACP's Youth Council and the migrant school represented a significant departure from the strategies and tactics adopted during the movement's earlier waves.[82]

In the months following the rebellion, black working-class youths increasingly shifted the movement's primary focus from integrating existing institutions to developing autonomous institutions of their own. Rather than petitioning for admission to the all-white Oriac Center (a.k.a. Teen Town), teenagers working with the NAACP's Youth Council began raising funds to purchase and renovate a building that could be used as a recreational center for black youth. Students at the migrant school also adopted a self-help approach, forming the Southern Illinois Cooperative Association (SICA) in the fall of 1967, through which students operated a cooperative buying program and market that allowed black workers to avoid white merchants, create new jobs, and redirect profits back into the black community. Members also began developing plans for a cooperative day care center, a record store, a newspaper, a radio station, a housing construction program, a thrift store, and a credit union that would lend at a lower interest rate than local banks.[83]

Underpinning this strategy of black self-help and institution building was a broader transformation in the outlook of black working-class youth. Mirroring similar ideological shifts taking place within liberal civil rights organizations such as SNCC and CORE during the late 1960s, black youths would increasingly abandon calls for liberal integration in favor of a black power politics rooted in black nationalism. The city's black working-class youths began to view racial oppression as a fixed and immutable reality that necessitated racial solidarity, self-reliance, and collective action. Members of the NAACP Youth Council, for example, cautioned their peers against the futile hope that white Cairoites might voluntarily cede to demands for meaningful change. "The past decade has shown that the Negro in Cairo cannot wait for the white man to solve his problems for him," members declared. In delineating a specific plan of action, they advocated greater racial solidarity among black Cairoites and a dual strategy of economic nationalism and black electoral power: "The Negro is going to have to take the initiative in speeding . . . change. He is going to have to take it first in expanding his black consciousness and unifying his effort. He is going to have to take it by using his vote where it will do him the most good just as other ethnic groups have done before him. He is going to have to do it by spending his money where possible in ways that will help businesses which give him a fair shake and will help black businesses flourish." Students and administrators at the migrant school supported this vision, viewing racial solidarity and the development of autonomous institutions as the only effective solution to the city's ongoing practices of economic discrimination.[84]

At the same time, Cairo's black congregations were beginning to contemplate their own place in this new phase of the struggle. After holding prominent positions in earlier civil rights campaigns, black congregations and activist church leaders now found themselves on the periphery of an emergent black power struggle in which unifying Christian discourses of philosophical nonviolence and racial reconciliation no longer played a central role. Black activists of all ideological stripes, however, recognized the importance of black church support to local protest traditions and saw the need to recruit activist clergy and lay leaders back into the movement. These efforts began in earnest the year following the rebellion; black power leaders staged a series of dialogues with congregations about the true meaning of scriptural conceptions of racial reconciliation and brotherhood. In March 1968 local activists invited Rev. J. Metz Rollins, executive director of the recently formed NCBC, to speak on the religious implications of black power. In a speech delivered at Ward Chapel, Rollins encouraged Cairo's established religious leaders not to fear black power, arguing that it "only means violence when violence is forced upon black people." In a more fundamental sense, Rollins argued that black power represented the same concept of "black unity [that] was used to build black churches" in the face of white exclusion and violence. While he acknowledged integration as a "godly way to live" founded on the Christian vision of "a single human race," Rollins argued that it was "necessary at this time for all black people to continue to identify [strongly with each other] until freedom from white inflicted injustices is a reality for all black brothers and sisters." Over the coming years black power activists would build on this foundation, forging strong ties between black power and black religious traditions that facilitated the black church's reemergence at the center of Cairo's black freedom struggle.[85]

3

From the Seminary to the Streets

Grassroots Black Theology and the Forging of a United Front

In September 1970 Rev. Charles Koen, leader of the Cairo United Front, joined delegates from across the African diaspora in Atlanta, Georgia, for the founding conference of the Congress of African Peoples (CAP).[1] Organized by Newark-based activist Amiri Baraka, the CAP conference took place at a watershed moment in the black power movement. Coming on the heels of a period marked by the intense sectarianism and internecine battles epitomized by the US Organization–Black Panther Party conflict on the West Coast, CAP represented an ambitious attempt to heal old wounds and bring together the disparate ideological wings of the movement into a single united front.

The concept of a national black united front—popularized by Malcolm X (later el-Hajj Malik el-Shabazz) and his Organization of Afro-American Unity (OAAU) and subsequently employed by others, including Stokely Carmichael (later Kwame Ture) and Baraka—was reinvigorated at the CAP conference, becoming both a hallmark for and an aspiration of what historian Peniel Joseph has called the "second wave" of the black power movement.[2] During the early 1970s, advocates of a united front strategy sought to mobilize black political leaders and activists of all ideological stripes behind a shared organizational structure and common political agenda. Nationally, these efforts were best represented by the work of Baraka and CAP, responsible for organizing a series of black political conventions, culminating in the landmark National Black Political Convention in Gary, Indiana, in 1972.[3] However, these broader initiatives grew out of and were informed by the struggles of grassroots activists committed to building united front organizations in communities across the country.[4]

Forging lasting alliances between cultural and revolutionary nationalists, not to mention mainstream civil rights organizations and black power
radicals, was no easy feat. For this reason conference attendees greatly
anticipated hearing from Koen, who like Baraka was a well-known prac-
titioner of the united front approach. Between 1969 and 1974 Koen's
organization could be counted among the nation's leading united front
movements, responsible for mounting one of the longest economic boycotts of the era and maintaining unprecedented levels of support within
the black community. In a speech entitled "How Long Must We Wait?,"
Koen emphasized the urgent need for black power organizations to move
beyond symbolic forms of racial solidarity and toward the formation of
tangible alliances capable of sustaining a national liberation movement.
"We must hook up from Cairo, Ill., to Atlanta and back to Chicago and
Newark. . . . Don't think for a minute it is going to be an easy struggle," Koen cautioned. "We must make a decision. Everybody is black,
everybody is yelling 'nation time,' everybody has a natural, an afro and a
beard," he teased. "You should know now who you really are. The point
is: Are you ready?" The crowd responded affirmatively. "Are we going to
move together now or wait a little longer?" The crowd responded again.
"If we can hook ourselves together, if we can deal with defense; if we can
unite under a banner of redefined, relevant Christianity," he explained,
"then we will have an over-all struggle."[5] These final words, spoken
before an audience of black leaders from across the diaspora, reflected
the distinctive contribution of Koen and the Cairo United Front to black
power politics. During a period when the black church's role in the black
freedom struggle was increasingly questioned by movement participants,
Koen insisted on the continued relevance of black Christian traditions
and the pivotal role they might play in forging a national black front.

Koen's belief in the ability of a "redefined, relevant Christianity" to
unify the disparate wings of the black power movement stemmed from his
practical efforts to build a grassroots united front in Cairo. This chapter
chronicles the formation of the Cairo United Front, an organization that
brought together black Cairoites from across organizational, class, generational, and ideological lines in support of a broad-based and inclusive
movement for racial change and social justice. In contrast to other forms
of coalitional and alliance-based organizing, the united front strategy

had its roots in both black nationalist and radical intellectual traditions and reflected the specific political aspirations of black power's militant wing in response to narrowing political opportunities and brutal repression. A united front approach afforded Cairo's black radicals a degree of insulation from external pressure and a broader platform from which to organize. However, as national black power leaders would quickly learn, maintaining a united front was remarkably difficult, because it tied radical activists to multiple competing constituencies that frequently differed in their interpretations of the movement's goals and tactics. It was in navigating these potential pitfalls that the Cairo United Front was most successful. By building on the shared religious culture of black Cairoites as well as emergent theological trends, United Front leaders constructed a grassroots black power theology and movement culture capable of bridging intraracial divisions and sustaining the movement over the long haul.

The Genesis of a Strategy

If the politics of civil rights liberalism took clearest shape in the crucible of the postwar Jim Crow South and that of the new nationalism in the more cosmopolitan urban north of the 1960s, the united front strategy that strove to fuse these two strains into a single struggle was perhaps best articulated at the border in Cairo, Illinois. For black Cairoites, adopting a united front strategy was a logical and necessary response to local conditions. Organizing in this northern borderland city carried the perpetual risk of persecution and racial violence at the hands of organized white supremacist groups, including the Klan, the John Birch Society, and the WCC. During the mid-1950s, cross burnings and bombings had forced the local NAACP chapter underground, effectively stalling civil rights protest. When the movement regained steam during the early 1960s, teenage protestors were savagely beaten in the streets. Cut off from the rest of the state and trapped behind the city's fortresslike walls, black freedom fighters faced the prospect of a dangerous and isolating struggle. Accordingly, activists emphasized the need to reach outward, building broad-based movements and strategic alliances that would draw national attention to the embattled city. While black professionals had historically held leadership roles in civil rights organizations, the rigidity of Cairo's color line and the consignment of the majority of African Americans to the lowest rungs of the city's social and economic hierarchy solidified conceptions of "linked fate" between the black working and middle classes. Though the two groups often diverged in their understandings of appropriate strategies and tactics, they were united by a sense of the fragility of their struggle and the need for solidarity in the face of white opposition.[6]

While local imperatives justified broad-based and inclusive organizational approaches, the decision to adopt a distinctive brand of united front politics hinged on the intellectual and organizational labor of skilled activists. Black power leaders recovered the strategy from a longer genealogy of united front initiatives aimed at transcending fissures of ideology in service of a unified black freedom struggle. The strategy's roots can be traced to the formation of the National Negro Convention movement in the 1830s and T. Thomas Fortune's subsequent attempt to forge a National Afro-American League at the height of the nadir.[7] Between World Wars I and II black leftists were inspired by the front-style tactics employed by Communists to forge common cause against fascism and used the strategy to build mass movements around police brutality, jobs, and housing. These efforts culminated in the creation of the Sanhedrin All-Race Conference in 1922 and the National Negro Congress in 1936, both of which forged alliances between black leftists, nationalists, and liberal reform organizations.[8] United Front organizations were later developed in response to revolutionary anticolonial struggles in Africa, Asia, and Latin America. Black power radicals often came to learn of the strategy by way of these earlier black organizing traditions or through Mao Tse-tung's writings on the Chinese Revolution and Ghanaian revolutionary Kwame Nkrumah's expositions on pan-African struggles.[9]

After his 1964 visit with the leaders of national liberation movements in Africa, Malcolm X promoted a united front strategy for the black liberation movement in the United States. This approach promised to bring together the movement's disparate ideological wings under a single umbrella. All parties would work together to forge a common agenda while simultaneously respecting the autonomy of each constitutive group. In this manner Malcolm hoped that black radicals and black nationalists could form a strategic front with more traditional civil rights organizations without compromising either group's unique tactical approach. However, in contrast to more traditional political alliances, Malcolm's articulation of a black united front strategy carried a radical connotation in which revolutionary nationalists were positioned as key agents in the eventual reorientation of constituent groups toward a pan-African and leftist critique. Consistent with these aims, Malcolm founded the OAAU in 1964 with the goal of reinforcing "the common bond of purpose between [people of African descent] . . . by submerging all of our differences and establishing a non-religious and non-sectarian constructive program for Human Rights." While the realization of a united front eluded Malcolm in his lifetime, the concept continued to resonate with black power radicals who followed him, most prominently the Los Angeles–based Black Congress, formed in 1967, and the Washington, DC–based Black United Front established by former SNCC leader Stokely Carmichael in 1968. Like Malcolm, Carmichael hoped these efforts would provide the organizational philosophy and framework for a broader front with civil rights leaders at the national level.[10]

It was in this context that Charles Koen learned of the united front strategy and became its key advocate in Cairo. In many ways Koen's political development mirrored that of Carmichael. In 1962, at the age of sixteen, Koen had collaborated with experienced SNCC organizers in mounting the organization's first northern nonviolent direct-action campaign against Jim Crow accommodations in Cairo. He remained in SNCC's orbit while attending McKendree College, formally joining the organization in 1966 during Carmichael's tenure as chairman.[11] Koen's membership coincided with the organization's dramatic turn toward black power struggles in northern cities and its brief alliance with the BPP. Scholars have tended to view this period of SNCC's history as one marked by militant rhetoric and internal conflict at the expense of a workable program for northern cities. While there is much truth in this claim, SNCC also provided a generation of grassroots activists with new ideological and strategic resources at a key turning point in the black freedom movement. Struggling to address rapidly changing social and political realities, SNCC members engaged with a wide range of conceptual frameworks, including liberalism, black nationalism, pan-Africanism, black feminism, Marxism, and third-world internationalism. In this moment of political and intellectual experimentation, SNCC members often vacillated between approaches, and their public statements reflected a fundamental ambivalence that contributed to black power's increasingly amorphous character. However, the stark ideological divisions that would eventually come to characterize the movement had not yet solidified. Thus, SNCC—as a participatory democratic organization—became a key discursive space for activists hoping to give meaning to black power.[12]

For Koen, who had come of age in a struggle rooted in discourses of racial reconciliation and nonviolence, SNCC offered alternative frameworks that were formative to his political development. In turn, SNCC's expansive intellectual and organizational networks encouraged Koen—a working-class activist from a comparatively remote part of the United States—to view local struggles as part of broader pan-African and internationalist movements. After the rebellion of 1967, Koen began to expand his sphere of influence, forming alliances with organizations across Southern Illinois and Missouri. Particularly drawn to Carmichael's vision of cooperative economics, Koen exported the model of the Southern Illinois Cooperative Association (SICA) to other downstate communities, resulting in the formation of a number of black-owned and operated enterprises across the region. As a result of this work, Koen was invited to serve as spokesperson for the Black Economic Union (BEU), a coalition of antipoverty, youth, and cultural organizations in the metro St. Louis area.

SNCC leaders, looking for ways to penetrate black urban communities in the North, rewarded Koen for his efforts, electing him to the position of Midwest deputy chairman in June 1968. Under the leadership of Philip Hutchings, SNCC increasingly embraced electoral politics, encouraging local organizers to forge black political fronts with the goal of solidifying a national black political party. It was on this basis that SNCC leaders formed a tenuous alliance with the Oakland-based BPP in February 1968, a move that inspired Koen to establish the St. Louis–based Black Liberators later that summer. Like the BPP, the Black Liberators were a revolutionary nationalist organization that recruited members from the ranks of the city's black poor and working-class youth. With Koen at the helm, the Liberators advocated an eclectic program that combined cooperative economics and Pantheresque "survival programs" with a political strategy that focused on multiracial coalition building and electoral strategies. However, it was the Liberators' fierce commitment to armed self-defense that garnered the most attention, resulting in a coordinated crackdown by law enforcement agencies that led to the organization's dissolution less than six months after its formation. During those six months, Koen had been arrested on twelve separate occasions for charges ranging from minor traffic violations to unlawful assembly and, finally, possession of a controlled substance. "They tried framing me on trumped-up charges which restricted me to the state of Illinois," Koen explained. "So I left Missouri and returned to Cairo in 1968 on a full-time basis although I was still living in Carbondale, East St. Louis, and Chicago."[13]

Upon returning to Cairo, Koen found ample support for a united front strategy among local activists. The civil rights battles of the 1950s and early 1960s had resulted in the gradual integration of Cairo's schools, medical facilities, and some public accommodations. However, Jim Crow and racially exclusionary practices persisted in many areas of community life, including the city's segregated public housing projects, all-white civic and religious organizations, and strict color bars locking black workers out of city jobs and confining them to the lowest rungs of private sector employment. "There was discrimination in every area of life just about," Preston Ewing explained. "You name it, there's discrimination. . . . Everything was separate." In 1971 the Chicago-based advocacy group Alliance to End Repression reported that Cairo had the highest levels of poverty, unemployment, and substandard housing in Illinois; black Cairoites bore the brunt of these hardships.[14]

Efforts to forge a united front were given added impetus by repeated incidents of racial violence. In January 1968, only a few months after the suspicious death of Robert Hunt Jr. in police custody, local Baptist minister and White Hats leader Larry Potts admitted to killing Marshall Morris, a seventy-three-year-old black veteran of World War I. Testifying before a coroner's inquest, thirty-three-year-old Potts claimed he had arrived home to discover the elderly veteran attempting to sexually assault his wife. When his initial efforts to subdue Morris failed, Potts picked up a baseball bat and beat him to death. Potts was never arrested or charged with a crime, angering Morris's family and the wider black community, who refused to accept the young minister's account. "Things were already disturbed and then this white preacher beat this old . . . colored man to death," Kendrick recalled. "I doubt if we ever get over that."[15] The following spring these acts of wanton and unpunished violence culminated with White Hats firing shots from the Mississippi River levee into a segregated black public housing project, the Pyramid Courts, forcing Gov. Richard Ogilvie to deploy the National Guard.[16] "By then," Koen explained, "the black organization[s] in Cairo realized the importance of moving toward a kind of united front structure. . . . It was black unity or black annihilation." He concluded, "We chose black unity." As an experienced and respected organizer, Koen was well situated to assist in the formation of an alliance. In April the Cairo United Front was founded as an umbrella group representing all of the black organizations in the city, including the local branch of the NAACP, SICA, the migrant school, the Interdenominational Ministerial Alliance, black youth organizations, and an interracial and ecumenical group of ministers and nuns from across Illinois known as the Concerned Clergy. Shortly after, the Cairo United Front began hosting regular rallies at St. Columba's Catholic Church, and Koen, as the organization's chairman, announced the initiation of an economic boycott of all white-owned businesses that refused to hire black workers.[17]

While the United Front maintained strong support from all segments of the black community, the organization's mass base was firmly rooted in the black working class. The Pyramid Court housing project served as a central locus of the United Front's activities, and residents played prominent on-the-ground roles in the weekly rallies, picketing, and demonstrations. Koen also recruited a large group of black working-class youths and young adults to serve as the organization's core activists (fig. 3.1). This group included unemployed and underemployed laborers such as Clarence Dossie, James Whitfield, Frank Hollis, and James "Switch" Wilson, all of whom lived in Pyramid Courts and played active roles in local organizing through SICA and the IMC school. Others, like Joyce Gilkey and Mable Hollis, had as children also served alongside Koen in SNCC's 1962 nonviolent direct-action campaign in the city. In addition to these young working-class activists, Koen also forged a strong alliance with NAACP branch president Preston Ewing, whose legal and administrative skills had been invaluable to local struggles.[18]

Joining these homegrown activists were two other primary constit-

Figure 3.1. Children picket in support of a boycott of white merchants in Cairo, May 2, 1969. AP Photo/Fred Jewell.

uencies. The first and smallest constituency was a group of white professional allies that relocated to Cairo to lend the United Front legal, technical, and moral support. This group included a number of young progressive clergymen such as Fr. Gerald Montroy and Fr. Ben Bodewes from the Belleville diocese and Rev. Manker Harris, a Church of God minister from Decatur, Illinois. Originally from Chattanooga, Tennessee, Harris had taken an active role in earlier civil rights battles, including the 1965 Selma campaign, resulting in his forced resignation as president of the Decatur Council of Churches in 1969. Shortly after, Koen invited Harris to come to Cairo and serve as the United Front's press secretary. Harris left his wife and two young daughters in Decatur and took up living quarters with Montroy and Bodewes at St. Columba's, where they were joined by a number of attorneys, among them Larry Aschenbrenner, Martha Jenkins, and Michael Seng, who were working for the Lawyers' Committee for Civil Rights Under Law (whose operations are discussed in chapter 4). Consistent with earlier phases of the Cairo black freedom struggle, local white support was virtually nonexistent, with the notable exception of local attorneys and longtime NAACP members Robert and David Lansden.[19]

The last constituency was a slightly larger cohort of young, educated African American organizers from urban communities and college campuses across the region. Among them were Leon Page, a former East St. Louis CORE and Black Economic Union (BEU) activist, and Bobby Williams, an organizer from Cape Girardeau, Missouri, who had overseen OEO antipoverty programs in the Missouri Bootheel. These more experienced and cosmopolitan organizers brought a technical expertise and, in Page's case particularly, an ideological sophistication that informed the United Front's philosophy. Always dressed in a serape and sandals, Page was described by his peers as a "philosopher" and "the United Front's Frantz Fanon." Interestingly, although both men embraced Koen's left nationalism, neither shared his religious worldviews. As Manker Harris described, "They got on board because the whole purpose wasn't to expound on or to push a religious movement, but a real civil rights thing where people were being mistreated, abused, discriminated against like crazy, and it was time to do something about it. All had that thing in common, that no matter what else they were, they had that in common: 'We'll do what we need to do to get this job done.'"[20]

Ewing, who was also nonreligious and a civil rights liberal, agreed, emphasizing the effectiveness of front-based politics despite what he described as the "varying degrees of militancy" among the organization's core leadership. "I did learn that you have to respect that [diversity] and see how that can bring together people moving in the same direction. . . . In retrospect you look back and they worked in absolute harmony because they had common goals." For Ewing, forging a united front with black power radicals like Koen and Page was particularly important in a midsized community with tight social networks like Cairo. "Small town, you know everybody. So, you know, you go to school with people. You know their families. You have lived on the same block and different things like that. So, we saw the racism as our common enemy," Ewing explained. "So it wasn't really a time for us to act out some individual things or differences with people like, 'You go to this church and I go to this church, we don't go to the same church,' or something like that. We didn't have that." It was on this same pragmatic basis and with the express purpose of solidifying a united front that secular humanists like Page and Williams partnered with Koen in creatively fusing aspects of both cultural and revolutionary nationalism with the shared religious traditions of Cairo's black residents.[21]

A Shared Religious Tradition

While racial violence provided the initial impetus for the formation of a united front, sustaining the strategy required a unifying philosophy and cohesive movement culture. For this, Cairo United Front leaders looked to the oppositional culture of the black working class as an organic ideological tradition capable of inspiring, motivating, and disciplining movement participants as well as bridging intraracial barriers of generation, class, and ideology that might undercut racial solidarity. One tradition that black Cairoites tended to share was a familiarity with the discourses and practices of the black church. As chapter 1 demonstrated, African American Christian traditions in Cairo exhibited greater homogeneity in comparison to larger northern cities where the processes of migration, urbanization, and industrialization had generated religious plurality and secularization among certain segments of the black population. In contrast, church attendance and membership in Cairo remained high, and the vast majority of black residents came into contact with the institution whether it was for regular Sunday worship, childhood Sunday school classes, or the church's extensive social and cultural programming. Most black Cairoites, like their counterparts across the Ohio River Valley, shared an evangelical Protestant faith and belonged largely to historically black Baptist and Methodist denominations or one of the city's three Pentecostal congregations. While these traditions diverged along social and ecclesiastical lines, all three shared a belief in the centrality of scripture as the inspired word of God, the primacy of conversion and a personal relationship with Christ, and the power of the divine as a present and active force in the world desirous of the deliverance of his chosen people from oppression.[22]

In addition to these deep theological bonds, black Christians in Cairo were united by a set of shared cultural practices rooted in the black church, including call-and-response oratory, communal prayer, congregational worship, and charismatic sermonizing. Shared religious traditions had historically functioned as an important source of ecumenicalism, binding together black Cairoites of different social classes and generations. Ministers from different denominational backgrounds joined hands to form a citywide black ministerial alliance; community choirs brought Christians together in ecumenical displays of worship; and periodic revivals served to unite believers around a shared evangelistic mission to reach "lost" friends and relatives as well as rededicate their own lives to personal holiness and righteousness. Despite important differences in denominational affiliation and worship style, black Christianity in Cairo was a pervasive and comparatively homogenous tradition that, as sociologist Mary Patillo-McCoy argues, "culturally and religiously [bound] together the black middle-class and the black poor," both young and old.[23]

Coming out of this tradition, Koen recognized the importance of securing the support of black clergy and congregants to build an effective movement. Black congregations such as Ward Chapel AME and the First Missionary Baptist Church had functioned as important staging grounds for earlier civil rights struggles, as well as a source of political leadership. During the black power era, many of the more established black civic and political leaders remained prominent churchgoers. Foremost among them was retired schoolteacher and former NAACP president Hattie Kendrick, whose extensive experience and personal sacrifice ensured that she was the object of almost universal respect among black residents. Maintaining her support and that of other older community leaders such as Rev. J. I. Cobb (pastor of the Pulaski COGIC congregation), Rev. Sherman Jones (First Missionary Baptist Church), and retired minister Rev. Levi Garrett would be important if the United Front hoped to gain legitimacy among the community's elders and generate mass support in a close-knit community.

Koen's interest in mobilizing black churches into the United Front set him apart from many other black power activists. For black radicals in particular, Christianity conjured Marx's dictum that religion was the "opiate of the masses," an ideology that promoted quiescence and distracted from what Huey P. Newton referred to as "a more concrete understanding of social conditions" rooted in dialectical materialism.[24] Such critiques also found support among cultural nationalists like Maulana Karenga, leader of the US Organization, who frequently referred to Christianity as a form of "spookism." Karenga and his sometime protégé Amiri Baraka offered the secular humanist tradition of Kawaida as an alternative that resonated with many of the cultural practices of former black Christians while rejecting what they viewed as Christianity's Eurocentric and "otherworldly" theology. In addition to these ideological critiques, the autobiographies and memoirs of many black power radicals reveal a strong anticlericalism forged through numerous personal encounters with the antidemocratic and opportunistic behaviors of black ministers. Revolutionary and cultural nationalists roundly criticized black clergy, including more progressive members of the NCBC, which had formed in the wake of the urban rebellions as an expression of resurgent black nationalism within church circles. Speaking to NCBC members in St. Louis in November 1968, Karenga accused ministers of being "a liability" in the black community, more concerned with ruling than with revolution and content with providing "comfort not change." More crudely, BPP chief of staff David Hilliard denounced NCBC members at a 1970 event in Berkeley as "a bunch of bootlicking pimps and motherfuckers." During the late 1960s, the repudiation of the black church as a harbinger of false hope and unprincipled and opportunistic leadership was a common refrain among black power activists.[25]

However, during black power's second wave, many leading activists would come to reconsider their earlier criticisms of the black church, if not their anticlericalism, as the movement's militant wing struggled to overcome a tide of state repression and political isolation. Having worked on the ground in the rural South with SNCC, Stokely Carmichael early on grasped the importance of the black church to community organizing traditions. "I instinctively understood that if my struggle was to be among my people then any talk of atheism and the rejection of God just wasn't gonna cut it. I just knew that. My early political work in the rural South would confirm this. All our meetings were held in churches. They all began with prayer. When they approved, people would say, 'Son, you doing the Lord's work.' . . . I did not want to be alienated from my people because of Marxist atheism."[26] Activists working in the urban north, where religious traditions were more diverse, often took longer to reach this conclusion. Among the most memorable of these instances was BPP leader Huey Newton's 1971 speech "On the Relevance of the Church" at the University of California, Berkeley. Presented in the same location where Hilliard had made his infamous remarks to NCBC just a few months prior, Newton offered what many viewed as a dramatic reversal of the BPP's position on the black church. By rejecting this key institution, Newton argued, the Panthers had cast themselves into "a void alienated from the whole community."

> We said the church is only a ritual, it is irrelevant, and therefore we will have nothing to do with it. We said this in the context of the whole community being involved with the church on one level or another. That is one way of defecting from the community, and that is exactly what we did. Once we stepped outside of the church with that criticism, we stepped outside of the whole thing that the community was involved in and we said, "You follow our example; your reality is not true and you don't need it."

Facing marginalization, Newton explained that BPP members had reevaluated their earlier position and that many were now church attendees and participants.[27]

While some dismissed Newton's speech as purely strategic, it also reflected the BPP's recent adoption of revolutionary intercommunalism—an ideology that, like the United Front's, shifted emphasis away from vanguardist, small-cadre politics and toward the development of a practical political agenda rooted within black communities.[28] Incorporating the black church was critical to these broad-based initiatives, culminating in the BPP's formation of the Son of Man Temple in Oakland in 1973, a nonsectarian church that served as a clearinghouse for the organization's survival programs and public forums. However, the practical significance of the BPP's embrace of the black church was still unclear. While Newton's statements lent greater legitimacy to the ongoing reliance of local BPP chapters on church resources, the role that religious practices and beliefs would play in the movement itself was not fully elaborated. Moreover, Newton offered no indication that the organization had reneged on its interpretation of Christianity as an opiate, leaving listeners to infer that the Panthers were willing to tolerate such abstractions only if it helped achieve their broader goals.[29]

While Newton tried to find space for black Christian institutions and traditions in the black liberation struggle and others proposed substituting secular humanist alternatives, Koen joined a growing cohort of activist ministers, including Rev. Jesse Jackson in Chicago, Rev. Albert Cleage in Detroit, Rev. Leon Sullivan in Philadelphia, and Rev. Benjamin Chavis in Wilmington, in advocating the continued relevance of the black church and moral politics to black power struggles.[30] Although Koen's political ideology had altered significantly in the years following his early activism, his personal faith persisted. Koen's small-town roots grounded him in the intimate yet potent social networks of the black church, infusing his politics with a grassroots religious revivalism that distinguished him from many of his radical peers who had come of age in larger northern cities. Koen's emergence as a nationally renowned black power leader took place within this unique cultural milieu, and like many southern and border-state radicals before him, he approached radical frameworks through the lens of a prophetic black working-class faith (fig. 3.2). In turn, Koen's

Figure 3.2. Rev. Charles Koen, ca. 1969. Courtesy of the Manuscript Division of the Library of Congress.

embrace of radical frameworks played a key role in his effort to transform the dominant civil rights theology of racial reconciliation and nonviolence in order to make grassroots religious traditions amenable to the new realities of black power politics. Koen's centrality to this process of reworking and radicalizing grassroots religious traditions cannot be overstated. A Baptist minister by training, Koen possessed the necessary skills and was invested in reframing religious beliefs and practices to serve radical ends. From his position as chairman of the United Front, he situated Christian discourses at the center of the organization's philosophy and infused the movement with the cultural practices of the black church. In doing so, he called on the existing religious cultures of black Cairoites as well as new theological traditions emerging from the nation's seminaries.[31]

Spiritual Rallies and the Crafting of a Movement Culture

Visitors were captivated by the religious dynamics of the Cairo struggle. Their reports conveyed a vivid image that clashed with popular conceptions of black power. Writing for the *New York Times* magazine in February 1971, Pulitzer Prize–winning investigative journalist J. Anthony Lukas strove to capture the unique tone and cadence of the United Front's Saturday spiritual rallies. Lukas opened his article with an image of the United Front choir "bobbing and weaving" to the sound of a church organ while the packed crowd at St. Columba's clapped "to the driving, syncopated beat" of a familiar gospel tune. As the music ended Koen rose to the pulpit, his "Afro outlined like a warrior's helmet against the blue-green of the stained-glass window," and he began to speak. "The essence of our struggle today," he exclaimed, "is that we got one more river to cross. . . . We crossed the Nile. We crossed the Mississippi. We crossed the mighty Ohio. But the river we're going to cross downtown today isn't a physical river. It's a river of the spirit." He continued, "You might see some brothers fall, but no matter how many folks they kill, no matter how many armored cars they bring in, we got to have faith," he urged. With that, the young minister motioned for the crowd to join him at the altar in prayer before taking to the streets of downtown Cairo in protest.[32]

Lukas's article drew national attention to the emergence of a distinctive "movement culture" in Cairo that drew heavily from the ritualistic world of the city's black churches.[33] The fascination of social commentators with these manifestations of popular religiosity reflected broader assumptions regarding black power's secular quality in contrast to earlier civil rights struggles. The juxtaposition left commentators scrambling for ways to explain Cairo's confounding combination of "old-time religion and revolutionary thought."[34] However, for local activists less interested in demarcating themselves from the legacy of civil rights than in building broad-based alliances, embracing religious rituals was a conscious and deliberate act that positioned the United Front favorably within a longer tradition of struggle steeped in religious meaning and mores. By pulling from the black church's cultural "toolkit" of call-and-response oratory, communal prayer, and congregational worship, the United Front situated itself in continuity with earlier phases of the black freedom struggle, garnering the organization considerable legitimacy among black residents.[35]

Cultural continuities between the United Front and earlier civil rights struggles played an important role in securing the support and participation of an older generation of established community leaders. Spiritual rallies provided respected community elders with a familiar and comfortable context for participation. Local black clergymen of all denominational stripes were invited to provide words of inspiration and instruction to United Front members at the weekly spiritual rallies. Rev. Sherman Jones, pastor of the First Missionary Baptist Church, and Rev. Blaine Ramsey, former pastor of Ward Chapel, were frequent speakers who would later play active roles on the United Front's advisory board. Joining them were older churchwomen such as Hattie Kendrick and Carmel Fowler, who gave regular updates on local organizing efforts (fig. 3.3). The organization also maintained an ecumenical choir that performed a familiar selection of spirituals, hymns, and gospel songs. Local church music directors and accompanists, including Rice Whitfield, Hernean Mallory, and Gradie McMillen, were invited to lead the United Front choir and in the process formed close bonds with younger activists.[36]

By inviting community elders to participate, the United Front's radical wing sought to build on the unique intergenerational milieu of the black church that had historically provided a valuable context for the development of mentoring relationships between younger and older activists, men and women.[37] Through her extensive church networks,

Figure 3.3. Hattie Kendrick joins a United Front march, ca. 1970. Courtesy of the Manuscript Division of the Library of Congress.

Kendrick had forged close relationships with many of the younger men and women in the movement. Her enigmatic protégé at the NAACP, Preston Ewing Jr., was the son of fellow Ward Chapel member Nancy Ewing and a former student at Washington Junior School. Koen had also been a member of Ward Chapel, serving with Kendrick on the church's steward board. During the civil rights struggles of the early 1960s, Kendrick and Blaine Ramsey had "recruited and mentored" Koen, taking him under their wing and teaching him "how to do church work." After their marriage, Koen's wife Clydia joined Ward Chapel, where she worked closely with Kendrick on church hospitality and social programs. Carmel Fowler, a fellow church member and NAACP leader, became godmother to the young couple's children. The centrality of churches to black life in Cairo, and the intergenerational bonds fostered within them, ensured that strong ties existed between the city's established civil rights leaders and key black power activists.[38]

Far from rejecting these bonds, black power activists—as in earlier

SNCC campaigns—further institutionalized them within the United Front's structure, bridging generations and casting community elders as much-needed advisors. Black women elders such as Kendrick and Fowler served as what sociologist Belinda Robnett has called "community bridge leaders," specializing in linking social movement organizations to each other and to indigenous community networks. Robnett provides the concept of bridge leadership as a way of theorizing black women's key roles in social movement mobilization in the context of their gendered exclusion from formal leadership positions.[39] However, in Cairo black women activists like Kendrick and Fowler had served as elected officers within the NAACP during the campaigns of the postwar era. In this context, their designation as informal advisors to the United Front was a role they embraced as elders deeply invested in passing the torch to a new generation of leaders. While informal, the role of advisor was a privileged position that afforded Kendrick and Fowler a powerful voice and influence in the organization's decision making. Described by United Front leaders as "the Mother of the Struggle,"[40] Kendrick's long history as a church leader and community activist provided her with an excellent understanding of local people, their attitudes, and interests. Clydia Koen described Kendrick as "just a storehouse of knowledge that she . . . imparted to people." In turn, her work with the NAACP allowed Kendrick to establish a vast network of contacts within the broader civil rights community that proved invaluable to younger activists. As Preston Ewing explained, "She knew who to contact . . . not only her state NAACP contacts, but she had her national contacts. So she knew people, who to call." As a result, younger activists "sort of piggy-backed on [Kendrick] . . . and her resources," according to Ewing. Like Ella Baker, Kendrick used her capacity as an advisor to mentor and guide younger activists as well as to bridge different generations and organizations.[41]

Despite Kendrick's prominence as an advisor, the United Front's leadership structure was occupied almost exclusively by men and reflected forms of male chauvinism common to both secular black power organizations and black churches. At the United Front's headquarters, labor was divided along white- and pink-collar lines; men filled the executive and field positions while women performed traditionally feminized clerical duties as secretaries and typists. Manker Harris described the organization's leadership as "basically male-oriented" but emphasized that black women activists—including Floretta Avant, Deborah Flowers, Joyce Gilkey, Mable Hollis, Geneva Whitfield, and others—"let their voices be heard and be known." Indeed, beyond the ranks of official leadership black women were very visible and performed critical work related to the day-to-day activities of the organization. Foremost among these tasks was the mobilization of the picket lines designed to sustain the boycott of downtown stores. Many former United Front members recall women's central role in "organizing the lines" and ensuring that picketers were in strict compliance with various laws and ordinances. "There were times," Preston Ewing recalled, "when maybe most of the people picketing were women." Black female activists also took the lead in establishing many of the United Front's emergent "survival programs" aimed at meeting the educational, nutritional, healthcare, childcare, and clothing needs of community members. Historian Tracye Matthews has observed similar patterns of female leadership in the BPP's "survival programs" and aptly argues that such activities "represented an extension of 'traditional' roles for women in the family" as mothers, nurturers, and transmitters of culture. In the United Front's case, the development of "survival programs" also built on the longstanding charitable and mutual-aid activities of African American churchwomen. These types of movement work were essential to the United Front's program and constituted an invaluable source of grassroots leadership despite the absence of a formal title or salary.[42]

While the United Front's official publications provide little direct insight into the organization's gender ideology, Koen's personal writings reveal considerable concern about sexual politics and the relative roles of men and women in the black family and the freedom struggle. As a left nationalist, Koen rejected the more conservative rhetoric espoused by cultural nationalists who argued that black women should play a "complementary" and subordinate role.[43] "The black woman's role in the struggle," Koen insisted, "is parallel to that of the black man's. . . . As far as I am concerned she is an individual who must be instructed and must escalate her struggle to that of the man." In practice, however, conventional notions of "women's work" as nurturers and homemakers remained unreformed; such notions, when combined with the reality of women's low-paid employment, made equitable participation in the movement virtually impossible. Moreover, several of the United Front's most prominent male leaders had left their families behind to join the Cairo struggle, while others actively discouraged their spouses from participating. Clydia Koen, for example, had been active as a teenager in earlier civil rights campaigns but stepped back during the black power era at the request of her husband. As she explained to a reporter in September 1971, "We've never believed in husband and wife working together. As he became more active, I stepped back. He wanted it that way." The pressure to remain behind the scenes was something Koen confesses she did not "really understand" or "accept" at the time, especially considering that she was frequently called on to perform clerical responsibilities for the United Front and was eventually hired as a paralegal for another movement organization. In retrospect, Koen attributes her husband's opposition to her involvement as being motivated by a desire to protect his family. Although such fears were prevalent and well founded, Charles Koen's personal writings also echoed anxieties about black matriarchy and black manhood popularized by the 1965 Moynihan Report. Koen cautioned black women activists against moving "beyond the black man," viewing this type of gendered self-assertion as individualistic and destructive. The black woman activist, he asserted, should "be aware" and "not allow herself to be used by the system, or the black man will feel that he has to look up to [her] in terms of obedience."[44]

Koen's vision of ideal gender relations was built on the foundation of stable, heteronormative family units—the production of which he asserted was a central goal of the movement itself. Citing his own childhood as an example, Koen argued for the importance of "strong families" and extended kinship structures as the basis for raising "strong black child[ren]" capable of continuing the struggle for generations to come. The United Front's extension of the intergenerational milieu of the black church into the movement, as well as its incorporation of religious practices, ensured that youth involvement would be widely accepted and encouraged by parents. In the years following Cairo's 1967 urban rebellion, addressing the lack of constructive social activities for black youths became a central concern of parents and community organizations. Historically, Jim Crow practices had locked black children and teenagers out of whites-only organizations like the Boy Scouts and had excluded them from popular youth hangouts like the Oriac Center (a.k.a. Teen Town), the Roller Bowl, and the swimming pool. By the end of the decade most of these recreational spaces had closed, succumbing to dwindling financial resources while still resisting pressure to integrate. Black working-class parents in particular worried that their children were being left to roam the streets unsupervised, where they could easily fall prey to injury, illicit activities, and police harassment. In this context, the United Front's weekly rallies offered a much-needed social space for all generations within black families to participate collectively. Many of the United Front's "strong sisters" and "strong brothers," as local activist Clarence Dossie described them, came from a few, core, black working-class families including the Garretts, the Whitfields, and the Mallories.[45] In each case multiple generations of a single family joined the United Front, taking on active roles in the movement. The sight of "grandmothers with canes, middle-aged parents with children, and teenagers with dogs" all amassing at St. Columba's to join in worship surprised many out-of-town visitors, who tended to view black power as a predominantly black urban youth phenomenon.[46]

While the United Front's mass meetings built on the cultural conventions and networks of the black church, they also challenged some of the institution's less democratic aspects. United Front leaders embraced the black church's tradition of charismatic leadership, recognizing its ability to galvanize and empower members. Saturday rallies were held just prior to the organization's weekly demonstrations and were designed to meet the deeper emotional and spiritual needs of members, binding them together in preparation for the obstacles they might face downtown. In these moments Koen's pastoral voice elevated above others, taking on the quality and tone of the prophetic tradition so familiar to many movement participants. However, United Front radicals, including Koen, firmly believed that the legitimacy of their leadership hinged not on divine calling alone but on the sanction and support of the rank and file. Accordingly, the United Front's mass meetings functioned as democratic assemblies serving to "unite the people spiritually," "inform" them, and "allow for community expression."[47] *Ramparts* reporter Howard Kohn aptly described the meetings as "a combination [of] religious service and experiment in participatory democracy."[48]

In implementing democratic practices at mass meetings, the United Front built on the limited traditions of democratic exchange present in many black congregations. While decision making in evangelical congregations tended to be hierarchical and gendered, laity exerted a limited degree of influence through a system of internal committees and boards as well as through call-and-response rhetorical practices. By volunteering to serve on church steward boards, women's auxiliaries, and mission societies, the laity played an active role in shaping discrete components of the church's overall program. The United Front expanded on this existing tradition by asking members to engage in Christian service by joining committees focused on specific areas of their political program such as housing, education, or cooperative economics. Interspersed between the hymns and sermons at the weekly spiritual rallies, leaders would report back from these committees and provide opportunities for those in attendance to ask questions, offer testimonies, and register complaints. Building on the established rhetorical practice of witnessing and testifying employed by black women churchgoers from the pews, the United Front fostered dynamic intergenerational and cross-gender dialogue that centered the divine in the organization's activities. In allowing this kind of democratic feedback, United Front leaders expanded on call-and-response traditions typically utilized for the purpose of affirming and uplifting. However, members were encouraged to offer testimonies not only of support and encouragement but also of disagreement and criticism. In turn, major questions of strategy and tactics were put to a formal vote in which all members were permitted to participate, irrespective of class, gender, or generation. Accordingly, United Front radicals deepened the church's existing democratic practices by challenging conformist tendencies and opening the possibility of mass participation.[49]

While radicals like Koen and Page viewed the aspirations and interests of the rank and file as central, they did not romanticize their position. Mass meetings were imagined as a site of dynamic exchange, where radical intellectuals skilled in the art of persuasion played an active role. In his writings Koen emphasized the importance of providing activists with "correct political training" through immersion and the systematic study of local conditions and "the science, art, and works of others who have been actively engaged in struggle." This knowledge, he argued, should then be mobilized to persuade the people through "rational arguments" at mass meetings and in the United Front's various committees. In accordance with their political training, radicals viewed themselves as playing an active role in raising the political consciousness of the black working class and pushing its members, through criticism and rational exchange, to a more advanced level of organization. In reality, however, rational arguments were rivaled if not surpassed by discourses of a more spiritual tenor.[50]

A Handbook for the Revolution

The significance of biblical scripture to the United Front's political ideology and programming cannot be overstated. In the organization's publications the King James Bible was cast as a vital tool and central focus of the struggle. In political education scriptures took their place alongside the words of Malcolm X, Nkrumah, and Mao. Koen referred to the holy book as a "handbook for the revolution," insisting that he personally looked "to the Bible for divine guidance."[51] Visitors to the city noted a broader reliance on the scriptures by rank-and-file movement participants. John H. Britton, managing editor of *Jet* magazine, described seeing Bibles prominently displayed in the homes of United Front members during his visit to the city in 1970. "Typically," he said, "it [the Bible] shows telltale signs of having been opened, leafed through repeatedly and closed shut many times." United Front members, Britton argued, were clearly employing this "instrument of salvation" to "bargain for a few days more sanity, or life itself" in the midst of violence and terror. While the Bible did function as an important source of reassurance and comfort, Britton's statements obscured the very important way in which local activists called on scriptures not only to survive Cairo but also to transform it.[52]

Christian discourses had played an important role in earlier civil rights struggles, functioning as a source of transcendent motivation and imbuing the movement with religious meaning. Cairo's liberal integration campaigns of the postwar era were underpinned by a civil rights theology of racial reconciliation and nonviolence that appealed to black Cairoites across class and generational lines and legitimated their participation in direct-action tactics. As a teenager Koen had come of age in a movement shaped by a philosophy that emphasized the redemptive quality of non-violent acts and their ability to transform hate through love. Nonviolent protest, he had hoped, would prompt white Cairoites to repent of their sin and join in the creation of a Beloved Community where black and white community members would be reconciled. However, the refusal of white Cairoites to accede to the demands of peaceful protest and their continued reliance on racial violence to maintain relationships of power and privilege prompted Koen and other movement participants to develop not only new strategies and tactics but also new scriptural referents by which black power could be better articulated and actualized.

The United Front's leadership utilized biblical narratives to frame their practical organizing efforts, which represented a creative blend of the legal and nonviolent direct-action tactics of earlier civil rights struggles with a black nationalist program that emphasized community control, institution building, and armed self-defense. The tremendous diversity of approaches employed by black power activists in Cairo reflected the United Front's broad-based membership and distinctive organizational structure. Within days of the United Front's formation in April 1969, members initiated an economic boycott of white-owned businesses that refused to hire black workers. The boycott, which would last for almost three years, was among the longest of the era and was critical to reigniting mass protest in Cairo as well as unifying the movement's ideological wings behind a shared tactical agenda. However, as a united front organization, constituent groups were also granted considerable autonomy to pursue their own tactics independently. Thus, the NAACP continued its robust legal campaign against the city's discriminatory practices, and SICA remained committed to the development of separate cooperative institutions. In this context, the United Front deployed biblical narratives of exodus, exile, and nation building to provide an overarching sense of unity and purpose to the varied organizing efforts of black Cairoites.[53]

The story from the book of Exodus that had been so central to national civil rights struggles continued to play a prominent role in black Cairoites' understanding of their place and purpose during the black power era. Accounts of the oppression of the Israelites at the hands of their Egyptian rulers and their deliverance into a Promised Land resonated with the collective experience of African Americans living in Egypt. It was frequently retold by United Front leaders at the organization's spiritual rallies and in its publications.

> And God said: "LET MY PEOPLE GO!" The people left Cairo, Egypt, a prosperous land, a fertile land, a land of security. They left for an unknown land, an unknown future, but they left for FREEDOM. When they left the greatness of Cairo left with them. Cairo gained its might through the misuse of God's children as the Egyptians found their power through the enslavement of God's people. Their economy was built around slavery. And then there was Little Egypt, in the United States of America, State of Illinois. Little Egypt, a prosperous land, a fertile land, a land of security. Its major city and capital city was Cairo. It too became great and prosperous and maintained its power through Slavery of God's children. But throughout history God's children kept hearing His Voice proclaiming "Let my People Go!" The voice grew louder, the message became clearer to His people. But as in Egypt, the Pharaohs hardened their hearts as the people heard and moved slowly, but surely toward Freedom's Land.[54]

As this retelling of the Exodus story shows, black Cairoites drew significant parallels between the Israelites' plight and their own. Particular emphasis was placed on the unjust and immoral foundation on which the Egyptians had built their society. United Front leaders contended that Cairo's wealth and prosperity had been established "through the enslavement of God's children."[55] In turn, "Pharaohs" of the past and present had "hardened their hearts" to the cries of the people, placing the pharaohs at odds with God and the inexorable drive toward freedom. "Just as time caught up with the Pharaohs of Egypt," United Front leaders contended, "time surely has caught up with the Pharaohs of Little Egypt." The sin and pride of the city's white officials ensured their position on the wrong side of history and the wrong side of God's active work within Cairo as a liberating force on behalf of the oppressed.[56]

However, in their retelling of the Exodus story, United Front activists drew important distinctions between the biblical account and their visions of freedom. Most evidently, they rejected a literal interpretation of the Exodus that might have tied them to an emigrationist or territorial nationalist politics. While the Israelites had "sought their freedom outside of Cairo," the United Front interpreted God's proclamation of "let my people go" to mean "let my people find their freedom in Cairo." Realizing this vision, United Front leaders argued, would involve overturning the city's exploitative system of rule and "rebuilding" the city on a godly foundation of "justice," "equality," "brotherhood," and "Freedom."[57] Echoing a longer ecclesiastical tradition in African American Christian thought that scholar Eddie Glaude terms the "ideology of chosenness," Koen situated black Cairoites as "a chosen people" called by God to radically reorder society so that "the top shall become the bottom, and the bottom shall become the top." Importantly, this interpretation situated black Cairoites at an exilic moment, the promise of liberation yet to be fulfilled.[58] For this reason many contemporaries likened Reverend Koen not to Moses, the prophet who led the Israelites out from under slavery, but to Joshua, the prophet called to lead his people through the wilderness to the building of a new nation. Indeed, after performing at one of the United Front's spiritual rallies, jazz drummer Max Roach dedicated the song "Joshua" on his 1971 album, *Lift Every Voice and Sing*, to Koen.[59]

Exodus and exilic narratives provided a powerful discursive frame for the United Front's economic boycott against white merchants. While United Front leaders recognized that these small family-owned businesses could not address the full extent of the crisis facing the city's black workers, the boycott's targeted moral critique proved particularly effective in mobilizing large numbers of black Cairoites into the movement. Cairo's economy, United Front leaders argued, was so "totally engulfed with exploitation" that "we can no longer support it." New recruits viewed their exodus from downtown stores as a clear repudiation of the unjust and immoral practices of the city's white elite. By withholding the "black dollar," African Americans expressed their unwillingness to be complicit in a system of racial discrimination and economic exploitation that had kept people in "Little Egypt" oppressed for generations. "After we pulled back the economic wealth," Koen argued, "it was like the children of Israel leaving the camp after they pulled out the economic wealth of Egypt. Pharaoh was in serious trouble." "We didn't pull out physically," he explained, "but we pulled out in terms of our economic support." In this manner, black Cairoites took on what religious studies scholar Cheryl Sanders calls an "exilic identity," separating themselves from a sinful society until God's restorative work had been performed.[60]

The boycott placed moral responsibility for the city's restoration in the hands of its rulers. Initially, the boycott was framed as a moral appeal to the pharaohs of the day to take a public stance against racial discrimination in Cairo. In June 1969 members presented city officials with a list of demands and expressed a willingness to "meet today or any day at whatever time and place . . . to begin meaningful discussions." The demands were wide-ranging, calling for "public acknowledgement of the injustices black people live under in Cairo, fair representation of black people in the judicial system and equal and fair redistribution of the city's economic and political power." Once city leaders met these demands, the boycott would be called off and true reconciliation could begin. However, as illustrated in the next chapter, local merchants and city officials refused to comply, denouncing the boycott and ushering in a reign of terror led by members of a newly formed chapter of the WCC known locally as the United Citizens for Community Action (UCCA). Accordingly, United Front leaders called on Republican governor Richard Ogilvie to intervene, petitioning him to declare Cairo a disaster area, initiate job creation and training programs, and solicit federal support for the resolution of the city's legal, economic, and political problems. United Front members reinforced these demands by staging a series of sit-ins, wait-ins, and pray-ins at the governor's office in Springfield during the summer of 1969.[61]

These demonstrations of nonviolent direct action were designed to dramatize the moral aspect of the United Front's struggle and draw out important continuities with earlier civil rights campaigns. During a period when many black power activists were distancing themselves from the legacy of the civil rights era, United Front leaders did exactly the opposite, describing their nonviolent methods as "consistent with the philosophy of the late Dr. Martin Luther King." This was a strategic move on the part of radicals like Koen, who recognized the privileged position King held among black Cairoites and, more importantly, understood how King's spiritual philosophy of racial reconciliation and nonviolence had not fully exhausted its utility. By deploying nonviolent direct-action tactics at this early stage in the movement, United Front leaders were able to solidify broad-based support. In addition, these approaches also appealed to liberal clergy, particularly members of the Illinois Conference of Churches (ICC), who played an active role in the demonstrations at the governor's office.[62]

Governor Ogilvie took an oppositional stance to the United Front, refusing to meet with the organization's leaders and greeting protestors with mass arrests. By the end of the summer of 1969, more than two hundred people, including large numbers of nuns and ministers, had been jailed as a result of the demonstrations in Springfield. These actions prompted the United Front to brand the governor "Pharaoh Ogilvie," drawing explicit parallels between him and the biblical ruler of the Exodus story. While the United Front had previously utilized the "pharaoh" moniker to frame their own moral appeal to political leaders as "Let My People Go," the governor's failure to restore the city ensured that the label would be increasingly used as an expression of judgment that marked him as an enemy of God's children, "more concerned about . . . money than . . . the poor and oppressed." "When we distinguished him as Pharaoh," Koen explained, "the whole realm of oppression became a total reality. The enemy had been defined: he was symbolic of the whole creation of the existence of the oppression."[63]

This rhetorical shift reflected a broader loss of hope among United Front members that nonviolent direct-action tactics would result in any meaningful concessions from intractable white officials. Over the coming months this sentiment would solidify as local merchants, who were willing to go out of business before hiring black workers, rendered discourses of racial reconciliation irrelevant. The United Front, however, refused to abandon the boycott, instead rearticulating it as a sign of God's judgment and the impending destruction of Egypt. "Without money," United Front leaders explained, "their entire program of destruction and overall exploitation is doomed to failure." Borrowing from another exilic story, Reverend Koen described the boycott as akin to Joshua's battle against Jericho, predicting that the "walls of hatred, pride, bias and oppression would fall in Cairo through the efforts of black residents as they struggled to be free from their white oppressors." By withholding their money,

United Front members and supporters now viewed themselves as God's agents in an uncompromising battle against injustice that would result in the overthrow of Cairo's corrupt system of rule whether local rulers repented or not.[64]

The Exodus story was the most salient biblical narrative for civil rights activists, and by deploying it black power radicals forged a discursive bridge between themselves and those who still subscribed to a politics that placed primacy on racial reconciliation, redemptive suffering, and nonviolence. When "Pharaoh" hardened his heart to the plight of the oppressed, the United Front's use of the Exodus story allowed them to transform what might have been construed as a sign of defeat into an act of prophetic fulfillment. However, the Exodus story proved much less germane to activists' practical efforts to develop new and galvanizing strategies to liberate an exilic people. Accordingly, stories of exodus were supplemented and at times supplanted by other stories, particularly postexilic ones focused on the practical work of (re)building a nation. Religious studies scholar Allen Dwight Callahan explores how the story of Nehemiah, in particular, has offered many African Americans "an alternative to a grandiose hope of freedom, the deferral of which had made black folks heartsick with political disappointment." The story's depiction of Nehemiah's return to Jerusalem to rebuild the city's walls and reform oppressive political and economic institutions in the wake of Babylonian captivity has historically struck a chord with both black nationalist and black radical ministers. During the nadir, the black socialist minister Rev. George Washington Woodbey cast Nehemiah as a priest filled with righteous indignation at the unjust treatment of the poor by rulers who sought to extract usury for their own personal gain. For Woodbey, Nehemiah's godly anger at the robbery of the poor echoed that of contemporary socialists who called for an end to the sharecropping system in the South. In their efforts to move beyond a nonviolent direct-action strategy, United Front leaders also looked to Nehemiah as a scriptural guide that could legitimize a grassroots politics that blended black nationalist visions of nation building with a radical critique of capitalism.[65]

The biblical concept of rebuilding the city was central to the United Front's political and spiritual philosophy.[66] Like Jerusalem in the age of Nehemiah, Cairo was cast as a city plagued by corruption and strife stemming from city administrators' failure to adhere to godly precepts. The notion of the "fallen" or sinful nation pervaded black Cairoites' representations of the city. In a poem entitled "Cairo Will Die!" published in the *East St. Louis Monitor* in March 1968, an unnamed local author provided an exemplary representation of how many black Cairoites viewed the city's sin and the imminent nature of God's wrath and judgment.

> Cairo will die because of its
> own creation of fear and hate.
> Cairo will die from its
> malignant cancer of racism, prejudice, bigotry and injustice.
> Cairo will die because of its
> incompetent city administrators.
> Cairo will die because of its
> Russian type police force and illiterate chief.
> Cairo will die because of its
> economical and industrial starvation.
> Cairo will die because of its
> retail merchants exploitativeness.
> Cairo will die because of its
> hypocrisy in Christianity.
> Cairo will die because all men, women, and children can not
> work, live and play together.

Some drew more explicit parallels between Cairo and other "fallen" cities in the Bible whose imperial power had collapsed under the weight of divine judgment. In a poem entitled "Cairo" published in the *Monitor* in February 1968, local poet and migrant school student Ed Riddick drew parallels between Cairo and Babylon's spiritual sin that led to physical destruction:

> Shout aloud all ye people
> for old Cairo
> like ancient Babylon falls
> to rise
> no more

and Migrants unite to arise
and stoop no more
and hope surfaces to
die no more
die no more!!

While the Exodus narrative motivated black Cairoites to remove all support for the city's existing institutions, United Front leaders argued that Nehemiah represented their divine calling to return to the city and rebuild it on a more just and righteous foundation. At the organization's spiritual rallies, speakers frequently drew parallels between Nehemiah's mission to mend the broken walls of Jerusalem and black Cairoites' divine calling to rebuild a sinful city. Speaking at a rally in September 1970, Reverend Ramsey called on United Front members to be like Nehemiah, who "returned to that rebel, that torn down community, and said, we are on this wall, we are going to do our work, and we can't come down." Through the Nehemiah story the restoration of Cairo was now rearticulated not as the prerogative of the pharaohs but as the divine calling of a formerly captive people.[67]

The phrase "build the wall" took on multiple meanings for black Cairoites, but its most prominent usage was in reference to the development of parallel cooperative institutions. The failure of the economic boycott and demonstrations to secure meaningful concessions from political and economic leaders further encouraged the United Front's shift toward a black nationalist politics of self-help and cooperative economics inspired by Tanzanian leader Julius Nyerere's economic philosophy of Ujamaa. SICA had already pioneered efforts in this area, founding a cooperative store and market; in the wake of the failed demonstrations of the summer of 1969 the United Front increasingly embraced these efforts, elevating cooperative institution building to the top of the organization's political agenda. In the United Front's year-end report, this shift in strategy was framed explicitly in the language of the Nehemiah story. Finding themselves "unable to move either from an economic or political base," United Front members had been "forced to recognize that it is the order of finite man which has things in its present state" and not divine will. "Therefore," United Front leaders argued, "we must now begin to relate to a higher order" by "rebuilding a community that has been dying under the white administration." In a direct reference to Nehemiah 4:17, the United Front called on black Cairoites to "assume . . . the burdens of one another and the responsibilities for one another" by establishing "an economic base on the cooperative principal [sic]." In contrast to the old system, the United Front's parallel economic institutions would be responsive not just to "the needs of a few but for the masses." By adopting practices of profit sharing and cooperative marketing, the United Front hoped to develop "an independent economy" without duplicating the unjust and exploitative dynamics of Cairo's ruling elite.[68]

Working closely with its constituent groups, the United Front initiated an extensive network of cooperative institutions designed to distribute jobs and wealth more equitably within the community as well as to provide much-needed alternatives to the services offered by white business owners. Programs included a cooperative day care center, a women's clothing store, a grocery store, a taxi service, a pig farming project, and a prefabricated housing factory. These programs emerged from dialogues with black Cairoites, who were expected to cooperatively own and operate them. To become part owners, community members were required to purchase low-cost shares that allowed them to vote and collect profits at a rate proportional to their investment. This emphasis on democratic ownership and participation gained scriptural reinforcement from the Nehemiah story, which cast the rebuilding of the city's walls not as an individual act of heroic leadership but as a community-wide responsibility. "The role of Nehemiah," South African theologian J. N. K. Mugambi explains, "is very different from that of Moses." While Moses was situated as the indispensable leader, Nehemiah "encourages the people and facilitates their work." In this sense the shift from Exodus to postexilic scriptural referents was also indicative of black power's embrace of a radical tradition that called for the broadening of democratic rights, powers, and responsibilities.[69]

While cooperative programs met many of the immediate needs of black residents by creating new jobs and affordable goods and services, they also served as a powerful expression of the United Front's broader political and moral critique of American capitalism. In Cairo the black radical tradition was informed by African Americans' position as a largely superfluous labor force. While black power radicals in larger urban areas were predicting that black labor would soon become expendable in the context of a deindustrialized national economy, Cairo's position as a declining river city had already sealed black workers' fate as surplus labor, making the city an important barometer for future trends. For the United Front's radical wing, black life in Cairo raised contradictions inherent in the capitalist system and the moral discourses utilized to bolster it. "Black people are struggling desperately to live a philosophy commonly known as the 'White Protestant Ethic,'" United Front leaders argued. "This philosophy [states]: 'Work long, hard and honestly and someday the great reward will be yours.'" However, despite their best efforts most black Cairoites were stuck "drawing Social Security" or "struggling for a dollar an hour or less." In fact, United Front leaders argued, the only lesson black Cairoites had learned from "capitalistic white America" was that "if you can't build yourself up, the rest of America will leave you on the ground—making life in America one long . . . death march for poor people."[70]

The United Front's critique of capitalism was, at its core, a moral one that characterized the system's reliance on racial and class inequalities as inconsistent with the Christian message. In his speeches and written works, Koen took aim at what he termed the "white value system" of "dollarbillism" that prioritized the individual over the collective, the material over the spiritual, and profits over people. White merchants in search of higher profits were targeted for capitalizing on the shortage of competition by driving up prices on the poor. So-called "black profiteers" were also singled out for their treatment of the black community as "an endless market" to be exploited for their own personal gain. "No man can serve two masters," Koen cautioned. "Ye cannot serve God and money." In this context, cooperatives were viewed as an ethical alternative because they were "people orientated" and in God's eyes, "men are so much more valuable than property" (Matthew 12:12). United Front leaders did not oppose for-profit initiatives, only the inequitable distribution of their fruits. "Capital," United Front member Reggie Brown argued, "is not inherently evil, but is made so only in the hands of those who want it to be." Instead, cooperative programs were designed to operate at a smaller profit margin, allowing goods and services to be purchased at affordable prices and surpluses to be redirected back into the community. In the longer view United Front leaders hoped that these new institutions would provide the foundation for a new economy and reinforce a new black value system rooted in a culture of mutuality and cooperation, or what local activists referred to as "soulism." "We must replace the white value system," Koen argued, "with a black system [based on] the cooperative principal [sic]. . . . When the whole essence of dollarbillism ceases to exist then Soulism will become the essence of the day."[71]

In many ways Koen's moral critique of American capitalism paralleled that of Martin Luther King, who denounced the "moral and spiritual famine in Western civilization" brought on by a rejection of Christ's teachings in favor of "secularism" and "materialism."[72] However, Koen also channeled the leading pan-Africanist and cultural nationalist thinkers of his generation who railed against the moral bankruptcy of the Eurocentric ethos of the West. Amiri Baraka, for example, depicted America as a place of the "dead" and the "dying"; a people absent of spirituality. The West, he argued, had traded in its gods for "material comfort"; the "worship . . . [of] things" at the expense of humanity. It was this anti-Christian value system, which Stokely Carmichael defined as "antihumanism," that Koen claimed had caused Cairo's fall and portended the coming fate of the nation. "Everything this society creates," he explained, "it turns against the universe and mankind. Man has become so involved in self, until he thinks he is God."[73] In his groundbreaking 1967 treatise, *Black Power: The Politics of Liberation*, Carmichael and coauthor Charles Hamilton issued a plea for "the creation of new values," with an "emphasis on the dignity of man, not on the sanctity of property" and on "'free people' not 'free enterprise.'" During black power's second wave, cultural nationalists Karenga and Baraka championed Kawaida as an alternative African-centered value system and promoted the doctrine of Nguzo Saba, or the "Seven Principles of Blackness," as a "code of common morality" for black people. These US-based projects in ethical reorientation were influenced in part by the earlier work of African national liberation leaders, particularly Nkrumah, who in 1964 articulated philosophical conscien-cism as an African humanist alternative to the inherited Christian morality and ideology of British colonialism. United Front radicals embraced cultural nationalists' conception of black liberation as both an internal and external struggle that necessitated the overhauling of values as much as institutions. However, while cultural nationalists often looked to a shared African history and culture for inspiration, the United Front's understanding of soulism or soul power emanated from the existing religious worldviews of black Cairoites.[74]

In the Cairo United Front's foundational document, *United Front Philosophy*, the organization's value system was described as "taken directly from the Book of Matthew, 25th Chapter," which "deals with the feeding of the hungry, clothing of the naked, and providing housing for the needy, also administering unto the sick, taking in strangers, and visiting those in captivity."[75] As the previous chapter illustrated, this scriptural mandate served as the bedrock of Hattie Kendrick's earlier church-based activism as well as that of the Ward Chapel's social action commission, out of which many of the civil rights leaders of the early 1960s had emerged. Koen recognized the salience of this scriptural mandate and its deep roots within a black Christian politics of racial uplift and self-help. In the black power era, Jesus's appeal to his followers to meet the needs of the poor and oppressed was easily refashioned to legitimate a programmatic agenda targeted at empowering Cairo's black and poor residents. This program included cooperative institutions as well as survival programs aimed at meeting the immediate needs of Cairo's poorest residents. Consistent with revolutionary nationalists' call for survival pending revolution, the United Front organized a free medical clinic, a clothing and food distribution program, and free legal aid services. Examined in more detail in chapter 4, these programs helped black working-class people survive the daily battles of life in Cairo and sustain the boycott. However, survival programs also served as a powerful expression of soulism's alternative values of mutuality and cooperation. As United Front activist Mable Hollis put it, people participated in these programs "because the Scripture of Matthew inspired them." "They wanted to feed the hungry, to clothe the naked, and to provide shelter to the homeless." By building cooperative and survival programs, black Cairoites viewed themselves as fulfilling Christ's mandate as well as heeding Nehemiah's call to "assume the burdens" and responsibilities of one another. For radicals, Matthew 25 also evoked Mao's call for revolutionaries to "serve the people"—a dictum that was aptly printed alongside scripture in the organization's political education materials.[76]

Serving the people, Koen argued, also meant being "prepared to protect and defend the community from all forms of evilness," whether directed from within or without. Internally, the organization established an independent system of justice known as the regional council and imposed a strict code of ethics adapted by Koen and Page from Nkrumah's *Handbook of Revolutionary Warfare* (1969). Disciplinary codes were employed by many radical black power organizations and were viewed as important tools for maintaining the internal discipline and unity essential to successful movements. Many United Front members, however, also embraced these codes of ethical conduct—which prohibited drug use, excessive drinking, theft, intraracial violence, and the sexual exploitation of black women—because they promoted an alternative value system that, as historians Robin D. G. Kelley and Betsy Esch have pointed out, "resonated with black religious traditions." Speaking with a reporter from the *Los Angeles Times* about the code of ethics, Koen argued: "I can take you to the Bible and show you where it says the very same thing." Community members who witnessed violations of the code were encouraged to contact United Front leaders immediately to ensure that justice was served. Bobby Williams, as a member of the regional council, recalled rank-and-file members frequently contacting him about incidents of intraracial and domestic violence. Individuals who were suspected of engaging in such acts were brought before the regional council and put on trial before a jury of their peers. "They tried to take care of it internally, absolutely," Manker Harris explained, "because they never trusted the police enough for anybody to go there. . . . The only way they were involved with the judicial system, [was] when the judicial brought them into it. They didn't go to it."[77]

United Front members were also expected to defend the black community against external threats, the most visible coming from local law enforcement and white vigilantes who engaged in near nightly armed assaults on the Pyramid Courts. In response, United Front members formed the Liberators, an armed self-defense unit led by James "Switch" Wilson that was charged with performing nightly "survival patrols" to protect the black community from vigilante attack. While participation in the Liberators was restricted exclusively to men, many of whom conceptualized their activities as being in defense of black women and children, female activists also played important roles in protecting their communities from outside assault. According to Manker Harris, "Everybody had guns in their home." Some, like Geneva Whitfield, operated civilian band radio networks out of their homes in the Pyramid Courts to monitor police activities and keep the Liberators abreast of their movements.

Citing an urgent need for patrols, a number of the United Front's younger members had formed an all-female defense unit, the Liberettes, by the spring of 1971. While exigency certainly contributed to the Liberettes' formation, press coverage also indicates the decisive influence of the wider black feminist movement. Several Liberettes, including their leader, Joyce Gilkey, had participated in earlier SNCC-led campaigns and were no doubt familiar with that organization's creation of a black women's caucus, as well as with the more recent emergence of independent black feminist organizations such as the Black Women's Alliance and the Third World Women's Alliance. Addressing United Front members, the Liberettes expressed a specific interest in organizing black women in Cairo to take a more "active role in the struggle" and to "improve conditions for black people." There is some evidence that the Liberettes spurred a broader reevaluation of the organization's position on gender ideology and praxis. At a Chicago rally in March 1971, Bobby Williams, the United Front's economic development coordinator, announced the organization's "support for women's liberation" and noted the "need for women to fight side by side with the men of Cairo," figuratively and literally. In addition to developing gender-segregated defense units, the United Front also withdrew support for the city's existing law enforcement agencies. Consistent with its philosophy of exodus and nation building, the United Front banned local and state police from the Pyramid Courts and set up barricades and checkpoints at the entrance.[78]

For the vast majority of black Cairoites, armed self-defense was a logical and necessary measure warranting little justification. Philosophical nonviolence, while popular with members of SNCC and the CNVFC during the sit-ins of 1962, did not gain broad-based support among black

Cairoites. While many participated in organized nonviolent direct-action tactics during the movement's "heroic" phase, black Cairoites—like African Americans in other communities across the South and the borderland—viewed armed self-defense as a legitimate response to acts of racial terror and violence. Although a small number of black Cairoites, such as COGIC minister Rev. J. I. Cobb, described themselves as "against all violence, either physical or psychological," most others drew ethical distinctions between offensive violence and armed self-defense. "What they used to say all the time was we're nonviolent, but we will defend ourselves," Manker Harris explained. "That was a big phrase they'd used all the time, so they wouldn't go after somebody with a gun, but if somebody came after them, they would be ready for it." United Front leaders, however, were also cognizant of the more popular tendency among white officials to conflate acts of armed self-defense, when performed by African Americans, with offensive violence. Governmental officials at the local and state level frequently accused the United Front of engaging in an "orgy of violence" and in displays of "outward para-military aggression." Accordingly, Chicago Deacons for Defense leader Fats Crawford was brought in to provide training on armed self-defense to local residents, while Page and Koen worked hard to provide a clear conceptual framework for its use.[79]

Any number of legal or philosophical traditions could have been used by United Front leaders to frame armed self-defense as a legitimate tactic. In Southern Illinois, like the Deep South, gun ownership was for many a way of life and a fiercely held constitutional right. However, the United Front did not appeal to legal or rights-based discourses but rather to scriptural mandates rooted in the Nehemiah story. Like the United Front, Nehemiah's efforts to rebuild the walls of Jerusalem had drawn the ire of corrupt administrators who had benefited from the city's rampant inequalities and unjust practices. According to the United Front, these men engaged in repeated attempts to deceive and even kill Nehemiah. Thus, in chapter 4 Nehemiah established that his supporters built the wall under the cover of night while carrying weapons to protect themselves. United Front leaders frequently cited Nehemiah 4:17–18 as evidence that armed self-defense was morally sound and a necessary precaution for activists engaged in the God-ordained work of rebuilding a city. "Like Nehemiah," Koen exclaimed, "we will carry the Bible in one hand and the gun to protect ourselves in the other."[80]

Biblical justifications for armed self-defense were also visually represented through the organization's symbol of "The Bible and the Gun," which was proudly displayed on the United Front choir's album cover, above the altar of St. Columba's Church, and in the homes of many members (fig. 3.4). This provocative image played cleverly on popular understandings of black power as having jettisoned the spiritual moorings of earlier civil rights struggles by embracing "violent" tactics. Contradicting these binaries, the United Front represented both the Bible and the gun as essential and harmonious components of the black activist's toolkit. For local organizers, the meaning of the image was apparent. "The gun," United Front activist Clarence Dossie explained, "was for your protection and the Bible was for your direction." By positioning the gun on top of the Bible, the image suggests that its use had not been taken lightly but rather incorporated after prayerful consideration and study.[81]

Through such religious imagery United Front leaders endeavored to clearly distinguish between moral acts of disciplined armed self-defense performed by black Cairoites and the unrestrained use of offensive violence by local whites. As the subsequent chapter shows, drawing this distinction became increasingly important as the United Front came to rely on funding from church-based agencies that were prohibited from extending grants to organizations that advocated the use of violence. However, scriptural interpretations of armed self-defense were also used to discipline United Front members regarding the ethical use of force. Because black Cairoites faced an onslaught of violence from police and white vigilantes, tensions could easily flare, resulting in retaliation and counterattacks. Keeping passions in check and preventing uncontrolled outbursts of anger that might be used by officials to validate further acts of repression were critical. In this context, the ability of United Front leaders to frame the use of violence in explicitly moral terms played an important role in legitimizing armed self-defense while characterizing retaliation or offensive violence as unacceptable. "If they [law enforcement] are trying to intimidate us, they won't succeed," Koen insisted. While members would "defend themselves," Koen insisted that they "[would] not attack

Figure 3.4. United Front, *On the Battlefield in Cairo, Illinois* (n.d.).

anyone." Bobby Williams recalled the success of this strategy in curbing potential offensive or retaliatory violence: "It was never aggressive. There'd never been where anyone in Cairo went and attacked the white housin' projects or where the white folks lived. Isn't that amazin'?"[82]

By "assuming the burdens" and responsibilities of one another through the extension of cooperative programming, survival programs, and armed self-defense, United Front members envisioned a new society emerging out of the ashes of the old. While the biblical cities of Cairo,

Babylon, and Jerusalem functioned as powerful symbols of the experience of captivity within a fallen or sinful city, "Soul Valley" came to embody the United Front's vision of the new society they were building. In the organization's communications, Soul Valley became common parlance for Cairo and its surrounding areas, serving as an almost prophetic expression of their "freedom dreams."[83] United Front leaders used this language to inspire others and encourage them to begin to imagine and build a world beyond slavery, oppression, and captivity.

> Mighty Egypt Has Fallen!
> A New Creation is Being Born!
> "Little Egypt" is no more! Cairo is now in Soul Valley!
> Thank God Almighty, Free at Last—in Soul Valley!

Consistent with Exodus and exilic narratives, Soul Valley was cast as "God's promised land of milk and honey." However, United Front members firmly rejected what they referred to as "pie-in-the-sky" religion, insisting that Soul Valley's realization hinged on the active work of God's children. "We are not just going to walk upon freedom," Koen exclaimed. "We aren't just going to pray upon freedom. It is going to take blood, sweat and determination." Using scriptural terms, United Front leaders depicted black Cairoites' progression from "Little Egypt to Soul Valley" as a "long journey" and a "narrow way," a language that resonated with radical understandings of revolution as an ongoing evolutionary process. "Your freedom and liberation," Koen insisted, "depends [sic] upon your commitment and purpose."[84]

A Grassroots Black Theology

The United Front's distinctive brand of black power radicalism quickly drew the attention of nationally prominent black clergy engaged in their own battles to preserve the church's relevance to black urban communities struggling for freedom. At the heart of this endeavor was NCBC, an ecumenical organization of black clergy founded in 1966 in direct response to the urban rebellions and the rise of black power. In the years immediately following the rebellions, NCBC's members—including

many national church executives within predominantly white denominations—worked hard to reorient the nation's churches toward the plight of
black urban communities. These efforts contributed to the birth of new
denominational task forces aimed at addressing the urban crisis by funding grassroots community organizations. However, members of NCBC
were also deeply invested in the broader theological implications of black
power, a concern that prompted the publication of James Cone's landmark *Black Theology and Black Power* (1968) and led to the formation of
NCBC's theological commission (1967) and the Black Theology Project
(1976), all aimed at the development of a systematic black theology. In
this context, the United Front's radical grassroots theology was a source
of inspiration that laid the foundation for strong alliances between NCBC
and the United Front.[85]

During the late 1960s and early 1970s, black church executives visited Cairo in droves to extend their support and witness firsthand the
movement's distinctive spiritual character. Among those attending the
United Front's events were Father Robert Chapman, executive director
of the Department of Social Justice for the National Council of Churches
(NCC); Rev. J. Metz Rollins, executive director of NCBC; Leon Modeste,
director of the Episcopal Church's General Convention Special Program;
Rev. Charles Cobb, executive director of the United Church of Christ's
Commission for Racial Justice (UCC-CRJ); and Rev. Benjamin Chavis,
a UCC-CRJ field secretary working out of Wilmington, North Carolina. Rev. Albert Cleage, pastor of the Shrine of the Black Madonna in
Detroit and author of *The Black Messiah* (1968), was a regular and popular speaker whose theology of black Christian nationalism resonated with
many United Front members. During the summer of 1970, Cleage's sermons on Christ as "a revolutionary messiah" and the black church as "a
power base for the struggle" were well received by audiences at the spiritual rallies. For those unable to attend, summaries of the sermons were
published in the *Monitor* and the *United Front News*. In this sense the
United Front's spiritual rallies and the follow-up publicity they generated
functioned as important media for the transmission and consumption of
emergent black theologies by grassroots black power activists.[86]

The leadership of the United Front embraced these new relationships with enthusiasm, viewing black church executives as logical allies

capable of bringing vital resources to the city. The next chapter explores how black church executives did just that, using their positions within predominantly white denominations to leverage the churches' extensive financial and legal resources on behalf of the United Front. However, in contrast to many other black power organizations that relied heavily on church funding for their survival, the United Front also accessed the church's theological resources. The United Front's leadership placed primacy on political education and the development of a disciplined and educated leadership cadre. The organization's "hard-core workers," as Clarence Dossie described them, were expected to receive training not only in radical theory and praxis but also in theological study. Recognizing this need for formal training, Reverend Cobb and George Bell of the UCC-CRJ invited United Front members to participate in the commission's in-service training program in community organization and black theology at Columbia University in New York. The program, which was cosponsored by IFCO and Riverside Church, offered students the opportunity to receive ordination in the UCC as well as to take classes specifically targeted toward ministry in black urban communities. The United Front's leadership agreed, viewing the program as an opportunity to develop a second tier of leadership. In the summer of 1970, Randy Robinson was the first black Cairoite to participate in the program, followed in the fall by a cohort of twelve additional students, including Clarence Dossie and Johnny Garrett. All of the participants in the program were men, indicative of the masculinist bias of both the United Front's leadership and the emergent black theology, a critique levied potently in the coming years by womanist clergy, including Pauli Murray and Jacquelyn Grant.[87]

Through these programs and the regular visits of leading black clergy and church executives, United Front members became active participants in a broader national dialogue about black theology's character and role in protest and community-building traditions. The enthusiasm with which grassroots activists engaged these theologies challenges not only assumptions about the secular quality of black power but also popular characterizations of black theology as a primarily academic pursuit. This is not to suggest that the United Front adopted these formal theologies wholesale. Rather, the United Front's distinctive religious worldview represented an eclectic bricolage of formal black theologies, radical political ideologies, and the organic religious traditions of black Cairoites themselves. As community organizers, United Front leaders intuitively fused formal academic theologies with African American folk traditions, presaging the important work of theologians such as Dwight Hopkins.[88] In turn, Koen's blending of grassroots revivalism and radical politics produced a strong emphasis on social class and expressed a critique of US capitalism neglected by many early works in black theology. Indeed, Clydia Koen recalls noting the significant theological differences between Cleage's distinctive brand of black Christian nationalism and her husband's faith that centered more heavily on issues of poverty and class exploitation.[89] Accordingly, Charles Koen and other grassroots movement theorists should be understood as pioneers and cocontributors in the effort to develop a systematic black theology during the late 1960s and 1970s. In Cairo these religious discourses ultimately proved invaluable to black power politics. The vision of a religiously grounded black united front was Rev. Charles Koen's most important contribution to the national black power movement. A little-examined and undervalued movement theorist, Koen skillfully navigated the organizational rifts and thorny political debates of black power's second wave, building an effective local united front organization on the foundation of a "redefined, relevant Christianity."

4

Straight from the Offering Plate

Church Resources and the New Black Power Coalition

On April 20, 1971, hundreds of black clergy from across the nation converged on St. Columba's Catholic Church in Cairo for the spring convocation of NCBC. Cairo's nationally recognized black power struggle and its leader Charles Koen's conscious engagement with black theology made the city an ideal site for the premier conference of radical black clergy. Chaired by NCBC's executive director, Rev. J. Metz Rollins, the convocation constituted a veritable who's who of the black church; representatives from almost all of the major historically black and predominantly white denominations were in attendance. Among them were more than twenty state and national church executives responsible for overseeing recently established black caucuses and powerful denominational task forces designed to address the growing urban crisis and its disproportionate effect on working-class black and Latino communities.

Seeking to capitalize on this extraordinary gathering, United Front leaders arranged for the visitors to be hosted by local residents and provided a guided tour of the embattled downstate community. Koen also requested a private, closed-door meeting with church executives to discuss the United Front's work and to develop a national church strategy to help sustain the local movement. NCBC director Rollins agreed to participate in a dialogue on April 22, along with Father Robert C. Chapman, executive director of the NCC's Department of Social Justice; Rev. Gayraud Wilmore, executive director of the United Presbyterian Church's Commission on Religion and Race (CORAR); and Rev. Blaine Ramsey Jr., executive director of the ICC's Special Task Force Committee. Since accepting the ICC post in 1969, Ramsey, former pastor of Cairo's Ward Chapel AME Church, had been a staunch ally of Koen and the United Front. Using his ecumenical contacts, Ramsey solicited financial and moral support for the organization and played a pivotal role in bringing NCBC to Cairo. Ramsey opened the meeting by recounting the political and economic challenges facing African Americans in the city and citing the efforts already made by his agency in collaboration with United Front leaders. At this point Ramsey turned the meeting over to Koen, who petitioned the church executives "to utilize their resources and call upon the interreligious communities to respond with funds and other resources, such as staff, to help alleviate the causes of the strife." By the meeting's end those in attendance had pledged further support from the nation's largest denominations and asked Ramsey and the ICC's Special Task Force to function as a "conduit through which funds and resources can be channeled to assist Cairo."[1]

The image of prominent church executives descending on the small border city of Cairo, Illinois, while perhaps surprising to contemporary readers, was not uncommon during the late 1960s and early 1970s. As the previous chapter illustrated, the United Front's skillful deployment of black religious traditions put the organization in close relationship with leading black theologians and ministers determined to render the black church relevant to black power. However, as Koen's statements at NCBC's spring convocation suggest, grassroots activists—in Cairo and in communities across the nation—expected that this "new breed" of activist clergy contribute in ways that extended beyond rhetorical forms of solidarity. Koen urged clergy, particularly those in predominantly white denominations, to make the tremendous organizational resources of the nation's churches available to the black power movement.

This chapter explores those efforts and demonstrates the remarkable success of the United Front in securing the transfer of organizational resources from state and national denominational structures to black power initiatives at the local level. Between 1969 and 1974 the United Front secured more than half a million dollars in grants from church-based organizations as well as garnering extensive lobbying, consultancy, and staff support for their political programming. As financial support for traditional civil rights organizations waned during the 1960s and local civic elites obstructed governmental funds, these new organizational resources proved invaluable and ensured that churches would become a significant, albeit overlooked, source of coalitional support for the black power movement in Cairo and beyond.

The extraction of church resources by grassroots black power organizations hinged on the support of black clergy and their progressive white allies. Using their newly acquired power in denominational caucuses, task forces, and ecumenical agencies, black church executives pushed for a more active social ministry and refocused denominational contributions to the black freedom movement, transitioning from a traditional emphasis on resolutions and lobbying to the more tangible extension of financial aid directly to community-based organizations. In contrast to federal or corporate support, church-based grants came with comparatively few strings attached, making them particularly attractive to black power organizations. As a result churches made critical contributions to those components of the United Front's daily operations that governmental or corporate agencies either could not or would not support, including staff salaries, office space, travel expenses, and legal fees. Further, the largest of these church-based grant awarding agencies extended seed-money for the initiation of the United Front's economic development programs, a factor that increased the likelihood that such initiatives would eventually receive additional governmental sponsorship from state and federal agencies. However, church-based resources were not without their limitations, and despite their comparative malleability, they offered a highly unstable foundation. As chapter 5 will demonstrate, the liberal distribution of church funds to black power organizations, when combined with a rising conservative political climate in the early 1970s, left the United Front and the nation's largest denominations vulnerable to unique forms of state repression and shifting political sentiments within the churches themselves.

Early Alliances with the New Breed of Activist Clergy

Locating and securing external resources was an essential aspect of the United Front's work. Though local activists had shown remarkable skill in mobilizing the indigenous cultural resources of Cairo's African American residents, building a movement among the jobless and working poor in a declining river city presented unique challenges that were only exacerbated in the black power era. Earlier civil rights campaigns had focused narrowly on the integration of public accommodations through a combination of legal and nonviolent direct-action tactics, an approach that incurred relatively few costs and those associated primarily with legal defense. In contrast, the United Front's embrace of a black power ideology defined by a commitment to black self-determination, cooperative economics, and the advocacy of armed resistance engendered new and sizable expenses that necessitated almost constant fundraising efforts on the part of local activists. Despite mobilizing a broad-based coalition of the city's black residents and securing the support of all of the black community's civic, religious, and political organizations, United Front leaders proved unable to meet these costs without significant external support.

In Cairo these fundraising challenges were further compounded by popular white animosity and the intractability of civic elites. In other communities shortages of indigenous resources might be overcome through a combination of state and federal aid and local interracial alliances. In Cairo, however, city officials had a long history of racial bias in the disbursement of federal contracts and OEO projects, and they had repeatedly refused to comply with federal antidiscrimination requirements, effectively blocking access to War on Poverty funds. In turn, the near universal opposition of white Cairoites to the United Front's efforts ensured that interracial coalitions with local religious or labor organizations would be virtually nonexistent. In fact, militant white opposition to black power, as chapter 5 will illustrate, actually exacerbated the United Front's dependence on external funding sources by fostering a culture of popular vigilantism and state repression that resulted in mass arrests and costly criminal proceedings. As a result, between 1969 and 1974, the leadership of the United Front was compelled to look outwards for new coalitional partners and sources of support.[2]

For Koen, forging alliances with church-based organizations was a natural, though by no means uncomplicated, method to address the United Front's funding concerns. The religious tenor of the United Front's program combined with the deep ties of its membership to local congregations ensured that church authorities would eventually be drawn into the movement's orbit. However, even before the United Front's formation a number of religious agencies demonstrated coalitional potential by launching programs among the city's black working class. These initial church-based efforts included the IMC, which opened its school for migrant workers in Cairo in January 1967, and the Catholic diocese of Belleville, which assigned Father Gerald Montroy to minister to the city's poor and black residents the following year. Both of these initiatives—like similar ones across the nation—were spurred by the harsh realities exposed by the urban rebellions, criticism of Christendom's response (or lack thereof), and the emergence of what theologian Harvey Cox observed in 1967 as a "New Breed" of activist clergy "bent on moving the church toward a more direct role in supporting and inducing social change."[3]

Father Montroy's path to Cairo is instructive as to how these broader religious transformations informed early collaborations between religious agencies and Cairo's black community. The child of working-class white parents, Montroy was raised a devout Catholic in rural Southern Illinois. Central to his family's sense of faith was an egalitarian ethic that countered the racial and class rigidity of their surroundings. "Both my parents," Montroy explained, "believed and taught us that we were no better than anyone else regardless of color or station in life."[4] Montroy's seminary years in Northwest Missouri coincided with the Second Vatican Council convened by Pope John XXIII in Rome between 1962 and 1965. At these historic talks delegates from across the globe issued a radical call for church democratization, ecumenical cooperation, and greater engagement with modern society, particularly in service to the poor and oppressed. The Benedictine monks who oversaw Montroy's education embraced these principles and reaffirmed his nascent childhood values. "We were taught that religion was helping people who were hungry, helping people who were disadvantaged. Helping people like that, and we figured that . . . you were blessed by doing that."[5] Under their tutelage Montroy developed a distinctive brand of theology that would shape his future ministry. "While we did not call it liberation theology," he explained, "it was a theology that concentrated on social justice. . . . We thought more about the disposed [sic] and the poor." In their spare time Montroy and his peers read the works of Martin Luther King and Malcolm X, simultaneously keeping close watch on developing civil rights campaigns. Upon his ordination in 1965, Montroy described himself as having "a completely different Christian outlook" than the generation of priests that preceded him and looked forward to making his own contribution to the social transformations sweeping the nation.[6]

Montroy and his peers entered the priesthood in a moment marked not only by significant shifts in doctrine but also by demographic changes. The preceding decades had witnessed a great migration of African Americans to northern cities and the onset of white flight, transforming some urban parishes almost overnight. In many communities church attendance precipitously dropped, and parish authorities were increasingly perceived as being out of touch with the lived realities of a changing populace.[7] Montroy's first assignment was to a parish in East St. Louis that was interracial but increasingly black. He quickly put his training to use, working closely with parishioners and joining a local chapter of CORE. During his tenure, the city—beset by discrimination and poverty—erupted into a powerful rebellion. "I sat on my balcony," Montroy recalled, "and watched the blacks march by." Overcome with waves of "empathy for the frustrations the majority of the population of East St. Louis had endured," the young priest began to dream of starting "a social work type ministry in the poorest areas" of the city.[8] However, Bishop Albert Zuroweste had other plans and reassigned Montroy to Cairo, a community that the diocesan leader described as having "many economic, social and race problems" that "necessarily disturb every Christian conscience."[9]

Montroy arrived in Cairo in August 1968 with a group of young Vatican II priests and laymen and set about renovating the abandoned St. Columba's rectory. The diocese had decided to close the segregated mission after the nonviolent integration campaigns of the early 1960s, but hopes that the all-white St. Patrick's Church would voluntarily integrate failed, leaving black parishioners without a church home. Montroy began by visiting Father Hugh Kilfoil at St. Patrick's to assess whether reconciliation was a possibility, but the meeting did not go well and left Montroy convinced that the priest "had no real interest in integrating his church." Now with few options, Montroy decided to take measures into his own hands. "I decided I would reopen St. Columba's for Sunday services and gathered a few black Catholics who wished to worship in a welcoming setting." Upon familiarizing himself with his new parishioners, other needs quickly became clear, prompting Montroy to establish a thrift store and tutoring program in the rectory. In the process of performing these duties, the young priest forged a close relationship with NAACP branch president Preston Ewing, IMC coordinator Charles Koen, and many of the other future leaders of the United Front. He soon would invite these young activists to use St. Columba's for meeting and office space. "He was very accommodating to the movement, and . . . he offered [us] the space there," Clydia Koen recalled. Montroy's decision was timely, as Ward Chapel, the traditional base of civil rights activities in the city, was having "economic problems," and its members were divided over the building's use by political organizations.[10]

Montroy's solidarity with Cairo's black working class, particularly political leaders like Ewing and Koen, quickly alienated him from many white Cairoites and provoked an organized campaign to remove him from the city. "I have been told to get out of town," he commented, "and great pressure is being brought by laymen to have me removed from Cairo."[11] Peyton Berbling, Alexander County state's attorney and cofounder of the White Hats, complained that Montroy was a "rabble rouser" and "the Father Groppi of Southern Illinois," referring to James Groppi, the white priest who gained national attention for his role in the Milwaukee black freedom struggle during the same period.[12] Father Kilfoil agreed, accusing Montroy of "consorting with the lower element" and "preaching militancy to blacks."[13] Tensions came to a head in February 1969 after the young priest witnessed members of the White Hats armed with shotguns and police dogs terrorizing black students from the recently integrated junior high school. Montroy, Ewing, and several tutors from St. Columba's formed a human shield and escorted the children back to their homes in the Pyramid Courts. "That night I lay in my bed and was absolutely aghast [at what I] had seen and heard," Montroy recalled. With Ewing's permission he contacted the *St. Louis Post-Dispatch*, and several weeks later reporter Robert Collins published the story under the headline, "Priest Makes Charge: Vigilante Corps in Cairo, Ill." "TV news media and other papers chased the headline," Montroy recalled. Within a few short days journalists from media outlets across the country arrived to cover the story. NBC news embedded reporters in Cairo for a week, interviewing local residents for the primetime syndicated show the *Huntley-Brinkley Report*.[14]

The arrival of the national press angered white Cairoites, but it also drew the attention of progressive young clergy, giving rise to a broader ecumenical and interracial coalition. In March 1969 a new group called the Concerned Clergy, constituted by nearly thirty Protestant and Catholic clergymen from across Southern Illinois, spontaneously formed in defense of Father Montroy's ministry. At the forefront were a number of young Vatican II priests, including Fathers Raphael Middeke and Stanley Roth, the latter a teacher at St. Teresa's Academy in East St. Louis who also served as the group's spokesperson. Several young Protestant clergymen from both historically black and predominantly white denominations also joined the group. Among them were United Methodist Church ministers Rev. Roger Knox and Rev. Charles Napier; Lutheran ministers Rev. Keith Davis and Rev. Gerald Pipping; and Rev. Blaine Ramsey, now pastor of an AME congregation in Peoria, Illinois.

While Vatican II influenced the Concerned Clergy's Catholic participants, their peers in the Protestant denominations took inspiration from a resurgent social gospel tradition in seminaries that placed primacy on working for social justice among the poor and oppressed. Many shared Montroy's calling to new and experimental forms of urban ministry and worried that if the priest's efforts were derailed a similar fate might be visited on them. Rev. Keith Davis, for example, was the pastor of First Lutheran Church in East St. Louis, where he had formed close relations with members of the Imperial War Lords street gang, involving them in community education and job training programs. Similarly, Reverend Napier was the director of the Inner City United Methodist Parish in East St. Louis and worried, "If Father Montroy cannot minister there unmolested today, who is to say that Charles Napier will be able to minister in East St. Louis tomorrow without intimidation."[15] Such fears were not unfounded. Despite offering a general statement of support to Montroy, Bishop Zuroweste's first public statement included the important qualification that he "did not agree with all of Father's methods." The Concerned Clergy feared that if the bishop distanced himself from the young priest it would set a dangerous precedent whereby church authorities might withdraw support for controversial urban ministries at the first sight of lay opposition.[16]

The Concerned Clergy visited Cairo for almost three weeks in March and April 1969 and sought to open lines of communication with city officials in a spirit of reconciliation. Civic leaders complained that Montroy was an "irreverent and irresponsible priest" who had "attack[ed] the image, character and reputation of Cairo" by spreading misinformation and outright lies to reporters. Members of the chamber of commerce argued that Cairo was "not a racist town" and that prior to Montroy's arrival the town had been making significant progress. Brazenly appropriating the hard-fought civil rights victories of the last decade, the chamber insisted that the "school system is completely integrated" and that "no establishment in Cairo is off-limits to a Negro." Local leaders also disputed the characterization of the White Hats as a racist vigilante organization, arguing that it was a legitimate civil defense group mobilized after the urban rebellion to protect private property.[17] Any hopes of equanimity, however, evaporated when vigilantes fired on the Pyramid Courts. "Sure enough gunfire erupted in the streets on our third night there," Napier recalled. "We experienced what it means to live in this hostile community with no visible means of protection. Immediately we contacted the Lieutenant Governor, and two hours later the State Police were in evidence."[18]

The Concerned Clergy also sought to build a rapport with local ministers by appealing to a sense of Christian brotherhood and shared mission. However, many white clergy joined Father Kilfoil and Rev. Larry Potts in actively supporting the White Hats, while others lived in fear of being labeled a "liberal" or "militant." "We realized that no minister who had antagonized the white Christian community in Cairo in the past had ever been allowed to remain," Father Middeke explained.[19] Indeed, only a few years earlier, Methodist ministers Rev. Boyd Wagner and Rev. William Fester had been forced to resign their respective posts at First Methodist and Tigert Memorial for championing an integrated ministerial association. Their replacement, Rev. William Warner, was a progressive minister responsible for cofounding the East St. Louis Inner City parish and leading a variety of initiatives in the region aimed at promoting interracial cooperation. Warner had tried "to develop the same type of work" in Cairo but found himself consistently "hamstrung" by what he described as "intercongregational conflict" and "racial tones."[20] As Hattie Kendrick aptly surmised in a letter to her sister, "The [United]

Methodist Church is trying to work here—no success. I went up and had an interview with the Bishop. He said whenever he sends a pastor here to preach love & compassion etc., the peckerwoods quit coming to church and won't let him come back."[21] Another local Lutheran pastor met very briefly with the Concerned Clergy. "His fear was evident," Napier explained, "and he left as quickly as he could after telling us that he would pay for just coming even though the President of his Synod was, at that time, in St. Columba's Church." This trepidation was not exclusive to white ministers. According to Father Middeke, "The non-involvement of the majority of the black Christian churches was as obvious and painful as the collaboration of the majority of the white churches in the racism of the community." As in earlier periods of repression, the city's black congregations had turned inward, undercutting the development of a mass movement.[22]

However, the Concerned Clergy's visit represented a watershed moment both for the ministers that participated and the local black freedom struggle. On April 3 a reluctant Bishop Zuroweste, now under pressure from other progressive Catholic agencies (including the Southern Illinois Association of Priests [SIAP] and the Catholic Council on Working Life), met with members of the Concerned Clergy and released a public statement in which he "amplified" his support for Father Montroy's work. The bishop urged local parishioners to "be patient" with the "new type of ministry" initiated by the young priest, arguing that while it represented "a new thrust and departure from the Church," it was also "a modern expression of an age-old concern . . . for the poor and oppressed."[23] Bishop Zuroweste also assigned Montroy's seminary classmate Father Benjamin Bodewes to assist at St. Columba's. While many of the clergy viewed the bishop's actions as a reluctant compromise at best, the diocesan leader had afforded Montroy's ministry institutional legitimacy, paving the way for more expansive church-based initiatives in Cairo. "Young priests, religious orders of nuns, especially the Sisters Adorers of the Precious Blood in Ruma, Illinois, along with many Catholic laymen, came to Cairo and worked for social justice there during the summer and fall of 1969," Montroy explained. Emboldened by their new coalitional partners and outraged by escalating violence, Cairo's black political leaders formed the United Front in April. In turn the new breed of Concerned Clergy returned to their own communities determined to secure the moral and financial resources necessary to sustain the United Front's work.[24]

The ICC and the Making of a Black Power Coalition

When Blaine Ramsey departed Cairo following the Concerned Clergy's visit in April 1969, he drove directly to the state capitol in Springfield to begin his tenure as the director of the ICC's Special Task Force Committee. Since the urban rebellions of the mid-1960s, the ICC—like its parent organization the NCC—had responded to allegations of culpability from both within and outside the church by pledging their support to initiatives aimed at addressing the root causes of the conflagrations. To this end the NCC established the Crisis in the Nation program in September 1967, declaring the agency's goal of *channeling* the "massive resources of our society into ghetto communities." To demonstrate the sincerity of this grandiose commitment, the general board of the NCC also directed the general administration and finance committee to "make available a minimum of ten percent of its unrestricted capital funds" to be used for "development programs in ghetto communities which are planned and directed by representatives of those communities for maximum benefit of the communities."[25] Though the program was subsequently characterized as little more than a "public relations ploy,"[26] staff members at the state level often took the mandate of the Crisis in the Nation program seriously, endeavoring to implement its recommendations. Between 1969 and 1973 Blaine Ramsey and the ICC's Special Task Force Committee were responsible for coordinating these efforts in Illinois.[27]

Until the late 1960s the ICC's work on race and poverty, like that of many church organizations, had focused almost exclusively on behind-the-scenes lobbying in support of civil rights legislation. As one member described in June 1966, the organization had participated in the work of "making quiet contacts with key people in government to help get good laws in[to] being."[28] While critical to the landmark legislative victories of the mid-1960s, these experiences did not prepare the ICC to respond to the growing demands of black power activists and the new breed of clergy working in some of the state's most impoverished communities after the urban rebellions. In March 1966 the ICC did participate with other religious bodies in forming the IMC, an agency responsible for opening adult education programs in Cairo and several other communities across the state.[29] However the ICC's broader efforts were hampered by inexperience and a failure to develop meaningful connections with black clergy and activists working on the ground. Rev. William K. Fox of the Christian Church (Disciples of Christ) laid bare these problems in a January 1968 study of black participation in the ICC. His findings indicated that the ICC's response to the Crisis in the Nation program had been "curtailed by the lack of meaningful rapport or functional relationships with the black sector of the church which largely resided in the midst of the Core City which so often is the foundation of the urban crisis." If contacts with black clergy were weak, relationships with secular community organizations were virtually nonexistent, and very few local councils maintained relationships with "black nationalist groups or radical civil rights organizations."[30]

With Fox's findings fresh on their minds, delegates at the ICC's thirty-eighth general assembly in January 1968 voted to create the Special Task Force Committee, charged with developing "an ecumenical statewide strategy" to address "the problems of race and poverty that exist in Illinois." Specific areas of focus included the provision of adequate and nondiscriminatory housing, equal justice under the law, and the extension of adult education and vocational training programs designed to improve employment opportunities. Importantly, the general assembly directed the task force to coordinate their efforts with secular grassroots organizations but failed to elaborate how this might be achieved in light of Fox's criticisms.[31] Given this lack of guidance, task force members initially struggled to make good on this mission. However, the ICC's rhetorical commitment to addressing the urban crisis provided an important contradiction that the savviest black power leaders would exploit. At a meeting of the task force in April 1968, members discussed an ultimatum they had received from Charles Koen in his capacity as spokesperson for the East St. Louis–based BEU. Since his appointment as the IMC's area coordinator, Koen's influence had broadened to include the metro St. Louis area, where he was working with a number of black power organizations. According to Koen, the BEU had requested financial support from church-based organizations on numerous occasions, but little had been forthcoming. Accordingly, almost a year before James Forman and the Black Economic Development Conference (BEDC) issued the Black Manifesto (which demanded $500 million in reparations from predominantly white denominations), Koen made "one last appeal" to the churches to put their money where their mouths were.[32]

As pressure increased to extend resources directly to local black power organizations, ICC executive secretary Frederick Roblee was forced to address the issue directly. Speaking with representatives from local councils, Roblee stated that he "did not want to undersell or oversell what the Illinois Council of Churches can do," emphasizing that "immediate funds" were not available. However, he did suggest that "it might be possible to go to certain foundations or organizations that are set to channel funds into needed areas," referencing the recent formation of several grant-awarding programs by some of the nation's largest denominations.[33] Foremost among them were the Episcopal Church's GCSP and IFCO, both established in 1967 for the purpose of redirecting denominational resources to local organizations working to address racism and poverty in communities across the country.[34] Three years later the United Presbyterian Church launched its own experimental initiative, the National Committee on the Self Development of People (SDOP), that would allow affected communities to "use their own efforts to gain material, social, political and spiritual freedom." Members of the task force affirmed Roblee's suggestion, developing a proposal to hire a permanent staff member capable of establishing firmer relations with local black power organizations as well as identifying potential resources and funds for their use. The proposal found widespread support at the ICC's thirty-ninth general assembly in January 1969, where delegates determined that the task force's efforts should be "continued, strengthened and enlarged" and a permanent director installed.[35]

Blaine Ramsey was an ideal choice for director of the ICC's most engaged committee on race and poverty. Since leaving Cairo in 1962, the young minister had remained a staunch advocate of an activist ministry, despite finding himself relocated to several downstate communities. Although the AME Church's itinerancy system could hinder some ministers from putting down the kinds of roots necessary to build effective local movements, it also had the paradoxical effect of providing activist ministers like Ramsey with extensive statewide networks and a comprehensive understanding of the challenges facing black Illinoisans. After leaving Cairo, Ramsey had pastored Champaign's Bethel AME Church (1963–1966) and Peoria's Ward Chapel (1966–1969), in addition to serving a brief stint as vice president of the Illinois chapter of the NAACP. In both communities Ramsey refocused local congregations toward civil rights activities, challenging both clergy and laity to reconceptualize the meaning of their faith in the context of the struggle for black freedom. Ramsey also exhibited a willingness to work alongside younger black nationalists, taking some of the earliest steps toward opening up church buildings to secular black power organizations. In Peoria, for example, Ramsey worked closely with local Black Panther Party leader Mark Clark, permitting the organization to use Ward Chapel for its free breakfast program. In the spring of 1969, Ramsey brought this flexibility and expertise to his new role as director of the ICC's Special Task Force Committee.[36]

Under Ramsey's leadership the task force was transformed. Prior to his appointment participation was largely confined to the executive officers of the ICC and a small group of white liberal representatives of the mainline denominations. However, by drawing on his own extensive networks Ramsey was able to secure the participation of leading clergy from the state's historically black denominations. This new group of task force members represented well-established congregations in some of the state's largest cities and included, among others, Rev. William Newell Guy, pastor of St. Peter AME Church in Springfield; Dr. Carroll McCoy Felton, pastor of Blackwell Memorial AME Zion Church in Chicago; Rev. Negil McPherson, pastor of Zion Missionary Baptist Church in Springfield; and Rev. Norman Owens, pastor of Macedonia Baptist Church in East St. Louis. Ramsey challenged the ministers to return to their respective communities and forge working relationships with local black power organizations in order to better present their needs and interests to the task force. These efforts quickly bore fruit, allowing Ramsey to boast in his year-end report that the task force was "now related to community organizations and ad hoc committees in Rockford, Kankakee, Rock Island, Peoria, Bloomington, Champaign, Decatur, Springfield, Alton, East St. Louis, and Cairo." As the relationship between clergy and local activists deepened, representatives from community organizations began to attend task force meetings in person to translate their concerns and ask for support. In this way the task force quickly emerged as a key site for coalition building not only between clergy and grassroots activists but also between civil rights and black power organizations from different parts of the state.[37]

Ramsey cast the task force's role in religious terms; it was to be "an advocate, enabler, and reconciler." In their capacity as *advocates,* task force members were called to stand "with the disinherited in their struggle against the forces of racism, poverty, and exploitation." In practical terms advocacy entailed crafting resolutions and lobbying public officials, methods that resonated with the ICC's conventional approach to black freedom struggles. As *enablers,* however, task force members were challenged to move beyond traditional forms of rhetorical support toward the identification of tangible resources that might better facilitate the work of the community organizations they served. The task force's contributions included the provision of consultancy and staff support, assistance in program development, and service as a liaison between local groups and larger religious and governmental entities. However, the task force's most important and controversial enabling efforts involved leveraging church funding for local black power organizations. Only through this work, Ramsey argued, could the task force contribute to the possibility of an authentic reconciliation. "It is . . . necessary," he explained, "to understand that the role of reconciler is not to compromise the evil but to stand firm for justice and righteousness. These are the prerequisites for peace and the new humanity."[38]

While task force members focused on building relationships with grassroots black power organizations, Ramsey began the difficult work of persuading ICC executives to use their own ecumenical networks to secure funding and other essential resources. At the end of his first year as director, Ramsey reported an urgent "need for denominations at [the] state and national levels to respond above the token level for funding community organizations and projects." Such support, he argued, was "very necessary" in terms of establishing "the kind of base upon which real economic and political power can be built." Ramsey also took aim at what he perceived as a "pernicious paternalism on the part of white churches

. . . characterized by ambivalent attitudes toward self-determining groups, feigned ignorance as to what the issues are, [and] limited financial commitments bordering on tokenism." Accordingly, he challenged ICC executives to "revamp" their funding guidelines to allow for a more direct, "no-strings" approach to funding local groups. To this end Ramsey was responsible for establishing the Special Task Force's brokerage system, which served as a conduit for church-based donations to community organizations across Illinois. This brokerage system allowed task force members to circulate funding requests to a comprehensive network of potential sponsors, including the ICC's constituent members as well as new national funding agencies like IFCO, GCSP, and SDOP. Sponsoring agencies in turn were able to channel their donations through the task force, which committed to account for and review all disbursements. Through this brokerage system Ramsey oversaw a significant expansion in the ICC's antipoverty activities and played a critical gatekeeping role in leveraging resources for black power groups.[39]

Between 1969 and 1974 Cairo was consistently at the top of the task force's list of priorities for funding and resources. In part this was a consequence of the national attention garnered by events in the embattled community. However, it was also a very tangible product of Ramsey's unique relationship with the city and its leading black power activists. When Ramsey became the director of the task force, it was natural that he continually foreground the city's concerns and link the United Front to grant-awarding agencies in state and national denominational structures. Indeed, Ramsey maintained an extraordinarily close relationship with events and actors on the ground, visiting Cairo regularly and assisting United Front leaders in the development of their political program.

In the spring of 1969, shortly after the Concerned Clergy's visit to Cairo, Ramsey began to encourage representatives from Cairo's various community organizations to attend the task force's meetings and make their needs known. During these early interactions, a pattern was quickly established that solidified the task force's role as a primary vehicle in the mobilization of external church-based resources for grassroots struggles in Cairo. Initial support came primarily from regional and state denominational bodies that were constituent members of the ICC and had direct jurisdictional ties to Cairo: SIAP, the Southern Illinois Conference of the United Methodist Church, and the ICC's South Conference. By the end of 1969, the task force had transferred close to $15,000 in small, one-time donations to the United Front and other community organizations working in the city. However, the escalation of violence in the summer of 1969 and the subsequent deployment of National Guard and state police units to Cairo drew national attention that over the coming months would serve to expand and broaden church-based support for the city's black power struggle.[40]

Advocates

The ICC's offices in Springfield were within walking distance of the state capitol building and were ideally situated to actualize Ramsey's vision of clergy as *advocates*. In April 1969, while the nation's attention was focused on events in Cairo, Ramsey coordinated private meetings between state officials and a small delegation of black residents and Concerned Clergy to address allegations of vigilantism and racial violence. The delegation met with Illinois's Republican governor Richard Ogilvie and with a bipartisan group of African American legislators, fourteen of whom subsequently agreed to cosponsor a resolution calling for a legislative investigation into conditions in the city. The resolution passed the Illinois House with only one opposing vote, and a special investigative committee was formed to conduct a series of public hearings in Springfield and Cairo during April and May.[41] Governor Ogilvie also responded to the delegation's appeals, throwing his support behind a successful legislative effort to repeal an 1885 law that allowed for the formation of vigilante groups and sending Lt. Gov. Paul Simon on a fact-finding mission to Cairo on April 17. Upon his return Simon published a lengthy report that offered wide-ranging recommendations, including the dissolution of the White Hats, the removal of the chief of police, and the appointment of African Americans to governmental committees and boards. Officials in Springfield cautioned city leaders that if they did not comply, access to state and federal assistance would almost certainly be blocked. The ICC's Special Task Force's nascent advocacy efforts were gaining traction.[42]

In Cairo, however, the intervention of state officials combined with the United Front's boycott of downtown stores stoked animosities and exposed deep rifts among the white citizenry. In April and May 1969, members of the White Hats, deputized by the county sheriff and coroner and armed with high-powered police rifles, staged near nightly assaults on hubs of United Front activity, including the Pyramid Courts, St. Columba's Church, and the migrant school. Speaking with state officials, Koen attributed the violence to local merchants determined to put an end to the boycott. Black residents fought back, exchanging defensive gunfire and in some cases staging retaliatory attacks on white-owned businesses.[43] With the prospect of open warfare looming, Governor Ogilvie was forced to deploy the National Guard, and Mayor Lee Stenzel released an eight-point plan responding to Lieutenant Governor Simon's recommendations. Viewing the mayor's plan as an act of capitulation, the White Hats and their supporters flooded city council meetings, demanding that more be done to end the boycott, rid the city of "outside agitators," and enforce the law against black militants.[44] In the weeks that followed, the White Hats continued to abuse their special deputy status by patrolling the streets, stopping and searching black residents, and conducting armed raids on centers of movement activity.[45]

In response Ramsey and the ICC task force continued to exert pressure on state officials to enforce the recommendations of Lieutenant Governor Simon and the special investigative committee. In June these efforts were bolstered by news that Rev. Jesse Jackson, leader of the SCLC's Operation Breadbasket, had selected Cairo as a stop on the organization's March Against Hunger. The enigmatic civil rights leader arrived in Cairo on June 17 and was accompanied by Rep. Corneal A. Davis and SCLC president Rev. Ralph Abernathy. Joined by Koen, the civil rights leaders led a march of nearly two thousand people from city hall to the Pyramid Courts.[46] That same week Illinois attorney general William Scott and six of his staffers drove to Cairo to meet with Koen, Jackson, and Abernathy. Shortly after, Governor Ogilvie directed state police to assume responsibility for law enforcement in Cairo and revoke the special deputy status of the White Hats. Scott also met with State's Attorney Berbling and ordered that the White Hats voluntarily dissolve or be subject to a legal injunction. Finding himself cornered, Berbling agreed but proved unprepared for the subsequent backlash from the White Hats and their supporters. White Cairoites, taking to the streets in the hundreds, marched from St. Mary's Park to the Cairo police station, where a Confederate flag was unfolded and hoisted atop a flagpole as the crowd sang "Dixie." Afterward, female protestors stormed the hotel where Scott and his staffers were staying, demanding an audience with the attorney general. According to Charles Gaines, one of Scott's aides, "They were chanting and using all kinds of vile epithets because their husbands' deputy sheriff badges had been taken away." For the next three nights, hundreds of angry white citizens assembled in St. Mary's Park, culminating on June 30 in the formation of a new organization, the UCCA, whose leaders would subsequently establish a formal alliance with the Citizens' Councils of America.[47]

United Front leaders observed the rise of the UCCA with trepidation but remained encouraged by the success of the boycott and their coalitional lobbying efforts. By partnering with the Concerned Clergy and allies on the ICC task force, they had succeeded in focusing the attention of state officials on Cairo, resulting in the revocation of a longstanding vigilante law, the dissolution of the White Hats, and a written commitment by Mayor Stenzel to further reforms. With these gains in mind, United Front leaders met with Ramsey and members of the ICC task force in July to discuss the next step in their lobbying strategy. Dubbed the "Drive to Save Cairo," the plan that emerged from these discussions proposed the delivery of a comprehensive list of demands to Governor Ogilvie's office in Springfield—backed up, if necessary, by clergy-led sit-ins. Though wide-ranging, the demands focused chiefly on addressing racial inequalities in the legal system and promoting economic development through expanded governmental investment. When initial attempts to reach the governor by phone failed, United Front leaders and members of the ICC task force coordinated a convoy of nearly one hundred clergy and black residents from across Southern Illinois to rally at the capitol. Though Koen secured a meeting with the governor, the ensuing talks collapsed, prompting clergy to begin sit-ins at the governor's office on July 15. Each morning the protestors returned, occupying Governor Ogilvie's reception where they chanted and sang freedom songs until they were evicted at the end of work hours.[48]

As the sit-ins entered a second week, Governor Ogilvie quickly lost patience and ordered capitol police to forcibly remove the protestors and arrest any resisters. On July 22, in full view of journalists and photographers, police entered the reception area and began to drag the occupants out, handcuffing them and escorting them to county jail. Speaking with reporters, the governor insisted that "the proper place to find solutions to the problems of Cairo" was not in Springfield but "in the town itself." "I would suggest," he scolded, "that there are better ways of helping Cairo than by creating insupportable disorder in a public place." Among those arrested were Father Montroy, Father Michael Lucey of SIAP, and Rev. Manker Harris, a white Church of God minister recently appointed director of the Decatur Council of Churches. "I was arrested under a table and carried out of there," Harris recalled. "I wasn't having it, and they had to carry me out and took me to county jail, and a bunch of nuns were arrested at the same time." Harris, along with many others, refused bail, opting to wait in jail until a local judge dismissed the charges against him. Undeterred, groups of protestors returned to the governor's office on July 23 and August 1, resulting in more than twenty additional arrests. A frustrated Ogilvie took to the airwaves, pleading with the clergy to return to their communities and minister to the spiritual needs of their own congregants. "Cairo," he insisted, "is not a religious issue."[49]

The growing ranks of Concerned Clergy begged to differ. From August 7–11 nearly fifty assembled at the Episcopal Diocesan Center in Springfield to meet with United Front leaders and take stock of the events of the summer. During these dialogues, Koen commended the ministers for their commitment and sacrifice, insisting that their advocacy had provoked a "crisis of conscience" in Springfield. "Folks now see the real image of Jesus, a walking Jesus, a street Jesus, an activist Christ, calling upon his ministers to follow him." Koen cautioned, however, against any backward steps, arguing that to "lose Cairo" would result in the loss of "the whole state for the poor." "Cairo," he explained, "has now become the symbol for getting the governor to alleviate poverty. If the movement of ministers, priests, nuns, black people, students, young and old, fail, then nothing else could win." With these stakes in mind, Koen proposed the formation of a statewide coalition of clergy and activist laypersons capable of coordinating ecumenical support at a moment's notice. The group agreed, forming the United Christian Front (UCF) and electing Koen as executive director, Rev. Charles Napier as president, and Father

Montroy as vice president. Though the Springfield protests had served to galvanize clergy, everyone at the Diocesan Center conceded that Governor Ogilvie had adopted a hard stance toward the United Front and was unlikely to meet demands for legal reform and economic development in the short term. With this in mind Koen insisted that UCF's first call of duty be to partner with the ICC task force in leveraging denominational resources to help meet the United Front's operational costs, legal expenses, and economic development initiatives in the interim.[50]

Enablers

The first sign of this expansion in church-based funding took place just prior to the UCF's formation and was led by the group's soon-to-be president Charles Napier. After visiting Cairo as part of the Concerned Clergy, Napier returned to his parish in East St. Louis determined to use his position to advance the United Front's work. His first opportunity came in June when he attended the annual convention of the Southern Illinois Conference of the United Methodist Church (UMC). Taking the convention floor, Napier petitioned his fellow Methodists to form an ad hoc committee aimed at coordinating a response to events in Cairo and other communities where the conference lacked a ministry to poor and black residents. "Time is short," Napier warned. "We are a white racist institution. These are God's people and we have an obligation to minister to them." Dr. Lowell Hazzard, a Methodist theologian from Washington, DC, agreed, calling on delegates to "quicken the pace of reconciliation with the black man, not slow it down." These appeals resonated with delegates who, after much discussion, voted to create a task force and allocated $10,000 for the creation of a legal aid office in Cairo to be staffed by an attorney and legal secretary.[51]

Reports of the conference's decision were followed closely in Cairo, where the abuse of legal power had served as a central tool in the repression of the black freedom struggle. On July 3, 1969, Montroy and Bodewes wrote a letter on behalf of the United Front to Rev. John Adams, director of UMC's Department of Law, Justice, and Community Relations, to ensure that the denomination followed through on its commitment. The priests explained that governmental officials had made "many promises" to black Cairoites regarding legal support that had gone unful-filled. What the United Front needed now, they explained, was not prom-ises but immediate "help and action from you and [other] concerned agencies who are willing to work for Justice." Specifically, Montroy and Bodewes requested that Adams secure the services of a lawyer who could work in Cairo "over an extended time, not just for one or two cases." It appears that their subtle prodding worked; shortly after the UMC's General Board of Christian Social Concerns began exploring a variety of potential nonprofit legal aid providers that might be willing to open an office in Cairo. They eventually settled on the Lawyers' Committee for Civil Rights Under Law, a nonprofit advocacy group that specialized in racial discrimination cases and had been working on the ground for sev-eral years in the US South and South Africa.[52] After a brief investigative trip to the city, representatives from the Lawyers' Committee concluded that "the administration of justice in Cairo is indeed terribly defective" and that legal services were necessary "to insure that the black people there are accorded their constitutional rights." The Lawyers' Commit-tee estimated that it would require a budget of $14,500 to establish and operate a legal office in Cairo for the first six months. After receiving assurances from UMC staffers that financial support would be obtained, Lawrence Aschenbrenner, chief counsel for the Lawyers' Committee in Jackson, Mississippi, arrived in Cairo in October 1969 to set up the office and deal with initial cases. Shortly after, a second attorney, Martha Jen-kins of Fayette, Mississippi, joined Aschenbrenner.[53]

The arrival of the Lawyers' Committee transformed Cairo's legal land-scape in a number of important ways. Most immediately, Aschenbrenner filed injunctions quashing the most egregious measures employed by city officials to halt the United Front's activities. Foremost among them was Mayor Stenzel's declaration on September 11, 1969, that Cairo was in a state of civil emergency and that all parades, picketing, and pub-lic "gatherings of . . . two or more individuals" were now prohibited by city ordinance. Under the auspices of this controversial declaration, local police had been arresting United Front members participating in weekly marches and walking the picket lines at downtown stores. On his first day in Cairo, Aschenbrenner drove to the federal court in Danville and secured a temporary restraining order to protect the civil liberties of black

Cairoites and ensure that peaceful demonstrations could continue without interference. Subsequently, Aschenbrenner turned his attention to Cairo's court system, halting all jury trials until a representative jury pool could be established. Such victories counteracted efforts of the United Front's opponents to railroad local activists and challenged longstanding discriminatory practices in Cairo's criminal justice system. Over the coming months the Lawyers' Committee would broaden the scope of its work, fighting and winning landmark civil rights suits against discrimination in education, housing, employment, and political representation. In the absence of support from Springfield, the United Front had found a new ally to forward their cause through legal channels.[54]

The UMC's role in establishing the Cairo legal aid office seemed to exemplify the type of enabling social ministry that the new breed of clergy and black power activists envisioned. A regional conference of the UMC had been challenged to address the very real problems facing black residents in its jurisdiction and had boldly stepped forward to provide a solution. In turn, the national denomination had thrown its weight behind the initiative and offered to assist in securing funding. Behind the scenes, however, the project was plagued by financial challenges that quickly strained the relationship between church sponsors and local activists. Though UMC executives had promised to support the legal aid office, initial funding came almost exclusively from private donations made by Methodist laypeople and a number of small nonrenewable grants as opposed to more sustainable sources of institutional revenue. Attempts were made by UMC executive John Adams to build a more stable ecumenical funding base, but he met with little success. Writing to NCC executive Robert Chapman in December 1969, Adams complained that despite his best efforts, "only Methodist money" had been received "for a project that was assumed to be inter-denominational and ecumenical from the beginning." According to Adams, "The Methodist sources have [now] been explored and exploited to their fullest." With the first installment of funding for the Lawyers' Committee now almost exhausted, Adams feared that "unless there are other expressions of support soon the Project unfortunately will have to be terminated."[55]

In reality, the legal aid office was a Methodist-inspired project and one that, despite Adams's protestations, had not received significant support from denominational authorities. At the time Adams wrote his letter, the UMC's national office had transferred just two thousand dollars to the Lawyers' Committee through a one-time donation made by the Women's Division of the Board of Missions. Clearly the UMC, an organization with an operating budget totaling in the millions, had not depleted its resources. Lacking adequate financial support, the legal aid office was forced to operate at a deficit, and United Front leaders were burdened with the task of identifying alternative funding streams. Rev. Manker Harris—now serving in Cairo as the United Front's press secretary—wrote to Adams in January 1970 to express his concern. The Lawyers' Committee, he argued, had been of "inestimable value" to those seeking "equal justice" in Cairo and to "pick up and leave" at this early stage "would be insane." Harris apologized for the "hostile" tone of his letter but emphasized that too many "well-intentioned" people had "set back the day of reconciliation by unwise, premature and what have turned out to be abortive attempts to 'mediate' and reconcile."[56]

Ultimately, the Lawyers' Committee's funding concerns were addressed not by church-based funding but by the extension of governmental money. In July 1970 the OEO awarded a $90,000 annually renewable grant to the organization for the provision of free legal services to poor residents in Alexander, Pulaski, and Union counties. Subsequently, thousands of working-class people—black and white—were able to obtain legal support for civil cases involving divorce, adoption, employment discrimination, child support, social security, and public aid. Upon the extension of federal aid, the Lawyers' Committee also received the first significant donations from major denominations, including $5,000 from the UMC's Board of Missions and $8,000 from the Illinois Synod of the United Presbyterian Church. With the Lawyers' Committee now well supported, Koen immediately contacted church authorities to request that these donations be redirected to the United Front to address other, more pressing needs for legal defense and bail bonds. However, these requests went unheeded, exacerbating underlying tensions between United Front leaders and church executives.[57]

In September Koen directed letters to both the Methodist and Presbyterian Church, rebuking denominational authorities for their failure to be responsive to the needs of grassroots activists. "It has always been our feeling," Koen explained, "that the white church should always desire to talk with black citizens who are involved in the struggle when grants are being made in a city on the assumption these monies would aid blacks." Instead, Koen charged that church executives had acted paternalistically by refusing to "divert funds" to the United Front and, in the process, disregarded the right of black Cairoites to self-determination. Local African Americans, not white clergy, Koen argued, "must determine the priorities, at a given time, as to how and to whom funds must be spent. . . . The white church cannot and must not pick a white person or a committee with a majority of whites to make these determinations for blacks." Koen concluded by cautioning his readers that black Cairoites would not break their "covenant with the Lord to fight racism at all levels" by becoming "part of a goodwill program" that allowed church leaders to "buy off their guilt," without addressing institutional racism in the nation's largest denominations.[58] Koen subsequently relayed these concerns to Peter Connell, director of the Lawyers' Committee, explaining that while predominantly white denominations provided "much of our [the United Front's] funding," they would prefer to "fund us indirectly" and through organizations like the Lawyers' Committee, which "they feel would 'safely' administer their monies." In light of these concerns, Koen asked Connell to channel the Presbyterian and Methodist funds to a bail bond initiative designed to assist United Front members facing criminal prosecution. In the interim United Front members took up offerings, and Rev. Blaine Ramsey extended his home as collateral to keep local activists out of jail.[59]

Within days of penning these anxious letters, Koen received news from Ramsey of a major breakthrough. The previous summer members of the ICC task force had assisted United Front leaders in submitting a substantial grant proposal to IFCO, a nonprofit ecumenical foundation that under the leadership of Baptist minister Rev. Lucius Walker had funded other community organizations to the tune of $1.5 million in the first two years of operations. In October 1969 Walker and other IFCO representatives assembled in Cairo to examine conditions in the city and better understand the United Front's work. Now, Ramsey could report with considerable relief the IFCO's board members had approved the proposal and the United Front would receive a grant of $229,660.[60]

The IFCO grant was the largest single church-based donation received by the United Front, and it underwrote much of the organization's work for the coming year. In addition to constituting a significant cash injection, the grant targeted aspects of the United Front's program that other governmental and denominational donations would not, including day-to-day operational expenses such as staff salaries and office space. After struggling for almost a year with limited resources, the United Front was now able to employ a full-time professional staff capable of devoting their undivided attention to the development of the organization's political program. Paid staff positions included an executive director, program coordinator, public relations officer, field organizers, and secretarial staff. In most cases local black activists were hired in acknowledgment of their longstanding commitment and loyalty. However, the organization's gendered division of labor continued. Male activists were hired to fill executive and field organizer positions, while Mable Hollis and two Southern Illinois University Carbondale (SIU) college students, May Francis Brown and Janice Stewart, were brought on board in clerical capacities. One noteworthy exception was Deborah "D.J." Jackson, a student at SIU who was appointed to the position of national campus coordinator. The IFCO grant created jobs for local activists and ensured that people familiar with local conditions were at the center of the United Front's operations. With their salaries coming from church-based donors outside of the city, the United Front's staff was also relatively autonomous and insulated from the economic pressure of Cairo's white elite. This independence was especially important in Cairo, where active participation in the black freedom struggle carried the risk of harassment at the hands of the UCCA, whose ranks included key figures in business, government, and law enforcement.[61]

Hiring a permanent staff also carried important programmatic implications for the United Front. Without paid staffers, black power organizations could easily exhaust themselves performing what local activists referred to as "survival work": staging self-defense patrols, ensuring community members were clothed and fed, and keeping activists out of jail. However, a paid staff structure afforded the United Front—for the first time—the stability and resources essential to the development of a long-term political agenda for black empowerment. Crucial to this long-term

planning was the earmarking of IFCO grant monies for a separate economic development corporation to be headed by Bobby Williams and
charged with building a variety of black-owned and -operated cooperative
institutions. IFCO also extended $60,000 in seed money that Williams
and his staff utilized to launch a cooperative shopping plaza, food market,
prefabricated housing factory, clothing store, and laundry. These innova-
tive projects were designed to create jobs for local black workers, provide
consumers with an alternative to discriminatory white business owners,
and redirect accumulated wealth back into the black community.[62]

Riding high on the success of the IFCO grant, Ramsey assisted
United Front staffers in submitting additional proposals to the Episcopal Church's GCSP and the United Presbyterian Church's SDOP, both
grant-awarding agencies directed by progressive African Americans with
a strong track record of supporting grassroots black power initiatives.
Under Leon Modeste's leadership the GCSP championed a "no strings"
approach to funding that resulted in more than $7.5 million in disburse-
ments to local projects between 1967 and 1973.[63] Similarly, in the SDOP's
first year of operations, Executive Director Rev. St. Paul Epps sponsored
a wide range of local initiatives, including a wood products company in
Lowndes County, Alabama ($62,500), the Black People's Unity Move-
ment in Camden, New Jersey ($150,000), the San Diego Welfare Rights
Organization ($29,000), and a cooperative feeder pig program run by
the Southeast Alabama Self-Help Association ($50,000).[64] After visiting
the city and meeting with United Front leaders in 1970, Modeste and
the GCSP awarded $68,000 to help "sustain [the United Front's] office
and staff expenses, develop its economic program further, continue political organizing, and finance leadership training classes."[65] The following
year, representatives from the SDOP also visited Cairo and subsequently
awarded the United Front two separate grants totaling $127,000 to
address the organization's "urgent needs of personnel and operating capital to establish a transit system, design a welfare program, protect tenants
rights, settle union and employment problems, and design and implement an education plan for children." By the end of 1971 the United
Front had received almost half a million dollars in direct aid from IFCO,
GCSP, and SDOP alone.[66]

While predominantly white denominations played an important role in addressing the United Front's operational costs and economic development programs, members of the ICC task force from historically black denominations used their own networks to sustain the organization's survival programs. Leading black churchwomen from across Chicago mobilized their congregations behind Operation Need, the United Front's emergency food and clothing distribution service, and by early 1970 their donations were sizable and consistent enough to warrant the opening of an office in the city. From Operation Need's new headquarters in Chicago's Hyde Park Bank Building, program director Edna Williams coordinated the churches' donations and arranged for regular convoys to transport the goods to Cairo.[67]

Joining one of those convoys in January 1970 was Dr. Leonidas Berry, chairman of the AME Church's health commission and a leading physician at Chicago's Provident Hospital. Upon hearing reports of African Americans being routinely denied medical treatment at St. Mary's Hospital—or if treated, receiving a grossly inadequate standard of care—Berry developed the Flying Black Medics—a team of black physicians and nurses that would make regular trips to Cairo to bring immediate medical assistance and focus national attention on the city's health crisis. After his initial visit Berry returned to Chicago to solicit the participation of black nurses, technicians, and doctors. In turn, he met with Bishop H. Thomas Primm of the Fourth Episcopal District of the AME Church and secured permission to solicit medical supplies through the health groups and missionary societies of Chicago's Woodlawn, Grant, and Coppin AME churches for distribution through Cairo's Ward Chapel. Additional support came from the black-owned Williams Clinic in Chicago, which provided over $10,000 of laboratory equipment. Finally, Berry and other black doctors from across Chicago pooled their resources and financed two charter planes to transport the staff and supplies to Cairo.

On a cold February day the Flying Black Medics landed in Paducah, where they were met by Reverend Koen and other United Front leaders. The team of thirty-two doctors, nurses, technicians, social workers, and dieticians were loaded onto a United Front bus and transported across the river into Cairo. Awaiting the group at Ward Chapel AME were hundreds of patients who had been organized and registered in advance by the church's social action committee chair Hattie Kendrick. As they met with the patients, the doctors were alarmed by the tragic human cost of Cairo's grossly inadequate medical services. Dr. Audley Connor of the Chicago Board of Health stated that twelve of the first fifteen adults he examined had "serious medical problems which needed immediate medical treatment." Men and women suffering from treatable conditions all but wiped out elsewhere came to the clinic and received medical attention for the first time before the gaze of the national news media. Most notably, reporters from NBC's *Huntley-Brinkley Report* returned to Cairo and broadcast the unfolding scene at Ward Chapel to a national audience.[68]

Upon completing their duties, Berry and the Flying Black Medics sought to capitalize on the media attention to secure a more long-term solution to the city's health-care problems. According to Berry, "the medical power structure of the state was greatly upset" by what they had seen in Cairo and even more so by the wave of bad publicity that had followed. Accordingly, Berry partnered with the ICC task force and United Front leaders in lobbying state officials to provide OEO funds for the establishment of a black-owned and -operated medical center in Cairo. However, Berry complained that the project was "bogged down by state, medical, and local politics" from the start, and a year after the Flying Black Medics had visited the city, state officials opted to extend an OEO grant totaling $100,000 to St. Mary's Hospital instead. Despite these challenges, St. Mary's opened a walk-in clinic in January 1971, serving over 650 patients in the first three months of operations and launching a mobile health unit and three outreach program centers in the city's public housing projects. By helping to get the medical program up and running, Leonidas Berry and the Flying Black Medics had increased the likelihood that the initiative would receive state and federal governmental awards, as was the case with the United Front's legal aid office and housing project.[69]

When members of NCBC arrived in Cairo in April 1971 for the organization's spring convocation, they could be proud of the advocacy and enabling efforts already made on the United Front's behalf. Over the past two years, black church executives at both the state and national level had played crucial roles in mobilizing the organizational resources essential to the operations of the United Front and many other grassroots black power groups across the country. Though a comprehensive accounting of church-based donations is still needed, even the most cursory examination suggests that mainline denominations constituted an important, albeit overlooked, source of coalitional support for black power organizations. At the forefront of these endeavors was Leon Modeste and the Episcopal Church's GCSP, which distributed $7.5 million between 1967 and 1973, followed closely by the Presbyterian Church's SDOP, which allocated $1.6 million in 1971 alone. Both denominations also contributed to IFCO's ecumenical fund, which disbursed $4.17 million in grants to hundreds of domestic and international projects between 1967 and 1975. The scope and scale of these financial contributions demonstrate that mainline denominations, under pressure from black power activists and the new breed of clergy, actually deepened their support for the black freedom movement after 1967, shifting from a traditional strategy that emphasized lobbying and legislative action to the direct-funding of social movement organizations.[70]

As this chapter has shown, the relationship between church executives and United Front leaders, though contentious at times, was ultimately a productive one. Church sponsorship allowed United Front leaders to meet the day-to-day operational expenses that other corporate and governmental donors would not support, including office space, legal costs, and the creation of a permanent staff structure. By hiring a paid staff the United Front was able to move beyond survival tactics to the development of a long-term political strategy for black empowerment centered on the establishment of parallel institutions in the medical, legal, housing, and consumer sectors. Seed money from church-based donors aided in getting these programs off the ground, which in turn increased the likelihood of more significant awards from state and federal governmental entities.

However, in an era of conservative ascendancy, the United Front's heavy reliance on funding from predominantly white denominations proved a double-edged sword. When Koen and NCBC executives sat down in April 1971 to discuss the prospects for additional funding, they could not have known that church-based donations for the United Front had already peaked and would soon enter a period of rapid and permanent decline. During those meetings, NCBC leaders pledged their continued support to the United Front, but within a few short months all of the major grant-awarding agencies came under attack from opponents both within and outside the church, prompting denominational authorities to scale back or terminate their operations. The subsequent chapter explores this assault on church-based donors and the corollary effect the decline in funding had on Cairo's black power struggle.

The Recession of National Spirit

The Decline of the Cairo Black Power Movement

Since its founding in the summer of 1969, the United Front had waged a powerful assault on Cairo's unique system of racial oppression, catapulting the organization into the national spotlight. In a period so often characterized by sectarianism and internecine battles, the United Front had forged a surprisingly broad-based coalition under the banner of a new spiritual philosophy and a set of shared cultural practices rooted in the black church. This distinctive approach served to promote great solidarity among black Cairoites and opened the door to new and important coalitional relationships, particularly with the new breed of clergy who championed the United Front's cause in the nation's sacred edifices. Building on these relationships, the United Front mounted one of the country's longest and most effective economic boycotts, overturned longstanding practices of discrimination, and established a series of parallel institutions that catered to some of the most basic needs of the city's poor and black residents. These successes ensured that many black power activists looked to Cairo as a model for organizational unity and a key bellwether of national trends.

However, by January 1972 the *Chicago Sun-Times* reported that Cairo had "all but vanished from the news."[1] Picket signs disappeared from city streets. The United Front's Saturday rallies were sporadic at best, and the economic boycott was, for all intents and purposes, broken. Black residents returned to a downtown business district decimated by intractable white merchants who in many cases favored bankruptcy over hiring African Americans and extending courtesy titles to all of their customers. Writing for the *Washington Post*, journalist Andrew Wilson observed that despite the failure of local business owners to meet the United Front's demands, the organization had "allowed the boycott to peter out," and local activists had seemingly abandoned "the practice of holding weekend rallies and parades." However, Wilson was quick to note that the United Front was "hardly on its last legs," arguing that the organization had simply "redirected its energy." The United Front's executive director Charles Koen agreed, insisting, "The social aspect of the struggle has been won. . . . Now we're interested in economics— in housing and building up the black community, in self-help and self-development."[2] Indeed, beginning in the winter of 1971, United Front leaders increasingly shifted organizational focus away from mass mobilization and direct action and toward state-sponsored economic development, electoral politics, and the mountain of ongoing legal cases still awaiting trial. While this strategic decision was made in earnest by United Front leaders determined to both protect and further the local movement, it was also a critical signpost that marked the United Front's final hours as a mass-based organization engaged in the "noninstitutionalized discourses and practices of change" that sociologist Roberta Garner identifies as the key hallmark of any social movement.[3]

This chapter traces the closing stages of the Cairo black power movement, drawing out those factors that contributed most significantly to its decline. In contrast to many other grassroots black power organizations, the United Front had survived the narrowing structure of political opportunities as well as the initial wave of state repression that characterized the late 1960s. The peak of the United Front's activities coincided with the Nixon administration (1969–1974), whose distinctive brand of new right politics undermined the War on Poverty, slashed domestic spending, and ushered in a law-and-order agenda. As this chapter will show, United Front leaders—like other black power activists across the country—were subject to a systematic campaign of repression at the hands of federal agencies, including the FBI and the IRS. Conditions at the state and municipal level were similarly bleak, as black Cairoites encountered an unsympathetic Republican governor and a powerful local chapter of the WCC, whose influence reached into law enforcement, business, and governmental affairs. The Cairo movement survived—in spite of these challenges—by adopting a united front strategy fused by a potent grassroots black power theology and by new and powerful coalitional partners within the nation's leading religious institutions. Thus, conventional interpretations of black power's decline—as a product of the movement's retreat from community organizing traditions, as the result of internal disorganization and a narrowing structure of opportunities, or as the consequence of external repression—are, by themselves, less persuasive in Cairo's case.[4]

Rather, this chapter contends that interpretations of black power's decline must be tested on the ground by examining local movements as they evolved over time in response to changing social and political conditions. At the grassroots level, the story of decline was often a gradual one in which small but significant changes in the structure of opportunities, the character of repression, and importantly, the availability of organizational resources, contributed to a movement's rise and fall. While previous studies have tended to emphasize the cumulative pressure these factors placed on the black power movement, as though each added a little more weight to an already weak foundation, I argue that it was often the dynamic interplay between specific factors that mattered most. This interplay is especially evident in the Cairo black power movement's decline, whose origins can be traced to 1971 and the election of members of the WCC to key governmental posts; to an escalation in the repressive moves of local, state, and federal authorities; and most importantly, to the collapse of the church-based resources that underpinned much of the United Front's political program. Rather than upping their support at this crucial juncture, the United Front's primary donors—predominantly white, mainline denominations—pulled back under internal pressure from conservative white congregants and external pressure from governmental agencies. This "recession of national spirit," as Rev. Blaine Ramsey so aptly termed it,[5] forced Koen and other United Front leaders to make difficult choices about their political program, culminating in a shift away from mass mobilization and toward other institutionalized means of securing racial change. Thus, in Cairo the fall of black power as a coherent social movement is a story of the conscious *tactical innovations* of local activists in response to a combination of narrowing opportunities, external repression, and dwindling resources.[6]

Black Power against All Odds

In October 1971 freelance journalist Michael Watson penned an article for the St. Louis–based magazine *PROUD* detailing his recent visit to Cairo. Clearly shaken by his brief sojourn in the borderland, Watson cast Cairo as "the seat of racism and oppression" and the foremost "battleground for Black Survival in the country." Here, he cautioned, the "polarization of the races is complete" and "the white forces of business, government, and the military have joined in their efforts to stamp out black insurrections in a raw, overt display of power." For this reason, Watson explained, black power leaders across the nation "view [Cairo] as a microcosm of America—a forecast of what is to become in the not too distant future." Visions of the nation's future through a Cairo-shaped lens conjured a sense of foreboding and terror. "I am frightened," Watson admitted. "I am afraid that Death will win in Cairo and that we will all be lost. . . . If white violence is allowed to destroy them then white violence will destroy us all."[7]

Watson's comments capture the remarkably repressive conditions and narrow structure of opportunities faced by black power activists in Cairo. Although political opposition handcuffed black power organizations across the country, United Front leaders had to negotiate the triple threat of a conservative president, an unsympathetic Republican governor, and an intractable civic elite dominated by members of a formidable local chapter of the WCC. Founded in 1969 by local businessmen Carl Helt and Bob Cunningham, the homegrown UCCA boasted a broad-based membership that included many of the city's leading business owners, trade unionists, religious leaders, and public employees. Membership estimates ranged from 1,200 to 2,000, constituting somewhere between 30 and 50 percent of the city's white population. It was from the ranks of these hardcore segregationists that third-party candidate George Wallace was able to secure 30 percent of all Cairo votes cast in the 1968 presidential election, an unprecedented number considering that African Americans constituted nearly 40 percent of the town's population at the time.[8] During the early 1970s, the UCCA headquarters on Washington Avenue emerged as an important hub of regional white supremacist activities, drawing visitors from WCC chapters across the borderland and the US

South; it also attracted members of the Chicago branch of the American Nazi Party. The UCCA headquarters, blazoned with a Confederate flag and the WCC motto ("State's Rights—Racial Integrity"), was also home to the organization's monthly publication, the *Tri-State Informer*, which by October 1971 claimed a circulation reaching twenty-eight states.[9]

The UCCA functioned at once as a mass-based political organization, an economic pressure group, and a paramilitary vigilante force. Members of the UCCA regularly attended city council meetings, exerting pressure on white political leaders to adopt a heavy-handed "no compromise" approach in their dealings with the United Front. As the previous chapter illustrated, the organization's members pressed Mayor Lee Stenzel to declare a state of civil emergency in September 1969, prohibiting all nonviolent demonstrations by city ordinance. However, when city leaders refused to comply with the UCCA's demands, members harangued them and forced them to resign. UCCA members also leveraged their own power as proprietors, employers, and property owners to punish anyone viewed as supporting the United Front's efforts. Black Cairoites and their allies risked being fired or laid off from their jobs, denied credit, evicted from their homes, expelled from school, and threatened with removal from welfare rolls. Preston Ewing reasoned that it was this pattern of economic harassment combined with the threat of social ostracism that contributed to the virtual absence of indigenous white moderates and interracial cooperation in Cairo. "The white people here were not free," Ewing explained. "Here are people that . . . live on your block and they will speak to you but in the larger environment where there are white people they couldn't even be friendly and stop and have a conversation." According to Ewing, even potentially sympathetic whites were "held hostage" by the UCCA's militancy and "couldn't break away from it because they felt that was the social agenda for white people."[10]

The UCCA's real stronghold, however, was in law enforcement, where the line between police officers and vigilantes often blurred due to the continued practice of deputizing white citizens. Following Illinois Attorney General William Scott's revocation of their special deputy status in June 1969, UCCA members successfully lobbied for a new city ordinance allowing for the formation of an auxiliary police force.[11] During a visit to the city in December 1970, *New York Times* reporter

188 FAITH IN BLACK POWER

J. Anthony Lukas obtained a list of these auxiliary officers, proving that only a handful were professionally trained and that a significant number were known to be active members of the UCCA. One of them was Bob Hogan, who in 1953 pled guilty to a malicious mischief charge stemming from the bombing of the home of African American physician Urbane Bass. "Today," Lukas stated, "he [Hogan] is a sheriff's deputy authorized to patrol the streets of Cairo with a rifle or submachine gun and keep racial peace." Lukas also interviewed Wilbert Beard, a black police officer who resigned his post in disgust over the department's infiltration by white vigilantes. During his three and a half years on the force, Beard witnessed what he described as a "real chummy" relationship between white officers and vigilantes, who he believed were "in and out of the police station all of the time." One former police chief even admitted to Beard that "most of the white policemen" were UCCA members.[12] Seeking to dispel allegations of collusion, city leaders contracted the International Association of Chiefs of Police to perform an independent study of local law enforcement. The final report bluntly concluded that the Cairo Police Department was "insensitive to the racial conditions confronting them" and had failed to demonstrate "the ability to maintain order with justice or to achieve the traditional objectives of a police agency."[13]

When UCCA members viewed the police as being "too soft on militants," they took aggressive action by forcing the resignation of three police chiefs and a county sheriff in less than two years.[14] In September 1969 William Petersen resigned a record-setting ninety days after taking the position as chief of police, citing the pressure of the Concerned Mothers of Cairo and Vicinity, a UCCA affiliate constituted by white women. "When people of the entire community, white and black, state that they are going to arm themselves and take the law into their own hands," Petersen declared, "then I as a professional policeman cannot continue to head this police department."[15] The vast majority of city officials, however, either openly or tacitly endorsed this arrangement, affording vigilantes weapons and the legal cover of deputy status as they mounted an extralegal campaign of terror against the city's black residents. As one city official admitted to a reporter from the *St. Louis Post-Dispatch*, "We send out the police and let them fire on the [Pyramid Court] project to keep the whites satisfied."[16]

Between 1969 and 1971 arson and sporadic gunfire were an almost daily experience for black Cairoites. White vigilantes firebombed black businesses, shot into black homes, and burned black churches to the ground. According to Wilbert Beard, white officers often had advance knowledge of such acts. "It was uncanny," he explained, "but they'd already have men on stand-by." Unsurprisingly, the perpetrators were never prosecuted for their crimes. A 1971 report by the Chicago-based advocacy group the Alliance to End Repression indicates that between March 3, 1969, and June 1, 1971, only three white suspects were arrested and none were convicted. During the same period, the United Front received reports of more than 140 incidents of shooting or firebombing directed at the homes and businesses of black residents.[17]

Republican governor Richard Ogilvie's periodic deployment of state police did little to rectify these inequities. Instead, state troopers played a key role in enforcing the city's repressive ordinances, arresting black protestors in droves and sparking new allegations of discriminatory treatment and brutality. United Front activists accused state police of failing to investigate the complaints of black residents and of standing by as local law enforcement and white vigilantes harassed and shot into their communities. At the same time state police heavily patrolled the Pyramid Courts and secured blanket search warrants to raid the homes of black residents in search of weapons. Many local activists believed that this harassment was an attempt to bait the black community into acts of retaliatory violence that would serve to justify a full-scale assault on the housing project. "The State Police," United Front leaders proclaimed, "are not here to protect Black citizens of this community, but they are here to harass, intimidate, incite and finally to try to destroy Black leaders and other Black people of Cairo." While a full-scale assault was averted, black residents living in the Pyramid Courts continued to live in fear, arming themselves and sleeping in bathtubs or under beds for protection.[18]

Indeed, the laxity with which local and state police enforced the law against white vigilantes only highlighted the severe and unjust manner with which the same officers handled black Cairoites and their allies in the United Front. An Alliance to End Repression report showed that a total of 266 African Americans, in contrast to 3 whites, were arrested between March 3, 1969, and June 1, 1971. Many were arrested for small ordinance and vehicular infractions.[19] However, in June 1970 local and state police began targeting the United Front's leaders, arresting several on trumped-up felony charges. "Well, they arrested me for attempted murder," United Front press secretary Manker Harris recalled. "I said, 'My God, what are you talking about?' . . . Now isn't this something? I get shot at by cops, and I get charged with attempted murder."[20] Also rounded up in the June sweep were Koen (aggravated battery charges); James Chairs, the United Front's chief of staff (disorderly conduct); James "Switch" Wilson, head of the United Front Liberators (criminal destruction of property); and field organizer Herman Whitfield (assault with a deadly weapon—the weapon being a charm bracelet). In August, after listening to State's Attorney Peyton Berbling present the prosecution's case, an Alexander County grand jury handed down indictments. "They have indicted persons who are working for social change," Koen declared. "We recognize if we are going to survive this type of judicial system, we will have to depend on God and ourselves."[21] With the support of the Lawyers' Committee, the United Front was successful in securing acquittals in the vast majority of cases. In fact, the 1971 Alliance to End Repression report indicated that only 2 of the 266 arrests had resulted in a conviction prior to June 1, 1971. However, the arrests continued unabated, and toward the end of the year the city's latest mayor, Pete Thomas, ratcheted up the tension by issuing a "shoot-to-kill" order if racial disturbances occurred. "And when I say we're gonna kill 'em," Mayor Thomas explained, "I mean we're gonna kill 'em."[22]

When vigilante violence and police harassment failed to halt the United Front's activities, the FBI colluded with local officials in an effort to destroy the organization's leadership and internal unity. Under the auspices of the Counterintelligence Program (COINTELPRO), FBI agents had closely monitored Charles Koen's activities since his time with the Black Liberators in St. Louis in 1968. Koen was placed on the agency's Security and Agitator Index of so-called "black extremists," and FBI Director J. Edgar Hoover authorized agents from the St. Louis field office to utilize counterintelligence measures to undermine his leadership and create disunity between the Liberators and other black nationalist and student groups. In fact, Koen's return to Cairo in the spring of 1969 was spurred, at least in part, by the FBI's efforts to foster marital tensions between the young leader and his wife Clydia Koen. "I can remember getting a letter from them," Clydia Koen recalled. "A poison pen letter is what they call it." FBI memos show that the anonymous letter contained accusations of infidelity intended "to alienate him from his wife" and "cast a [negative] reflection upon him with the white ministers in the area who are sympathic [*sic*] and . . . helpful to him." Agents in the St. Louis field office expressed hope that the letter would "draw [Koen] back to his wife" in Cairo, ending the Liberators' activities. When it became clear, however, that Koen intended to build a new movement in Cairo, agents in the Springfield and Chicago field offices reopened their investigations, starting separate case files on other Cairo-based activists.[23]

Initially the FBI's efforts centered on the development of local informants who might provide accurate and up-to-date intelligence on the United Front's activities. However, field agents frequently complained that the "tightly knit" organization was virtually impossible to infiltrate. Six months into the investigation, Hoover penned a series of frustrated memos that criticized the Springfield field office for their failure to identify a single informant "knowledgeable in the affairs of [Koen] or the UF." Hoover demanded that agents exert "more effort, more imagination and supervisory direction" toward the "development of racial informants in Cairo." Spurred by Hoover's criticism, Springfield agents intensified their efforts to identify potential informants, focusing on residents of the Pyramid Courts. By the end of 1970, they had developed at least three so-called "ghetto informants" who provided regular information regarding the United Front's activities. According to FBI records, all three informants were African American and had access to the United Front's public meetings and events. From the quality of the information received, none appears to have been part of the organization's inner core. Local activists' adoption of broad-based organizing approaches and reliance on preexisting social networks hindered FBI efforts at infiltration and the development of agents provocateurs.[24]

However, information obtained from confidential informants did assist the FBI in disrupting the United Front's operations. Beginning in November 1970, FBI agents targeted local black businessman James Avery as a potential informant. A former boxer and state police officer, Avery had been on friendly terms with black power leaders before he elected to go to local police and not the United Front's regional council with information regarding a break-in at his tavern. Branded a traitor, Avery became the only black business owner targeted by the boycott, and Sam's Tavern was forced to close. FBI records indicate that Springfield agents approached Avery shortly afterward and "encouraged" him to "attempt to discredit the United Front." Avery allegedly responded with some enthusiasm, explaining to FBI agents that he intended to file criminal charges against United Front leaders for intimidation and "air an appeal to the black people in Cairo to no longer follow the dictate of [Koen] and the United Front." Springfield agents notified Hoover that Avery was "confident that with backing he will be able to break the United Front hold on Cairo and gain a peaceful settlement of all difficulties." However, when Avery launched his first public attack on Koen during a United Front rally at St. Columba's in January 1971, he was quickly booed out of the hall. Following this failed attempt, Avery took to the airwaves and called on black Cairoites to participate in an election on January 16 to determine the future leadership of the black community. Once again Avery's efforts fell on deaf ears. Writing shortly after Avery's failed coup, IFCO assistant director Lorenzo Freeman described Cairo as "the most cohesive Black community" he had ever encountered. "All elements seem to be represented in the [United Front] hierarchy and no polarization is evident within the organization. The ranks are well closed."[25]

Indeed, by the start of 1971 it seemed that the United Front had beaten the odds, making Cairo a lone bright spot in the struggle for freedom and justice. Reviewing the events of the last twelve months, the *Chicago Daily Defender* lamented that 1970 had been "a slow year for civil rights." Movement activity had "dropped to a murmur" as "more militant organizations either changed their modus operandi or went completely underground." Many black power activists had reportedly "redirected their energies from the podium to the backroom," rendering demonstrations and direct action obsolete. "Nowhere," the article concluded, "is anybody doing anything, except in Cairo and the political arena." While somewhat exaggerated, these statements illustrate the impact of heightened repression and a narrowing structure of opportunities on black power struggles, forcing many activists to abandon mass mobilization in favor of black officialdom. In this context, the Cairo United Front appeared to be a throwback to the militancy of a prior and quickly fading tradition. In the face of a coordinated pattern of repression, the organization had not fragmented or collapsed but had continued to make significant strides in its effort to empower poor and black residents. Taking to his pulpit at St. Columba's, Koen equated the harassment of United Front leaders with the trials and persecutions of Jesus, whom the young minister described as "fearless" in facing the legal and political rulers of his time. "This," Koen insisted, "must be the attitude of persons today who are involved as Jesus was in the freeing of the minds, bodies and spirits of God's children."[26]

However, the United Front had not escaped 1970 unscathed. The organization entered the New Year in dire financial straits after being saddled with the burden of skyrocketing bail bonds accumulated during the law enforcement sweeps of the preceding months. On a single day in December 1970, fifteen United Front members were arrested and jailed, resulting in over $100,000 in bail bond costs for the organization. Once again, many of those targeted were United Front leaders, a fact that placed added pressure on the activist community. The arrests continued in January as James Chairs, chief of staff for the United Front, was picked up at the governor's office in Springfield while protesting discriminatory police practices. In February state police raided the Pyramid Courts, arresting Frank Hollis, Deborah Flowers, and "Switch" Wilson on federal gun charges. In March the courts ruled the search warrants used in the state police raid were illegal, but the damage had already been done. Large segments of the United Front leadership were now awaiting trial, and the organization was floundering under a mountain of legal bills.[27]

Backlash from the Pews

The United Front's ability to meet bail bonds and keep key activists out of jail hinged on the organization's relationship with their external donors, particularly church-based grant-awarding bodies like IFCO, GCSP, and SDOP. However, by 1971 United Front activists and their network of allies within denominational hierarchies began to express concern about the reliability of church-based funding. Rev. Blaine Ramsey was among the first to spot the warning signs. As chair of the ICC's Special Task

Force, Ramsey was well situated to observe broader trends within the nation's largest denominations, and as early as May 1970 he sounded the alarm that funding for local black power struggles was unstable. In a report written that month, Ramsey informed the leadership of the ICC that the "greatest problem" facing his agency was that predominantly white denominations would "cop out" on funding black power organizations. This concern, according to Ramsey, was already "evidenced by an increased reluctance on the part of some to work ecumenically with programs which the Task Force designates as being necessary to accomplish a reconciled community." While task force staff were doing their best "to maintain financial and moral support" for such initiatives, Ramsey argued that they were dealing with church executives who were often reluctant to extend resources due to their own "polarized constituency," "dwindling funds," and "reordering of denominational priorities." In addition to these internal factors, Ramsey also pointed to the increased burden imposed on church resources by what he perceived as competing struggles. "National events related to pollution, campus unrest and national violence, aggravated by the Vietnam War and the Cambodian incursion have not helped," Ramsey explained. "These events have overshadowed the unresolved problems of black people in the nation's ghettos." These issues, combined with the fact that churches were planning "to cut back in areas of social action and ecumenical relations," gave Ramsey little reason for optimism. "The unhappy picture of the ecumenical church in Illinois," he concluded, "reflects the recession of national spirit." Over the next few months, Ramsey's immediate fears for the United Front were allayed by IFCO's extension of a substantial grant to the organization. However, his report was prescient in that it highlighted major shifts taking place within mainline denominations that in the coming years would place new pressure on the United Front.[28]

The 1960s and 1970s represented a moment of ecclesiastical upheaval as a white "Christian Silent Minority" expressed growing concerns about the direction of church affairs.[29] An abundance of sociological studies published during the era warned of the latent conflict burning just beneath the surface of many Protestant and Catholic congregations. In his 1969 bestseller *The Gathering Storm in the Churches,* Jeffrey Hadden described how the new breed of clergy and church executives, radicalized in the crucible of civil rights and the War on Poverty, were now finding themselves polarized from a more conservative laity. Tensions between clergy and laity had roots in longstanding theological debates over the social gospel and higher criticism as well as in more recent social debates over anticommunism and school prayer; the polarity was exacerbated by the very visible involvement of progressive clergy in the civil rights struggles of the 1960s. A 1967 national opinion poll showed that while less than 10 percent of mainline Protestant clergy "basically disapproved of the Civil Rights movement in America," almost half of all church attenders polled were opposed. When asked specifically about clergy's participation in picketing and demonstrations, almost three-quarters of church attenders indicated that such activity did "more harm than good" and that they would be personally "upset" if they were to discover their own minister or priest was participating.

Importantly, these findings split down racial lines; black parishioners were much more likely to support the activist ministry advocated by the new breed of clergy. For example, a 1968 study of UCC members indicated that 77 percent of African American respondents felt that their church leaders should spend a lot of time "working for social justice" compared to just 20 percent of white respondents. Moreover, while white respondents ranked "working for social justice" tenth in frequency among twelve ministerial roles, African American respondents ranked it first. Thus, even in the most liberal of Protestant denominations, important divisions existed between both laity and clergy and black and white parishioners as to the role and responsibility of ministers in regard to social justice. As Hadden explains, these disparities constituted "a very significant source of conflict within the churches" and put activist clergy on "a collision course" with a large segment of the laity.[30]

As denominational support expanded during the black power era, these underlying tensions quickly rose to the surface. Most controversial was the decision by church executives to allocate denominational revenues for grant-awarding bodies aimed at addressing the effects of the urban crisis. "There is a growing fear," commentator Will Oursler explained, "that the churches are moving too far into the questionable action programs." Many conservative laypersons simply recoiled at the idea of being "committed as individuals or a congregation to the support of groups and causes with which they may not sympathize—and which they may actively oppose." A May 1969 Gallup poll indicated that 92 percent of all churchgoers opposed James Forman's Black Manifesto, which called for $500 million in reparations from predominantly white denominations. As Forman supporters occupied the NCC's headquarters, parishioners flooded church executives with angry letters, insisting that they not cave to the activist's demands. The fact that decisions about funding black power initiatives tended to be made by new breed church executives with little input from local white congregants was a source of considerable antagonism. As Jeffrey Hadden explained, the new breed of clergy "saturated virtually every non-parish structure within the church" including denominational administration, college and seminary instruction, and inner-city experimental ministries. These positions, Hadden explained, allowed radical clergy to "maximize their power to bring about innovation and change" and insulated them from "direct reprisals from laity." However, this insulation of activist clergy fostered a significant rift between local, predominantly white congregations and national church structures.[31]

In an ironic twist, conservative critics from within mainline denominations mobilized the participatory democracy discourse of sixties liberal activists to expose what they perceived as the unrepresentative mechanisms by which denominational policy and funding decisions were made. In his 1967 polemic *The Protestant Revolt*, fundamentalist clergyman James DeForest Murch railed against "clerical domination which treats them [laypeople] as sheep, demanding their complete acquiescence in . . . distasteful programs." According to Murch, laity deeply "resent being lumped into a mass of faceless automatons and delivered by the liberal establishment as in favor or not in favor of this or that social or political position, without ever bothering to consult them or to get their approval."[32] Fueled by such concerns, conservative laypeople across mainline denominations formed dissident lay committees in an effort "to thwart the steam-roller power of the ecumenical high command." Organized in 1965, the Presbyterian Lay Committee described its work as "a silent revolution" that incorporated "an increasing number of church members who are getting tired of paying for all the radicalism and secularism of their church leaders." Others withheld financial contributions and in some cases opted to leave denominations entirely. By 1971 Oursler and other social commentators were beginning to observe a general "retreat in gifts and giving," often targeted at the new task forces and grant-awarding agencies developed to address the urban crisis. The following year these claims were bolstered by NCC executive Dean Kelley, who claimed that the decline in mainline Protestant church membership was being prompted by the social justice activities of new breed clergy. By the early 1970s concerns over what Blaine Ramsey had aptly defined as a "polarized constituency" and talk of "dwindling funds" dominated the national conventions of all of the mainline denominations, forcing church executives to either face down conservative factions or engage in a "reordering of denominational priorities." On the whole, the churches opted for the latter.[33]

The scaling back of church support for social justice ministries was swift, disproportionately affecting task forces and grant-awarding agencies designed to address the urban crisis. The Episcopal Church's GCSP, a program that had extended significant resources to the United Front, was one of the first to feel the backlash. Since its founding in 1967, the program had come under consistent attack from conservative clergy and laypeople for extending grants to grassroots black power organizations. In particular, opponents honed in on GCSP's failure to incorporate diocesan leaders into the decision-making process and the program's sponsorship of initiatives that were alleged to have advocated violence. One controversial case was the GCSP's extension of a grant to the Jackson Human Rights Project in Mississippi. Concerns were raised that far from embracing racial reconciliation, the organization was a black separatist group that promoted the use of violence against whites. Conservative clergy also asserted that the funding should not be granted because the local bishop had objected. The GCSP's director, Leon Modeste, granted the funding despite local opposition and concerns regarding the organization's goals and tactics. Further controversy was fostered in 1970 when the GCSP awarded a grant, against the wishes of a local bishop, to the Malcolm X Liberation University in Durham, North Carolina. In response, white conservative Episcopalians slashed their financial contributions, costing the North Carolina diocese nearly $165,000. Consequently, the diocese reduced its donation to the national church by nearly 40 percent that year. As tensions mounted, twenty-five diocesan conventions passed resolutions requesting that local bishops be permitted to veto potential grants within their diocese, a power they secured at the 1970 general convention. Bishops were now given thirty days to object to any proposed grant in their diocese. If the bishop objected, only a full majority of the executive council could override it. By mobilizing discourses rooted in democratic localism, conservative clergy and laity radically undercut the power of the GCSP and its director, Leon Modeste, who had functioned as a key gatekeeper to church resources.[34]

By 1973 the GCSP's very survival was threatened as the executive council, according to Modeste, increasingly felt that it must respond to the demands of the "folks back home."[35] On October 18 the entire African American staff of the GCSP received notices of termination, and in December the program was officially closed. Since its creation at the height of the urban rebellions, the program had funded projects totaling $7.5 million in urban areas across the country. However, heightened hostility toward the program from conservative laity and clergy ensured that it had become a liability for liberal church executives. The Community Action and Human Development section replaced the program. However, in his annual address Bishop John E. Hines conceded that the resources allocated to the group would be considerably less than in previous years and its mission broader than originally defined. Given a small budget, no permanent full-time director, and only two staff members, the program was now charged with addressing the concerns of all ethnic and racial "minorities." Hines gave the GCSP a begrudging and defiant farewell, describing it as "a moment in the conscience of men" that had served to broaden understandings of the church's role and responsibility in the world. In contrast, Modeste blamed the program's closure on church executives' lack of commitment and capitulation to white Episcopal laypeople who, when asked in a series of hearings in 1973, insisted that the program was "causing a schism in the church, and had to go." Reflecting on his experiences, Modeste concluded that reliance on the church had been a mistake. "There is no question in my mind," Modeste stated, "that Blacks will never be free as long as we are dependent upon white institutions for resources. For at the most crucial time for us, the white institution will always withdraw the resources in favor of self-interest."

Accordingly, Modeste argued, "Blacks must build and maintain our own institutions and control those agencies which provide services in our communities."[36]

As the Episcopal Church moved to close down its largest grant-awarding body, the Presbyterian Church's SDOP was also struggling to stay afloat. By July 1972 the program was forced to order a moratorium on all new funding awards due to declining donations and a backlog of unpaid bills. The committee's director, Rev. St. Paul Epps, bemoaned the fact that donations were dramatically lower than the anticipated $10 million per year required to reach the denomination's target of raising "70 million in the 70s toward overcoming poverty." According to Epps, donations for the program barely reached $2 million, prompting a scaling back of programming and expectations. In 1973 these financial realities forced Epps and his staff to reject more than two hundred grant applications so that the committee could meet more than $1 million in outstanding commitments to programs that had been validated the previous year. The moratorium was not lifted until early 1975.[37]

Another key Presbyterian agency charged with addressing issues of race and poverty, CORAR, also came under heavy attack and by 1972 had witnessed a dramatic curtailment in its power and autonomy. At the 1972 general convention, widespread opposition to CORAR's recent extension of a $10,000 grant from the Emergency Fund for Legal Aid to the Angela Davis defense fund erupted into protests, prompting a series of proposals from local synods demanding that black-led task forces like CORAR come under greater supervision from the general convention, be governed by stricter guidelines, or be stripped of their autonomous funding capacity. These efforts were voted down by the convention; however, tensions over the dissemination of funds, particularly without the consent of local presbyteries, persisted. As a result, many synods, including the Synod of Illinois, began to impose stricter measures of their own regarding the dissemination of funds, and they increasingly granted local presbyteries greater say in the decision-making process.[38]

Ecumenical bodies like IFCO and the NCC were also affected by these broader denominational cutbacks. IFCO, an organization heavily dependent on denominational contributions, quickly saw its resources dwindle. In January 1971 IFCO director Lucius Walker was forced to declare a moratorium on grants, cautioning that if donations did not bounce back the organization's survival was at stake.[39] At the NCC Father Robert C. Chapman, the CME minister who had worked as the organization's director for racial justice from 1969 to 1971 and had been recently promoted to director of the social justice department, was fired in July 1973, prompting sit-down protests from supporters at the organization's headquarters in New York. While the NCC claimed that Chapman had been discharged for "lack of concurrence with policy," his supporters alleged that Chapman had fallen out of favor with the organization as its priorities had shifted. Close to fifty protestors participated in a sit-in at the NCC's offices at the Interchurch Center, demanding that the organization fire its general secretary, apologize to Father Chapman, and set up a separate and autonomous division on criminal, racial, and social justice that would be financed by one-tenth of the organization's overall operating budget. At an earlier moment this proposal might have gained some support from within the denomination. However, by 1973 the tide was turning and the plea fell on deaf ears.[40]

Back at ICC headquarters in Springfield, Blaine Ramsey began to observe a similar pattern. What had initially been a cause for concern by 1971 had turned into a full-scale funding crisis that struck at the heart of the organization's ability to meet the needs of the state's poor and black communities. In a report submitted to ICC executives, Ramsey asserted that the Special Task Force's resources had "dwindled and in some instances . . . dried up entirely." From conversations with church executives, Ramsey deduced that the shortage of funds was connected to a precipitous decline in lay giving for benevolent projects. "People have been turned off by what they call a preoccupation in political affairs," he explained. "This situation," he continued, "has greatly jeopardized the morale of staff and hindered the development and execution of programs designed to meet the needs of people in areas where poverty and racism are acute." Ramsey insisted that the cause of this decline in support was a lack of commitment to racial justice and antipoverty initiatives by church leaders and members. "Benign neglect," he informed ICC executives, "seems to be the posture now taken by funding groups." Accordingly, Ramsey joined Modeste in concluding that the nation's churches could "no longer be depended upon to adequately fund Community Action

Programs." The fragile coalition between liberal white church executives, progressive black clergy, and black power activists forged in the wake of the urban rebellions was rapidly disintegrating.[41]

The collapse of this fragile coalition was felt most severely at the local level, where many black power organizations had relied heavily on church resources to build effective movements and institutions. Between 1971 and 1974, the United Front witnessed a precipitous decline in funding from church-based organizations. While comprehensive financial records for the United Front are unavailable, an examination of donations made to the organization by the three largest funding bodies—IFCO, the Episcopal Church's GCSP, and the Presbyterian's SDOP—indicates that annual donations fell from a peak of $297,660 in 1970 to $127,000 in 1971 before drying up completely the following year. Additional donations were not forthcoming in subsequent years.[42]

These fiscal woes were compounded by the inability of many grant-awarding agencies to meet even preexisting commitments. In the fall of 1971, the SDOP found itself unable to transfer the second half of an $112,000 grant to the United Front due to a shortage of funds. While the grant was eventually received, its delay created a crisis of liquidity that hampered the United Front's ability to cover immediate expenses. Efforts to secure the money from alternative sources ran up against fierce resistance from the Southern Illinois Presbytery, whose members were often hostile to the United Front's activities. "Many of the southern Illinois and Cairo Presbyterians," the *Monitor* reported, "look at the Cairo blacks as a dangerous group of militants willing to answer shot for shot the gunfire from police and white vigilantes into the black community." The wider funding scene was not much brighter, as denominational programs targeting the urban crisis had their budgets slashed. Meanwhile, the UMC's ongoing support for the Lawyers' Committee galvanized a backlash from white Methodists in Cairo, who according to United Front member Hattie Kendrick were threatening to halt tithes and offerings if church executives persisted in "taking their money . . . to help the niggers fight them." In an effort to dissuade church executives from funding the United Front, UCCA members—many of whom were leading ministers and laypersons—projected an image of Koen and the United Front as religious hypocrites and criminals motivated by self-interest and greed.

The fall 1971 issue of the *Tri-State Informer*, for example, featured a caricature of the United Front's "The Bible and the Gun" symbol in which a pair of hands grasps for a weapon placed atop a King James Bible with alcohol and ammunition strewn about. "This [illustration]," the caption reads, "shows better than words the mockery of religion of the 'Rev.' [Koen]."[43]

Heavily reliant on church-based resources, the United Front began to experience financial difficulties almost immediately. As the previous chapter showed, the "no strings" model of funding championed by many black clergy made church funds indispensable in meeting expenses that corporate and governmental grants prohibited, such as legal bills and daily operational costs. Unsurprisingly, these two areas were the most immediately affected by the scaling back of church support and the concomitant collapse in the United Front's liquidity. The fact that the United Front faced a rapid decline in church resources at the exact moment its key activists were facing criminal prosecution only served to exacerbate the emerging crisis. Black power activists responded to the lethal combination of legal repression and declining resources by engaging in a vigorous fundraising campaign and by redirecting all available funds to legal aid. At this early stage it was far from clear that the decline in church funding was going to be a permanent feature of the landscape. However, donations would never again reach 1970 levels, despite the best efforts of black church executives.

Tensions over the church's support for black power were not confined to Protestant denominations. In fact, for black Cairoites one of the year's most visible signs of retrenchment came from the Belleville diocese of the Roman Catholic Church. Just two years earlier, progressive forces within the diocese had succeeded in opening up St. Columba's to black parishioners and social service organizations, including the United Front. However, by 1971 St. Columba's had come to serve as a controversial symbol of Catholic support for black power, and pressure was mounting on diocesan leaders to evict the United Front. "Complaints from older clergy and a few laymen reached the Chancery Office," Gerald Montroy explained. "Instead of responding to these complaints by teaching or preaching social justice and racial equality, they took the easy way out." In December 1970 Bishop Albert Zuroweste succumbed to the pressure

and ordered the United Front, NAACP, IMC, and several other community organizations to vacate their offices no later than February 1. Further, the bishop terminated Father Ben Bodewes and ordered an end to
all religious ministries at St. Columba's. After February 1 black parishioners would be expected to transfer to the all-white St. Patrick's Church
pastored by Father Casper Deis. According to the bishop, these changes
were necessary to make room for the Cairo Recreational Committee
(CRC), an interracial arts and crafts program initiated by Flora Cham-
bliss, a middle-class black parishioner who the United Front accused of
breaking the boycott and opposing their work. The CRC, the bishop
argued, better reflected the church's reconciliation mission and represented a positive step toward healing the embattled community. Father
Deis supported what he called the bishop's "Gospel-spirited decision"
and pointed to the bad reputation brought upon the parish as a result
of the United Front's use of St. Columba's. "Our concern," Father Deis
informed reporters, "must be that the Catholic Church disassociate itself
from even the appearance of violence." Father Deis agreed that the CRC
was more consistent with the church's reconciliationist goals, arguing
that the program was better situated than the United Front to promote
cultural programs that afforded "opportunities for blacks and whites to
develop understanding for each other."[44]

United Front leaders vehemently opposed Bishop Zuroweste's decision, lobbying the diocesan leader to rescind his eviction order. Reverend
Ramsey organized an emergency meeting with the bishop in January, but
talks quickly broke down. In a follow-up letter Ramsey questioned the
bishop's plan to integrate St. Patrick's, stating that it was unrealistic and
suggestive of a "false sense of optimism . . . about the changed attitudes
of the white people in Cairo, especially those who make up the Catholic constituency." Ramsey also challenged the bishop's assertion that the
CRC offered a pathway to reconciliation, stating that he had performed
his own investigation into the group and found that the biracial character
of its leadership was "not solid" and that several of the group's assumed
black leaders had either declined to participate or resigned. The bishop
also received a strongly worded letter from Hattie Kendrick, who insisted
that the United Front's work was wholly consistent with biblical teachings. "The [United Front] only wants of you a place to have their meet-

ings, keep their records and assist the needy. Do you knowingly deprive them of this opportunity or are you like Pilot [*sic*] listening to the angry mob outside as they scream 'crucify them'?" Kendrick signed her letter "A discouraged Christian."[45]

When these petitions fell on deaf ears, local activists decided to resist eviction. In an open letter published in the *Monitor,* Father Bodewes announced his decision to continue his parish duties without pay and in defiance of the bishop's orders. "I will stay in St. Columba and the United Front and the other [six] organizations, the food distribution and clothing distribution will remain and continue to use the building and services. . . . I shall not be moved." The eviction deadline loomed and local activists dug in their heels as expressions of support flooded in from progressive Catholic organizations, including SIAP, the National Coalition of American Nuns, the National Conference of Interracial Justice, the National Federation of Priests Councils, and the Catholic Interracial Council of Chicago. Members of SIAP offered to join local parishioners in resisting eviction through nonviolent demonstrations. In response Bishop Zuroweste offered to allow the NAACP and IMC to use the building if the United Front agreed to leave, an offer that the organizations' respective leaders rejected.[46]

When February 1 arrived no evictions took place, but struggles over control of St. Columba's continued. In early September 1971 Bishop Zuroweste ordered that all utilities in the church be shut off, leaving occupants to face the winter without lights, hot water, or heat. When this tactic failed, the bishop filed the appropriate paperwork to transmit ownership of St. Columba's to St. Patrick's Church. Subsequently, Father Deis announced that St. Columba's was slated for demolition and that the land would be given to "two poor Catholic families" to build homes on. United Front coordinator Leon Page and NAACP president Preston Ewing met with Father Deis and challenged both his legal right to evict the tenants and his claim that two Catholic families wanted to build homes on the parish lot. Pointing out that St. Columba's was located in a predominantly poor and black area that had witnessed considerable violence over the past three years, Ewing argued that this was not the real motive and offered to extend the families sites in a better neighborhood. Father Deis rejected the offer. These struggles continued for several months before a coalition of progressive Catholic leaders finally purchased the building on the United Front's behalf.[47]

The United Front's struggle to secure ongoing access to church facilities and funding took a significant toll, diverting energy away from the organization's wider political program. Moreover, the collapse in church support rendered the United Front increasingly vulnerable to new forms of economic repression. The support of predominantly white religious institutions had afforded United Front activists a modicum of independence from local whites. The organization's paid staff structure, funded almost exclusively by church grants, allowed leading activists protection from economic discrimination at the hands of local employers and welfare officers. Bail bond donations and the opening of the Lawyers' Committee provided important legal protections to activists who were picked up and pushed through the criminal justice system. Moreover, the Catholic Church had provided the organization with office and meeting space beyond the control of local landlords. For these reasons, resisting eviction from St. Columba's was essential, since United Front leaders would almost certainly find themselves unable to purchase or rent another building in the city. Thus, by retracting their support, church leaders had removed an important "umbrella of protection," as Southern Illinois priest Father James Genisio put it.[48]

Making sense of this retraction of support was something that frustrated many black power activists and radical clergy. Most viewed liberal church executives as having succumbed to internal opposition from conservative white laity and a few firebrand clergymen. Some, like Leon Modeste, began to interpret white church executives' failure to take a principled stance as an almost inevitable consequence of their positionality as leaders of white racist institutions. Future programs, he argued, would have to be developed independent of their support or risk a similar outcome. For others, like Father Genisio, "money was the prime motive," and church executives had opted to prioritize tithes and offerings over their commitment to the poor and oppressed. However, the United Front case is particularly instructive because it reveals both the internal and external opposition church executives faced for their support of black power organizations. While the precipitous decline of the church-based coalition was sparked by broader ecumenical debates over the appropriate role of the church in political affairs, these tensions were exacerbated by external pressure from state agencies, including the IRS and the FBI.[49]

The Chilling Effect

During the early 1970s, black power activists and their church-based funders came under fire as the IRS began to demonstrate what one contemporary described as "an unprecedented interest in the civil rights, anti-poverty, and anti-war activities of certain religious organizations." Several national denominations and ecumenical bodies were investigated concerning allegations that they had violated the provisions of their tax-exempt status by "carrying on propaganda or attempting to influence legislation." The NCC and IFCO were audited in response to allegations that the organizations were funneling church funds to subversive groups. In IFCO's case the IRS quickly expanded the audits to include half of the approximately one hundred community groups that had been sponsored by the organization as well as the personal returns of the foundation's board members. Between 1970 and 1973 the IRS performed similar investigations of the accounts of more than a dozen church organizations. Writing for the *Nation,* attorney Joseph Ruskay described the IRS investigations as "the covert weapon" employed by the Nixon administration to "discourage its critics within the churches." According to Ruskay, "The legal basis for this alarming intrusion of the government in church affairs is dubious at best" and at worst "a clear abridgment of First Amendment guarantees." Dean Kelley, director of religious and civil liberties at the NCC, agreed, stating that the Nixon administration had used the IRS as "the chief but not only means" to threaten "religious groups which engage in dissident secular activities outside their own walls."[50]

Declining resources certainly made the United Front vulnerable to this kind of harassment, and for several years UCCA members angered by church donations to the United Front petitioned state officials to investigate the organization's finances. Indeed, a central tool in the arsenal of the United Front's opponents was spreading rumors of financial impropriety. Local officials mocked the so-called "bleeding hearts" at the ICC and other religious groups across the country who had "poured tons of money" into the United Front for failing to recognize that they were being manipulated by criminals and militants. In the winter of 1971 the Illinois Attorney General's office demanded that the United Front file an audit. Because external funds had dwindled and previous donations were tied up in bail bonds, the United Front was in no position to advance the six to ten thousand dollars required to perform an audit. Consequently, the United Front lost its charitable status, preventing activists from soliciting donations until the fall of 1972.[51]

That same year the IRS's intelligence division began a major investigation into Charles Koen's personal finances. Alleging that Koen had diverted thousands of dollars in funds from the United Front for his own personal use without declaring the money as income, the IRS honed its investigation on the United Front's church donors, filing summons in person at the national headquarters of the UMC, the Episcopal Church, UCC, the United Presbyterian Church, the Christian Church, and the NCC. The summons demanded copies of "cancelled checks, money orders or other means to payment" to Charles Koen; any "correspondence, notes, memoranda, or other documents" related to those contributions; and, more broadly, "any other records relating to the activities of Charles E. Koen, the United Front, Inc., and/or other officers, employees, or members of the United Front, Inc." National church executives—among them Dean Kelley and Robert Chapman of the NCC; George Granger, treasurer of the UMC; Charles Lockyear, treasurer of the UCC; and Gayraud Wilmore of the Presbyterian Church—immediately met with Leon Page of the United Front to discuss the investigation and coordinate a strategy. None of the groups had given money directly to Koen. However, the final component of the summons cast a broader net to include information related to funds that had been extended to the United Front. Deeming this beyond the scope of the investigation, church executives decided to comply with the first two parts of the summons but not the final one.[52]

Local black power activists and allied black church executives viewed the IRS inquiry with skepticism and tried their best to persuade other denominational leaders it was part of a broader pattern of state repression. Gayraud Wilmore reminded church executives that many other African American activists had been "the objects of inquiry by IRS and other governmental agencies in recent years." Father Robert Chapman echoed Wilmore's claims, calling the IRS inquiry "just another in a long series of efforts to crush the United Front." Chapman also suggested that local whites might have "sparked" the IRS investigation, since on his many trips to Cairo he had observed that "rumors circulate freely that large sums of money have been pouring into the Front" from church-based organizations. Those rumors also cast Koen as a "rip-off artist" who was capitalizing on church-based donations for his own purposes.[53] Blaine Ramsey agreed with Chapman's assessment, stating that the investigations were "the result of strong pressure brought to bear on the United Front by the local power structure to short circuit funding channels." Like Chapman, Ramsey had observed "all sorts of rumors . . . swirling in the Cairo community about the financial accountability of the United Front," and while he conceded that the organization may have not "employed the best bookkeeping procedures," the accusation that Koen was siphoning large sums for his personal use was patently false. The United Front leadership agreed with Ramsey's interpretation, characterizing the tax investigations as a new spin on older forms of harassment.[54]

While many church executives took a principled stance in relation to the IRS's harassment of the United Front, the general effect was to further dampen church-based funding for black power. Dean Kelley argued that the IRS investigations had "a chilling effect" on the churches' social justice activities: "Even if the investigated organizations get a clean bill of health, it will often have spent several thousand dollars in legal and other fees to defend itself and will be a little less eager to do anything which might precipitate another complaint and investigation." According to Kelley, these investigations only served to exacerbate the "growing mood of quiescence, consolidation, disenchantment and loss-of-nerve" taking place in churches throughout the country. This quiescence, Kelley argued, "is a sign that the government's efforts to discourage boatrocking and trouble-making were not altogether failures."[55]

The IRS was not the only federal agency devoting considerable energy and resources to breaking the ties between the United Front and their church donors. FBI records show that agents were particularly concerned with the United Front's ability to leverage church resources, and they kept close tabs on the organization's denominational sponsors. When it was discovered that the United Front was receiving significant donations from the Episcopal Church, FBI director Hoover ordered agents in the Washington field office to launch a counterintelligence initiative aimed at "having these funds cut off."[56] Agents crafted a letter to an unidentified leader in the Episcopal Church posing as "a Vestreyman of one of the largest downtown Episcopal Churches in Chicago." In the letter, the supposed "vestreyman" informed the reader that he was "aware that the Episcopal Church funded the United Front of Cairo in amount of $50,000.00 for the year 1970" and that one of the organization's leaders had been "given an opportunity to speak" before the church's general convention. The author warned that the church's funding of the United Front had prompted "many members" to "cut their pledges, thus forcing a cut of funds for local parish programs as well as funds for National Church programs." Accordingly, the author asked his reader, "for the good of our church, to withhold funds from the United Front of Cairo." The author concluded his letter by assuring Episcopal authorities that while he agreed with "most of the Church's program," he disagreed with sponsoring organizations like the United Front "that resort to violence in order to obtain their objectives."[57]

Hoover also ordered agents in the Springfield field office to develop and circulate an anonymous flyer aimed at "lessening . . . [Koen's] support in the black community of Cairo and elsewhere." Exploiting notions of Koen as a charlatan and fraud that were popular among local white supremacists, the FBI flyer sought to highlight Koen's "expensive taste" and other "opportunistic traits," by caricaturing him in "expensive mod clothing" and jewelry surrounded by a group of "ordinary" and "poor" black men. "It is anticipated," field agents reasoned, "that circulation of this would further latent resentment against [Koen] in the black community and assist in neutralizing him." These counterintelligence efforts angered local activists, who knew Koen as a principled leader who also lived in poverty. "He was poor," Manker Harris recalls. "He didn't have money. He didn't spend that much on clothes either. A lot of times he would go through some of the clothes that were brought in [through Operation Need], like a lot of the brothers and sisters did."[58]

Survival by Any Means

By the summer of 1971 the full extent of this bleak financial picture had set in, leaving United Front leaders to face some difficult decisions. All remaining funds were now being diverted to attorney fees and bail bonds, casting the organization's long-term political program into jeopardy and necessitating a fundamental reevaluation of strategies and tactics. Further complicating matters was the election of leading UCCA members to municipal office in April. In a hard-fought campaign, three UCCA candidates—Allen Moss, James Walder, and James Dale—secured spots on the city council, beating out black candidates Rev. Sherman Jones, Ed Wade, and Preston Ewing Sr. Incumbent mayor Pete Thomas, fearing "extremists" might seize political office, declared that he would run for reelection, ultimately defeating UCCA candidate E. J. Walder and African American Alphonso Farmer. However, once the ballots were counted and the extent of the UCCA victory was realized, Thomas came under pressure to resign and was quickly replaced by James Walder, a downtown merchant and the UCCA's treasurer. All three commissioners secured reelection in 1975, marking a fundamental realignment in political power.[59]

The election of Walder, Dale, and Moss stunned black power activists. "These men," Charles Koen declared, "are the most extreme of the extremists" and "have vowed to keep blacks in their place." The election served as a referendum of sorts, ending any hopes of dialogue or compromise. During their tenure, Mayor Walder and his commissioners brought the UCCA's "no compromise" approach to the city government. Faced with a mountain of civil suits, they dug in their heels and pursued the cases at a tremendous expense to the city even when it was clear that the courts would rule in the United Front's favor. "Yeah, I give them credit. . . . They were comprehensive in their opposition," Preston Ewing Jr. joked. "They didn't leave a stone unturned. They would oppose [us] on every little thing." UCCA council members also refused to accept federal and state funds aimed at assisting poor and black residents, taking their lead from Carl Helt's *Tri-State Informer*, which characterized such initiatives as "hand-out programs" run by "fat necked Negro administrators" designed to "bribe-off" black power activists. When the United Front sought to work independently to secure federal and state grants for economic development, city leaders repeatedly stymied their efforts. A particularly egregious example of this obstructionism was the city council's refusal to sell lots to the United Cairo Housing Corporation (UCHC) for use in new home developments. Now a state-sponsored agency, the UCHC sought to purchase city lots to build new homes projected to bring $1.9 million to the local economy, increase the tax base, and create new jobs. However, UCHC's close ties to the United Front provoked opposition from city council members, who closed ranks against the sale and forced the organization to reevaluate its initiative. Meanwhile, council members continued to approve increases in the police department's budget, believing that "law and order" was the only way to end the boycott that was devastating their businesses. Increasingly, it appeared that the city council was willing to bankrupt the city rather than negotiate. As one UCCA member stated to a journalist from *Ramparts* magazine, "We would rather see the town wiped off the map than turn it over to those revolutionaries from the United Front."[60]

The UCCA's rise to political power played an important role in the United Front's discussions of the need for tactical innovation. Black power activists in Cairo had always adopted a multipronged approach to addressing discrimination in the city: filing legal suits, engaging in nonviolent direct action, running candidates for political office, and developing autonomous parallel institutions. For some, however, these new political realities appeared to render many of the older tactics obsolete. Most obviously, the UCCA victory had demonstrated the limitations of an electoral strategy to achieve black power in Cairo. Until the discriminatory at-large commission system could be dismantled, black Cairoites would find themselves locked out of city government and unable to capitalize on their latent voting power. This exclusion of black Cairoites from formal avenues of power was not new, and between 1969 and 1971 local activists had become particularly adept at operating through noninstitutionalized channels, mounting boycotts, sit-ins, and demonstrations in an effort to extract concessions from local and state officials. However, UCCA members now controlled city government, the business district, and law enforcement, and serious questions were raised about the viability of such strategies in achieving the United Front's goals. Almost two years into one of the nation's best-organized boycotts, local merchants showed no signs of breaking their resolve. If anything their determination seemed steelier than ever, making the costs associated with these tactics harder to bear. Church funds were drying up and key leaders faced jail time; unsurprisingly black power activists began to question whether the picketing and protests associated with the boycott were still worth the cost. Shortly after the election, some United Front leaders began to advance the argument that their best chance of eradicating longstanding practices of discrimination was in state-sponsored economic development and in the courts.

These strategic debates intensified during the summer of 1971 as police resumed their assaults on the United Front. Heavy police patrols returned to Cairo's streets. An armored truck was deployed. Conflict seemed imminent. In June violence erupted after Commissioner Dale ordered police to launch an assault on St. Columba's Church after receiving unsubstantiated reports of sniper fire. The only people inside the church were Fathers Bodewes and Montroy and Helen Belsheim, an attorney for the Lawyers' Committee. Disillusioned with the ministry, Montroy had left Cairo a year prior and had returned to celebrate completing his first year of law school. Now the former priest found himself "hunched down in the church pews" as police officers and vigilantes fired at them, blowing "out the window casings, breaking glass and knocking softball size holes in the walls" of the rectory. "We crawled on the floor to the front of the church thinking we might be able to escape through the front door," Montroy recalled. Pushed back by gunfire, the two men crawled to a phone and made a direct call to Lt. Gov. Paul Simon. "I told him I thought we were going to be killed by the police and citizens' council." Lt. Governor Simon ordered state police to the church and Montroy, Bodewes, and Belsheim were thrown into the back of an armored truck and escorted from the scene. Having nowhere to go, the two priests and the lawyer were left in the care of a reluctant Father Deis at St. Patrick's. "He said we could stay there for the rest of the night but must be gone by daylight," Montroy explained.[61]

The United Front had survived police repression in the past, but this time they would have to cope without the assistance of several key leaders. Over the course of the summer of 1971, a number of United Front activists faced trial dates: some lost appeals and others were sentenced to jail. The organization's economic development coordinator, Bobby Williams, was trapped in a protracted legal battle stemming from his arrest on weapons charges in Cape Girardeau in 1969. Although Williams was exonerated on appeal, he was picked up again in June 1971, this time for violating the Federal Gun Control Act. Two convictions and two successful appeals later, representatives from the Internal Security Division of the US Justice Department were brought in to prosecute the case against Williams one more time. Williams was found guilty in 1974 and surrendered to the federal marshal in St. Louis to begin serving a five-year prison sentence in federal prison in Terre Haute, Indiana.[62]

In the summer of 1971 Koen was also facing sentencing for charges dating back to his stint with the Black Liberators in St. Louis. In July Koen surrendered to officers and began serving a six-month sentence at the St. Louis county jail for disorderly conduct and resisting arrest. Koen's incarceration was greeted by outrage from the United Front's allies across the country. In September supporters staged protests in twelve different cities, calling on President Nixon to pardon Koen immediately. During his incarceration, Koen began a fast to protest his unjust imprisonment and those of other black power activists. By the time he was paroled in September, Koen had lost almost sixty pounds, his body wracked by the effects of malnutrition (fig. 5.1). It took months for Koen to gain the strength to even leave his home, and when he did he was unable to walk without the assistance of a cane. "A modern-day Moses with the staff," Bobby Williams recalled, "but he never did regain his sense of balance."[63]

Koen's incarceration had a visible effect on the United Front. Despite preparing for his absence for several months, the organization was left reeling by dwindling resources combined with narrow political opportunities and the loss of Koen's charismatic and energizing leadership style. Although the NAACP and the Lawyers' Committee continued their legal battles, the direct-action arm of the United Front was stagnating. Picketing ground to a halt and black shoppers trickled back to some of the stores. The end of picketing and protesting in Cairo could have easily demoralized local activists and resulted in a complete dissipation of the United Front's activities. However, United Front leaders took the opportunity presented by the deescalation to initiate what they described as "a new stage" in the black power struggle. Koen's replacement, Leon Page,

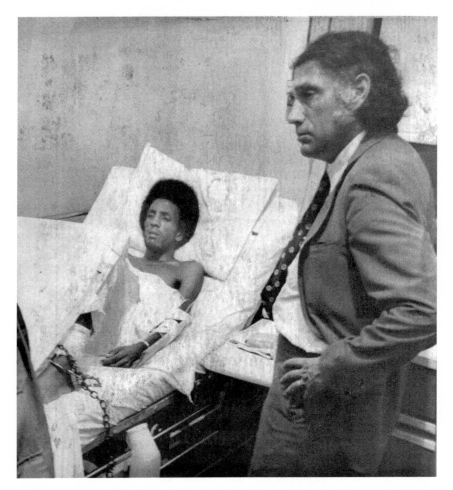

Figure 5.1. Lawyer William Kunstler visits Charles Koen in Homer G. Phillips Hospital on August 31, 1971. Permission of Corbis Images.

held a series of meetings with the United Front's members to discuss the future direction of the movement. While the NAACP and the Lawyers' Committee were engaged in what promised to be a very slow and arduous legal struggle, Page and Williams continued to champion the alternative strategy of independent economic development.[64]

In its efforts to locate more stable sources of revenue for economic development projects, the United Front turned its attention increasingly toward state government. For the past three years the United Front had struggled to make headway with Republican governor Richard Ogilvie. However, in 1972 Ogilvie faced an uphill reelection battle against his Democratic opponent, Daniel Walker. Seeing the potential for a shift in power, Reverend Koen stepped out in early support for Walker, denouncing Ogilvie's record and describing the sitting governor's administration as "the most repressive in Illinois' history." Speaking at a press conference in November, Koen encouraged black voters across the state to join forces in casting a collective vote for Walker. "We must get ourselves together," he appealed. "At the ballot box we're not going to be turned around." Using the United Front's statewide infrastructure, Koen brought together a powerful coalition of black leaders behind Walker's campaign, including representation from twenty-four downstate communities. When the election results came, the coalition claimed success as Ogilvie was ousted from the governor's office; black voters played an important role in several Illinois communities.[65]

United Front leaders anticipated that their support for Walker would afford them political patronage and influence over the new governor, and when Walker assumed office the lines of communication certainly became more open than they had been under the Ogilvie administration. Moreover, some tangible gains for black Cairoites were secured, including a commitment to prevent the closure of St. Mary's Hospital (which had been facing serious financial difficulties) and the extension of $50,000 in economic development grants to a new United Front initiative focused on assisting in the development of small business enterprises. Indeed, by the fall of 1973, United Front leaders expressed some optimism about their community development initiatives, seeing small but significant progress. Building on these initial successes, the United Front's coalition organized a series of local forums aimed at highlighting the concerns facing the state's poorest communities. A comprehensive state project was discussed that would bring significant economic development and social service programming to Southern Illinois, including expanded funding for the OEO agencies to allow for job training. "We went to Springfield with a master plan," United Front chief of staff James Chairs explained, "and they listened."[66]

However, over the next year very little progress was made, and the relationship between the United Front's coalition and the Walker administration ultimately broke down when the governor supported a series of regressive welfare policies. United Front activist Geneva Whitfield had actively campaigned for Walker but now lamented her decision. "I could claw my eyes out now," she declared. "Walker brainwashed us. I figured if a man wore out his shoes going around talking to people and if he didn't drive a limousine, I figured we had a chance with that man. But now, I don't see nothing that he has done to help the poor people. People are suffering under the administration of Walker."[67] In March 1974 members of the United Front electoral coalition showed up at a joint session of the legislature to protest the fact that the governor had turned a "deaf ear" toward the plight of the poor. As the coalition collapsed, so did hopes that electoral politics could address the plight of black Cairoites. "They kept telling us to try the political process," Koen declared, "and we tried the political process only to get cheated again." Bobby Williams was more blunt in his assessment, "[When we] went into the political arena, I think that's where we . . . lost control. We got co-opted."[68]

The Cairo United Front's attempts at tactical innovation between 1971 and 1974 had produced mixed results for local black power activists. Prompted by what Rev. Blaine Ramsey called a "recession of national spirit," the United Front had been forced to make some difficult decisions after their primary source of funding retracted support. This decline in church resources was compounded in the summer of 1971 by a further narrowing of political opportunities when members of the WCC rose to political power and several of the United Front's leaders faced incarceration. It was in this context that United Front leaders decided to deemphasize the high-profile mass mobilizations and direct-action campaigns that had characterized the organization's first three years. Instead, local activists opted to shift their focus to the organization's ongoing legal battles and the leveraging of political patronage through involvement in electoral politics at the state level. The latter proved largely ineffective as a tool to expand the United Front's fledgling economic programs, although some limited progress was made. On the other hand, legal strategies, as the concluding chapter shows, were remarkably successful in transforming the city's longstanding patterns of racial discrimination in politics, hiring, and law enforcement. However, the onset of a primarily legal and electoral battle over the rights and opportunities of black Cairoites also marked the end of mass mobilization in Cairo, Illinois. While local leaders like Rev. Charles Koen, Clydia Koen, and Preston Ewing Jr. continued to devote considerable energy to the struggle for black empowerment, the days of rallies, picketing, and protest had drawn to a close. In December 1985 the *St. Louis Post-Dispatch* poignantly characterized the impact of these tactical innovations. While the United Front had survived, the paper reported that "in a touch of irony" the organization was now "part of the establishment," functioning as a "clearinghouse for federal and state social services grants."[69]

Conclusion

In the spring of 1972, the United States Commission on Civil Rights held a three-day public hearing in Cairo to investigate, in the words of Commissioner Frankie Freeman, "allegations from individuals and organizations all over the country that extensive and overt racial discrimination exists here." For almost five years events in Cairo had dominated national headlines, prompting commentators to ask whether the city was a "bizarre anomaly" or if its story offered "an ominous portent of the future." Commissioner Freeman explained that information gathered during the hearing would be used "to examine and evaluate not only the problems of Cairo, but . . . of cities throughout the Nation that are also troubled by poverty [and] racial strife." After hearing from representatives from city government, state and federal agencies, private business, and the black community, the commission made nineteen recommendations. Among them were proposals to overhaul the policies and practices of the Cairo Police Department, which the commission condemned as having been "both unprofessional and biased"; to appoint black residents to serve on all county and city boards and commissions; to immediately integrate public housing; and to initiate investigations into discriminatory practices in public and private employment. Governmental agencies at the local, state, and federal level were tasked with ensuring that these recommendations were carried out.[1]

Two years later staff members from the commission's Illinois State Advisory Committee returned to Cairo to evaluate what progress had been made. Despite the cessation of open hostilities, committee members quickly discerned that the relative calm did not stem from meaningful changes in the city's racial practices. Under Mayor James Walder's UCCA-dominated city council, local government remained a bastion of white power. Black Cairoites held only 5 of the 126 positions available on city and county boards and commissions, and they continued to experience chronic underrepresentation in municipal employment. The city still had no black firemen, and only two black police officers were charged with patrolling the still rigidly segregated Pyramid Courts. Investigations performed by the Illinois Fair Employment Practices Commission and the US Equal Employment Opportunities Commission (EEOC) confirmed widespread discriminatory practices in public and private employment, but both agencies reported that statutory and budgetary constraints had prevented effective action. Perhaps most disconcertingly, the committee found that "no action" had been taken "to prevent a recurrence of the breakdown of law and justice which occurred in Cairo during the late 1960s and early 1970s." The policies and practices of the Cairo Police Department remained wholly unchanged. Almost a decade after the committee's first visit to the city in 1966, members concluded that the "impact of civil rights legislation has still not reached Cairo."[2]

The findings of the US Commission on Civil Rights in 1972 and the Illinois State Advisory Committee in 1974 revealed the extent and resiliency of Cairo's racial and economic problems. Despite mounting one of the longest and best-organized campaigns of the black power era, the United Front had struggled to pierce a solid wall of white intransigence and naked terror. In turn, these local challenges had been exacerbated by the refusal of public officials at all levels of government to use their authority to force compliance with civil rights legislation, opting instead to use the punitive arm of the state to quash protests. However, despite the bleak picture rendered by the hearings, the United Front's efforts had not been in vain. As protests waned, legal suits filed at the height of the struggle continued to make their way through the courts, culminating, by the decade's end, in a series of landmark victories that would irrevocably transform racial practices in the city.

A key turning point in the legal battle took place in October 1974 when a resolution was finally reached in *Young v. Alexander County Housing Authority*, a suit filed five years earlier addressing segregation in public housing. The consent decree that followed resulted in the integration of public housing and the allocation of federal funds for renovations necessary to bring accommodations up to equal standards. Importantly, the consent decree also stipulated that members of the Alexander County board should retain two black representatives to serve on the housing authority, establishing a precedent for affirmative action appointments to other boards and commissions. The following year a settlement was reached in *Ewing v. Walder*, mandating black representation on the boards of a number of municipal agencies, including the county welfare commission, land commission, building commission, airport commission, and health department as well as the city board of zoning appeals, library board, police pension board, and board of fire and police commissioners. In February 1976 a resolution was also reached in the seven-year-old *Hollis v. Emerson* case, resulting in the appointment of a black representative to the four-member public utilities commission. Collectively, these legal rulings contributed to a significant expansion of formal black political power in the city, affording African Americans a greater role in the administration of governmental programs and agencies. "What's changed," Preston Ewing explains, "is some of the decision making [power] . . . was wrestled away from them. So there has been a diminished amount of power in the hands of a few people."[3]

The biggest political victory, however, came in March 1980 when the district court ruled on *Kendrick v. Walder*, a class-action suit filed by Hattie Kendrick in 1973 charging that Cairo's at-large city council system violated the Fourteenth and Fifteenth Amendments as well as the Voting Rights Act of 1965 by diluting and canceling out the votes of black citizens. After seven years of legal wrangling, a consent decree was imposed abolishing the at-large city council system of governance and replacing it with an aldermanic system in which the city was divided into five wards, two of which were predominantly African American. In November 1980 two black Cairoites—Bobbie Whitaker (Second Ward) and Earl Wade (Third Ward)—were elected to the city council, becoming the first African American council members in almost seventy years. In the next election United Front chairman Charles Koen would join them, symbolizing a transition of movement leadership from protest to black officialdom.[4]

Beyond the political sphere, black Cairoites also made some significant strides in the battle against employment discrimination, increasing the number of municipal and county-level jobs held by black workers. In February 1976, under pressure from the EEOC, the city agreed to maintain a 17 percent black workforce as well as employ two African Americans on the fire department and three on the police department. That same year Charles Bridges became the city's first African American firefighter. "Back then you had some bad bigots in this department," Bridges recalled. "But I knew I had to fight it. Either blacks were going to be here or I was going to go down swinging." Legal action also prompted a number of county agencies, including the department of corrections, the housing authority, the highway department, and the public aid office, to begin hiring black workers in skilled and semiskilled positions. Former United Front activist Clarence Dossie pointed to the significance of these gains for black workers. "If it wasn't for the movement . . . a lot of brothers that were around here they wouldn't have gotten jobs . . . because we were instrumental in helping them get jobs on the highway department and the prison jobs."[5]

The Lawyers' Committee was central to securing these victories and continued to provide the only free legal services available to poor black and white citizens in the county. In 1972 the committee played a prominent role in the formation of the Land of Lincoln Legal Assistance Foundation, which took over operations in the city and went on to provide free legal services in sixty-five counties across central and Southern Illinois. Among the organization's founders were local attorney Robert Lansden and Preston Ewing Jr. In this manner black power struggles contributed to the development of what Ewing describes as a vast "network of legal services" across the state of Illinois.[6]

In tandem with these important legal gains, the United Front and its many organizational offshoots were responsible for the city's only substantive economic development efforts of the 1970s. In addition to their earlier cooperative ventures, United Front activists worked with the Pulaski-Alexander Development Corporation to attract a small number of new industries and provide technical assistance to individuals seeking to start businesses of their own. In conjunction with the latter, United Front members also formed Help Your Brother Inc., a nonprofit organization that leveraged state and federal grants to assist in small-business development. The United Front's housing initiative, UCHC—renamed the Egyptian Housing Development Corporation—was particularly effective, resulting in the construction of over 160 homes for low-income residents as well as the creation of jobs for local carpenters and laborers. While modest, these programs represented the only meaningful local efforts to counteract capital flight, job losses, and growing poverty.[7]

Beyond these tangible gains, black power also facilitated a potent transformation in the consciousness and identity of black Cairoites, particularly the working-class activists who had been at the forefront of local struggles. In oral interviews and autobiographies, United Front members stress the role that the movement played in fostering a powerful sense of racial solidarity, empowerment, and pride. For many, memories of the years immediately preceding the black power movement were marked by feelings of shame, embarrassment, and even self-hatred. For Koen these feelings stemmed from his youthful inability to comprehend the roots of racial inequality combined with an uncritical embrace of Eurocentric standards of beauty and value. "It was part of the white image we strived for from the bottom of our feet to the top of our heads. We were just that confused." As he aged, Koen's understanding of the wider society sharpened, but with that understanding came a new sense of shame for what he perceived as black Cairoites' accommodation to the status quo out of fear. Ewing describes having similar feelings when his relatives and friends came to visit from larger black communities further North. "It was almost like . . . we were embarrassed in the presence of people that lived in other places that were not living with these indignities and racism. . . . So, that [for] me was a kind of source of oppression." In this context, black power represented an important watershed in the self-concept of many movement participants as they overcame fear by devoting energy to the destruction of Jim Crow and the creation of new institutions *by* and *for* black people. According to Koen, these activities produced a powerful "sense of oneness" that unified black Cairoites across intraracial divisions of color and class, fostering feelings of self-esteem and confidence.[8]

The United Front's democratic organizing model was uniquely effective in affording black working-class and poor people the opportunity to articulate their grievances and cultivate a sense of agency necessary for collective action. Parallel institutions afforded the unschooled and unemployed new knowledge and skills, instilling pride and a belief in the capacity for self-determination. In Hattie Kendrick's classroom at the migrant school, a new generation of black adults gained access to basic literacy skills and a black studies education that grounded them in the history and culture of African-descended people. "I wanted to teach them about themselves . . . make them feel proud of themselves," Kendrick wrote to her family. "It really does my heart good to see their eyes glow as I have incidentally brought in facts about the Negro." One Friday night after completing her class, a student grabbed Kendrick's hand and whispered, "Miss Kendrick, I hate to see you leave us all the time. You tell us so much about our people that I never knew." Kendrick left the room hurriedly, in tears. "What kind of teacher would I be letting my students see me cry?" Clarence Dossie's participation in the movement similarly afforded him the opportunity to obtain a formal education in black theology and to visit other parts of the country, forging connections with leaders in a broader movement for racial justice and social change. "I would never have gone anywhere if it hadn't been for the [movement]," Dossie states. "I never would have traveled the highways. . . . I would never have had a chance to meet César Chávez . . . Dick Gregory . . . Louis Farrakhan." Emboldened and inspired by these types of experiences, United Front activists would continue to organize around the challenges faced by black workers in Cairo even after the broader movement had dissipated. Dossie eventually became a master craftsman and turned his attention to addressing discrimination in local craft unions. Others entered local politics, organized around welfare and tenants rights, and championed equitable taxation policy. The United Front—now a registered NPO— also "continued . . . to help people," according to its last director, Clydia Koen. "We provided help with paying rent, help with paying utility bills" as well as offering youth mentoring and vocational training programs.[9]

Importantly, *Faith in Black Power* shows that these cultural, political, and economic transformations were possible in large measure due to the United Front's ability to mobilize the organizational resources of the black church. Challenging notions of black power's de-Christianization, grassroots activists in Cairo successfully counteracted the narrowing political opportunities and sectarianism of the late 1960s and early 1970s by forging a surprisingly broad-based and inclusive coalition under the banner of a new spiritual philosophy and a set of shared cultural practices rooted in the black church. Building on the unrivaled social and cultural power of Cairo's black churches, local activists mobilized religious discourses and cultures to bridge potent intraracial divisions rooted in class, generation, and ideology. In the hands of grassroots activists, black religious traditions operated as a kind of glue, binding together disparate peoples in a common struggle for social justice and racial change. Primarily because of this broad-based and cohesive foundation, the United Front was able to survive state repression and vigilante violence, mounting one of the longest and most potent black power campaigns of the era.

This vision of a religiously grounded black united front was Rev. Charles Koen's most important contribution to the national black power movement. A little-examined and undervalued movement theorist, Koen skillfully navigated the organizational rifts and thorny political debates of black power's second wave to build an effective local united front organization and solidify ties with offshoots in communities across Illinois and Missouri. By 1971 Koen—with the aid of his extensive political allies—had succeeded in developing a national political structure, foreshadowing the emergence of the National Black United Front by decade's end. Koen also brought his united front strategy into the electoral arena, cofounding the United Black Voters of Illinois in 1976 and launching a failed gubernatorial bid against Adlai Stephenson in 1986. Two years later, Koen threw his weight behind Jesse Jackson's presidential campaign.

Central to all of Koen's political projects was a belief in the unifying power of a religious tradition that emphasized the poor and oppressed. *Faith in Black Power* demonstrates that far from being disconnected from the emergent black theology, Koen and other United Front activists were key agents in its production, consumption, and transmission. Engaging the latest religious literature, inviting theologians to speak at weekly rallies, and obtaining training at seminaries and universities across the country, Cairo's black power activists were significant participants in a broader dialogue about black theology's character and role in protest and community-building traditions. In many ways grassroots activists anticipated a number of the more recent turns in black theology, and they should be recognized as pioneers and cocontributors in the effort to develop a systematic black theology during the late 1960s and 1970s.

Faith in Black Power illustrates that just as grassroots activists were formative to the development of black liberation theology, black theologians and church executives made vital contributions to local black power struggles. Emboldened by the "new nationalism" of the postrebellion era, black clergy developed their own caucuses and ecumenical bodies, exerting pressure on predominantly white denominations to extend resources directly to black power organizations. As a result of these efforts, the United Front was able to secure more than half a million dollars in grants from church-based sponsors between 1969 and 1974 as well as obtaining vital technical and legal support. Accordingly, the nation's churches represent an important and overlooked source of coalitional support for black power, challenging traditional periodizations of the liberal civil rights coalition's decline.

However, in an era of conservative ascendancy the United Front's reliance on such funds proved to be a double-edged sword, and by the mid-1970s churches retreated under mounting opposition from state agencies and white congregants. When combined with ongoing repression at the local level, the collapse in church funding compelled United Front leaders to redirect energy away from mass direct-action strategies and toward legal gradualism and state-sponsored economic development projects, resulting in the decline of the Cairo movement. Thus, *Faith in Black Power* also contributes to broader debates about black power's decline as well as the rise of modern conservatism, situating the nation's churches at the center.

While the shift away from mass direct action signaled the end of the black power movement in Cairo, the aforementioned legal and political victories were secured in the quieter years that followed, serving to expand black political power and access to municipal employment. However, victories in the battle against economic decline, capital flight, and black deproletarianization were harder to come by, indicative of a broader national problem. In the forty years following the black power struggle, Cairo has continued to decline; its population plummeted from just over six thousand in 1970 to fewer than three thousand in 2010. Downtown stores are closed, industry has relocated, and the city itself is in dire financial straits. Reflecting back on his years in the struggle, Dossie surmised that the United Front had "won the battle but we lost the war."[10]

In turn, many United Front leaders paid a steep price for their movement activities as US social policy took a punitive course that gave rise to "the new Jim Crow" of mass incarceration. After serving five years in prison on federal weapons charges, Bobby Williams—now saddled with a felony conviction—struggled to secure stable employment and housing in St. Louis, where he continues to be active in battles around eminent domain, labor rights, and police brutality. Charles and Clydia Koen remained in Cairo to build the United Front's social service programs, but they faced near continual pressure from state agencies and law enforcement. In 1991 Charles Koen was convicted and sentenced to serve twelve years in federal prison on charges of setting fire to the United Front's headquarters to collect insurance money and hide evidence of his embezzlement of government funds. In 2011 Koen was convicted and sentenced to twelve additional years in prison on new charges of theft and forgery related to the United Front's operations. Koen insists that the allegations are false and represent "a national conspiracy to isolate and silence black leadership." When I met with Clydia Koen in 2014, her husband had been incarcerated for more than two years. Two weeks prior he had been relocated to a different prison closer to their family home, but she had been unable to contact him since. We sat down together at the kitchen table, where a King James Bible lay open alongside a letter she had crafted to her husband earlier that morning. "[The harassment] never did end," she explained. "That's been our lives." When I asked how she found the strength to continue, Koen pointed to the well-worn Bible. "You pray and you go on. God has been the source of our strength. We wouldn't have made it. There's no way I could have made it and not believe in God."[11]

Acknowledgments

Writing this book has been a solitary endeavor, but one in which I have incurred many debts. For the privilege of engaging in intellectual labor, I am beholden to many teachers. At Kings College London I had the honor of working under the excellent supervision of John Howard. During a study abroad opportunity at the University of Illinois, I met Mark H. Leff—an impeccable historian and unmatched educator—who mentored and recruited me into the profession. I returned to the University of Illinois for my doctoral years, where I continued to work with Leff and a cohort of other remarkable historians and black studies scholars, foremost among them James Barrett, Sundiata Keita Cha-Jua, Clarence Lang, Erik McDuffie, Kathryn Oberdeck, David Roediger, and Ken Salo. These scholars helped cultivate and mold my intellectual curiosities, methodological approaches, and theoretical perspectives. As coadvisors of my dissertation committee, Lang and Leff played especially important roles, spending countless hours reading over drafts and offering friendship and mentorship.

I have also received guidance and support from many colleagues, allies, and friends. From my Kings College years, special thanks are due to Jo Burgin, Sophia Khan, Clare McLeish, Althea Legal-Miller, Adeola Sheehy-Adekale, and Claudine Vega. At the University of Illinois I was welcomed into a number of different intellectual and activist communities that sharpened my analysis and sustained me over the long haul. From the Odyssey Project, I thank Michael Burns, James Kilgore, and John Marsh for the opportunity to build equitable and inclusive educational initiatives for low-income and working-class people. I am also thankful for the members of the Champaign-Urbana Citizens for Peace and Justice—Sister Carol Ammons, Aaron "A-Dub" Ammons, Deacon Clayborne, Brian Dolinar, Belden Fields, and Martel Miller—who provided me with a second education on building movements for racial change and social justice. That second education was continued in the local labor movement, where Treva Ellison, John Gergely, and Natalie

Havlin brought me into the struggle and grounded me in a radical tradition of broad-based and democratic grassroots unionism. Joining me in these overlapping movements were my closest friends and intellectual compatriots in African American studies at Illinois—David Bates, Heidi Dodson, Ashley Howard, Anna Kurhajec, Stephanie Seawell Fortado, and Alonzo Ward. In addition to taking classes, bargaining contracts, and walking picket lines together, several of these individuals read multiple drafts of this manuscript, and the final product is stronger as a result. This excellent support continued at the University of Wyoming, where I benefited from the guidance of faculty and staff in the African American and Diaspora Studies Program and Department of History. Special mention is afforded to members of the interdisciplinary faculty reading circle—Darrell Jackson, Tracey Owens Patton, Amanda Stow, and Marcus Watson—who provided helpful insight on several chapters.

This project would not have been possible without the generous support of a variety of programs and institutions. Funding came from a number of sources, including the University of Illinois Graduate College, the University of Illinois Department of African American Studies, the Doris G. Quinn Foundation, the Illinois Historic Preservation Agency, the Illinois State Historical Society, and the University of Wyoming African American and Diaspora Studies program. My research also benefited significantly from the guidance of librarians and archivists across the nation. I thank Thomas Weissenger of the African American Research Center at the University of Illinois and John Hoffman of the Illinois History and Lincoln collections for their research support. Several other libraries and archives facilitated my research, and I appreciate their assistance: Special Collections Research Center, Southern Illinois University; Cairo Public Library; Vivian G. Harsh Research Collection of Afro-American History and Literature, Chicago Public Library; Illinois State Archives; Abraham Lincoln Presidential Library; General Commission on Archives and History of the University Methodist Church; Schomburg Center for Research in Black Culture; State Historical Society of Missouri; National Archives; and the Library of Congress Manuscript Division. I also thank the staff at Cairo City Hall who graciously allowed me to use their facilities during numerous research trips to the city.

As a study of a local black freedom movement, this book could not have been written without the assistance of the grassroots activists responsible for mounting that struggle. For entrusting me with their memories, I thank Clarence Dossie, Preston Ewing Jr., Rev. Eugene Fowler, Manker Harris, Clydia Koen, Gerald Montroy, and Bobby Williams. Special thanks are due Ewing and Harris for providing copies of newspaper articles, photographs, and other documentary evidence helpful to the project.

For providing forums for presentation and discussion of my ideas, I am grateful to several professional organizations: the Association for the Study of African American Life and History; the Association for the Study of the Worldwide African Diaspora; the National Council for Black Studies; and the Organization of American Historians. I would also like to thank the anonymous reviewers and editorial staff at University Press of Kentucky for their commitment to seeing this book published.

Finally, I would like to thank my parents, Kevin and Ann Pimblott, and my husband, Ray Mitchell, for their love and support. I owe an immeasurable debt to my mother and father for always encouraging me to walk my own path, ask difficult questions, and persevere in the face of hardships. Ray has lived and breathed this project with me for nearly a decade, and his contributions are second to none. He has read every chapter (some of them several times) and his critical feedback is almost always on point.

Notes

Introduction

1. Karen Rice, "The Movement, God and Me," *United Front News*, 13 Mar. 1971.

2. On the black political ideology of radical egalitarianism, see Michael C. Dawson, *Black Visions: The Roots of Contemporary African-American Political Ideologies* (Chicago: University of Chicago Press, 2001). In arguing that radical egalitarianism was the *predominant* ideology of the civil rights movement, I do not intend to ignore the important contributions of historians such as Peniel Joseph, Robin D. G. Kelley, and others who have documented the coexistence of a smaller cohort of black nationalists and radicals. Rather, I agree with Sundiata Cha-Jua and Clarence Lang's characterization of black nationalism and radicalism as "a submerged tendency in the 1950s and early 1960s with few proponents and institutional bases" when contrasted with their liberal counterparts. For further discussion, see Cha-Jua and Lang, "The 'Long Movement' as Vampire: Temporal and Spatial Fallacies in Recent Black Freedom Studies," *Journal of African American History* 92, no. 2 (Spring 2007): 265–88 [279]; Peniel E. Joseph, "Waiting Till the Midnight Hour: Reconceptualizing the Heroic Period of the Civil Rights Movement, 1954–1965," *Souls* 2 (Spring 2000): 6–17; and Robin D. G. Kelley, "Stormy Weather: Reconsidering Black (Inter)Nationalism in the Cold War Era," in *Is It Nation Time? Contemporary Essays on Black Power and Black Nationalism*, ed. Eddie S. Glaude Jr. (Chicago: University of Chicago Press, 2002), 67–90.

3. Wesley C. Hogan, *Many Minds, One Heart: SNCC's Dream for a New America* (Chapel Hill: University of North Carolina Press, 2007), 36; Cleveland Sellers and Robert L. Terrell, *The River of No Return: The Autobiography of a Black Militant and the Life and Death of SNCC* (New York: Morrow, 1973), 147; Anne Moody, *Coming of Age in Mississippi* (New York: Laurel Press, 1968), 317–18; Amiri Baraka, "From Parks to Marxism: A Political Evolution," *Crisis* 105, no. 6 (Dec. 1998), 21.

4. Huey P. Newton, *Revolutionary Suicide* (New York: Harcourt Brace Jovanovich, 1973), 71. On black nationalism and radicalism, see Dawson, *Black Visions*.

5. I use the term "black church" to reference black Christians and predominantly African American congregations whether they belong to a historically black or predominantly white denomination.

6. Mark L. Chapman, *Christianity on Trial: African American Religious*

Thought before and after Black Power (Maryknoll, NY: Orbis Books, 1996), 42.

7. Alex Haley, "Playboy Interview: Malcolm X" (May 1963), reprinted in *Malcolm X: As They Knew Him*, by David Gallen (New York: Ballantine Books, 1995), 109–30; Chapman, *Christianity on Trial*, 70.

8. J. L. Jeffries, *Black Power in the Belly of the Beast* (Urbana: University of Illinois Press, 2006), 8.

9. Two landmark works on the black church in the modern civil rights movement are Aldon D. Morris, *The Origins of the Civil Rights Movement: Black Communities Organizing for Change* (New York: Free Press, 1984), and Doug McAdam, *Political Process and the Development of Black Insurgency, 1930–1970* (Chicago: University of Chicago Press, 1982). Both Morris and McAdam focus on the invaluable organizational resources that the black church provided to civil rights struggles, including charismatic leadership, financial resources, a preexisting membership base, communications networks, meeting spaces, and administrative facilities. More recently, scholars have also explored the transformative effect of religious worldviews on the ideologies and activism of specific organizations and grassroots activists. Such works include Charles Marsh, *The Beloved Community: How Faith Shapes Social Justice, from the Civil Rights Movement to Today* (New York: Basic Books, 2005); Johnny E. Williams, *African American Religion and the Civil Rights Movement in Arkansas* (Jackson: University Press of Mississippi, 2003); and Johnny E. Williams, "Linking Beliefs to Collective Action: Politicized Religious Beliefs and the Civil Rights Movement," *Sociological Forum* 17, no. 2 (June 2002): 203–22.

10. Religious studies scholar Gayraud Wilmore coined the term "de-Christianization" in *Black Religion and Black Radicalism: An Interpretation of the Religious History of Afro-American People*, 2nd ed. (Maryknoll, NY: Orbis Books, 1983). For accounts that characterize the shift from civil rights to black power as the de-Christianization of the movement, see Gayraud S. Wilmore, ed., *African American Religious Studies: An Interdisciplinary Anthology*, 4th ed. (Durham, NC: Duke University Press, 2000), 182; Charles Marsh, *God's Long Summer: Stories of Faith and Civil Rights* (Princeton, NJ: Princeton University Press, 1997); Marsh, *Beloved Community*.

11. Charles M. Payne, *I've Got the Light of Freedom: The Organizing Tradition and the Mississippi Freedom Struggle* (Berkeley: University of California Press, 1995), 366.

12. Peniel Joseph called for greater examination of the relationship between the black church and black power in "The Black Power Movement: A State of the Field," *Journal of American History* 96, no. 3 (Dec. 2009): 751–76, and in "Perspectives on the New Black Power Scholarship," paper presented at the 93rd annual meeting of the Association for the Study of African American Life and History, Birmingham, AL, Oct. 2008.

13. See William L. Van Deburg, *New Day in Babylon: The Black Power Move-*

ment and American Culture, 1965–1975 (Chicago: University of Chicago Press, 1993); Yohuru Williams, *Black Politics/White Power: Civil Rights, Black Power, and the Black Panthers in New Haven* (St. James, NY: Brandywine Press, 2000); Bettye Collier-Thomas and V. P. Franklin, eds., *Sisters in the Struggle: African American Women in the Civil Rights–Black Power Movement* (New York: New York University Press, 2001); Scot Brown, *Fighting for US: Maulana Karenga, the US Organization, and Black Cultural Nationalism* (New York: New York University Press, 2003); Rhonda Y. Williams, *The Politics of Public Housing: Black Women's Struggles against Urban Inequality* (New York: Oxford University Press, 2004); Jeffrey O. G. Ogbar, *Black Power: Radical Politics and African American Identity* (Baltimore: John Hopkins University Press, 2005); Charles E. Jones, ed., *The Black Panther Party Reconsidered* (Baltimore: Black Classic Press, 1998); Jeffries, *Black Power in the Belly of the Beast*; Peniel E. Joseph, *Waiting 'Til the Midnight Hour: A Narrative History of Black Power in America* (New York: Holt Paperbacks, 2006); Peniel E. Joseph, ed., *The Black Power Movement: Rethinking the Civil Rights–Black Power Era* (New York: Routledge, 2006); Matthew J. Countryman, *Up South: Civil Rights and Black Power in Philadelphia* (Philadelphia: University of Pennsylvania Press, 2007); Hasan Kwame Jeffries, *Bloody Lowndes: Civil Rights and Black Power in Alabama's Black Belt* (New York: New York University Press, 2009); Clarence Lang, *Grassroots at the Gateway: Class Politics and Black Freedom Struggle in St. Louis, 1936–75* (Ann Arbor: University of Michigan Press, 2009); Donna Jean Murch, *Living for the City: Migration, Education, and the Rise of the Black Panther Party in Oakland, California* (Chapel Hill: University of North Carolina Press, 2010); Akinyele Omowale Umoja, *We Will Shoot Back: Armed Resistance in the Mississippi Freedom Movement* (New York: New York University Press, 2013); Jakobi Williams, *From the Bullet to the Ballot: The Illinois Chapter of the Black Panther Party and Racial Coalition Politics in Chicago* (Chapel Hill: University of North Carolina Press, 2013).

14. Rhonda Y. Williams, "Black Women, Urban Politics, and Engendering Black Power," in *Black Power Movement*, ed. Peniel E. Joseph, 79–104; Angela D. Dillard, *Faith in the City: Preaching Radical Social Change in Detroit* (Ann Arbor: University of Michigan Press, 2007); Patrick D. Jones, *Selma of the North: Civil Rights Insurgency in Milwaukee* (Cambridge, MA: Harvard University Press, 2009).

15. Wilmore, *Black Religion and Black Radicalism*; C. Eric Lincoln and Lawrence H. Mamiya, *The Black Church in the African American Experience* (Durham, NC: Duke University Press, 1990).

16. On black caucuses, see Peter C. Murray, *Methodists and the Crucible of Race, 1930–1975* (Columbia: University of Missouri Press, 2004), 201; Gayraud S. Wilmore, *Pragmatic Spirituality: The Christian Faith through the Africentric Lens* (New York: New York University Press, 2004), 191–92; Mary R. Sawyer, *Black Ecumenism: Implementing the Demands of Justice* (Valley Forge, PA: Trin-

ity Press International, 1994). On the National Conference of Black Churchmen, see Sawyer, *Black Ecumenism*, 66–87; Anthony B. Pinn, *The Black Church in the Post–Civil Rights Era* (Maryknoll, NY: Orbis Books, 2002), 15; Lincoln and Mamiya, *Black Church*, 192–93; Dwight N. Hopkins, "A Transatlantic Comparison of a Black Theology of Liberation," in *Freedom's Distant Shores: American Protestants and Postcolonial Alliances with Africa*, ed. R. Drew Smith (Waco, TX: Baylor University Press, 2006), 85.

17. Albert B. Cleage, *Black Messiah* (New York: Sheed and Ward, 1968); James H. Cone, *Black Theology and Black Power* (New York: Seabury Press, 1969); Albert B. Cleage, *Black Christian Nationalism: New Directions for the Black Church* (New York: Morrow, 1972).

18. For example, see Wilmore, *Pragmatic Spirituality*, 193–94, and Dale P. Andrews, *Practical Theology for Black Churches: Bridging Black Theology and African American Folk Religion* (Louisville, KY: Westminster John Knox Press, 2002), 23.

19. Rev. Charles Koen utilized the terms "soul," "soulism," and "soul power" to distinguish between the United Front's spiritual philosophy of mutuality and cooperation and its negative counterpart in American individualism, materialism, and militarism. United Front members would often shout "soul" or "soul power" in chorus. For example, see "How Long Must We Wait?," *United Front News*, Sept. 12, 1970; "Blacks Vote Boycott On," *United Front News*, Sept. 26, 1970; "New Cairo March a Tense Standoff," *United Front News*, Dec. 19, 1970; J. Anthony Lukas, "Bad Day at Cairo, Ill.," *New York Times* magazine, Feb. 21, 1971. The chant "soul power" was first used in 1968 by Operation Breadbasket's leader Jesse Jackson during the Poor People's Campaign as a spiritual alternative to "black power," because it was flexible enough to incorporate poor people irrespective of race and ethnicity. See "Poor People Vow Last Peaceful March in Plea for Aid from Congress," *Jet*, July 4, 1968. The term was later immortalized by James Brown on his live album *Revolution of the Mind: Recorded Live at the Apollo*, Polydor, 1971.

20. The quietist tendencies of black religion are emphasized in most of the early scholarship on black religion performed by African American sociologists and historians. See Carter G. Woodson, *The History of the Negro Church* (Washington, DC: Associated Publishers, 1945), 224–33; Edward Franklin Frazier, *The Negro Church in America* (New York: Schocken Books, 1974), 51, 56; Joseph R. Washington, *The Politics of God* (Boston: Beacon Cross, 1967); Gunnar Myrdal, *An American Dilemma: The Negro Problem and Modern Democracy*, 2nd ed. (New York: Harper & Brothers, 1944).

21. Payne, *I've Got the Light*, 274.

22. For criticism of the tendency to romanticize and exaggerate church and clergy participation in the civil rights movement, see Ronny E. Turner, "The Black Minister: Uncle Tom or Abolitionist?," *Phylon* 34, no. 1 (1973): 86–95; Adolph

Reed, *The Jesse Jackson Phenomenon: The Crisis of Purpose in Afro-American Politics* (New Haven: Yale University Press, 1986).

23. See Adam Fairclough, "The Southern Christian Leadership Conference and the Second Reconstruction, 1957–1973," *South Atlantic Quarterly* 80 (1981): 183; William Brink and Louis Harris, *Black and White: A Study of U.S. Racial Attitudes Today* (New York: Simon and Schuster, 1967); Payne, *I've Got the Light*, 191.

24. Allison Calhoun-Brown, "Upon This Rock: The Black Church, Nonviolence, and the Civil Rights Movement," *PS: Political Science and Politics* 33, no. 2 (June 2000): 172.

25. See McAdam, *Political Process and Black Insurgency*; Morris, *Origins of the Civil Rights Movement*.

26. McAdam, *Political Process and Black Insurgency*, 48.

27. Calhoun-Brown, "Upon This Rock," 171.

28. For key works on frame theory, see Erving Goffman, *Frame Analysis: An Essay on the Organization of Experience* (New York: Harper and Row, 1974); David Snow, Burke Rochford Jr., Steven K. Worden, and Robert D. Benford, "Frame Alignment Processes, Micromobilization, and Movement Participation," *American Sociological Review* 51, no. 4 (Aug. 1986): 464–81; Robert D. Benford and David Snow, "Framing Processes and Social Movements: An Overview and Assessment," *Annual Review of Sociology* 26 (2000): 611–39; William A. Gamson and David S. Meyer, "The Framing of Political Opportunity," in *Comparative Perspectives on Social Movements*, ed. Doug McAdam, John D. McCarthy, and Mayer N. Zald (New York: Cambridge University Press, 1996), 275–90; Doug McAdam, "The Framing Function of Movement Tactics: Strategic Dramaturgy in the American Civil Rights Movement," in *Comparative Perspectives on Social Movements*, ed. McAdam et al., 223–55.

29. Snow et al., "Frame Alignment Processes," 464–81.

30. Morris, *Origins of the Civil Rights Movement*, 97; McAdam, *Political Process and Black Insurgency*, esp. 108–11, 161–63.

31. Calhoun-Brown, "Upon This Rock."

32. Martha Biondi, *To Stand and Fight: The Struggle for Civil Rights in Postwar New York City* (Cambridge, MA: Harvard University Press, 2003); Jeanne F. Theoharis and Komozi Woodard, eds., *Freedom North: Black Freedom Struggles Outside the South, 1940–1980* (New York: Palgrave Macmillan, 2003); Robert O. Self, *American Babylon: Race and the Struggle for Postwar Oakland* (Princeton, NJ: Princeton University Press, 2003); Countryman, *Up South*.

33. The concept of the "borderland" is taken from Henry Louis Taylor Jr., *Race and the City: Work, Community, and Protest in Cincinnati, 1820–1970* (Urbana: University of Illinois Press, 1993). For studies of the black freedom movement in the borderland, see Peter B. Levy, *Civil War on Race Street: The Civil Rights Movement in Cambridge, Maryland* (Gainesville: University Press of

Florida, 2003); Tracey E. K'Meyer, *Civil Rights in the Gateway to the South: Louisville, Kentucky, 1945–1980* (Lexington: University Press of Kentucky, 2009); Lang, *Grassroots at the Gateway.*

34. Darrel Dexter, *Bondage in Egypt: Slavery in Southern Illinois* (Cape Girardeau: Southeast Missouri State University, 2011); Nicole Etcheson, *The Emerging Midwest: Upland Southerners and the Political Culture of the Old Northwest, 1787–1861* (Bloomington: Indiana University Press, 1996), 70–71; Taylor, *Race and the City*; K'Meyer, *Civil Rights in the Gateway to the South*, 3; Levy, *Civil War on Race Street*, 10–11; Christopher Phillips, *Missouri's Confederate: Clairborne Fox Jackson and the Creation of Southern Identity in the Border West* (Columbia: University of Missouri Press, 2000), 16; Edward Franklin Frazier, *The Negro in the United States* (New York: Macmillan, 1957), 242.

35. K'Meyer, *Civil Rights in the Gateway to the South*, 5; Kenneth S. Jolly, *Black Liberation in the Midwest: The Struggle in St. Louis, Missouri, 1964–1970* (New York: Routledge, 2006), xiv.

36. K'Meyer, *Civil Rights in the Gateway to the South*, 9, 39, 42; Darrel E. Bigham, *We Ask Only a Fair Trial: A History of the Black Community of Evansville, Indiana* (Bloomington: Indiana University Press, 1987), 100, 138.

37. George C. Wright, *Life behind the Veil: Blacks in Louisville, Kentucky, 1865–1930* (Baton Rouge: Louisiana State University Press, 1985), 76; Joe William Trotter, *River Jordan: African American Urban Life in the Ohio River Valley* (Lexington: University Press of Kentucky, 1998), xiv, 35; Taylor, *Race and the City*, xv; Bigham, *We Ask Only a Fair Trial*, 14–33, 105–7, 138.

38. Wright, *Life behind the Veil*, 4; K'Meyer, *Civil Rights in the Gateway to the South*, 11, 43; Levy, *Civil War on Race Street*, 1–2, 7.

39. For an especially effective analysis of the role of region in shaping black freedom struggles, see Clarence Lang, "Locating the Civil Rights Movement: An Essay on the Deep South, Midwest, and Border South in Black Freedom Studies," *Journal of Social History* 47, no. 3 (Winter 2013): 371–400.

40. Taylor, *Race and the City*, xviii.

41. Wright, *Life behind the Veil*, 9.

42. Joanne Wheeler, "Together in Egypt: A Pattern of Race Relations in Cairo, Illinois, 1865–1915," in *Toward a New South? Studies in Post–Civil War Southern Communities*, ed. Orville Vernon Burton and Robert C. McMath (Westport, CT: Greenwood Press, 1982), 103–34; Christopher K. Hays, "Way Down in Egypt Land: Conflict and Community in Cairo, Illinois, 1850–1910," (PhD diss., University of Missouri–Columbia, 1996); Christopher K. Hays, "The African American Struggle for Equality and Justice in Cairo, Illinois, 1865–1900," *Illinois Historical Journal* 90, no. 4 (Winter 1997): 265–84; Darrel E. Bigham, *On Jordan's Banks: Emancipation and Its Aftermath in the Ohio River Valley* (Lexington: University Press of Kentucky, 2006); Jon C. Teaford, *Cities of the Heartland: The Rise and Fall of the Industrial Midwest* (Bloomington: Indi-

ana University Press, 1993); Trotter, *River Jordan*; Bigham, *We Ask Only a Fair Trial*.

43. Quote taken from Bernard Gavzer, "Fear and Hate Abound: Gap Is Widening," *Chronicle Telegram* (Elyria, Ohio), Mar. 15, 1970.

44. For further discussion of early European American migratory patterns in Southern Illinois, see Frederick M. Wirt, "The Changing Social Bases of Regionalism: Peoples, Cultures, and Politics in Illinois," in *Diversity, Conflict, and State Politics: Regionalism in Illinois*, ed. Peter F. Nardulli (Urbana: University of Illinois Press, 1989), 37; Cullom Davis, "Illinois: Crossroads and Cross Section," in *Heartland: Comparative Histories of the Midwestern States*, ed. James H. Madison, 127–57 (Bloomington: Indiana University Press, 1988); John Asa Beadles, *A History of Southernmost Illinois* (Karnak, IL: Shawnee Development Council, 1990), 16–17.

45. Scholars have noted the cultural influences of native-born white migrants from the Upland South on Southern Illinois through examinations of architecture, speech, food, and religion. See Etcheson, *Emerging Midwest*, 4; Wirt, "Changing Social Bases," 33–34, 37–39; Davis, "Illinois: Crossroads."

46. As referenced in this book, "Egypt" includes the southern thirty-four counties of Illinois: Alexander, Bond, Clay, Clinton, Crawford, Edwards, Effingham, Fayette, Franklin, Gallatin, Hamilton, Hardin, Jackson, Jasper, Jefferson, Johnson, Lawrence, Madison, Marion, Massac, Monroe, Perry, Pope, Pulaski, Randolph, Richland, Saline, St. Clair, Union, Wabash, Washington, Wayne, White, and Williamson. Other scholarship cited in this study may use the term "Egypt" to refer to the sixteen southernmost Illinois counties.

47. Davis, "Illinois: Crossroads," 146–47; Jacque Voegeli, *Free but Not Equal: The Midwest and the Negro during the Civil War* (Chicago: University of Chicago Press, 1967); Ed Gleeson, *Illinois Rebels: A Civil War Unit History of G Company, Fifteenth Tennessee Regiment, Volunteer Infantry: The Story of the Confederacy's Southern Illinois Company, Men from Marion and Carbondale* (Carmel, IN: Guild Press of Indiana, 1996); John McMurray Lansden, *A History of the City of Cairo, Illinois* (Carbondale: Southern Illinois University Press, 1976), 129; William Henry Perrin, *History of Alexander, Union, and Pulaski Counties, Illinois* (Chicago: O. L. Baskin, 1883), 55; Herman R. Lantz, *A Community in Search of Itself: A Case History of Cairo, Illinois* (Carbondale: Southern Illinois University Press, 1972), 24; Victor Hicken, *Illinois in the Civil War* (Urbana: University of Illinois Press, 1991).

48. Hays, "African American Struggle," 265; Hays, "Way Down in Egypt Land," 174–94; Leslie A. Schwalm, "'Overrun with Free Negroes': Emancipation and Wartime Migration in the Upper Midwest," *Civil War History* 50, no. 2 (2004): 145–74; Wheeler, "Together in Egypt," 106–8; United States Sanitary Commission, "*The U.S. Sanitary Commission in the Valley of the Mississippi, during the War of the Rebellion, 1861–1866: Final Report of Dr. J. S. Newberry* (Cleveland, OH: Fairbanks, Benedict, 1871); John Eaton and Ethel Osgood

Mason, *Grant, Lincoln, and the Freedmen: Reminiscences of the Civil War, with Special Reference to the Work for the Contrabands and Freedmen of the Mississippi Valley* (New York: Negro Universities Press, 1969), 37–38; Edward Noyes, "The Contraband Camp at Cairo, Illinois," in *Selected Proceedings of the Sixth Northern Great Plains History Conference*, ed. Lysle E. Meyer (Moorhead, MN: n.p., 1972), 203–17; Levi Coffin, *Reminiscences of Levi Coffin* (New York: Arno Press, 1968); Laura S. Haviland, *A Woman's Life-Work: Labors and Experiences of Laura S. Haviland* (Salem, NH: Ayer, 1984).

49. Scholars disagree as to how quickly segregation was established as practice in Cairo. However, there is general agreement that by the turn of the twentieth century an elaborate system of social segregation was in place. See Wheeler, "Together in Egypt," 119–21; Hays, "African American Struggle," 279–81; Hays, "Way Down in Egypt Land," 238–46, 449–50.

50. Frazier, *Negro in the United States*, 252; Bigham, *We Ask Only a Fair Trial*, 65, 129, 172; Hays, "Way Down in Egypt Land," 298–300.

51. Hays, "Way Down in Egypt Land," 380.

52. K'Meyer, *Civil Rights in the Gateway to the South*, 7.

53. The data in this section comes from the National Council of Churches, *Churches and Church Membership in the United States: An Enumeration and Analysis by Counties, States, and Regions, Series C, No. 14–15* (New York: n.p., 1957). Unfortunately, this study did not include data on churches or church membership from historically black denominations, including the "two large Negro Baptist bodies nor the three Negro Methodist bodies."

54. The report defined the US South as including Delaware, Maryland, the District of Columbia, Virginia, West Virginia, North Carolina, South Carolina, Georgia, Florida, Kentucky, Tennessee, Alabama, Mississippi, Arkansas, Louisiana, Oklahoma, and Texas.

55. Trotter, *River Jordan*, 82.

1. On Jordan's Banks

1. Lansden, *History of Cairo*, 31–33; Terri K. Wright, "The Upper Circle: The History, Society and Architecture of Nineteenth-Century Cairo, Illinois" (PhD diss., Southern Illinois University Carbondale, 1995), 8–12.

2. Lansden, *History of Cairo*, 33–42, 258–59; Federal Writers' Project, *Cairo Guide* (Cairo: Cairo Public Library, 1938), 15–17; C. P. Greene, Thomas H. Bacon, and Sidney J. Roy, *A Mirror of Hannibal* (Hannibal, MO: C. P. Greene, 1905), 84–85; H. C. Bradsby, "History of Cairo," in *History of Alexander, Union and Pulaski Counties*, ed. Perrin, 15–16, 22–23, 90, 267.

3. Charles Dickens, *American Notes and Pictures from Italy* (New York: Charles Scribner's Sons, 1900), 203, 222. On Cairo as an example of nineteenth-century "paper town," see Lara Langer Cohen, *The Fabrication of American Lit-*

erature: Fraudulence and Antebellum Print Culture (Philadelphia: University of Pennsylvania Press, 2012).

4. Holbrook quote taken from Bradsby, "History of Cairo," 28. For a discussion of Holbrook's failed initiative, see Lansden, *History of Cairo*, 41–57; Lantz, *Community in Search*, 8–13.

5. Executive Committee on Southern Illinois, *Southern Illinois: Resources and Potentials of the Sixteen Southernmost Counties* (Urbana: University of Illinois Press, 1949), 146.

6. Taylor, *Race and the City*, xiv.

7. For further discussion of Cairo during this period of antebellum expansion, see Hays, "Way Down in Egypt Land," esp. 42–117, and Wright, "Upper Circle," esp. 29–66. On the formation of Cairo's Catholic parishes, see Lansden, *History of Cairo*, 138–39, 143, 152, and Robert Newton Barger, *Ethnicity in the Cairo Catholic Schools: An Historical Investigation* (Illinois Historical Survey, 1975), 12, 20.

8. On slavery in Southern Illinois, see Dexter, *Bondage in Egypt*, and Voegeli, *Free but Not Equal*.

9. After the passage of the Fugitive Slave Law in 1850, Cairo authorities regularly captured and returned escaped slaves to their owners: see Dexter, *Bondage in Egypt*, 363–64; Flora H. Sedberry, "Arrest of runaway slaves, Thebes, Illinois, 1856," July 10, 1941, box 4, folder 12, Negro in Illinois Papers, Vivian Harsh Research Collection of Afro-American History and Literature, Illinois Writers' Project, Chicago Public Library (hereafter IWP); Flora H. Sedberry, "Runaway slaves arrested in Alexander County, Illinois, 1852," June 16, 1941, IWP, box 4, folder 22. On similar practices across the northern borderland, see Bigham, *On Jordan's Banks*, 42–45.

10. Sundiata Keita Cha-Jua, *America's First Black Town: Brooklyn, Illinois, 1830–1915* (Urbana: University of Illinois Press, 2000), 63; Maxine E. Wormer, *Alexander County, Illinois, 1850 Census* (Thomson, IL: Heritage House, n.d.).

11. US Census Bureau, *Eighth Census: 1860*, Alexander County, Illinois, population schedule, Cairo, p. 52, dwelling 342, family 342, George Williams, digital image, Ancestry.com, accessed Feb. 18, 2015, http://ancestry.com; Nannie Glenn, "Housing for Negroes in Alexander County," n.d., IWP, box 37, folder 29; Dexter, *Bondage in Egypt*, 305, 309, 319–28.

12. *Cairo Weekly Times and Delta*, July 29, 1857, quoted in Dexter, *Bondage in Egypt*, 363–64.

13. Dexter, *Bondage in Egypt*, 363–64, 381; "Excitement at Cairo," *National Emporium*, July 30, 1857; Lloyd W. Owens, "The Beginning, 1853–1900," IWP, box 14, folder 5.

14. On the divided loyalties of Cairo and Southern Illinois during the Civil War, see Lansden, *History of Cairo*, 128–37; James Pickett Jones, *Black Jack: John A. Logan and Southern Illinois in the Civil War Era* (Tallahassee: Florida State

University, 1967); T. K. Kionka, *Key Command: Ulysses S. Grant's District of Cairo* (Columbia: University of Missouri Press, 2006), esp. 27–42; Hays, "Way Down in Egypt Land," 118–95; Delores Archaimbault and Terry A. Barnhart, "Illinois Copperheads and the American Civil War," *Illinois History Teacher* 3, no. 1 (1996): 15–30.

15. *Cairo City Weekly Gazette*, July 25, 1861, quoted in Dexter, *Bondage in Egypt*, 301; Leslie A. Schwalm, *Emancipation's Diaspora: Race and Reconstruction in the Upper Midwest* (Chapel Hill: University of North Carolina, 2009), 74, 286.

16. W. E. B. Du Bois, *Black Reconstruction in America* (1935: reprint, New York: Free Press, 1998), 55. For an excellent discussion of the role of African American resistance to the fall of the Confederacy, see Armstead L. Robinson, *Bitter Fruits of Bondage: The Demise of Slavery and the Collapse of the Confederacy, 1861–1865* (Charlottesville: University of Virginia Press, 2005), esp. 37–57, 178–82.

17. H. Oscar to Frederick Douglass, Sept. 25, 1862, qtd. in *Illinois's War: The Civil War in Documents*, ed. Mark Hubbard (Athens: Ohio University Press, 2013), 93–94.

18. Coffin, *Reminiscences*, 619–20. For further discussion of the Cairo contraband camp, see Noyes, "Contraband Camp at Cairo"; Hays, "Way Down in Egypt Land," esp. 171–93; Schwalm, "'Overrun with Free Negroes,'" 145–74; Bigham, *On Jordan's Banks*, 84–93; Schwalm, *Emancipation's Diaspora*, 74–75.

19. Haviland, *Woman's Life-Work*, 246–47.

20. Maj. R. E. Lawder to Brig. Gen. J. Sprague, Sept. 4, 1865, Letters Received, Department of the Missouri, ser. 2593, Record Group 393, Records of US Army Continental Commands, 1821–1920, pt. 1, National Archives, Washington DC, qtd. in Schwalm, *Emancipation's Diaspora*, 75; H. Oscar to Frederick Douglass, Sept. 25, 1862, qtd. in Hubbard, *Illinois's War*, 94.

21. Federal Writers' Project, *Cairo Guide*, 42–44; *Attractions of Cairo, Illinois* (Cairo: The People Print, 1890). For further discussion of Cairo's postbellum economy, see Lantz, *Community in Search*, 20–50; Wright, "Upper Circle," 111–38; Hays, "Way Down in Egypt Land," esp. 131–46, 292–97.

22. US Census Bureau, 1880 census, Alexander County, Illinois, population schedule, Cairo, Ancestry.com, accessed Feb. 23, 2015, http://ancestry.com; Shirley J. Portwood, "African American Politics and Community in Cairo and Vicinity, 1863–1900," *Illinois History Teacher* 3 (1996): 13–15; Hays, "African American Struggle," 267, 270–71; Hays, "Way Down in Egypt Land," 224–25, 297–301.

23. US Census Bureau, *Census of Population: 1870*, vol. 1 (Washington, DC: GPO, 1872).

24. My analysis of black proletarianization in Cairo builds upon the seminal work of urban historian Joe William Trotter Jr.: see *Black Milwaukee: The Mak-*

ing of an Industrial Proletariat, 1915–45, 2nd ed. (Urbana: University of Illinois Press, 2007). Trotter situates proletarianization as a hallmark of the black urban experience that was central to the development of black urban communities during the late nineteenth and early twentieth centuries. According to Trotter, it was the rise of a black industrial proletariat that facilitated the formation of a new black middle class and community institutions after Word War I. Further, by examining proletarianization through the lens of the black working class, Trotter contributes to a reinterpretation of its effects. While labor historians traditionally viewed proletarianization as a downward shift for workers who had previously owned their own skill and labor, Trotter showed that for many African Americans wage-work represented a step up from peonage. My application of the proletarianization thesis to a river city complicates Trotter's periodization and traditional focus on industrial workers.

25. Hays, "African American Struggle," 267–68; Portwood, "African American Politics," 13, 16–17; Glenn, "Housing for Negroes"; Forest McClain, "Notes on Cairo, Illinois," Oct. 17, 1951, IWP, box 26, folders 22, 23; Nannie Glenn, "The Beginning and the Ending of the Colored Newspaper in Alexander County," n.d., IWP, box 42, folder 17. For an excellent biographical account of one of these early black entrepreneurs, see Bruce L. Mouser, *A Black Gambler's World of Liquor, Vice, and Presidential Politics: William Thomas Scott of Illinois, 1839–1917* (Madison: University of Wisconsin Press, 2014).

26. Most scholars agree that customs of racial segregation were already widely practiced in Cairo during the late nineteenth century. See Portwood, "African American Politics," 14–15; Hays, "Way Down in Egypt Land," 238–43; and Hays, "African American Struggle," 280–81. For an alternative perspective, see Wheeler, "Together in Egypt," 104, 110.

27. On the concept of counterpublics, see Nancy Fraser, "Rethinking the Public Sphere: A Contribution to the Critique of Actually Existing Democracy," in *Habermas and the Public Sphere*, ed. Craig Calhoun (Cambridge, MA: MIT Press, 1989): 109–42. On the concept of the black counterpublic, see Michael C. Dawson, "A Black Counterpublic? Economic Earthquakes, Racial Agenda(s), and Black Politics," *Public Culture* 7 (1994): 195–223; Dawson, *Black Visions*, 23–29.

28. On religious gatherings in the Cairo Contraband Camp, see Hays, "Way Down in Egypt Land," 326–27.

29. According to historian Joe Trotter, "Baptist and AME churches dominated the religious and institutional life of Ohio Valley blacks." *River Jordan*, 78. For further discussion of the development of black Baptist and Methodist congregations in borderland communities during the late nineteenth century, see Bigham, *On Jordan's Banks*, 247–61.

30. Hays, "Way Down in Egypt Land," 326–27; John J. Sheard, "Notes on Morning Star Free Will Baptist and Ward Chapel A.M.E. Churches in Cairo, Illi-

nois," July 26, 1941, IWP, box 17, folder 2; "Notes on New Hope Free Baptist Church in Cairo," n.d., IWP, box 17, folder 6; Bernice Hall, "Notes of Mt. Moriah Missionary Baptist Church in Cairo," June 2, 1941, IWP, box 17, folder 5; "Notes on Mt. Carmel Missionary Baptist Church in Cairo," n.d., IWP, box 17, folder 8.

31. Trotter, *River Jordan*, 78.

32. Hays, "Way Down in Egypt Land," 327–28, 353; Hays, "African American Struggle," 278; Lloyd W. Owens, "The Beginning, 1853–1900," n.d., IWP, box 14, folder 5; Anna Casey, Ann Williams, Flora Sedberry, "Notes on education in Cairo, Illinois, 1867–92," Mar. 28, 1941, IWP, box 14, folder 4; Bigham, *On Jordan's Banks*, 296–97.

33. For a discussion of the importance of class and color in congregational affiliation in the post–Civil War era, see Frazier, *Negro Church in America*, 36–37. Kimberley Phillips also traces the importance of kinship and origins to church membership in the context of the Great Migration, see *AlabamaNorth: African-American Migrants, Community, and Working-Class Activism in Cleveland, 1915–45* (Urbana: University of Illinois Press, 1999), 142.

34. The regional origins and class demography of congregations were ascertained by comparing church histories and membership rolls to census records. For partial membership rosters of Ward Chapel AME, see Sheard, "Notes on Morning Star Free Will Baptist," July 26, 1941, IWP, box 17, folder 2; Hattie Kendrick, untitled history of Ward Chapel A.M.E. Church, Mar. 18, 1976, Kendrick-Brooks Family Papers, box 21, folder 15, Library of Congress, Washington, DC (hereafter KBFP-LOC). On the theology and practices of the African Methodist Episcopal Church, see James T. Campbell, *Songs of Zion: The African Methodist Episcopal Church in the United States and South Africa* (New York: Oxford University Press, 1995). Also see Bigham, *On Jordan's Banks*, 249.

35. Quote from Hall, "Notes on Mt. Moriah Missionary Baptist Church in Cairo," June 2, 1941, IWP, box 17, folder 5. For partial membership rosters of Cairo's Baptist congregations, see "Notes on Mt. Carmel Missionary Baptist Church in Cairo," n.d., IWP, box 17, folder 8; Anna Casey, Flora Sedberry, Effie Kansden, "Notes on early Baptist churches in Cairo, 1869–73," Aug. 25, 1941, IWP, box 17, folder 4.

36. Hays, "Way Down in Egypt Land," 348.

37. Quote from Bradsby, "History of Cairo," 55; Hays, "Way Down in Egypt Land," 348–51; Hays, "African American Struggle," 274–75; Portwood, "African American Politics," 14–15; Wheeler, "Together in Egypt," 122–25; Bigham, *On Jordan's Banks*, 181.

38. Flora Sedberry, "Notes on African-Americans in Cairo, Illinois, 1866–1880," Sept. 18, 1941, IWP, box 29, folder 13; Hays, "Way Down in Egypt Land," 328–29; Hays, "African American Struggle," 274–75.

39. Hays, "Way Down in Egypt Land," 331–32; Campbell, *Songs of Zion*,

58–61; "Notes on Cairo, Illinois," IWP, box 26, folders 22, 23; Mouser, *Black Gambler*, 31–32; Kendrick, untitled history of Ward Chapel, KBFP-LOC, box 21, folder 15.

40. *Cairo Evening Bulletin*, Aug. 4, Sept. 14 and 25, 1869, qtd. in Hays, "Way Down in Egypt Land," 330. For further discussion of Reverend Bradley's conservatism, see Hays, "Way Down in Egypt Land," 329–31.

41. Portwood, "African American Politics," 14–15.

42. Lantz, *Community in Search*, 45.

43. Quote from Lantz, *Community in Search*, 68. For further discussion of Cairo's economic challenges during this period, see ibid., esp. 41–87; Hays, "Way Down in Egypt Land," 367, 390–91.

44. Rayford W. Logan, *The Negro in American Life and Thought: The Nadir, 1877–1901* (New York: Dial Press, 1954). John J. Sheard and Lloyd Owens, "Illegitimate Businesses," Oct. 3, 1941, IWP, box 35, folder 26; *Daily Telegram's Cairo City Directory* (1904); Hays, "Way Down in Egypt Land," 372–409; Wheeler, "Together in Egypt," 118–19; Mouser, *Black Gambler*, 24.

45. Wheeler, "Together in Egypt," 118–21; Hays, "Way Down in Egypt Land," 448–50; Herbert A. Eastman, "Speaking Truth to Power: The Language of Civil Rights Litigators," *Yale Law Journal* 104, no. 4 (Jan. 1995): 869–72; Barger, *Ethnicity in Cairo Catholic Schools*, 20, 37.

46. Office of the Superintendent of Public Instruction (OSPI), *Directory of Illinois Schools, 1928–1929* (Springfield: OSPI, 1929); Taylor H. A. Bell, *Sweet Charlie, Dike, Cazzie, and Bobby Joe: High School Basketball in Illinois* (Urbana: University of Illinois Press, 2004), 41; "Crack School Bias in Second Illinois City," *Chicago Defender*, Sept. 27, 1952.

47. Quote from Davison M. Douglas, *Jim Crow Moves North: The Battle Over Northern School Desegregation, 1865–1954* (New York: Cambridge University Press, 2005), 3. During the 1920s, sociologist Hannibal Gerald Duncan also observed the distinctive quality of school segregation in the northern borderland. "There is . . . along the southern border of Pennsylvania, Ohio, Indiana, Illinois, and Kansas a semi-legal segregation in the schools in force. At least, it amounts to a tacit understanding, in some of the towns, that the colored children must go to the colored schools and that they will not be admitted to the schools attended by white children." See Duncan, "The Changing Relationship in the Border and Northern States" (PhD diss., University of Pennsylvania, 1922), 37. For further discussion of segregation patterns in the northern borderland, see Bigham, *We Ask Only a Fair Trial*; Michael Washington, "The Stirrings of the Modern Civil Rights Movement in Cincinnati, Ohio, 1943–1953," in *Groundwork: Local Black Freedom Movements in America*, ed. Jeanne Theoharis and Komozi Woodard (New York: New York University Press, 2005), 215–34; Jayne R. Beilke, "The Complexity of School Desegregation in the Borderland: The Case of Indiana," in *With All Deliberate Speed: Implementing Brown v. Board of Education*,

ed. Brian J. Daugherity and Charles C. Bolton (Fayetteville: University of Arkansas Press, 2011), 199–216.

48. The analysis of residential segregation and housing patterns is taken from Wheeler, "Together in Egypt," 114, 120.

49. Quotes from Ida B. Wells-Barnett, "How Enfranchisement Stops Lynchings," *Original Rights* magazine, June 1910, 46; Stacy Pratt McDermott, "'An Outrageous Proceeding': A Northern Lynching and the Enforcement of Anti-Lynching Legislation in Illinois, 1905–1910," *Journal of Negro History* 84, no. 1 (Winter 1999): 61–78 [62].

50. For statistical information on lynchings in Illinois, see Michael J. Pfeifer, ed., *Lynching beyond Dixie: American Mob Violence outside the South* (Urbana: University of Illinois Press, 2013), 276–80.

51. Ida B. Wells-Barnett, "A Red Record: Tabulated Statistics and Alleged Causes of Lynchings in the United States, 1892, 1893, 1894," in *Selected Works of Ida B. Wells-Barnett*, comp. Trudier Harris (New York: Oxford University Press, 1991), 146.

52. US Census Bureau, *Census of Population: 1900*, vol. 1, pt. 1 (Washington, DC: GPO, 1901), p. 613, 615, 618–19, 626.

53. Manfred Burg, *Popular Justice: A History of Lynching in America* (Chicago: Ivan R. Dee, 2011), 116. For further discussion of black Cairoites' expanded political power during this period, see Wheeler, "Together in Egypt," 126–27; Bigham, *On Jordan's Banks*, 191, 309–10.

54. "What Father Downey Said," *Evening Citizen*, Nov. 11, 1909; McDermott, "'An Outrageous Proceeding,'" 62–64; "Last Rites Held over Dead Girl," *Evening Citizen*, Nov. 11, 1909; "How the Get-Away was Accomplished," *Evening Citizen*, Nov. 11, 1909.

55. Quotes from "Story of Wildest Night Cairo Ever Experienced," *Evening Citizen*, Nov. 12, 1909; Wells-Barnett, "How Enfranchisement Stops Lynchings," 46–48; "Mob Seizes Big Four Freight Train," *Evening Citizen*, Nov. 11, 1909; McDermott, "'An Outrageous Proceeding,'" 65; "Save Negro from Lynching," *Chicago Daily Tribune*, Nov. 11, 1909; "Few Evidences of Lynchings Left," *Cairo Evening Citizen*, Nov. 12, 1909.

56. "Lynch 2 at Cairo," *Daily Pantagraph* (Bloomington, IL), Nov. 12, 1909; Wells-Barnett, "How Enfranchisement Stops Lynchings," 46–48; "Soldiers Awe Mob: Negro Taken Away," *New York Times*, Nov. 13, 1909. "Few Evidences of Lynchings Left," *Cairo Evening Citizen*, Nov. 12, 1909.

57. "Soldiers Awe Mob," *New York Times*, Nov. 13, 1909.

58. W. L. Clanahan, "Cairo's Negroes," *New York Times*, Nov. 19, 1909.

59. Hays, "Way Down in Egypt Land," 405–9.

60. Alfreda M. Duster, ed., *Crusade for Justice: The Autobiography of Ida B. Wells* (Chicago: University of Chicago Press, 1972), 312–14.

61. Patricia A. Schechter, *Ida B. Wells-Barnett and American Reform* (Cha-

pel Hill: University of North Carolina Press, 2001), 141; McDermott, "'An Outrageous Proceeding,'" 74–75; Mia Bay, *To Tell the Truth Freely: The Life of Ida B. Wells* (New York: Hill and Wang, 2009), 280–81; Wells-Barnett, "How Enfranchisement Stops Lynchings," 49–52.

62. Quote from "Race War Is Plot," *Los Angeles Times*, Feb. 23, 1910; "Troops Rushed to Vienna to Check Mob," *Cairo Evening Citizen*, Jan. 12, 1910; "Vienna Citizens Wire Thanks to Gov. Deneen," *Cairo Evening Citizen*, Jan. 13, 1910; Lantz, *Community in Search*, 78; Wells-Barnett, "How Enfranchisement Stops Lynchings," 52; "Sheriff Shoots into Mob," *Columbus-Enquirer-Sun*, Feb. 19, 1910; "Cairo," *Belleville News-Democrat*, Feb. 19, 1910; "Cairo Cowers in Fear of Mob Rule," *Indianapolis Star*, Feb. 21, 1910; "Another Race Clash Is Feared in Cairo," *New York Times*, Feb. 21, 1910; "In Cairo, Ill.," *Crisis* 1 (Dec. 1910).

63. Quote from Lansden, *History of Cairo*, 146; Wheeler, "Together in Egypt," 126–27; Mouser, *Black Gambler*, 82–83; Hays, "African American Struggle," 276–77, 282; Bigham, *On Jordan's Banks*, 310; Hays, "Way Down in Egypt Land," 359, 380, 446–48; "Important Happenings in Cairo 1909," *Cairo Evening Citizen*, Jan. 3, 1910; "Election Notice," *Evening Citizen*, Aug. 9, 1909; "Election Law Had No Opposition," *Evening Citizen*, Nov. 3, 1909; "The Commission Form of Government," *Cairo Evening Citizen*, Dec. 10, 1910; Illinois Advisory Committee to the United States Commission on Civil Rights, *A Decade of Waiting in Cairo* (Washington: US Commission on Civil Rights, 1975), 310.

64. "Notes on New Hope Free Baptist Church in Cairo," n.d., IWP, box 17, folder 6; "Notes on First Missionary Baptist Church," Aug. 19, 1941, IWP, box 17, folder 7; Lantz, *Community in Search*, 47, 114.

65. "Notes on Cairo, Illinois," IWP, box 26, folder 23.

66. "The St. Paul Missionary Baptist Church," n.d., IWP, box 45, folder 26; John J. Sheard, "The History of Everdale Missionary Baptist Church of Cairo, Illinois," Aug. 30, 1941, IWP, box 45, folder 23; "First Central Baptist Church of Cairo, Illinois," n.d., IWP, box 45, folder 24; John J. Sheard, "Notes on Church of God in Christ," Aug. 3, 1941, IWP, box 17, folder 10. On the growth of Pentecostalism during the nadir, see Anthea D. Butler, *Women in the Church of God in Christ: Making a Sanctified World* (Chapel Hill: University of North Carolina, 2007).

67. "History of St. Columba's Catholic Parish," n.d., IWP, box 45, folder 25; Barger, *Ethnicity in the Cairo Catholic Schools*, 34–46; C. Goelz, *General History of the Diocese of Belleville* (East St. Louis, IL: The Messenger Press, 1939), 67–68, 81. On the Roman Catholic Church's ministry to African American migrants during this period, see Frazier, *Negro in the United States*, 363–64; Cyprian Davis, *The History of Black Catholics in the United States* (New York: Crossroad, 1990), 198.

68. Sheard, "Notes on Morning Star Free Will Baptist," July 26, 1941, IWP,

box 17, folder 2; "Notes of First Missionary Baptist Church in Cairo, Illinois," Aug. 19, 1941, IWP, box 17, folder 7; Nannie Glenn, "The Beginning and Ending of the Colored Newspaper in Alexander County," n.d., IWP, box 42, folder 17. For further discussion of the formation of the National Baptist Convention, USA, see James Melvin Washington, *Frustrated Fellowship: The Black Baptist Quest for Social Power* (Macon, GA: Mercer University Press, 1986).

69. Cairo Community Development Association, "Report of the Population Committee," Aug. 1957, Ephemera Collection, Special Collections Research Center, Morris Library, Southern Illinois University Carbondale (hereafter SCRC, SIU). On the growing diversity of black church traditions in the North during this period, see Arthur Huff Fauset, *Black Gods of the Metropolis: Negro Religious Cults of the Urban North* (New York: Octagon Books, 1974 [1944]); Wallace D. Best, *Passionately Human, No Less Divine: Religion and Culture in Black Chicago* (Princeton, NJ: Princeton University Press, 2005).

70. Most of the seminal works on the black community of the late nineteenth and early twentieth century argue that the black church's preeminence in political and social affairs was a product of disenfranchisement and the absence of competing institutions. For example, see Benjamin Mays, *The Negro's Church* (New York: Institute of Social and Religious Research, 1933), 8–9, and Frazier, *Negro Church in America*, 48–49. For a more recent articulation of this position, see Barbara Dianne Savage, *Your Spirits Walk beside Us: The Politics of Black Religion* (Cambridge: Harvard University Press, 2008), 9–10, 67. Some scholars maintain that the black church's emergence as an alternative political sphere refocused black political activity inward to denominational activities and, ultimately, accommodation. See Frazier, *Negro Church in America*, 49–51, and Reed, *Jesse Jackson Phenomenon*.

71. "Cairo's Women's Clubs Meet," *Chicago Defender*, June 19, 1915; "What the People Are Doing in Cairo," *Chicago Defender*, Nov. 21, 1914; "New Hospital Is Planned for Cairo, Ill.," *Chicago Defender*, May 15, 1915; "The NAACP of Cairo, Illinois," 1920, IWP, box 38, folder 2; Kendrick, untitled history of Ward Chapel, KBFP-LOC, box 21, folder 15. For further discussion of black churchwomen's activism during this period, see Evelyn Brooks Higginbotham, *Righteous Discontent: The Women's Movement in the Black Baptist Church, 1880–1920* (Cambridge, MA: Harvard University Press, 1993), and Bettye Collier-Thomas, *Jesus, Jobs, and Justice: African American Women and Religion* (New York: Knopf, 2010).

72. "G.O.P. Chief Hails Tuesday Vote as New Deal Blow," *Chicago Daily Tribune*, Nov. 7, 1935; Lantz, *Community in Search*, 53–54, 114; Wright, "Upper Circle," 193; Illinois Interracial Commission (hereafter IIC), *First Annual Report of the Illinois Inter-Racial Commission* (1944), 62; US Census Bureau, *Census of Population: 1940*, vol. 2, *Characteristics of the Population* (Washington, DC: GPO, 1943).

73. Draft manuscript by Kathryn Ward, KBFP-LOC, box 22, folder 2.

74. On Cairo's blues subculture, see Henry Townsend and Bill Greensmith, *A Blues Life* (Urbana: University of Illinois Press, 1999), and Sebastian Danchin, *Earl Hooker, Blues Master* (Oxford: University Press of Mississippi, 1999).

75. "Illinois Troops Oust Relief Sit-Downers," *New York Times*, Apr. 11, 1937; "Strikers Are Back at Work," *Pittsburgh Courier*, Nov. 11, 1933; "Minister Shot as Mob Storms Relief Office," *Chicago Defender*, Apr. 17, 1937; "Illinois Troops Called to Evict Relief Strikers," *Christian Science Monitor*, Apr. 10, 1937; "Labor Leader Wins Victory in Cairo, Ill.," *Chicago Defender*, July 22, 1939; "Cairo Appeals for Troops in Strike Slaying," *Chicago Daily Tribune*, Nov. 10, 1939; Cairo City Council minutes, Nov. 13 and 20, 1939.

76. "The Depression Era Art Projects in Illinois," *Illinois Heritage* (2000): 4–9; "The First Pulpit in Granville: The Story of the Village Age Post Office Mural," *Historical Times: Quarterly of the Granville, Ohio, Historical Society* 17, no. 2 (Spring 2003): 4.

77. Lantz, *Community in Search*, 55–58, 114; Charles C. Colby, *Pilot Study of Southern Illinois* (Carbondale: Southern Illinois University Press, 1956), 49; US Census Bureau, *Census of Population: 1950*, vol. 2, *Characteristics of the Population* (Washington, DC: GPO, 1952).

78. IIC, *Special Report on Employment Opportunities in Illinois* (Chicago: n.p., 1948), 8–9; Illinois State Advisory Committee, "I Reckon It's on Its Way But It Ain't Got Here Yet: A Report on Federal Civil Rights Program in Southern Illinois," 1966, box 40, Records Relating to Special Projects, 1960–70, Office of the Staff Director, USCCR, Record Group 453, National Archives, Washington, DC.

79. "Notes on Cairo, Illinois," n.d., IWP, box 26, folders 22, 23; *Negro City Directory of Cairo, Illinois* (Cairo: n.p., 1936), Manuscript, Archives, and Rare Book Library, Emory University; IIC, *Third Report of Illinois Interracial Commission* (1949), 8; IIC, *First Annual Report*, 83; IIC, *Sixth Report of Commission on Human Relations* (1955), 37; Illinois Commission on Human Relations, *Seventh Biennial Report* (n.p., 1957), 35; US Census Bureau, *Census of Population: 1960*, vol. 1, *Characteristics of the Population* (Washington, DC: GPO, 1963); Cairo Community Development Association "Report of the Population Committee," Aug. 1957, Ephemera Collection, SCRC, SIU.

80. Quotes from Sheard, "Notes on Morning Star Free Will Baptist," July 26, 1941, IWP, box 17, folder 2; "The St. Paul Missionary Baptist Church," n.d., IWP, box 45, folder 26; "First Central Baptist Church of Cairo, Illinois," n.d., IWP, box 45, folder 24; "Notes of First Missionary Baptist Church in Cairo, Illinois," Aug. 19, 1941, IWP, box 17, folder 7; "Notes on New Hope Free Baptist Church in Cairo," n.d., IWP, box 17, folder 6. A broader tendency toward union services during the Depression was noted by Mays in *Negro's Church*, 157.

81. The increasing administrative uniformity and ritualistic homogeneity of

Cairo's congregations during this period is apparent in the previously cited histories of local congregations preserved in the IWP papers at the Chicago Public Library.

82. On gospel music's incorporation into urban congregations during this period, see Clarence Taylor, *The Black Churches of Brooklyn* (New York: Columbia University Press, 1994), 67–99; Lawrence W. Levine, *Black Culture and Black Consciousness: Afro-American Folk Thought from Slavery to Freedom* (Oxford: Oxford University Press, 2007), 174–90.

83. Quote from Kendrick, untitled history of Ward Chapel, KBFP-LOC, box 21, folder 15; Sheard, "Notes on Morning Star Free Will Baptist," July 26, 1941, IWP, box 17, folder 2.

84. Cairo City Council minutes, Nov. 6, 1939, and Oct. 29, 1940, City Hall, Cairo, IL; Michael P. Seng, "The Cairo Experience: Civil Rights Litigation in a Racial Powder Keg," *Oregon Law Review* 285 (1982): 305.

2. Redemptive Love, Vigilante Terror, and Rebellion

1. On the lynching of Cleo Wright, see Dominic J. Capeci, *The Lynching of Cleo Wright* (Lexington: University Press of Kentucky, 1998).

2. Hattie Kendrick handwritten note, n.d., KBFP-LOC, box 22, folder 4.

3. Hattie Kendrick audiotape transcript no. 9, 1974, KBFP-LOC, box 19, folder 3; Charles E. Cobb Jr., "Traveling the Blues Highway," *National Geographic*, Apr. 1999, 46; Kendrick audiotape transcript no. 21, 1974, KBFP-LOC, box 19, folder 5.

4. Kendrick audiotape transcript no. 9, 1974, KBFP-LOC, box 19, folder 3; OSPI, *Illinois School Directory, 1946–1947* (Springfield, IL: OSPI, 1947); Corneal Davis et al., *Corneal A. Davis* (Springfield, IL: The Council, 1984), 42.

5. August Meier and John H. Bracey Jr., "The NAACP as a Reform Movement, 1909–1965: 'To Reach the Conscience of America,'" *Journal of Southern History* 59, no. 1 (Feb. 1993): 15; Andor Skotnes, *A New Deal for All? Race and Class Struggles in Depression-Era Baltimore* (Durham, NC: Duke University Press, 2013), 210.

6. Kendrick handwritten note, n.d., KBFP-LOC, box 22, folder 4; Davis, *Corneal A. Davis*, 42.

7. Davis, *Corneal A. Davis*, 43–45.

8. "Cairo Negro Teachers File Suit for Equal Pay," *Cairo Evening Citizen*, Jan. 30, 1945.

9. "Cairo Teachers Salary Hearing Set for April," *New York Amsterdam News*, Apr. 7, 1945; *Papers of the NAACP, Part 3: Campaign for Educational Equality, Series C, Legal Department and Central Office Records, 1951–1955*, Reel 23, 0799–0801; Davis, *Corneal A. Davis*, 47–50; Thurgood Marshall to Christopher C. Wimbush, Feb. 27, 1945, *Papers of the NAACP, Part 3*, Reel 23,

00799; Wimbush to Marshall, Feb. 23, 1945, *Papers of the NAACP, Part 3*, Reel 23, 00800; Wimbush to Marshall, Mar. 9, 1945, *Papers of the NAACP, Part 3*, Reel 23, 00801.

10. Thurgood Marshall quote taken from Douglas, *Jim Crow Moves North*, 238. On the NAACP's campaign to end northern school segregation during the 1940s, see Thomas J. Sugrue, *Sweet Land of Liberty: The Forgotten Struggle for Civil Rights in the North* (New York: Random House, 2008), 169–70, and Gilbert Jonas, *Freedom's Sword: The NAACP and the Struggle against Racism in America, 1909–1969* (New York: Routledge, 2005).

11. Thurgood Marshall qtd. in Douglas, *Jim Crow Moves North*, 247.

12. Douglas, *Jim Crow Moves North*, 247–49; IIC, *Third Report of Illinois Interracial Commission* (1949), 11–12; "No State Aid if Race Excluded," *Chicago Defender*, July 2, 1949.

13. Douglas, *Jim Crow Moves North*, 250; Gloster B. Current, "Exit Jim Crow Schools in East St. Louis," *Crisis* 57 (Apr. 1950): 209–14.

14. Report of Special Committee Appointed Pursuant to House Resolution No. 34, 1951, Superintendent of Public Instruction, Legal Department Correspondence, Colored Children File, Record Group 106.014, Illinois State Archives; June Shagaloff and Lester P. Bailey, "Cairo—Illinois Southern Exposure," *Crisis* 59 (Apr. 1952): 208–13; Douglas, *Jim Crow Moves North*, 252.

15. "Mass Meeting under NAACP Sponsorship," *Cairo Evening Citizen*, Jan. 16, 1952; "Guild Presents Program at Mt. Moriah Church," *Chicago Defender*, Feb. 15, 1947; "Cairo," *Chicago Defender*, Feb. 12, 1949; "Dentist," *Chicago Defender*, Feb. 12, 1949; Annual Report of Branch Activities for Cairo, Illinois, Dec. 22, 1952, *Papers of the NAACP, Part 25: Branch Department Files, Series A, Regional Fields, Special Projects, 1941–1955*, Reel 16, 0102; "FBI Enters Cairo School Row," *Jet*, Feb. 21, 1952.

16. Kendrick, untitled history of Ward Chapel, KBFP-LOC, box 21, folder 15.

17. Kendrick handwritten note, n.d., KBFP-LOC, box 22, folder 4.

18. Kendrick, untitled history of Ward Chapel, KBFP-LOC, box 21, folder 15; Annual Report of Branch Activities for Cairo, Illinois, Dec. 22, 1952, *Papers of the NAACP, Part 25*, Reel 16, 0102; "Cairo School Situation," *Crisis* 59 (Mar. 1952): 143–44.

19. Shagaloff and Bailey, "Cairo," 211–13; "Local Leaders Held Guilty of Cairo Bias," *New York Amsterdam News*, Feb. 16, 1952; "FBI Enters Cairo School Row," *Jet*, Feb. 21, 1952; "Crosses Burn in Cairo, Ill., Negro Areas," *Southern Illinoisan*, Jan. 28, 1952.

20. Quote taken from "Race Violence Flares in Cairo, Ill.," *Jet*, Feb. 14, 1952. These acts of racial terror were widely publicized in local and national newspapers. For select coverage, see "Crosses Burn in Cairo, Ill., Negro Areas," *Southern Illinoisan*, Jan. 28, 1952; "FBI Enters Cairo School Row," *Jet*, Feb. 21,

1952; "Cairo School Situation," *Crisis* 59 (Mar. 1952): 143–44; "Cairo Home of Negro Doctor Is Bombed," *Marion Daily Republican*, Jan. 30, 1952; "Bomb Blasts Illinois Negro Doctor's Home," *Washington Post*, Feb. 1, 1952; "Auto Salesman Arrested on Cairo Bombing Charge," *Atlanta Daily World*, Feb. 1, 1952; "Violence Running in Cairo, Ill., Community," *Atlanta Daily World*, Feb. 3, 1952; "Grand Jury to Hear 4 in Bombing," *New York Amsterdam News*, Feb. 9, 1952; "Nab Bomb Suspect," *Afro-American*, Feb. 9, 1952.

21. "Bomb Blasts Illinois Negro Doctor's Home," *Washington Post*, Feb. 1, 1952.

22. "Support the Businesses which Support Your Community," *Cairo Evening Citizen*, July 6, 1962; "Grand Jury Is Dismissed after Report," *Cairo Evening Citizen*, Feb. 22, 1952; "AFL Unions Work Out No-Strike Agreement for Quick Completion of Joppa, Ill., Electric Power Plant," *Southern Illinois Labor Tribune*, Aug. 27, 1953.

23. "Charged with Conspiracy," *Cairo Evening Citizen*, Feb. 8, 1952; "Hearings in Police Court Are Continued," *Cairo Evening Citizen*, Feb. 13, 1952; "Nine Arrested in Cairo Race Disturbances," *Marion Daily-Republican*, Feb. 8, 1952; Jonas, *Freedom's Sword*, 80.

24. "Grand Jury Is Dismissed after Report," *Cairo Evening Citizen*, Feb. 22, 1952.

25. Shagaloff and Bailey, "Cairo," 211.

26. Wright, *Life behind the Veil*, 4; Lang, "Locating the Civil Rights Movement," 387–88. On borderland cities and the politics of interracial civility, see K'Meyer, *Civil Rights in the Gateway to the South*, 11, 43; Levy, *Civil War on Race Street*, 1–2, 7.

27. Current, "Exit Jim Crow Schools."

28. Shagaloff and Bailey, "Cairo," 212.

29. Leo C. Schultz, "A Report of the Situation at Cairo," Superintendent of Public Instruction Records, Legal Department Correspondence, Segregation File, Record Group 106.014, Illinois State Archives.

30. Shagaloff and Bailey, "Cairo."

31. "NAACP Asks Dismissal of Cairo School Head," *Atlanta Daily World*, Mar. 11, 1952; "Cairo Free of Incidents as Schools Drop Segregation," *Atlanta Daily World*, Sept. 10, 1952; "Enroll Negro Students in Cairo Schools: Illinois City Quiet as Color Line Crashed," *Chicago Defender*, Sept. 13, 1952. Correspondence between Alexander County superintendent of public instruction Lucy Twente McPherson and state superintendent of public instruction Vernon Nickell regarding the desegregation lawsuit and the withholding of state funds is available in the Superintendent of Public Instruction Records at the Illinois State Archives, Springfield.

32. Barger, *Ethnicity in Cairo Catholic Schools*, 31, 45–46.

33. "School Doors Opening," *Chicago Defender*, Sept. 13, 1952.

34. June Shagaloff, "Progress Report on Northern Desegregation," *Equity & Excellence in Education* 4 (1966): 44–46 [45]; Illinois State Advisory Committee, Samuel J. Simmons to Walter Lewis, Aug. 22, 1966, box 40, Records Relating to Special Projects, 1960–1970, Office of the Staff Director, USCCR, Record Group 453, National Archives, Washington, DC; OSPI, *Illinois School Directory, 1966–67* and *1967–68* (Springfield, IL: OSPI, 1967).

35. W. A. Fingal to Thurgood Marshall, Sept. 10, 1953, *Papers of the NAACP, Part 3*, Reel 1, 0476–0479; "Cairo, Illinois, Schools Remain Segregated," *Washington Post*, June 28, 1956.

36. Langston Hughes, "A Sentimental Journey to Cairo, Illinois," *Chicago Defender*, May 15, 1954.

37. "Dynamite Arrow: Neighbor Points Out Foe of Segregation," *Life*, Feb. 1, 1954; Kendrick handwritten note, n.d., KBFP-LOC, box 22, folder 7.

38. Kendrick handwritten note, n.d., KBFP- LOC, box 22, folder 7; memorandum, "Decision of Cairo Board of Education, School District No. 1," July 28, 1954, KBFP-LOC, box 21, folder 12; Cairo City Council minutes, Feb. 20 and Mar. 5, 12, 1956; Ann Elizabeth Herda, "Black Women's Inspirational Leadership in the Civil Rights Movement: A Case Study" (master's thesis, Southern Illinois University Carbondale, 1994), 17. Sociologist Aldon Morris outlines a similar assault on southern NAACP branches in the wake of direct-action campaigns aimed at testing the 1954 *Brown* decision: see Morris, *Origins of the Civil Rights Movement*, 30–35.

39. W. A. Fingal to Thurgood Marshall, Sept. 10, 1953, *Papers of the NAACP, Part 3*, Reel 1, 0476–0479; "Cairo, Illinois, Schools Remain Segregated," *Washington Post*, June 28, 1956; draft manuscript by Kathryn Ward, KBFP-LOC, box 22, folder 2; Annual Reports of Branch Activities for Cairo, Illinois, *Papers of the NAACP, Part 25*, Reel 16, 0102–0121; "Cairo Movie House Ends Segregation," *Atlanta Daily World*, Jan. 17, 1954.

40. "Staying in Cairo, Says Dr. Wallace," *Chicago Defender*, Feb. 9, 1952; "Prince Hall Military Lodge Honors Illinois Dentist," *Atlanta Daily World*, Nov. 26, 1954; Annual Reports of Branch Activities for Cairo, Illinois, *Papers of the NAACP, Part 25*, 1941–1955, Reel 16, 0102–0121.

41. Kendrick, untitled history of Ward Chapel, KBFP-LOC, box 21, folder 15; Fingal to Marshall, Sept. 10, 1953, *Papers of the NAACP, Part 3*, Reel 1, 0476–0479. On the economic independence Methodist denominational structures afforded ministers during the civil rights struggle, see Payne, *I've Got the Light*, 189, 191.

42. University of Illinois, *Transactions of the Board of Trustees* (Urbana, IL: University of Illinois, 1958), 287; Kendrick, untitled history of Ward Chapel, KBFP-LOC, box 21, folder 15.

43. Transcripts of audiotapes 3 and 4 made by Hattie Kendrick, n.d., KBFP-LOC, box 19, folder 2; Kendrick, untitled history of Ward Chapel, KBFP-LOC,

box 21, folder 15; Kendrick, untitled script for a church play, n.d., KBFP-LOC, box 21, folder 15.

44. Collier-Thomas, *Jesus, Jobs, and Justice*; Higginbotham, *Righteous Discontent*. On black women's activism within the AME Church, see Jualynne E. Dodson, *Engendering Church: Women, Power, and the AME Church* (Lanham, MD: Rowman & Littlefield, 2002).

45. Hattie B. Kendrick, *Fourth Episcopal District African Methodist Episcopal Church Illinois-Iowa Conference Women's Missionary Society Guidelines*, n.d., KBFP-LOC, box 21, folder 15; Ronnie Woods to the family and friends of our dear departed sister, Miss Hattie B. Kendrick, June 22, 1989, KBFP-LOC, box 21, folder 3.

46. Kendrick, untitled script, KBFP-LOC, box 21, folder 15; transcripts of audiotapes 3 and 4 made by Hattie Kendrick, n.d., KBFP-LOC, box 19, folder 2.

47. Charles E. Koen, *The Cairo Story: And the Round-Up of Black Leadership* (Cairo, IL: Koen Press, n.d.), 41–43, 47; Kenneth C. Field, "Here's Why Southern Illinois Has Earned the Sad Title of 'Little Mississippi,'" *Chicago Defender*, July 7, 1962.

48. Koen, *Cairo Story*, 44–46.

49. Ibid., 46–48.

50. On black religious intellectuals and segregation as a moral sin, Dennis C. Dickerson, "African American Religious Intellectuals and the Theological Foundations of the Civil Rights Movement, 1930–55," *Church History* 74, no. 2 (June 2005): 217–35.

51. Transcripts of audiotapes 3 and 4 made by Hattie Kendrick, n.d., KBFP-LOC, box 19, folder 2; Cairo City Council minutes, Jan. 23, 1961; August Meier and Elliott M. Rudwick, *CORE: A Study in the Civil Rights Movement, 1942–1968* (Urbana: University of Illinois Press, 1975), 159–62; "20 SIU Students Attend Sit-In Meeting in Cairo," *Egyptian*, June 29, 1962; Koen, *Cairo Story*, 49; Commission on Human Relations, *Tenth Biennial Report* (Chicago: n.p., 1963).

52. James Peake Jr., "SNCC Report," Sept. 26, 1962, Student Nonviolent Coordinating Committee Papers, 1959–1972 (microform), Reel 8, 0298; John Lewis and Michael D'Orso, *Walking with the Wind: A Memoir of the Movement* (New York: Simon and Schuster, 1998), 190–91; "20 SIU Students Attend Sit-In," *Egyptian*, June 29, 1962; "Anti-Bias Group Formed," *Southern Illinoisan*, July 9, 1962; "John O'Neal Explains Non-Violence Committee," *Egyptian*, July 24, 1962; Koen, *Cairo Story*, 49; Student Nonviolent Freedom Committee, "A Report on Student Nonviolent Activities in Southern Illinois," Sept. 29, 1962, Student Nonviolent Coordinating Committee Papers, 1959–1972 (microform), Reel 9, 0347-50; Field, "Here's Why Southern Illinois Has Earned the Sad Title," *Chicago Daily Defender*, July 7, 1962.

53. Koen and other CNVFC members were part of a small minority in the

civil rights movement who subscribed to nonviolence as a philosophy as opposed to a strategy or tactic. On debates within SNCC over nonviolence as a philosophy versus strategy and the role of the Nashville contingent, see Payne, *I've Got the Light*, 98, 110; Howard Zinn, *SNCC: The New Abolitionists* (Boston: Beacon Press, 1964), 221–24; Cheryl Lynn Greenberg, *A Circle of Trust: Remembering SNCC* (New Brunswick, NJ: Rutgers University Press, 1998), 18–22, 34–35, 168–69; Hogan, *Many Minds, One Heart*, 16–38, 84, 156–58; Doug McAdam, *Freedom Summer* (New York: Oxford University Press, 1998), 121–23; Sellers, *River of No Return*, 35–39, 109, 146–47; David L. Chappell, *A Stone of Hope: Prophetic Religion and the Death of Jim Crow* (Chapel Hill: University of North Carolina Press, 2004), 67–87, 313. At the local level, nonviolent tactics were often deployed in tandem with a broader commitment to armed self-defense. See Simon Wendt, *The Spirit and the Shotgun: Armed Resistance and the Struggle for Civil Rights* (Gainesville: University Press of Florida, 2007); Christopher B. Strain, *Pure Fire: Self-Defense as Activism in the Civil Rights Era* (Athens: University of Georgia Press, 2005).

54. CNVFC, "Cairo Nonviolent Freedom Committee Newsletter," July 1962, James Forman Papers, LOC, box 69, folder 9.

55. CNVFC, "Nonviolence: Key to Dignity," Sept. 29, 1962, Student Nonviolent Coordinating Committee Papers, 1959–1972 (microform), Reel 9, 0350; "John O'Neal Explains Non-Violence Committee," *Egyptian*, July 24, 1962; CNVFC, untitled speech to local ministers, July 1962, James Forman Papers, LOC, box 69, folder 9; CNVFC, untitled speech, 1962, James Forman Papers, LOC, box 69, folder 9.

56. Koen, *Cairo Story*, 49–50; "Stabbing Claimed during Cairo Race Disturbance," *Southern Illinoisan*, June 27, 1962; Jim Wiggs, "She Accepts the Curses," *Southern Illinoisan*, June 27, 1962; "No Quitting, Negro Says," 1962, James Forman Papers, LOC, box 69, folder, 9; newsletter of the CNVFC, July 1962, James Forman Papers, LOC, box 69, folder 9; "Police Remain Alert for More Demonstrations," *Cairo Evening Citizen*, June 28, 1962; "Former Coed Says She Was Slashed during Sit-In at Cairo Restaurants," *Marion Daily Republican*, June 27, 1962; "Big Gathering at Restaurant Is Dispersed," *Cairo Evening Citizen*, June 27, 1962; "Negroes Soaked in Cairo Sit-In," *Southern Illinoisan*, June 28, 1962; "Cairo Mayor, Students to Huddle on Bias Charges," *Chicago Defender*, July 2, 1962; "Fourth Day of Demonstrations at Restaurant," *Cairo Evening Citizen*, June 30, 1962.

57. On Nashville's Operation Open City, see Benjamin Houston, *The Nashville Way: Racial Etiquette and the Struggle for Social Justice in a Southern City* (Athens: University of Georgia Press, 2012).

58. Press release from the CNVFC, June 30, 1962, James Forman Papers, LOC, box 69, folder 9; "Cairo Youth Committee Protests Despite Arrest of 23 Sit-Ins," *Chicago Daily Defender*, July 16, 1962.

59. James Peake Jr., "Freedom Fight Spreads to Cairo, Ill.," *Guardian*, July 1962, James Forman Papers, LOC, box 69, folder 9; "Integrationists Continue Their Hunger Strike," *Cairo Evening Citizen*, July 16, 1962; "Over 40 Arrested in Cairo," *Southern Illinoisan*, July 15, 1962; "Court Hearings for Sit-In Demonstrators Are Continued," *Cairo Evening Citizen*, July 17, 1962; Kenneth Field, "Convict 17 Kids in Cairo Protests," *Chicago Defender*, July 21, 1962; "21 Fined in Cairo," *Southern Illinoisan*, July 20, 1962; telegram from Martin Luther King Jr. to CNVFC, July 23, 1962, James Forman Papers, LOC, box 69, folder 9.

60. CNVFC untitled speech delivered to community members, July 1962, James Forman Papers, LOC, box 69, folder 9; "Cairo Tense: 5 Barred from Swimming Pool," *Chicago Daily Defender*, July 5, 1962; "300 Attend Interracial Cairo Meet," *Southern Illinoisan*, July 6, 1962; "Demonstrations Planned," *Southern Illinoisan*, July 26, 1962.

61. Kendrick handwritten note, n.d., KBFP-LOC, box 22, folder 3; "Boys Work by Some of the Club," *Rotarian*, July 1920, 19; "Club Notes," *Rotarian*, Aug. 1921, 135; report from the CNVFC, July 10, 1962, James Forman Papers, LOC, box 69, folder 9; "Attorney General Issues Ruling on Swimming Pool," *Cairo Evening Citizen*, Aug. 1, 1962; report from the CNVFC, Aug. 8, 1962, James Forman Papers, LOC, box 69, folder 9; "Cairo Action Report," n.d., *Papers of the NAACP, Part 19: Youth File, Series D, 1956–1965, Youth Department Files*, Reel 2, 0330–0332; Student Nonviolent Freedom Committee, "Report on Student Nonviolent Activities in Southern Illinois," Sept. 29, 1962, David Ibata Collection of Racial Strife, SCRC, SIU, box 1, folder 6; "Insist Kerner Act on Cairo Race Riots," *Chicago Daily Defender*, Aug. 20, 1962.

62. "Cairo Probe Pledged by Gov. Kerner," *Chicago Daily Defender*, Aug. 21, 1962; Student Nonviolent Coordinating Committee Papers, 1959–1972 (microform), Reel 9, 0349; Cairo City Council minutes, Aug. 20, 27, and Sept. 10, 1962.

63. "Negroes Skate at Integrated Cairo Rink," *Chicago Daily Defender*, Sept. 10, 1962; Barger, *Ethnicity in the Cairo Catholic Schools*, 45; Cairo City Council minutes, June 10, July 8, 15, and Aug. 12, 1963.

64. Robert L. Sands, "Cairo's Success Story," *Together*, Dec. 1964, Bonnie J. Krause Papers, SCRC, SIU, box 2, folder 9; minutes of the Christian Social Action Commission, May 13, 1963, Illinois Conference of Churches Records (1880–1997), box 10, folder 11, Abraham Lincoln Presidential Library (hereafter ICC Records, ALPL), Springfield, Illinois; "Cairo Commission at Work," *Illinois Human Relations* (May–June 1964); Estelle Merrifield and Erma Bridgewater, "History of Bethel AME Church, Champaign, IL," (Champaign: n.p., 1991); Special Task Force Committee on Cairo, "Biographical Sketch: Charles Enlow Koen," ICC Records, ALPL, box 11, 1969; McKendree University, *McKendrean 1964 Yearbook* (Lebanon, IL: McKendree College, 1964); Dan Clark, "Illinois, Cairo," *Chicago Defender*, Jan. 11, 1964. On the role that the

sit-ins and kneel-ins played in galvanizing white Methodist clergy, see Murray, *Methodists and the Crucible of Race*, 109, 147–49, 163–64.

65. Illinois Council of Churches, "Report of Visitation to Cairo, Illinois," July 9–10, 1964, Bonnie J. Krause Papers, SCRC, SIU, box 2, folder 9; Cairo City Council minutes, May 25, June 8 and 23, 1964, and Feb. 27, June 30, July 10, Sept. 5, 1967; "Swim Pool in Cairo Closes," *Southeast Missourian*, June 26, 1963; "Closing of Swimming Pool a Disgrace," *Monitor*, Aug. 15, 1968; "Pool Filled with Cement, Blacks Knee-Deep in Anger," *Jet*, May 26, 1968.

66. Koen, *Cairo Story*, 47–48. The CNVFC held a small number of pickets at local stores including the Wonder Market: see "Heavy Protests Lodged in Illinois Jailings," *Carolinian* (Raleigh, NC), Aug. 25, 1962; "Cairo, Ill., Supermarket Picketed after Student Is Beaten," *Louisville Defender*, Aug. 30, 1962.

67. "Charges 'Slave Labor,'" *Chicago Tribune*, July 24, 1966; Hattie Kendrick to Martha and Charles Cobb, Mar. 5, 1969, KBFP-LOC, box 20, folder 10; Illinois State Advisory Committee, "I Reckon It's on Its Way"; Frederick L. Bernstein to Ford Foundation, n.d., KBFP-LOC, box 21, folder 5.

68. "Biographical Sketch: Charles Enlow Koen," 1969, ICC Records, ALPL, box 11, Special Task Force Committee on Cairo, 1969; Koen, *Cairo Story*, 53; "Illinois Migrant School in Second Year," *Monitor*, Jan. 18, 1968; Frederick A. Roblee to Illinois Legislators and Illinois delegation in the Congress of the United States, Feb. 23, 1967, ICC Records, ALPL, box 10, folder 27; Cayetano Santiago, "Something Is Growing in Cairo," 1967, KBFP-LOC, box 21, folder 6; Hattie Kendrick to Martha and Charles Cobb, Mar. 5, 1969, KBFP-LOC, box 20, folder 10.

69. Preston Ewing Jr. interview with the author, Oct. 29, 2011, Cairo; souvenir program for the 94th Illinois Annual Conference of the African Methodist Episcopal Church, Fourth Episcopal District, held at Ward Chapel AME Church, Aug. 1965, KBFP-LOC, box 21, folder 15.

70. Cairo City Council minutes, Feb. 27, Mar. 13, May 22, and July 10, 1967; "Negroes Win 3 of 8 Nominations in Cairo Primary," *Chicago Tribune*, Mar. 1, 1967; Robert E. Kolze to Rev. Isaac Igarashi, Apr. 24, 1967, ICC Records, ALPL, box 19, folder 23. On the Port Gibson boycott, see Emilye Crosby, *A Little Taste of Freedom: The Black Freedom Struggle in Clairborne County, Mississippi* (Chapel Hill: University of North Carolina Press, 2005).

71. On the urban rebellions of the mid-1960s, see *Report of the National Advisory Commission on Civil Disorders* (New York: Bantam, 1968); Robert M. Fogelson, *Violence as Protest: A Study of Riots and Ghettos* (New York: Doubleday, 1971). For an important analysis of three midwestern rebellions in 1967, see Ashley Howard, "Prairie Fires: Urban Rebellions as Black Working-Class Politics in Three Midwestern Cities" (PhD diss., University of Illinois at Urbana-Champaign, 2012).

72. Koen, *Cairo Story*, 53; "Negro Youth Leaders Give Cairo 72 Hours to Meet Terms," *St. Louis Post-Dispatch*, July 20, 1967; "Racial Unrest, Fires, Looting at Cairo, Ill.," *St. Louis Post-Dispatch*, July 17, 1967; *The Cairo Project: A Report* (Carbondale: Southern Illinois University Carbondale, School of Journalism, 2007); McLaughlin, *Long, Hot Summer of 1967*, 6. On the Newark rebellion, see Kevin Mumford, *Newark: A History of Race, Rights, and Riots in America* (New York: New York University Press, 2008).

73. "Racial Unrest, Fires, Looting at Cairo, Ill.," *St. Louis Post-Dispatch*, July 17, 1967; "Cairo Hit by Wave of Fire Bombing and Vandalism," *Cairo Evening Citizen*, July 17, 1967; "Guardsmen Ordered to Action as Disturbances Flare Anew," *Cairo Evening Citizen*, July 19, 1967; "Hunt Weapons in Negro Homes," *Chicago Tribune*, July 20, 1967.

74. "Negro Youth Leaders Give Cairo 72 Hours to Meet Terms," *St. Louis Post-Dispatch*, July 20, 1967.

75. "Cairo to Study Grievances after Firebombing, Looting," *St. Louis Post-Dispatch*, July 18, 1967; "Reforms or Else, Cairo Negroes Say," *Southern Illinoisan*, July 21, 1967; "Mayor Appeals for End to Bombings, Vandalism," *Cairo Evening Citizen*, July 18, 1967; "Ewing Claims 100 Youth Involved," *Cairo Evening Citizen*, July 19, 1967.

76. Koen, *Cairo Story*, 53–54; "Negro Youth Leaders Give Cairo 72 Hours," *St. Louis Post-Dispatch*, July 20, 1967; "72-Hour Ultimatum Issued by Cairo Negro 'Leaders,'" *Cairo Evening Citizen*, July 21, 1967; Donald Janson, "Negroes Demand Action by Cairo, Ill.," *New York Times*, July 21, 1967.

77. Paul Good, *Cairo, Illinois: Racism at Floodtide* (Washington, DC: Commission on Civil Rights, 1973), 16; Jerome P. Curry, "Negroes Seek Jobs as Test of Promise by Plant in Cairo," *St. Louis Post-Dispatch*, July 24, 1967; "Cairo Leaders Meet, Believe Race Crisis Has Been Averted," *St. Louis Post-Dispatch*, July 23, 1967; "Mayor and City Council Members Issue Statement," *Cairo Evening Citizen*, July 24, 1967; "Council Makes Progress in Reply to Grievances," *Cairo Evening Citizen*, July 21, 1967.

78. Quotation from handbill printed in Preston Ewing Jr. and Jan Peterson Roddy, *Let My People Go: Cairo, Illinois, 1867–1973* (Carbondale: Southern Illinois University Press, 1996), 12; Cairo City Council minutes, July 24, 1967; "White Citizens Hold Mass Meeting," *Cairo Evening Citizen*, July 22, 1967; "Merchant Drive to Hire More Cairo Negroes," *St. Louis Post-Dispatch*, July 21, 1967; "Cairo Whites Urge Arrests of Arsonists and Snipers," *St. Louis Post-Dispatch*, July 22, 1967; "Cairo Posts $1000 Reward to Curb Violence," *St. Louis Post-Dispatch*, July 25, 1967; "Cairo Council Posts Reward for Those Guilty of Arson, Vandalism," *Cairo Evening Citizen*, July 25, 1967.

79. "Law Enforcement," n.d., Alliance to End Repression Records, Series 1, Operating Files, 1969–1986, Subseries 5, Council, Committees and Task Forces, 1970–1984, Chicago Historical Society, box 7, folder 34; "Chapter of Com-

mittee of 10 Million Formed in Cairo," *Cairo Evening Citizen*, July 31, 1967; "Cairo Organizes Unit to Control Disorders," *Southern Illinoisan*, July 31, 1967; Cairo City Council minutes, Aug. 14, 1967; "Cairo Residents Arming for Summer," *FOCUS/Midwest* (1968); Louis G. Heath, "Ghost Town Vigilantes: The Racial Pallor of Cairo," *Nation* 22 (Dec. 1969): 692–95; Illinois Advisory Committee, *A Decade of Waiting in Cairo*, 5–6; Good, *Cairo, Illinois*, 16–17.

80. On the Detroit rebellion of 1967, see Sidney Fine, *Violence in the Model City: The Cavanagh Administration, Race Relations, and the Detroit Riot of 1967* (Ann Arbor: University of Michigan Press, 1988); Thomas J. Sugrue, *The Origins of the Urban Crisis: Race and Inequality in Postwar Detroit* (Princeton, NJ: Princeton University Press, 1996).

81. "Another Group Asks Peaceful Cairo Settlement," *Cairo Evening Citizen*, July 24, 1967; "Cairo Has New Police Chief: Carl Clutts Resigns Post," *Cairo Evening Citizen*, May 27, 1969; Cairo City Council minutes, Aug. 17, 1942; "Racially Tense Cairo Slates Elections Today," *Herald-Journal*, Apr. 20, 1971; Cairo City Council minutes, June 13, 1966, Feb. 27, 1967, and Sept. 14, 1970.

82. "Youths on the Move," *Monitor*, Feb. 1, 1968; "Cairo NAACP Adopts 30-Point Program for 1968," *Monitor*, Feb. 1, 1968; "Cairo NAACP to Meet," *Monitor*, Feb. 29, 1968; "NAACP to Meet," *Monitor*, Oct. 31, 1968; "Cairo Today," *Monitor*, Jan. 18, 1968; "Announces Plans for 1969," *Monitor*, Jan. 3, 1969; "Cairo Youth Council Organized, Set Goals," *Monitor*, Jan. 18, 1968; "Youth Council Elect Officers," *Monitor*, Feb. 29, 1968.

83. "Cairo Youth Council Organized," *Monitor*, Jan. 18, 1968; "Youths on the Move," *Monitor*, Feb. 1, 1968; "Southern Illinois Co-Operative Assn. Teaches 'Importance of the Dollar,'" *Monitor*, Jan. 18, 1968; "S.I.C.A. Forms Credit Union," *Monitor*, Feb. 9, 1968; "Record-News Stand to Open," *Monitor*, Feb. 15, 1968; "SICA in Retrospect," *Monitor*, Jan. 3, 1969; Southern Illinois Cooperative Association Pilot Project Report, n.d., ICC Records, ALPL, box 19, folder 4; Illinois Migrant Council, "Analysis of S.I.C.A. Programs in Cairo, Illinois," May 20, 1968, ICC Records, ALPL, box 19, folder 4; "Thrift Shop Opens," *Monitor*, Jan. 9, 1969.

84. "The Cairo Youth Council," *Monitor*, Feb. 22, 1968.

85. "Church Official Visits Cairo, Explains Black Power," *Monitor*, Mar. 14, 1968; "Cairo Church News," *Monitor*, Feb. 29, 1968; "Church News," *Monitor*, Feb. 15, 1968.

3. From the Seminary to the Streets

1. To distinguish between the Cairo United Front organization and the broader concept of a united front strategy, I capitalize the former and not the latter.

2. For further discussion of the "second wave" of the black power move-

ment, see Joseph, *Waiting 'Til the Midnight Hour*, 254–55; and Peniel E. Joseph, "Introduction: Towards a Historiography of the Black Power Movement," in *Black Power Movement*, ed. Joseph, 7, 20–21.

3. On the founding conference of the Congress of Afrikan People and the broader effort to forge a national black united front during the early 1970s, see Cedric Johnson, *Revolutionaries to Race Leaders: Black Power and the Making of African American Politics* (Minneapolis: University of Minnesota Press, 2007); Komozi Woodard, *A Nation within a Nation: Amiri Baraka (LeRoi Jones) and Black Power Politics* (Chapel Hill: University of North Carolina Press, 1999), 159–218; Komozi Woodard, "Amiri Baraka, the Congress of African People, and Black Power Politics from the 1961 United Nations Protest to the 1972 Gary Convention," in *Black Power Movement*, ed. Joseph, 55–77; Komozi Woodard, "It's Nation Time in NewArk: Amiri Baraka and the Black Power Experiment in Newark, New Jersey," in *Freedom North: Black Freedom Struggles outside the South, 1940–1980*, ed. Jeanne Theoharis and Komozi Woodard (New York: Palgrave Macmillan, 2003), 287–313.

4. Black united front groups operated in a number of US communities, including Los Angeles; Washington, DC; Boston; West Point and Jackson, MS; and Newark. On the Mississippi united front organizations, see Umoja, *We Will Shoot Back*, 181–86. On the Congress of Afrikan People in Newark, see Woodard, *Nation within a Nation*. On the Los Angeles–based Black Congress, see Scot Brown, "The Politics of Culture: The US Organization and the Quest for Black 'Unity'," in *Freedom North*, ed. Theoharis and Komozi, 223–55; Darnell M. Hunt and Ana-Christina Ramon, eds., *Black Los Angeles: American Dreams and Racial Realities* (New York: New York University Press, 2010), 146–49; Brown, *Fighting for US*.

5. "How Long Must We Wait?," *United Front News* (Cairo, IL), Sept. 12, 1970.

6. On the concept of "linked fate," see Michael C. Dawson, *Behind the Mule: Race and Class in African American Politics* (Princeton, NJ: Princeton University Press, 1994).

7. On T. Thomas Fortune and the Afro-American League, see Benjamin R. Justesen, *Broken Brotherhood: The Rise and Fall of the National Afro-American Council* (Carbondale: Southern Illinois Press, 2008), and Shawn Leigh Alexander, *An Army of Lions: The Civil Rights Struggle before the NAACP* (Philadelphia: University of Pennsylvania Press, 2012).

8. On the united front politics of black leftists in the United States during the interwar years, see Mark Naison, *Communists in Harlem during the Depression* (Urbana: University of Illinois Press, 1983), esp. 126–59; Mark Solomon, *The Cry Was Unity: Communists and African Americans, 1917–1936* (Jackson: University Press of Mississippi, 1998); Gerald Horne, *Black Liberation/Red Scare: Ben Davis and the Communist Party* (Cranbury, NJ: Associated University Presses, 1994); George M. Frederickson, *Black Liberation: A Comparative His-*

tory of Black Ideologies (New York: Oxford University Press, 1995), esp. 202–24; Erik S. McDuffie, *Sojourning for Freedom: Black Women, American Communism, and the Making of Black Left Feminism* (Raleigh, NC: Duke University Press, 2011); Minkah Makalani, *In the Cause of Freedom: Radical Black Internationalism from Harlem to London, 1917–1939* (Chapel Hill: University of North Carolina Press, 2011); Erik S. Gellman, *Death Blow to Jim Crow: The National Negro Congress and the Rise of Militant Civil Rights* (Chapel Hill: University of North Carolina Press, 2012).

9. The work of anticolonial activists from Africa, Asia, and Latin America influenced proponents of a united front strategy in the United States. For key works, see Kwame Nkrumah, *Handbook of Revolutionary Warfare: A Guide to the Armed Phase of the African Revolution* (New York: International Publishers, 1969); Mao Tse-tung, *Selected Works of Mao Tse-tung* (Oxford, UK: Pergamon Press, 1969).

10. Malcolm X, "Organization of Afro-American Unity: A Statement of Basic Aims and Objectives," in *Malcolm X: The Man and His Times*, ed. John Henrik Clarke (Trenton, NJ: Africa World Press, 1990), 336. On the united front politics of Malcolm X and Stokely Carmichael, see William W. Sales Jr., *From Civil Rights to Black Liberation: Malcolm X and the Organization of Afro-American Unity* (Boston: South End Press, 1994), esp. 97–132, 192–96; Manning Marable, *Malcolm X: A Life of Reinvention* (New York: Viking, 2011), 191–93, 251, 260, 284, 354; Stokely Carmichael, *Ready for Revolution: The Life and Struggles of Stokely Carmichael (Kwame Ture)* (New York: Scribner's, 2003), 642–43, 648–50; Clayborne Carson, *In Struggle: SNCC and the Black Awakening of the 1960s* (Cambridge, MA: Harvard University Press, 1995), 288, 292; Peniel E. Joseph, *Stokely: A Life* (New York: Perseus Books, 2014): 231–32, 235–37, 269, 288, 297.

11. Benjamin Looker, *"Point from which creation begins": The Black Artists' Group of St. Louis* (Columbia: University of Missouri Press, 2004), 43–44; McKendree University, *McKendrean 1964 Yearbook, McKendrean 1966 Yearbook* (Lebanon, IL: McKendree College, 1966).

12. Scholarship on SNCC's work during the late 1960s depicts an organization plagued by internal conflict and disorganization that rendered the group ineffective. Historian Cheryl Greenberg, for example, claims that by 1967 SNCC's "existence as an effective force for social change had ended." Greenberg, *Circle of Trust*, 12. However, the autobiographies of former SNCC members and organizational histories suggest that SNCC also continued to be a site of dynamic intellectual engagement and ideological development. See Sellers and Terrell, *River of No Return*, 170–252; Carson, *In Struggle*, 215–306; Belinda Robnett, *How Long? How Long? African-American Women in the Struggle for Civil Rights* (New York: Oxford University Press, 1997), 173–89; James Forman, *The Making of Black Revolutionaries* (Seattle: University of Washington Press, 2000 [1972]),

411–533; Carmichael, *Ready for the Revolution*, 520–727; Stephen Ward, "The Third World Women's Alliance: Black Feminist Radicalism and Black Power Politics," in *Black Power Movement*, ed. Joseph, 119–44; Hogan, *Many Minds, One Heart*, 226–34.

13. Koen, *Cairo Story*, 56; "Koen to Appeal Verdict of St. Louis Jury," *Monitor*, Jan. 29, 1970. For more on Koen's political activities during this period, see Carson, *In Struggle*, 290–94; Jolly, *Black Liberation in the Midwest*, 63–65, 73–76; Looker, *"Point from which creation begins,"* 43–44; Lang, *Grassroots at the Gateway*, 207–9.

14. Preston Ewing Jr., interview with the author, Oct. 29, 2011, Cairo, IL; Alliance to End Repression, "Cairo, Ill.: Law with Justice?," 1972, David Ibata Collection, SCRC, SIU, box 1, folder 3.

15. Kendrick audiotape transcript no. 9, 1974, KBFP-LOC, box 19, folder 3; "Mystery Still Surrounds Marshall Morris' Death," *Monitor*, Feb. 15, 1968; "New Investigation Possible into Death of Morris," *Monitor*, Feb. 22, 1968.

16. "Whites Invade Black Community: Gunfire Disrupts Tense City," *Chicago Daily Defender*, Apr. 1, 1969; "Guns Blaze in Cairo, Ill., Racial Clash," *Chicago Tribune*, Apr. 1, 1969; "Gov. Ogilvie Orders Guardsmen to Cairo," *Cairo Evening Citizen*, Apr. 29, 1969.

17. Koen, *Cairo Story*, 57. On the formation of the United Front, see "Races: War in Little Egypt," *Time*, Sept. 26, 1969; "History of Struggle," *Chicago Daily Defender*, Dec. 10, 1970; Charles E. Koen, *United Front Philosophy* (Cairo, IL: n.p., n.d.), 7; "Progress Report from the United Front," 1969, ICC Records, ALPL, box 11, folder 8.

18. Manker Harris, interview with author, June 20, 2012, Springfield, IL; United States Commission on Civil Rights, *Hearing before the United States Commission on Civil Rights* (Cairo, IL: n.p., 1972), 232.

19. Manker Harris interview.

20. Manker Harris interview; Bobby Williams, interview with author, Dec. 1, 2013, St. Louis, MO. On Leon Page, see "C.O.R.E. Charges School 'Ignored' Negro Teacher's Request for Transfer: State Sit-in at East St. Louis High," *Monitor*, Feb. 9, 1968; Jolly, *Black Liberation in the Midwest*, 65–66. On Bobby Williams, see "Bobby Williams: A Civil Rights Leader Fights for His Freedom," *Win*, Dec. 26, 1974.

21. Preston Ewing Jr., interview with author, Oct. 29, 2011, Cairo, IL.

22. On the unifying tenets of black evangelicalism, see Milton G. Sernett, "Black Religion and the Question of Evangelical Identity," in *The Variety of American Evangelicalism*, ed. Donald W. Dayton and Robert J. Johnston (Knoxville: University of Tennessee Press, 1991), 135–47; Albert J. Raboteau, "The Black Experience in American Evangelicalism: The Meaning of Slavery," in *The Evangelical Tradition in America*, ed. Leonard I. Sweet (Macon: Mercer University Press, 1997), 181–89.

23. Mary Pattillo-McCoy, "Church Culture as a Strategy of Action in the Black Community," *American Sociological Review* 63, no. 6 (Dec. 1998): 768.

24. Newton quote taken from Newton, *Revolutionary Suicide*, 71. On the nature of the BPP's opposition to Christianity, see Steve McCutcheon, Judson L. Jeffries, and Omari L. Dyson, "The Black Panther Party and the Black Church," in *From Every Mountainside: Black Churches and the Broad Terrain of Civil Rights*, ed. R. Drew Smith (Albany: State University of New York Press, 2013), esp. 137–38.

25. "Karenga Urges Black Churchmen to Get Together and Help Develop Black Communities," *Monitor*, Nov. 7, 1968; Huey Newton, *To Die for the People: The Writings of Huey P. Newton*, ed. Toni Morrison (San Francisco: City Lights Books, 2009), 73; Ogbar, *Black Power*, 155; Brown, *Fighting for US*, 34–35.

26. Carmichael quoted in Savage, *Your Spirits Walk beside Us*, 260.

27. Newton, *To Die for the People*, 60–74.

28. For more on the BPP and revolutionary intercommunalism, see Floyd W. Hayes III and Francis A. Kiene III, "'All Power to the People': The Political Thought of Huey P. Newton and the Black Panther Party," in *Black Panther Party Reconsidered*, ed. Jones, 157–76; Robert O. Self, "The Black Panther Party and the Long Civil Rights Era," in *In Search of the Black Panther Party: New Perspectives on a Revolutionary Movement*, ed. Jama Lazerow and Yohuru Williams (Durham, NC: Duke University Press, 2006), 15–59.

29. On the BPP's changing relationship to the black church during black power's "second wave," see Newton, *To Die for the People*, 60–74, and McCutcheon et al., "Black Panther Party and the Black Church."

30. On Cleage, see Dillard, *Faith in the City*, esp. 237–85, and Heather Ann Thompson, *Whose Detroit? Politics, Labor, and Race in a Modern American City* (Ithaca, NY: Cornell University Press, 2004), esp. 84–85. On Benjamin Chavis in Wilmington, see James Lance Taylor, "The Reverend Benjamin Chavis-Muhammed: From Wilmington to Washington, from Chavis to Muhammed," in *Religious Leaders and Faith-Based Politics: Ten Profiles*, ed. Jo Renee Formicola and Hubert Morken (Lanham, MD: Rowman & Littlefield, 2001): 115–40. On Leon Sullivan in Philadelphia, see Countryman, *Up South*; V. P. Franklin, "'The Lion of Zion': Leon H. Sullivan and the Pursuit of Social and Economic Justice," *Journal of African American History* 96, no. 1 (Winter 2011): 39–43; Nathaniel Bracey, "Community Development: The Zion Non-Profit Charitable Trust," *Journal of African American History* 96, no. 1 (Winter 2011): 90–95; Stephanie Dyer, "Progress Plaza: Leon Sullivan, Zion Investment Associates, and Black Power in a Philadelphia Shopping Center," in *The Economic Civil Rights Movement: African Americans and the Struggle for Economic Power*, ed. Michael Ezra (New York: Routledge, 2013): 137–53.

31. On the fusion of radical ideologies and grassroots popular theologies by

African American activists in the borderland and Deep South, see Robin D. G. Kelley, "'Comrades, Praise Gawd for Lenin and Them!': Ideology and Culture among Black Communists in Alabama, 1930–1935," *Science & Society* 52, no. 1 (Spring 1988), 59–82; Robin D. G. Kelley, *Hammer and Hoe: Alabama Communists during the Great Depression* (Chapel Hill: University of North Carolina Press, 1990); Jarod Roll, *Spirit of Rebellion: Labor and Religion in the New Cotton South* (Urbana: University of Illinois Press, 2010); Mark Fannin, *Labor's Promised Land: Radical Visions of Gender, Race, and Religion in the South* (Knoxville: University of Tennessee Press, 2003).

32. Lukas, "Bad Day at Cairo, Ill.," *New York Times* magazine, Feb. 21, 1971.

33. On the concept of social movement cultures, see Verta Taylor and Nancy Whittier, "Analytical Approaches to Social Movement Culture: The Culture of the Women's Movement," in *Social Movements and Culture*, ed. Hank Johnston and Bert Klandermans (Minneapolis: University of Minnesota Press, 1995), 163–88.

34. Howard Kohn, "Civil War in Cairo, Ill.: A Dispatch from the Front," *Ramparts* 9, no. 9 (Apr. 1971): 46–51.

35. In referencing the "toolkit" provided by the black church, I build upon the important work of social movement scholars who have underscored the role of culture in protest movements and have drawn particular attention to the role of the black church. See Pattillo-McCoy, "Church Culture," 768; Sandra L. Barnes, "Black Church Culture and Community Action," *Social Forces* 84, no. 2 (Dec. 2005): 967–94; Johnny E. Williams, "Vanguards of Hope: The Role of Culture in Mobilizing African American Women's Social Activism in Arkansas," *Sociological Spectrum* 24 (2004): 129–56.

36. "Blacks Vote Boycott On," *United Front News*, Sept. 26, 1970; Kohn, "Civil War in Cairo"; "United Front Choir to Participate in Meet," *Monitor*, Apr. 16, 1970.

37. On generational cohorts and intergenerational movement mobilization in social movement theory, see Hank Johnston, "Age Cohorts, Cognition, and Collective Violence," in *Violent Protest, Contentious Politics, and the Neoliberal State*, ed. Seraphim Seferiades and Hank Johnston (Farnham, UK: Ashgate Publishing, 2012): 39–53.

38. Maryadi, "The Roles of Black Churches in the Cairo Civil Rights Movement (1960s–1970s)" (Master's thesis, Southern Illinois University Carbondale, 1995), 21–22; "Ward Chapel Host Successful Open House," *Monitor*, Jan. 23, 1969; "Church News," *Monitor*, Jan. 14, 1969.

39. Robnett, *How Long?*, 20–21.

40. Cairo United Front, Certificate of Award to Hattie B. Kendrick, Apr. 6, 1974, KBFP-LOC, box 20, folder 1.

41. Clydia Koen, interview with the author, May 21, 2014, Cairo, IL; Ann

Herda-Rapp, "The Power of Informal Leadership: Women Leaders in the Civil Rights Movement," *Sociological Focus* 31, no. 4 (Oct. 1998): 341–55 [351].

42. Manker Harris interview; Preston Ewing interview; Tracye Matthews, "'No One Ever Asks, What a Man's Place in the Revolution Is': Gender and the Politics of the Black Panther Party, 1966–1971," in *Black Panther Party Reconsidered*, ed. Jones, 291.

43. Matthews, "'No One Ever Asks,'" 272. For an excellent discussion of black nationalism and gender politics, see E. Frances White, "Africa on My Mind: Gender, Counter Discourse and African-American Nationalism," *Journal of Women's History* 2 (Spring 1990): 73–97.

44. Koen, *Cairo Story*, 81–82; "Mrs. Koen Keeps the Faith," *Monitor*, Sept. 9, 1971; Clydia Koen interview.

45. Clarence Dossie, interview with the author, Feb. 5, 2010, Cairo, IL.

46. Kohn, "Civil War in Cairo," 47.

47. Koen, *United Front Philosophy*, 10.

48. Kohn, "Civil War in Cairo."

49. "Blacks Vote Boycott On," *United Front News*, Sept. 26, 1970; "United Front Expanding Activities," *Monitor*, Jan. 15, 1970; Kohn, "Civil War in Cairo"; William R. Brinton, "The Story of Confrontation" *FOCUS/Midwest* 8, no. 54 (1971): 10–14; John H. Britton, "Blacks Rally to Fight Oppression in Cairo, Ill.," *Jet*, Mar. 5, 1970. On testifying in black women's church-based activism, see Rosetta E. Ross, *Witnessing and Testifying: Black Women, Religion, and Civil Rights* (Minneapolis, MN: Fortress Press, 2003).

50. Untitled article, *United Front News*, May 1971.

51. Kohn, "Civil War in Cairo," 50; Bernard Gavzer, "Fear and Hate Abound: Gap Is Widening," *Chronicle Telegram* (Elyria, Ohio), Mar. 15, 1970; "Basis of United Front Program," *United Front News*, Sept. 26, 1970.

52. Britton, "Blacks Rally to Fight Oppression," *Jet*, Mar. 5, 1970.

53. Religious studies scholar Eddie Glaude argues that "religious stories have provided an interpretative framework within which experiences can be made sense of and, for some, hope can be sustained." Eddie S. Glaude, *In a Shade of Blue: Pragmatism and the Politics of Black America* (Chicago: University of Chicago Press, 2008), 68.

54. "Progress Report from the United Front," ICC Records, ALPL, box 11, folder 8.

55. Britton, "Blacks Rally to Fight Oppression," *Jet*, Mar. 5, 1970.

56. "Progress Report from the United Front," ICC Records, ALPL, box 11, folder 8. For more on the Exodus narrative and its use by African Americans, see Allen Dwight Callahan, *The Talking Book: African Americans and the Bible* (New Haven, CT: Yale University Press, 2006), 83–138; Milton C. Sernett, *Bound for the Promised Land: African American Religion and the Great Migration* (Durham, NC: Duke University Press, 1997); Eddie S. Glaude, *Exodus! Religion,*

Race, and Nation in Early Nineteenth-Century Black America (Chicago: University of Chicago Press, 2000).

57. "Progress Report from the United Front," ICC Records, ALPL, box 11, folder 8.

58. "Blacks Vote Boycott On," *United Front News*, Sept. 26, 1970; on the notion of "chosenness" and black religious thought, see Glaude, *Exodus!*, 63–81.

59. Max Roach, *Lift Every Voice and Sing* (Atlantic Records, 1971).

60. Koen, *United Front Philosophy*, 11; Koen, *Cairo Story*, 91; Cheryl J. Sanders, *Saints in Exile: The Holiness-Pentecostal Experience in African American Religion and Culture* (New York: Oxford University Press, 1996), 128–29.

61. United Front of Cairo, "A Restatement of the Demands 'To Save Cairo,'" Oct. 19, 1969, ICC Records, ALPL, box 16, folder 1; Rev. Charles Koen, "Resolution," June 30, 1969, ICC Records, ALPL, box 16, folder 1.

62. "Boycott Will Continue, Preston Ewing Says," *Cairo Evening Citizen*, July 8, 1969.

63. "Shows Bias toward Blacks in Court," *United Front News*, July 18, 1970; "Progress Report from the United Front," ICC Records, ALPL, box 11, folder 8; "Governor Still Not Interested in People," *United Front News*, Jan. 16, 1971; Koen, *Cairo Story*, 94–95.

64. Koen, *United Front Philosophy*, 11; "United Front Expanding Activities," *Monitor*, Jan. 15, 1970.

65. Allen Dwight Callahan, "Remembering Nehemiah: A Note on Biblical Theology," in *Black Zion: African American Religious Encounters with Judaism*, ed. Yvonne Chireau and Nathaniel Deutsch (New York: Oxford University Press, 2000), 161; Philip S. Foner, ed., *Black Socialist Preacher* (San Francisco: Synthesis Publications, 1983), 119–25.

66. On the United Front's use of the Nehemiah story, see Kerry L. Pimblott, "Black Power and Black Theology in Cairo, Illinois," in *The Pew and the Picket Line: Christianity and the American Working Class*, ed. Christopher D. Cantwell, Heath W. Carter, and Janine Giordano Drake (Urbana: University of Illinois Press, 2016): 115–43.

67. "Cairo Will Die!," *Monitor*, Mar. 14, 1968; "Cairo," *Monitor*, Feb. 29, 1968; "Blacks Vote Boycott On," *United Front News*, Sept. 26, 1970; "Longest March of the Year," *Monitor*, Mar. 20, 1970.

68. "Longest March of the Year," *Monitor*, Mar. 20, 1970; "Progress Report from the United Front," ICC Records, ALPL, box 11, folder 8; Koen, *United Front Philosophy*, 11.

69. J. N. K. Mugambi, *Christian Theology and Social Reconstruction* (Nairobi: Action Publishers, 2003) 172–73; Koen, *United Front Philosophy*, "Progress Report from the United Front," ICC Records, ALPL, box 11, folder 8; "Cooperative Day Care Center to Open Monday in Cairo," *Cairo Evening Citizen*, Oct. 23, 1969; "Pre-Fabricated Housing Factory Developed in Cairo," *Monitor*, Aug.

20, 1970; "Operation of the Palace," *United Front News*, Oct. 3, 1970; "Migrant School Moves Ahead," *Monitor*, Feb. 19, 1970; "How Long Must We Wait?," *United Front News*, Sept. 12, 1970; "Capitalism Is Compared to Cooperatives," *United Front News*, Oct. 3, 1970.

70. "Progress Report from the United Front," ICC Records, ALPL, box 11, folder 8; "Editorial Notes," *United Front News*, May 1971.

71. "Black Congress Supports Cairo Blacks," *United Front News*, Sept. 12, 1971; "Capitalism Is Compared to Cooperatives," *United Front News*, Oct. 3, 1970; "Basis of United Front Program," *United Front News*, Sept. 26, 1970; untitled article, *United Front News*, Jan. 16, 1971; "Progress Report from the United Front," ICC Records, ALPL, box 11, folder 8.

72. Martin Luther King Jr., *Strength to Love* (New York: Harper and Row, 1963), 94.

73. Amiri Baraka, *Raise, Race, Rays, Raze: Essays since 1965* (New York: Random House, 1972), 18–19, 30; Stokely Carmichael and Charles V. Hamilton, *Black Power: The Politics of Liberation* (New York: Vintage Books, 1967 [1992]), 41; "This Society Creates Things to Use against Man," *United Front News*, Aug. 22, 1970.

74. Carmichael and Hamilton, *Black Power*, 41; Imanu Amiri Baraka, *A Black Value System* (Newark: Jihad Productions, 1969), 4; Amiri Baraka, "7 Principles of US Maulana Karenga & the Need for a Black Value System," in *Raise, Race, Rays, Raze*, 134–66; Kwame Nkrumah, *Consciencism* (New York: Monthly Review Press, 1964).

75. Koen, *United Front Philosophy*, 7.

76. Mable Hollis quote taken from Maryadi, "Roles of Black Churches," 30. For an excellent study of revolutionary nationalists' survival programs, see Alondra Nelson, *Body and Soul: The Black Panther Party and the Fight against Medical Discrimination* (Minneapolis: University of Minnesota Press, 2011).

77. Koen, *United Front Philosophy*, 16, 21; Nkrumah, *Handbook of Revolutionary Warfare*; Robin D. G. Kelley and Betsy Esch, "Black Like Mao: Red China and Black Revolution," in *Afro Asia: Revolutionary Political and Cultural Connections between African Americans and Asian Americans*, eds. Fred Ho and Bill V. Mullen (Durham, NC: Duke University Press, 2008), 113; Mao Tse-tung, "On the Reissue of the Three Main Rules of Discipline and the Eight Points for Attention—Instruction of the General Headquarters of the Chinese People's Liberation Army," in *Selected Works of Mao Tse-tung*, 3rd ed. (Peking: Foreign Languages Press, 1969) 155–56; "Three Main Rules of Discipline," *Black Panther Newspaper*, Aug. 9, 1969, 27; "Eight Points of Attention," *Black Panther Newspaper*, Aug. 9, 1969, 27; "Basis of United Front Program," *United Front News*, Sept. 26, 1970; Richard T. Cooper, "Cairo, Ill.—River Town Adrift on Tide of Racism," *Los Angeles Times*, Feb. 14, 1971; Manker Harris interview.

78. Manker Harris interview; "Females Organized to Support United

Front," *Monitor*, Feb. 23, 1971; "Chicago Rally Protests Cairo Raids," *United Front News*, Mar. 13, 1971; Koen, *United Front Philosophy*; "United Front Explains Curfew," *Monitor*, Feb. 5, 1970; Michael Watson, "Cairo," *PROUD*, Oct. 1971; "Cairo: The Legacy of Racism," *Washington Post*, Mar. 22, 1987. On black feminist organizations in this period, see Kimberly Springer, *Living for the Revolution: Black Feminist Organizations, 1968–1980* (Raleigh, NC: Duke University Press, 2005); Ward, "Third World Women's Alliance."

79. "Cairo Has New Police Chief," *Cairo Evening Citizen*, May 27, 1969; Manker Harris interview; "Statement by Leon Perry," n.d., James Forman Papers, LOC, box 60, folder 10; Koen, *United Front Philosophy*; Bobby Williams interview.

80. "United Front Explains Curfew," *Monitor*, Feb. 5, 1970.

81. Clarence Dossie interview; Kohn, "Civil War in Cairo"; Koen, *United Front Philosophy*; Lukas, "Bad Day at Cairo," *New York Times* magazine, Feb. 21, 1971; Britton, "Blacks Rally," *Jet*, Mar. 5, 1970; M.R.C. Coalition, "The Warzone" (1971).

82. "'Rebels Rule Cairo: UF," *Chicago Daily Defender*, Jan. 7, 1970; Bobby Williams interview.

83. Historian Robin D. G. Kelley speaks of the "freedom dreams" central to movements for racial justice and social change. "Progressive social movements do not simply produce statistics and narratives of oppression; rather, the best ones do what great poetry does: transport us to another place, compel us to relive horrors and, more importantly, enable us to imagine a new society." See Robin D. G. Kelley, *Freedom Dreams: The Black Radical Imagination* (Boston: Beacon Press, 2002), 9.

84. "Progress Report from the United Front," ICC Records, ALPL, box 11, folder 8; "Blacks Rally," *Jet*, Mar. 5, 1970; "This Society Creates Things," *United Front News*, Aug. 22, 1970.

85. On the National Conference of Black Churchmen (NCBC), see Sawyer, *Black Ecumenism*, 15; Robert S. Lecky and Elliott Wright, *Black Manifesto: Religion, Racism, and Reparations* (New York: Sheed and Ward, 1969), 7; Lincoln and Mamiya, *Black Church*, 192–93. Important early works in black theology include Cleage, *Black Messiah*; Cleage, *Black Christian Nationalism*; and Cone, *Black Theology*.

86. "Rev. Albert B. Cleage to Speak Saturday," *Monitor*, June 4, 1970; "Cairo Hears, 'Suffering Part of Freedom,'" *Chicago Daily Defender*, June 10, 1970; "Rev. Cleage Charms Weekly Rally," *Monitor*, June 11, 1970; "The Church Must Be a Power Base!" *United Front News*, July 18, 1970; "Special Observance for Dr. King Set Saturday, Jan. 16," *United Front News*, Jan. 16, 1971; United Front of Cairo Flyer, June 6, 1970, IFCO Papers, Schomburg Center of Research in Black Culture, New York Public Library, box 46, folder 32 (hereafter IFCO Papers); United Front of Cairo, "Rev. Albert B. Cleage,"

n.d., IFCO Papers, box 46, folder 32; United Front news release, May 29, 1970, IFCO Papers, box 46, folder 32; "Leon Modeste in Cairo July 25," *United Front News*, July 18, 1970.

87. Clarence Dossie interview; Koen, *United Front Philosophy*, untitled article, *United Front News*, May 1971; "United Church Supports Cairo," *United Front News*, Oct. 24, 1970; "Koen Says: Our Ship Is Rolling," *United Front News*, Aug. 29, 1970; "Rev. Robinson Examines White Theology," *United Front News*, Sept. 5, 1970. For an early womanist critique of the masculinist bias of black theology, see Jacquelyn Grant's 1979 essay "Black Theology and the Black Woman," republished in *African American Religious Thought: An Anthology*, ed. Cornel West and Eddie S. Glaude Jr. (Louisville, KY: Westminster John Knox Press, 2003): 831–48.

88. Dwight N. Hopkins, *Shoes That Fit Our Feet: Sources for a Constructive Black Theology* (Maryknoll, NY: Orbis Books, 1993).

89. Clydia Koen interview; Cornel West, *Prophesy Deliverance! An Afro-American Revolutionary Christianity* (Louisville, KY: Westminster John Knox Press, 1982).

4. Straight from the Offering Plate

1. Minutes of the Inter-Organization Task Force for Community Action, Apr. 22, 1971, ICC Records, ALPL, box 11, folder 25; "Rallies Dramatize Cairo Blacks' Lot," *New York Amsterdam News*, Apr. 17, 1971; "NCBC Sponsors 'Repression' Cairo Meet," *Afro-American* (Baltimore), Apr. 17, 1971; Blaine Ramsey Jr. to executives attending the Apr. 22 meeting in Cairo, June 9, 1971, ICC Records, ALPL, box 11, folder 25.

2. Illinois State Advisory Committee, "I Reckon It's On Its Way."

3. Harvey G. Cox, "The 'New Breed' in American Churches: Sources of Social Activism in American Religion," *Daedalus* 96 (Winter 1967): 135–50 [137].

4. Correspondence between Gerald Montroy and the author, Oct. 7, 2014.

5. Marybeth C. Stalp, "Comparative Responses to Activism: Catholic Religious in the Cairo Civil Rights Movement, 1967–1973" (Master's thesis, Southern Illinois University Carbondale, 1996), 12.

6. Correspondence between Gerald Montroy and the author, Jan. 21, 2015. On the Second Vatican Council, see Colleen McDannell, *Spirit of Vatican II: A History of Catholic Reform in America* (New York: Basic Books, 2011), esp. 73–118.

7. For more on these demographic changes in inner-city Catholic parishes and their social and cultural implications, see John T. McGreevy, *Parish Boundaries: The Catholic Encounter with Race in the Twentieth Century* (Chicago: University of Chicago Press, 1996).

8. Correspondence between Gerald Montroy and the author, Oct. 7, 2014.

9. Robert H. Collins, "Bishop Backs Fr. Montroy's Goals in Cairo But Not All of His Methods," *St. Louis Post-Dispatch*, Mar. 25, 1969; Ivan R. Levin of the Illinois Human Relations Commission to Roger W. Nathan, Apr. 15, 1969, ICC Records, ALPL, box 19, folder 3.

10. Correspondence between Gerald Montroy and the author, Oct. 7, 2014; Clydia Koen interview.

11. Robert H. Collins, "Priest Makes Charge: Vigilante Corps in Cairo, Ill.," *St. Louis Post-Dispatch*, Mar. 23, 1969.

12. "Clergymen in Cairo, Ill., Inquiry Seek Talks," *St. Louis Post-Dispatch*, Mar. 27, 1969; Collins, "Priest Makes Charge," *St. Louis Post-Dispatch*, Mar. 23, 1969. On Father Groppi's role in the Milwaukee black freedom struggle, see Jones, *Selma of the North*.

13. Thomas Powers, "Cairo Clerics Denounce Priest," *Chicago Tribune*, May 2, 1969; "Clergymen in Cairo, Ill., Inquiry Seek Talks," *St. Louis Post-Dispatch*, Mar. 27, 1969.

14. Correspondence between Gerald Montroy and the author, Oct. 7, 2014; Collins, "Priest Makes Charge," *St. Louis Post-Dispatch*, Mar. 23, 1969; memorandum from the Cairo Chamber of Commerce, "Cairo Story: And How It Could Happen to You!" Apr. 18, 1969, ICC Records, ALPL, box 11, folder 5.

15. Concerned Clergy, *Cairo: Were You There?* (East St. Louis, IL: Concerned Clergy, 1969), 4; Jolly, *Black Liberation in the Midwest*, 65, 68; Harold R. Piety, "Revolution Comes to East St. Louis," *FOCUS/Midwest* 6 (1968).

16. "Bishop Backs Fr. Montroy's Goals in Cairo," *St. Louis Post-Dispatch*, Mar. 25, 1969.

17. Cairo Chamber of Commerce, "Cairo Story: And How It Could Happen to You!"

18. Concerned Clergy, *Cairo: Were You There?*, 4.

19. Ibid., 3.

20. William R. Warner to John P. Adams, Sept. 9, 1969, Administrative Records of the Division of General Welfare Board of the General Board of Church and Society, 1887–2005 (hereafter Administration Records of the DGW), General Commission on Archive and History, United Methodist Church, Madison, NJ, 1477-3-2-08.

21. Hattie Kendrick to Martha Cobb, 1969, KBFP-LOC, box 20, folder 10.

22. Concerned Clergy, *Cairo: Were You There?*, 3–4.

23. Concerned Clergy, *Cairo: Were You There?*, 8; Robert A. Reicher to Gov. Richard Ogilvie, Apr. 2, 1969, ICC Records, ALPL, box 19, folder 8; "Illinois Priests' Group Backs Father at Cairo," *St. Louis Post-Dispatch*, Mar. 30, 1969.

24. Correspondence between Gerald Montroy and the author, Oct. 13, 2014; "Bishop Names Fr. Bodewes to Cairo Post," *Cairo Evening Citizen*, Apr. 21, 1969.

25. National Council of the Churches of Christ, "Resolution on the Crisis in the Nation," Sept. 14, 1967, ICC Records, ALPL, box 11, folder 5.

26. James R. Findlay, *Church People in the Struggle: The National Council of Churches and the Black Freedom Movement, 1950–1970* (New York: Oxford University Press, 1993), 188.

27. National Council of Churches, "Summary Report on 40 Councils of Churches Replying to the Questions on the Crisis in the Nation or Responding to Personal Interviews to Questions on the Crisis," Apr. 1968, ICC Records, ALPL, box 11, folder 4.

28. "A Progress Report from the Commission on Christian Social Action to the Board of Directors of the ICC," June 1, 1966, ICC Records, ALPL, box 10, folder 24.

29. The other agencies that participated in the formation of the Illinois Migrant Council included the Catholic Council on Working Life, the Church Federation of Greater Chicago, and the Bishops Committee for the Spanish Speaking; Frederick A. Roblee to Illinois Legislator and the Illinois Delegation in the Congress of the United States, Feb. 23, 1967, ICC Records, ALPL, box 10, folder 27; "A Proposal for the Alexander County Council of Community Organizations," Apr. 1969, ICC Records, ALPL, box 10, folder 30.

30. William K. Fox, "Black Participation in Council of Churches," Oct. 21, 1968, ICC Records, ALPL, box 11, folder 4.

31. Illinois Council of Churches, "The Inter-Organization Task Force for Community Action," Feb. 1970, ICC Records, ALPL, box 11, folder 8.

32. Minutes of the Task Force Committee, Apr. 29, 1968, ICC Records, ALPL, box 10, folder 31.

33. Ibid., Mar. 13, 1968, box 10, folder 29.

34. On the Interreligious Foundation for Community Organization (IFCO), see Lecky and Wright, *Black Manifesto*, 7–11, and Sawyer, *Black Ecumenism*, 84–86. On the Episcopal General Convention Special Program (GCSP), see Gardiner G. Shattuck Jr., *Episcopalians and Race: Civil War to Civil Rights* (Lexington: University Press of Kentucky, 2000), 179–212.

35. United Presbyterian Church, USA, *Minutes of the General Assembly of the United Presbyterian Church in the U.S.A.*, pt. 1 (Philadelphia: Office of the General Assembly, 1973), 671; "The Inter-Organization Task Force for Community Action," Feb. 1970, ICC Records, ALPL, box 11, folder 8.

36. Roger Ebert, "Taylor to Address Campus Protestors," *Daily Illini* (Urbana), Sept. 19, 1963; Paul Wood, "Black Churches Have History of Activism," *News-Gazette* (Champaign, IL), Feb. 22, 1987; Lawrence Maushard, "Black Panther Leader Mark Clark Remembered as 'Quiet Leader' on Anniversary of Infamous Police Raid," *Journal Star* (Peoria, IL), Dec. 12, 1999; Bad Subjects Production Team, *Bad Subjects: Political Education for Everyday Life* (New York: New York University Press, 1998), 86.

37. Blaine Ramsey Jr., "Report on the Special Task Force Committee," 1969, ICC Records, ALPL, box 11, folder 8; "Officers of the Special Task Force Committee," Mar. 28, 1969, ICC Records, ALPL, box 10, folder 29; minutes of the Special Task Force Committee, Apr. 14, 1969, ICC Records, ALPL, box 10, folder 29.

38. Blaine Ramsey Jr., "Report on the Special Task Force Committee," 1969, ICC Records, ALPL, box 11, folder 8.

39. Blaine Ramsey Jr., "Report on the Special Task Force Committee," 1969, ICC Records, ALPL, box 11, folder 8; "Functional and Structural Analysis of the Inter-Organization Task Force for Community Action," Apr. 11, 1971, ICC Records, ALPL, box 10, folder 30.

40. E. D. Bruegemann to Rev. Fay Smith, May 13, 1969, ICC Records, ALPL, box 19, folder 8; Task Force Committee, "Financial Report," 1969, ICC Records, ALPL, box 10, folder 29; "UF Gets $500 from Priests Organizations," *Cairo Evening Citizen*, Aug. 20, 1969; United Methodist Church (US) Southern Illinois Conference, *Official Journal and Yearbook of the 118th Session of the Southern Illinois Conference of the United Methodist Church* (Conference Committee on Journal Publications, 1969), 126–27.

41. "Legislature to Investigate Race Hate in Cairo," *Chicago Daily Defender*, Apr. 16, 1969; Joseph L. Turner, "Set First Hearing on Cairo," *Chicago Daily Defender*, Apr. 23, 1969; "Illinois House Committee to Move Hearings to Cairo," *Cairo Evening Citizen*, May 2, 1969.

42. "Simon to Arrive this Afternoon," *Cairo Evening Citizen*, Apr. 17, 1969; "Simon Seeks to End Racial Rift in Cairo," *St. Louis Post-Dispatch*, Apr. 18, 1969; "Lt. Gov. Simon's Report on Cairo," *Cairo Evening Citizen*, Apr. 22, 1969; "Senate Passes Measure to Outlaw Vigilantes," *Cairo Evening Citizen*, Apr. 16, 1969; "Repeal of Vigilante Bill Voted by Illinois Senate," *Cairo Evening Citizen*, May 6, 1969; "Vigilante Bill Sent to Ogilvie," *Cairo Evening Citizen*, June 19, 1969.

43. "Fire Damages Office at Pyramid Court," *Cairo Evening Citizen*, Apr. 25, 1969; "Violence Flares Anew in Cairo," *Chicago Daily Defender*, Aug. 26, 1969; "Violence Flares Anew in Strife-Torn Cairo," *Chicago Daily Defender*, Apr. 28, 1969; "Violence Flares in Cairo, Bombs Rock City," *Chicago Daily Defender*, Apr. 29, 1969; "Black Militants See More Violence as Guard Leaves," *Chicago Daily Defender*, May 5, 1969; "Fire-bombings Occur in Cairo over Weekend," *Cairo Evening Citizen*, Apr. 28, 1969; "White Hats: Good Guys or Hardcore Bigots?," *Chicago Daily Defender*, May 7, 1969.

44. "Stenzel Outlines Program to Relieve Cairo Tension," *Cairo Evening Citizen*, May 16, 1969; "Cairo Has New Police Chief: Carl Clutts Resigns Post," *Cairo Evening Citizen*, May 27, 1969.

45. "3 More Fire-bombings in Cairo," *Cairo Evening Citizen*, June 13, 1969; "Davis, Jackson Tour Cairo, Ill.," *Chicago Daily Defender*, June 18, 1969.

46. "Breadbasket to Launch Downstate Hunger Moves," *Chicago Daily Defender*, June 12, 1969; "Cairo a Feudal City: Jackson," *Chicago Daily Defender*, June 19, 1969; "Nation Eyes Violence in Black Areas," *Chicago Daily Defender*, June 28, 1969; "Photos Show Breadbasket Marchers' Anti-Hunger Drive," *Chicago Daily Defender*, July 14, 1969.

47. Quote from "Depression Blamed in Cairo Riot," *Chicago Daily Defender*, June 24, 1969; "Gov. Ogilvie Orders State Police to Patrol Cairo," *Chicago Daily Defender*, June 21, 1969; "Deputy Cards Being Collected," *Cairo Evening Citizen*, June 24, 1969; "Agreement on Dissolution of White Hats," *Cairo Evening Citizen*, June 23, 1969; "Whites in Cairo Make Promise to End White Hats," *Chicago Daily Defender*, June 24, 1969; "Mass Meeting Tonight at St. Mary's Park," *Cairo Evening Citizen*, June 30, 1969; "United Citizens for Community Action Formed in Cairo," *Cairo Evening Citizen*, July 1, 1969; "Tight Curfew in Cairo: Relatively Quiet Night," *Cairo Evening Citizen*, June 27, 1969.

48. ICC Special Task Force Committee, minutes for meeting, July 6, 1969, ICC Records, ALPL, box 19, folder 29; "Illinois Church Council Group Backs United Front Resolution," *Cairo Evening Citizen*, July 10, 1969; "United Front to Seek Meeting in Capital with Ogilvie, Scott," *Cairo Evening Citizen*, July 9, 1969; "United Front to Hold Rally Tonight at Cairo Church," *Cairo Evening Citizen*, July 9, 1969; Joseph L. Turner, "Gov. to Hear Cairo's Blacks," *Chicago Daily Defender*, July 14, 1969; "Cairo Leader Planning March on Springfield," *Chicago Daily Defender*, July 10, 1969; "Cairo Peace Pow-Wow Set," *Chicago Daily Defender*, July 7, 1969; "Representatives from Cairo Meet with Governor, Attorney General," *Cairo Evening Citizen*, July 16, 1969; "Seek Immediate Action by Ogilvie in Solution to Problems in Cairo," *Cairo Evening Citizen*, July 25, 1969.

49. "Ogilvie Says He Won't Let Sit-In Continue," *Cairo Evening Citizen*, July 24, 1969; Manker Harris interview; minutes from the first organizational meeting for the proposed United Christian Front, Aug. 7, 1969, ICC Records, ALPL, box 19, folder 15; "More Demonstrators Arrested: Several Refuse to Post Bond," *Cairo Evening Citizen*, July 24, 1969; "22 Are Arrested in Springfield 'Lay-in,'" *Cairo Evening Citizen*, Aug. 1, 1969.

50. Minutes from the second United Christian Front meeting, Aug. 11, 1969, ICC Papers, ALPL, box 19, folder 15; minutes from the first organizational meeting for the proposed United Christian Front, Aug. 7, 1969, ICC Records, ALPL, box 19, folder 15.

51. "Methodists Discuss Ministry to Black Community in Cairo," *Cairo Evening Citizen*, June 3, 1969; "Theologian Urges Quicker Reconciliation with Negroes," *Cairo Evening Citizen*, June 5, 1969; "Methodists Establish Task Force to Minister to Minority Groups," *Cairo Evening Citizen*, June 6, 1969; United Methodist Church, *Journal and Yearbook of the 118th Session*, 64, 77, 214; "The Southern Illinois Annual Conference of the United Methodist Church

and the Legal Aid Program in Cairo," June 1969, Administrative Records of the DGW, 1477-3-2-08.

52. Rev. Bernard Bodewes and Rev. Gerald Montroy to Rev. John P. Adams, July 3, 1969, Administrative Records of the DGW, 1477-3-2-07; John P. Adams to Dr. A. Dudley Ward and Dr. Grover C. Bagby, Aug. 21, 1969, Administrative Records of the DGW, 1477-3-2-07; John P. Adams to Milan C. Miskovsky, June 30, 1969, Administrative Records of the DGW, 1477-3-2-07.

53. James Robertson to Milan C. Miskovsky, July 29, 1969, Administrative Records of the DGW, 1477-3-2-07; "The Southern Illinois Annual Conference of the United Methodist Church and the Legal Aid Program in Cairo," June 1969, Administrative Records of the DGW, 1477-3-2-08; Milan C. Miskovsky to John P. Adams, Dec. 17, 1969, Administrative Records of the DGW, 1477-3-2-08; "Attorney Meeting Legal Needs of Blacks," *Monitor*, Feb. 5, 1970.

54. Seng, "Cairo Experience," 291, 295–96.

55. Letters from John P. Adams to Rev. Robert Chapman, Dec. 18, 1969, and Jan. 8, 1970, Administrative Records of the DGW, 1477-3-2-08.

56. Manker Harris to John P. Adams, Jan. 31, 1970, Administrative Records of the DGW, 1477-3-2-12.

57. Charles E. Koen to Lewis Andrew, Sept. 1, 1970, Administrative Records of the DGW, 1477-3-2-12; Peter J. Connell to Rev. Charles Koen, Oct. 2, 1970, Administrative Records of the DGW, 1477-3-2-08.

58. Charles E. Koen to Lewis Andrew, Sept. 1, 1970, Administrative Records of the DGW, 1477-3-2-12; Charles E. Koen to John Adams, Sept. 1, 1970, Administrative Records of the DGW, 1477-3-2-12.

59. Charles E. Koen to Peter Connell, Sept. 1, 1970, Administrative Records of the DGW, 1477-3-2-12; Charles E. Koen to John Adams, Sept. 1, 1970, Administrative Records of the DGW, 1477-3-2-12.

60. Lucius Walker, "IFCO and the Crisis of American Society," in *Black Manifesto: Religion, Racism, and Reparations*, ed. Robert S. Leckie and Elliott Wright (New York: Sheed & Ward, 1969), 134; proposal made by the United Christian Front to the Interreligious Federation of Community Organizations, 1969, ICC Records, ALPL, box 11, folder 8; United Front Community News Service, "Weekly News Summary," Oct. 4, 1969, ICC Records, ALPL, box 11, folder 8; "IFCO Grant Proposal Record: United Front of Cairo," Aug. 27, 1970, IFCO Papers, box 35, folder 78.

61. "IFCO Grant Proposal Record: United Front of Cairo," IFCO Papers, box 35, folder 78; untitled caption, *United Front News*, Oct. 24, 1970.

62. "A Proposal for the Funding of a Program in Economic Development for Cairo, Illinois," 1970, IFCO Papers, box 35, folder 78.

63. Leon Modeste, "The End of a Beginning," *Black World*, Jan. 1974, 86.

64. "Self-Development Fund Now Exceeds $1,600,000 Say Presbyterians," *New York Amsterdam News*, Dec. 4, 1971; "UPUSA Announces Grant for 'Self-Development,'" *Presbyterian Journal*, Dec. 8, 1971.

65. Episcopal Church Diocesan Press Service, "Twelve Grants Approved for Community Action Projects," Feb. 19, 1970.

66. "Cairo Blacks Get Church Funds," *Monitor*, Feb. 3, 1972; United Presbyterian Church, USA, *Minutes of the General Assembly of the United Presbyterian Church in the U.S.A.*, pt. 1 (Philadelphia: Office of the General Assembly, 1973), 98, 826–32, 836, 840–42; Bryant George to Blaine Ramsey, Aug. 10, 1972, ICC Records, ALPL, box 19, folder 14; "UPUSA Announces Grant," *Presbyterian Journal*, Dec. 8, 1971.

67. "Progress Report from the United Front," 1969, ICC Records, ALPL, box 11, folder 8; "United Front Inaugurates Operation Need," *Cairo Evening Citizen*, Oct. 14, 1969; "Operation Need Continues to Supply Food and Clothes," *Monitor*, Feb. 19, 1970; Renny Freeman, "The United Black Front of Cairo, Illinois, a Situational Report," Aug. 1971, New Detroit Inc. Collection, Archives of Labor and Urban Affairs, Walter P. Reuther Library, Wayne State University, box 195, folder 46; "Visitors Attend Weekly Rally," *Monitor*, Mar. 3, 1970.

68. Quote taken from "Cairo Shocks Medicos," *Chicago Daily Defender*, Feb. 18, 1970. On the Flying Black Medics, see Leonidas H. Berry, *I Wouldn't Take Nothin' for My Journey: Two Centuries of an Afro-American Minister's Family* (Chicago: Johnson Publishing, 1979), 409–11; "Medics, Aides Fly to Cairo," *Chicago Daily Defender*, Feb. 16, 1970; "Free Medical Clinic to Open," *Monitor*, Feb. 12, 1970; "Medical Clinic in Operation," *Monitor*, Feb. 19, 1970; "Chicago Black Churches Answer Cairo's Hunger Call," *Jet*, Jan. 22, 1970; "Flying Black Medics Dramatize Cairo's Poor Health Care," *Jet*, Mar. 5, 1970; "Flying Black Medics," *Ebony*, June 1970; "Disciples of Hippocrates," *Black Enterprise*, Feb. 1975.

69. Berry, *I Wouldn't Take Nothin'*, 409–11; "Disciples of Hippocrates," *Black Enterprise*, Feb. 1975; "Medical Clinic Open for the Needy," *Monitor*, Jan. 14, 1971; "Community Clinic Attracts Many Patients," *Monitor*, Apr. 8, 1971; "Mobile Health Unit Presented to St. Mary's Hospital," *Monitor*, Apr. 22, 1971.

70. Figures taken from Modeste, "End of a Beginning," *Black World*, Jan. 1974, 86–87; "UPUSA Announces Grant," *Presbyterian Journal*, Dec. 8, 1971; guide to the Interreligious Foundation for Community Organization Records, 1966–1984, Schomburg Center for Research in Black Culture, New York Public Library.

5. The Recession of National Spirit

1. "Problem Child Ignored Too Long," *Chicago Sun-Times*, Jan. 10, 1972.

2. Andrew Wilson, "Racially Tense Cairo, Ill., Quiet but Loathing," *Washington Post*, Sept. 25, 1972.

3. Roberta Garner, *Contemporary Movements and Ideologies* (New York: McGraw-Hill, 1996), 12.

4. Traditional interpretations of the black power movement's decline were hampered by a prevailing civil rights story that portrayed black power as a chaotic and violent aberration that served to undermine earlier civil rights struggles. According to such accounts, black power's demise followed shortly after and was the almost inevitable outcome of the movement's internal disorganization, overblown rhetoric, and failure to establish what political scientist Doug McAdam termed a "broad-based issue consensus" that could unify participants and mobilize coalitional support. Historian Clayborne Carson also underscored what he perceived as black power's fatal retreat from the community organizing tradition that typified earlier civil rights activism. When combined with narrowing political opportunities and rampant state repression, many scholars have contended that black power's obituary was all but written by the end of the sixties. See McAdam, *Political Process and Black Insurgency*, 186, and Carson, *In Struggle*, esp. 287–306.

5. Quotation taken from Blaine Ramsey, Report of the Inter-Organization Task Force for Community Action, May 28, 1970, ICC Records, ALPL, box 11, folder 20.

6. The concept of "tactical innovation" was developed by political scientist Doug McAdam and relates to the efforts of subjugated groups "to devise some way to overcome the basic powerlessness that has confined them to a position of institutionalized political impotence." According to McAdam, to secure concessions subjugated groups often deploy disruptive tactics such as strikes, boycotts, and demonstrations. McAdam cautions, however, "Even the most successful tactic is likely to be effectively countered by movement opponents if relied upon too long." Thus, activists must continually *innovate* in their tactics in response to the counter-moves of their opponents. See Doug McAdam, "Tactical Innovation and the Pace of Insurgency," *American Sociological Review* 48, no. 6 (Dec. 1983): 735–54 [736].

7. Watson, "Cairo," *PROUD*, Oct. 1971.

8. "United Citizens for Community Action formed in Cairo," *Cairo Evening Citizen*, July 1, 1969; "Statement of Policy and Position of United Citizens for Community Action," *Cairo Evening Citizen*, July 18, 1969; "White Citizens' Council Gains Strength in Cairo," *St. Louis Post-Dispatch*, Dec. 10, 1969; James N. Gregory, *The Southern Diaspora: How the Great Migrations of Black and White Southerners Transformed America* (Chapel Hill: University of North Carolina Press, 2005), 306.

9. Kohn, "Civil War in Cairo"; "White Citizens Council Founder to Speak in Cairo," *Monitor*, May 28, 1970; "Rap Nazis in Cairo Fray," *Chicago Daily Defender*, Aug. 18, 1970; "Responsibility for Riots Placed on Mayor, White Hats, and Nazis," *United Front News*, Aug. 15, 1970. "Nazis Surface," *United Front News*, Aug. 22, 1970; "American Nazi Party Supports Cairo Whites," *Monitor*, Aug. 20, 1970; "U.C.C.A. Plays Host to Shannon Meeting," *Tri-State Informer*, Jan. 1972; editorial, *Tri-State Informer*, Oct. 1971.

10. "Stenzel, Petersen Resign as Mayor, Police Chief," *Cairo Evening Citizen*, Sept. 16, 1969; Cairo City Council minutes, Sept. 15, 1969; Preston Ewing Jr. interview.

11. Cairo City Council minutes, Oct. 13, 1969.

12. Lukas, "Bad Day at Cairo," *New York Times* magazine, Feb. 21, 1971.

13. Quote taken from "Report Calls Cairo Police Incompetent," *Monitor*, Dec. 10, 1970.

14. Kohn, "Civil War in Cairo."

15. "Stenzel, Petersen Resign," *Cairo Evening Citizen*, Sept. 16, 1969.

16. Kohn, "Civil War in Cairo."

17. Lukas, "Bad Day at Cairo," *New York Times* magazine, Feb. 21, 1971; Cairo Task Force, "Chronology," 1971, Alliance to End Repression Records, Chicago Historical Society (hereafter AER-CHS), Chicago, box 7, folder 34; Cairo United Front, "Incidents of Violence, by Whites, against the Black Community since March 31, 1969," Oct. 30, 1970, James Forman Papers, LOC, box 69, folder 10.

18. "State Police Continue Harassment of Blacks," *United Front News*, Aug. 29, 1970; "State Police Plot to Kill Blacks," *Monitor*, Feb. 12, 1970; "State Police Try Sneak Attack into Pyramid Court," *United Front News*, Sept. 12, 1970; United Front of Cairo, "The History of State Police Activity in Cairo, Illinois, from March 1969," 1970, AER-CHS, box 7, folder 36.

19. Cairo Task Force, "Chronology," 1971, AER-CHS, box 7, folder 34; "Blacks Arrested between March 31, 1969–March 7, 1971," James Forman Papers, LOC, box 69, folder 11.

20. Manker Harris interview.

21. "15 Blacks in Cairo Indicted," *Chicago Daily Defender*, Aug. 24, 1970; "Blacks Arrested between March 31, 1969–March 7, 1971," James Forman Papers, LOC, box 69, folder 11; "Cairo Blacks Set Mammoth Demonstration," *Chicago Daily Defender*, July 8, 1970; "Violence Erupts in Cairo," *United Front News*, June 27, 1970; "Peyton Berbling Shirks His Duties," *United Front News*, Aug. 22, 1970.

22. "Bishop Orders Blacks to Leave Church," *National Catholic Reporter*, Jan. 8, 1971; Cairo Task Force, "Chronology," 1971, AER-CHS, box 7, folder 34; "Charges Dropped against Rev. Harris and Others," *Monitor*, Jan. 28, 1971.

23. Clydia Koen interview; Special Agent in Charge (SAC), St. Louis Field Office, letters to director FBI, Feb. 14 and 28, 1969, FBI Counterintelligence Program, File no. 100-448006, Federal Bureau of Investigation, Washington, DC; "Bare Smear Tactics OKd by Hoover," *Chicago Daily News*, Dec. 3, 1975; James Kirkpatrick Davis, *Assault on the Left: The FBI and the Sixties Antiwar Movement* (Westport, CT: Praeger, 1997), 96–97; Looker, *"Point from which creation begins,"* 44–45; SAC, Springfield Field Office, letter to director FBI, Aug. 31, 1970, FBI Freedom of Information Act file, Subject: Black United Front (Cairo, Illinois) (hereafter cited as BUF FOIA file).

24. SAC, Springfield Field Office, letters to director FBI, Nov. 27, 30 and Dec. 19, 21, 1970, BUF FOIA file; director FBI, letters to SAC Springfield Field Office, Dec. 1 and 4, 1970, BUF FOIA file.

25. SAC, Springfield Field Office, letters to director FBI, Jan. 8, 13, and 15, 1971, BUF FOIA file; Freeman, "United Black Front of Cairo," Aug. 1971, New Detroit Inc. Collection, Archives of Labor and Urban Affairs, Walter P. Reuther Library, Wayne State University, box 195, folder 46; Lukas, "Bad Day at Cairo," *New York Times* magazine, Feb. 21, 1971; Kohn, "Civil War in Cairo."

26. "'70 Was a Slow Year for Civil Rights," *Chicago Daily Defender*, Jan. 2, 1971; "United Front Marches On," *Monitor*, Feb. 26, 1970.

27. "More Money Needed for Bail Bonds," *United Front News*, Dec. 19, 1970; "James Chairs, Chief of Staff, First to Be Arrested at Governor's Office," *United Front News*, Jan. 16, 1971; "State Police Continues Actions against Blacks," *Monitor*, Feb. 18, 1971; "Court Says Police Raids Were Illegal," *Monitor*, Mar. 25, 1971.

28. Blaine Ramsey, "Report of the Inter-Organization Task Force for Community Action," May 28, 1970, ICC Records, ALPL, box 11, folder 20.

29. The term "Christian Silent Minority" was coined by Daniel K. Williams in *God's Own Party: The Making of the Christian Right* (New York: Oxford University Press, 2010), 80. For broader studies of grassroots religious conservatism during this period, see William Martin, *With God on Our Side: The Rise of the Religious Right in America* (New York: Broadway Books, 1996); Douglas E. Cowan, *The Remnant Spirit: Conservative Reform in Mainline Protestantism* (Westport, CT: Praeger, 2003); Darren Dochuk, *From Bible Belt to Sunbelt: Plain-Folk Religion, Grassroots Politics, and the Rise of Evangelical Conservatism* (New York: Norton, 2011).

30. Jeffrey K. Hadden, *The Gathering Storm in the Churches* (Garden City, NY: Doubleday, 1969) 111, 117–18, 142, 149–51, 180; Yoshio Fukuyama, "Parishioners' Attitudes toward Issues in the Civil Rights Movement," *Sociological Analysis* 29, no. 2 (Summer 1968), 97.

31. Will Oursler, *Protestant Power and the Coming Revolution* (Garden City, NY: Doubleday, 1971), 165, 181; Findlay, *Church People in the Struggle*, 206; Hadden, *Gathering Storm*, 185, 224.

32. James DeForest Murch, *The Protestant Revolt: The Road to Freedom for American Churches* (Arlington, VA: Crestwood Books, 1967), 86.

33. Oursler, *Protestant Power*, 17, 165, 182–83; Gardiner H. Shattuck Jr., *Episcopalians and Race: Civil War to Civil Rights* (Lexington: University Press of Kentucky, 2000), 206.

34. Shattuck, *Episcopalians and Race*, 190–91, 199–201; Mary Sudman Donovan, "Beyond the Parallel Church: Strategies of Separatism and Integration in the Governing Councils of the Episcopal Church," in *Episcopal Women: Gender, Spirituality, and Commitment in an American Mainline Denomination*, ed. Catherine M. Prelinger (New York: Oxford University Press, 1992) 147.

35. Leon Modeste, "The Church Ends a Good Program," *Amsterdam News*, Sept. 22, 1973.

36. Rt. Rev. John E. Hines, "Message from the Chair," *Diocesan Press Service*, Dec. 11, 1973; Modeste, "End of a Beginning," *Black World*, Jan. 1974, 86–87; Shattuck, *Episcopalians and Race*, 211; Modeste, "Church Ends a Good Program," *Amsterdam News*, Sept. 22, 1973.

37. "Clergy Calls for Fulfillment," *Los Angeles Sentinel*, Feb. 7, 1974; "Urge Presbyterians to Meet Human Development Pledge," *Chicago Defender*, Feb. 9, 1974; "Moratorium Lifted," *Washington Post*, Feb. 7, 1975.

38. United Presbyterian Church, USA, *Minutes of the General Assembly of the United Presbyterian Church in the U.S.A.*, part 1 (Philadelphia: Office of the General Assembly, 1972) 28, 32–33, 35–36, 37–42, 46–47, 52–54, 60, 65, 99, 199; Charles D. Hindman to Blaine Ramsey, July 31, 1972, ICC Records, ALPL, box 19, folder 4.

39. "IFCO Reflects Mood of Churches Retreat from Ecumenical Commitment," *Chicago Daily Defender*, Jan. 2, 1971.

40. "Church Council Dismissal Protested," *New York Times*, Feb. 21, 1974; "Church Council Sit-In Ends in Compromise after a Day," *New York Times*, Feb. 22, 1974; "Activists Take Over Offices of National Church Council," *New York Amsterdam News*, Feb. 23, 1974; "Salute to Father Chapman," *New York Amsterdam News*, Dec. 15, 1973.

41. Blaine Ramsey Jr., "New Directions for Funding Community Organizations," Jan. 26, 1971, ICC Records, ALPL, box 11, folder 25.

42. Bishop Albert A. Chambers to Charles McClellan, Nov. 5, 1968, ICC Records, ALPL, box 19, folder 4; "Twelve Grants Approved for Community Action Projects," Episcopal Church Diocesan Press Service, Feb. 19, 1970; United Front of Cairo, "IFCO Grant Proposal Records," Aug. 27, 1970, IFCO Papers, box 35, folder 78; United Presbyterian Church, USA, *Minutes of the General Assembly of the United Presbyterian Church in the U.S.A.*, pt. 1 (Philadelphia: Office of the General Assembly, 1972), 98, 836, 840–42; Bryant George to Blaine Ramsey Jr., Aug. 10, 1972, ICC Records, ALPL, box 19, folder 14; "UPUSA Announces Grant," *Presbyterian Journal*, Dec. 8, 1971.

43. Bryant George to Blaine Ramsey Jr., Aug. 10, 1972, ICC Records, ALPL, box 19, folder 14; "Cairo Blacks Get Church Funds," *Monitor*, Feb. 3, 1972; Hattie Kendrick to Charlotte Brooks, Sept. 1975, KBFP-LOC, box 22, folder 1; political cartoon, *Tri-State Informer*, Aug.–Sept. 1971.

44. Correspondence between Gerald Montroy and the author, Oct. 14, 2014; "Priest Speaks Out on Cairo Situation," *Monitor*, Jan. 28, 1971; "Bishop Orders Blacks to Leave Church," *National Catholic Reporter*, Jan. 8, 1971; "Black Group to Be Kicked Out by White Bishop," *Monitor*, Jan. 7, 1971.

45. Blaine Ramsey Jr. to Rev. Albert R. Zuroweste, Jan. 26, 1971, ICC Records, ALPL, box 19, folder 26; Hattie Kendrick to Bishop Albert R. Zuroweste, Jan. 8, 1971, KBFP-LOC, box 20, folder 12.

46. "An Important Message," *Monitor*, Jan. 7, 1971; "Priest Speaks Out," *Monitor*, Jan. 28, 1971; "Nuns Oppose Eviction of Black Group," *Monitor*, Feb. 4, 1971; "SIU Priests Speak against Bishop on Cairo," *Monitor*, Jan. 21, 1971; "Cairo Divides Catholics," *Monitor*, Mar. 4, 1971; "Eviction Negotiations Fail," *Monitor*, Feb. 18, 1971; "Eviction Back in Hands of Bishop," *Monitor*, Feb. 23, 1971.

47. "Black and White Catholics Disagree in Eviction Meeting," *Monitor*, June 1, 1972; "Bishop Turns Lights Out on Blacks," *Monitor*, Sept. 2, 1971; E. Charles Geittmann to the Cairo United Front, May 2, 1972, ICC Records, ALPL, box 19, folder 15; Leon Page to Father Casper Deis, May 8, 1972, ICC Records, ALPL, box 19, folder 15; "White Catholics Plan Eviction of Blacks," *Monitor*, May 4, 1972; "Church Property to Become Free Site for New Housing," *Cairo Evening Citizen*, Mar. 1972.

48. "Priest Speaks Out," *Monitor*, Jan. 28, 1971.

49. Ibid.

50. Joseph A. Ruskay, "New Muzzle for Churchmen," *Nation*, Oct. 2, 1972; Dean Kelley, "Freedom of Religion," in *Papers from the Conference on American Freedom* (Washington, DC: n.p., 1973), 55–59; Senate Committee on Appropriations, *Taxpayer Assistance and Compliance Programs: Hearings before the Subcommittee of the Department of the Treasury, U.S. Postal Service, and General Government Appropriations*, 93rd Cong., 1st sess. (Washington, DC: GPO, 1973), 587–88.

51. Transcription of interview with Mayor Pete Thomas of Cairo on WDZ, Decatur (IL), Jan. 20, 1970, ICC Records, ALPL, box 11, folder 8; minutes of the Inter-Organization Task Force for Community Action, Oct. 7, 1971, ICC Records, ALPL, box 11, folder 25; Blaine Ramsey Jr. to Carl C. Hoffman of the revenue office in Cairo, July 8, 1971, ICC Records, ALPL, box 19, folder 15; Blaine Ramsey Jr. to Atty. Gen. William J. Scott, Aug. 27, 1971, ICC Records, ALPL, box 19, folder 15; Atty. Gen. William J. Scott to Mable Hollis, Sept. 7, 1971, ICC Records, ALPL, box 19, folder 14.

52. Copies of the IRS summons issued to national church executives on July 26, 1972, are available in the Administrative Records of the DGW, 1477-3-2-10; minutes of meeting on Internal Revenue Service summonses, Aug. 2, 1972, ICC Records, ALPL, box 19, folder 15.

53. Minutes of meeting on Internal Revenue Service summonses, Aug. 2, 1972, ICC Records, ALPL, box 19, folder 15.

54. Blaine Ramsey Jr. to unknown recipient, Sept. 15, 1972, ICC Records, ALPL, box 19, folder 26; minutes of special meeting concerning Cairo, Illinois, Sept. 20, 1972, Administrative Records of the DGW, 1477-3-2-12.

55. Kelley, "Freedom of Religion," 59.

56. Director FBI letter to SAC, Washington Field Office, Dec. 18, 1970, FBI Files on Black Extremist Organizations, Pt. 1: COINTELPRO Files on

Black Hate Groups and Investigation of the Deacons for Defense and Justice (microform edition) Reel 6, 0367.

57. Letter from "A Concerned Episcopalian" to an unidentified Episcopal church executive, n.d., FBI Files on Black Extremist Organizations, Reel 6, 0369–70.

58. Director FBI letter to SAC, Springfield Field Office, Jan. 19, 1971, FBI Files on Black Extremist Organizations, Reel 6, 0463–64; SAC, Springfield Field Office, letter to director FBI, Jan. 7, 1971, FBI Files on Black Extremist Organizations, Reel 6, 0461–62; Manker Harris interview.

59. "Future of Cairo Rest on Election Tues." *Monitor*, Apr. 15, 1971; "Mayor Loses Control of City Council," *Monitor*, Apr. 22, 1971; Kohn, "Civil War in Cairo"; "Cairo Mayor Resigns," *Monitor*, Oct. 28, 1971; "No Hope of Progress under New Mayor," *Monitor*, Nov. 24, 1971; "James Walder Chosen Mayor," *Tri-State Informer*, Dec. 1971; "Great Day for Cairo Whites," *Monitor*, Apr. 29, 1971; "U.C.C.A. Plays Host To Shannon Meeting," *Tri-State Informer*, Jan. 1972; "Cairo Retains Responsible Leaders," *Citizen Informer*, May 1975.

60. "Vigilantes—Violence," *United Front News*, May 1971; "Cairo Mayor Thomas Resigns," *Tri-State Informer*, Nov. 1971; "Cairo Government about Broke," *Monitor*, Feb. 4, 1971; Kohn, "Civil War in Cairo"; "City Council Rejects New Housing," *Monitor*, May 13, 1971; "Housing Program to Be Explained to City Council," *Monitor*, May 20, 1971.

61. Gerald Montroy correspondence with the author, Oct. 2 and 7, 2014; "Three Whites Almost Killed by Police-Vigilantes," *Monitor*, June 3, 1971.

62. "Bobby Williams: A Civil Rights Leader Fights for His Freedom," *Win*, Dec. 26, 1974; "Bobby Williams Convicted," *United Front News*, Oct. 3, 1970; "Bobby Williams Convicted," *United Front News*, Sept. 26, 1970; "Blacks Fighting Court Actions," *Monitor*, July 8, 1971; "Guilty Verdict in Bobby Williams Case," *Monitor*, Nov. 4, 1971; "Given 5 Years Prison Term," *Monitor*, Dec. 2, 1971; "Williams Happy over Court's Decision," *Monitor*, June 15, 1972.

63. Bobby Williams interview; "Blacks Fighting Court Actions," *Monitor*, July 8, 1971; "Rev. Koen Begins Jail Term," *Monitor*, July 22, 1971; "Rev. Koen's Jailing Hit by Blacks Here," *Chicago Daily Defender*, Aug. 2, 1971; "Set Rallies to Help Jailed Rev. Koen," *Chicago Daily Defender*, Aug. 25, 1971; "Announce Move to Free Cairo's Rev. Koen from St. Louis Jail," *Chicago Daily Defender*, Aug. 12, 1971; "Koen on 'Water Fast,'" *Monitor*, July 29, 1971; "Koen Recovering from Illness," *Monitor*, Aug. 12, 1971; "Cairo Whites Angered by Koen's Release," *Monitor*, Sept. 9, 1971; "Koen Paroled: Is Hospitalized," *Chicago Daily Defender*, Sept. 7, 1971.

64. "The Cairo Scene Autumn 1971," *Tri-State Informer*, Oct. 1971; "New Plans for Black Movement Being Set," *Monitor*, Dec. 2, 1971; Koen, *Cairo Story*, 30–31; Wilson, "Racially-Tense Cairo," *Washington Post*, Sept. 25, 1972;

"8 Major Civil Rights Cases Pending," *Monitor*, Aug. 31, 1972; Bobby Williams interview.

65. "Koen Backs Walker," *Chicago Daily Defender*, Nov. 7, 1972; "United Front Maps Strategy," *Chicago Defender*, Sept. 15, 1972; "Koen Lauds State's Black Voters," *Chicago Daily Defender*, Nov. 9, 1972.

66. "3 County Medics to Cairo," *Chicago Defender*, Mar. 14, 1973; Joy Darrow, "Cairo Has Changed—For the Better?," *Chicago Defender*, Nov. 10, 1973; "United Front Maps Strategy," *Chicago Defender*, Sept. 15, 1972.

67. Bud Farrar, "Walker's Charisma Has Faded Away," *Southern Illinoisan*, May 19, 1974; "Say Walker Has Deaf Ear," *Chicago Defender*, Mar. 16, 1974.

68. Vernon Jarrett, "Battling for Voters' Rights," *Chicago Tribune*, Sept. 27, 1981; Bobby Williams interview.

69. Patrick E. Gauen, "Civil Rights Activist Seeks Role in Illinois Governor's Race," *St. Louis Post-Dispatch*, Dec. 26, 1985.

Conclusion

1. US Commission on Civil Rights, *Hearing before the Commission*, 3, 325; Lukas, "Bad Day at Cairo," *New York Times* magazine, Feb. 21, 1971; US Commission on Civil Rights, *Cairo, Illinois: A Symbol of Racial Polarization* (Washington, DC: n.p., 1973), 13.

2. Illinois Advisory Committee, *Decade of Waiting in Cairo*, 29, 32.

3. Preston Ewing Jr. interview; Seng, "Cairo Experience," 305–10.

4. Seng, "Cairo Experience," 310–12; Eastman, "Speaking Truth to Power"; "Rule At-Large Voting Hits Blacks in Cairo," *Chicago Defender*, Dec. 17, 1975; "Downstate Primary: 2 Black Aldermen for Cairo," *Chicago Sun-Times*, Aug. 25, 1980; "Charles Koen to Seek Spot on Cairo City Council," *Milwaukee Courier*, June 28, 1980; Cairo City Council minutes, May 27, June 10, and Aug. 28, 1980, and Jan. 13, 1981.

5. David Maraniss and Neil Henry, "Race 'War' in Cairo: Reconciliation Grows as Memories Recede," *Washington Post*, Mar. 22, 1987; Clarence Dossie interview; Seng, "Cairo Experience," 301–4; Illinois Advisory Committee, *Decade of Waiting in Cairo*, 16–17.

6. Preston Ewing Jr. interview; Hattie Kendrick to John Phipps Esq., Feb. 9, 1984, KBFP-LOC, box 20, folder 12; Land of Lincoln Legal Assistance Foundation Inc., "Handbook for Advisory Councilmembers" (1977), KBFP-LOC, box 21, folder 8.

7. Illinois Advisory Committee, *Decade of Waiting in Cairo*, 13, 33–34; minutes of the Illinois Consortium for Community Action, Oct. 11 and Nov. 15, 1973, ICC Records, ALPL, box 10, folder 31; Seng, "Cairo Experience," 305; Preston Ewing Jr. interview.

8. Koen, *Cairo Story*, 44; Preston Ewing Jr. interview.

9. Hattie Kendrick to Martha and Charles Cobb, Mar. 5, 1969, KBFP-LOC, box 20, folder 3; Hattie Kendrick to Martha Cobb, n.d., KBFP-LOC, box 20, folder 10; Clarence Dossie interview; Clydia Koen interview; Koen, *Cairo Story*, 25; Preston Ewing interview; "Tenant Orgn. to Be Formed," *Monitor*, May 13, 1971; Cairo City Council minutes, May 14 and 28, Nov. 26, 1974; "Blacks Want In on Housing Changes," *Monitor*, May 11, 1972; Cairo City Council minutes, Jan. 13 and 27, Feb. 10, and July 25, 1976.

10. Clarence Dossie interview.

11. Michelle Alexander, *The New Jim Crow: Mass Incarceration in the Age of Colorblindness* (New York: New Press, 2012); Koen, *Cairo Story*, 97; Clydia Koen interview.

Bibliography

Interviews and Correspondence

Clarence Dossie, interview with the author, Feb. 5, 2010, Cairo, IL.

Preston Ewing Jr., interview with the author, Oct. 29, 2011, Cairo, IL.

Manker Harris, interview with the author, June 20, 2012, Springfield, IL.

Clydia Koen, interview with the author, May 21, 2014, Cairo, IL.

Gerald Montroy, correspondence with the author, Jan. 21, Oct. 2, 7, and 13, 2014.

Bobby Williams, interview with the author, Dec. 1, 2013, St. Louis, MO.

Articles, Books, Dissertations, Manuscript Collections

Administrative Records of the Division of General Welfare Board of the General Board of Church and Society, 1887–2005. General Commission on Archive and History, United Methodist Church, Madison, NJ.

Alexander, Michelle. *The New Jim Crow: Mass Incarceration in the Age of Color-blindness.* New York: New Press, 2012.

Alexander, Shawn Leigh. *An Army of Lions: The Civil Rights Struggle before the NAACP.* Philadelphia: University of Pennsylvania Press, 2012.

Alliance to End Repression Records, Chicago Historical Society.

Andrews, Dale P. *Practical Theology for Black Churches: Bridging Black Theology and African American Folk Religion.* Louisville, KY: Westminster John Knox Press, 2002.

Archaimbault, Delores, and Terry A. Barnhart. "Illinois Copperheads and the American Civil War." *Illinois History Teacher* 3, no. 1 (1996): 15–30.

The Attractions of Cairo, Illinois. Cairo: The People Print, 1890.

Bad Subjects Production Team. *Bad Subjects: Political Education for Everyday Life.* New York: New York University Press, 1998.

Baraka, (Imanu) Amiri. *A Black Value System.* Newark, NJ: Jihad Productions, 1969.

———. "From Parks to Marxism: A Political Evolution." *Crisis* 105, no. 6 (Dec. 1998): 20–22.

———. *Raise, Race, Rays, Raze: Essays Since 1965.* New York: Random House, 1972.

Barger, Robert Newton. *Ethnicity in the Cairo Catholic Schools: An Historical Investigation.* Illinois Historical Survey, 1975.

Barnes, Sandra L. "Black Church Culture and Community Action." *Social Forces* 84, no. 2 (Dec. 2005): 967–94.

Bay, Mia. *To Tell the Truth Freely: The Life of Ida B. Wells*. New York: Hill and Wang, 2009.

Beadles, John Asa. *A History of Southernmost Illinois*. Karnak, IL: Shawnee Development Council, 1990.

Beilke, Jayne R. "The Complexity of School Desegregation in the Borderland: The Case of Indiana." In *With All Deliberate Speed: Implementing Brown v. Board of Education*, edited by Brian J. Daugherity and Charles C. Bolton, 199–216. Fayetteville: University of Arkansas Press, 2011.

Bell, Taylor H. A. *Sweet Charlie, Dike, Cazzie, and Bobby Joe: High School Basketball in Illinois*. Urbana: University of Illinois Press, 2004.

Benford, Robert D., and David Snow. "Framing Processes and Social Movement: An Overview and Assessment." *Annual Review of Sociology* 26 (2000): 611–39.

Berry, Leonidas H. *I Wouldn't Take Nothin' for My Journey: Two Centuries of an Afro-American Minister's Family*. Chicago: Johnson Publishing, 1981.

Best, Wallace D. *Passionately Human, No Less Divine: Religion and Culture in Black Chicago*. Princeton, NJ: Princeton University Press, 2005.

Bigham, Darrell E. *On Jordan's Banks: Emancipation and Its Aftermath in the Ohio River Valley*. Lexington: University Press of Kentucky, 2006.

———. *We Ask Only a Fair Trial: A History of the Black Community of Evansville, Indiana*. Bloomington: Indiana University Press, 1987.

Biondi, Martha. *To Stand and Fight: The Struggle for Civil Rights in Postwar New York City*. Cambridge, MA: Harvard University Press, 2003.

Bonnie J. Krause Papers, Special Collections Research Center, Morris Library, Southern Illinois University Carbondale.

Bracey, John H., Jr., and August Meier, eds. *Papers of the NAACP: Part 3, The Campaign for Educational Equality. Series C, Legal Department and Central Office Records*. Bethesda, MD: University Publications of America, 1995.

Bracey, Nathaniel. "Community Development: The Zion Non-Profit Charitable Trust." *Journal of African American History* 96, no. 1 (Winter 2011): 90–95.

Bradsby, H. C. "History of Cairo." In *History of Alexander, Union, and Pulaski Counties, Illinois*, edited by William Henry Perrin. Chicago: O. L. Baskin, 1883.

Brink, William, and Louis Harris. *Black and White: A Study of U.S. Racial Attitudes Today*. New York: Simon and Schuster, 1967.

Brinton, William R. "The Story of Confrontation." *FOCUS/Midwest* 8, no. 54 (1971): 10–14.

Brown, Scot. *Fighting for US: Maulana Karenga, the US Organization, and Black Cultural Nationalism*. New York: New York University Press, 2003.

———. "The Politics of Culture: The US Organization and the Quest for Black 'Unity.'" In *Freedom North: Black Freedom Struggles outside the South, 1940–1980*, edited by Jeanne Theoharis and Komozi Woodard, 223–55. New York: Palgrave Macmillan, 2003.

Burg, Manfred. *Popular Justice: A History of Lynching in America*. Chicago: Ivan R. Dee, 2011.

Butler, Anthea D. *Women in the Church of God in Christ: Making a Sanctified World*. Chapel Hill: University of North Carolina Press, 2007.

Cairo City Council Minutes. City Hall, Cairo, IL.

"Cairo School Situation." *Crisis* 59 (March 1952): 143–44.

Calhoun-Brown, Allison. "Upon This Rock: The Black Church, Nonviolence, and the Civil Rights Movement." *PS: Political Science and Politics* 33, no. 2 (June 2000): 168–74.

Callahan, Allen Dwight. "Remembering Nehemiah: A Note on Biblical Theology." In *Black Zion: African American Religious Encounters with Judaism*, edited by Yvonne Chireau and Nathaniel Deutsch. New York: Oxford University Press, 2000.

———. *The Talking Book: African Americans and the Bible*. New Haven, CT: Yale University Press, 2006.

Campbell, James T. *Songs of Zion: The African Methodist Episcopal Church in the United States and South Africa*. New York: Oxford University Press, 1995.

Capeci, Dominic J. *The Lynching of Cleo Wright*. Lexington: University Press of Kentucky, 1998.

Carmichael, Stokely. *Ready for Revolution: The Life and Struggles of Stokely Carmichael (Kwame Ture)*. New York: Scribner's, 2003.

Carmichael, Stokely, and Charles V. Hamilton. *Black Power: The Politics of Liberation*. New York: Vintage Books, 1967 [1992].

Carson, Clayborne. *In Struggle: SNCC and the Black Awakening of the 1960s*. Cambridge, MA: Harvard University Press, 1995.

Cha-Jua, Sundiata Keita. *America's First Black Town: Brooklyn, Illinois, 1830–1915*. Urbana: University of Illinois Press, 2000.

Cha-Jua, Sundiata Keita, and Clarence Lang. "The 'Long Movement' as Vampire: Temporal and Spatial Fallacies in Recent Black Freedom Studies." *Journal of African American History* 92 (Spring 2007): 265–88.

Chapman, Mark L. *Christianity on Trial: African American Religious Thought before and after Black Power*. Maryknoll, NY: Orbis Books, 1996.

Chappell, David L. *A Stone of Hope: Prophetic Religion and the Death of Jim Crow*. Chapel Hill: University of North Carolina Press, 2004.

Clark, John Henrik. *Malcolm X: The Man and His Times*. Trenton, NJ: Africa World Press, 1990.

Cleage, Albert B. *Black Christian Nationalism: New Directions for the Black Church*. New York: Morrow, 1972.

———. *The Black Messiah*. New York: Sheed and Ward, 1968.

Coffin, Levi. *Reminiscences of Levi Coffin*. New York: Arno Press, 1968.

Cohen, Lara Langer. *The Fabrication of American Literature: Fraudulence and Antebellum Print Culture*. Philadelphia: University of Pennsylvania Press, 2012.

Colby, Charles C. *Pilot Study of Southern Illinois.* Carbondale: Southern Illinois University Press, 1956.

Collier-Thomas, Bettye. *Jesus, Jobs, and Justice: African American Women and Religion.* New York: Knopf, 2010.

Collier-Thomas, Bettye, and V. P. Franklin, eds. *Sisters in the Struggle: African American Women in the Civil Rights–Black Power Movement.* New York: New York University Press, 2001.

Concerned Clergy. *Cairo: Were You There?* East St. Louis, IL: Concerned Clergy, 1969.

Cone, James H. *Black Theology and Black Power.* New York: Seabury Press, 1969.

Countryman, Matthew. *Up South: Civil Rights and Black Power in Philadelphia.* Philadelphia: University of Pennsylvania Press, 2006.

Cowan, Douglas E. *The Remnant Spirit: Conservative Reform in Mainline Protestantism.* Westport, CT: Praeger, 2003.

Cox, Harvey G. "The 'New Breed' in American Churches: Sources of Social Activism in American Religion." *Daedalus* 96 (Winter 1967): 135–50.

Crosby, Emilye. *A Little Taste of Freedom: The Black Freedom Struggle in Claiborne County, Mississippi.* Chapel Hill: University of North Carolina Press, 2005.

Current, Gloster B. "Exit Jim Crow Schools in East St. Louis." *Crisis* 57 (Apr. 1950): 209–14.

Danchin, Sebastian. *Earl Hooker, Blues Master.* Jackson: University Press of Mississippi, 1999.

David Ibata Collection of Racial Strife. Special Collections Research Center, Morris Library, Southern Illinois University Carbondale.

Davis, Corneal et al. *Corneal A. Davis.* Springfield, IL: The Council, 1984.

Davis, Cullom. "Illinois: Crossroads and Cross Section." In *Heartland: Comparative Histories of the Midwestern States,* edited by James H. Madison, 127–57. Bloomington: Indiana University Press, 1988.

Davis, Cyprian. *The History of Black Catholics in the United States.* New York: Crossroad, 1990.

Davis, James Kirkpatrick. *Assault on the Left: The FBI and the Sixties Antiwar Movement.* Westport, CT: Praeger, 1997.

Dawson, Michael C. *Behind the Mule: Race and Class in African American Politics.* Princeton, NJ: Princeton University Press, 1994.

———. "A Black Counterpublic? Economic Earthquakes, Racial Agenda(s), and Black Politics." *Public Culture* 7 (1994): 195–223.

———. *Black Visions: The Roots of Contemporary African-American Political Ideologies.* Chicago: University of Chicago Press, 2001.

"The Depression Era Art Projects in Illinois." *Illinois Heritage* (2000): 4–9.

Dexter, Darrel. *Bondage in Egypt: Slavery in Southern Illinois.* Cape Girardeau: Southeast Missouri State University, 2011.

Dickens, Charles. *American Notes and Pictures from Italy.* New York: Scribner's, 1900.

Dickerson, Dennis C. "African American Religious Intellectuals and the Theological Foundations of the Civil Rights Movement, 1930–55." *Church History* 74, no. 2 (June 2005): 217–35.

Dillard, Angela D. *Faith in the City: Preaching Radical Social Change in Detroit.* Ann Arbor: University of Michigan Press, 2007.

Dochuk, Darren. *From Bible Belt to Sunbelt: Plain-Folk Religion, Grassroots Politics, and the Rise of Evangelical Conservatism.* New York: Norton, 2011.

Dodson, Jualynne E. *Engendering Church: Women, Power, and the AME Church.* Lanham, MD: Rowman & Littlefield, 2002.

Donovan, Mary Sudman. "Beyond the Parallel Church: Strategies of Separatism and Integration in the Governing Councils of the Episcopal Church." In *Episcopal Women: Gender, Spirituality, and Commitment in an American Mainline Denomination*, edited by Catherine M. Prelinger, 133–63. New York: Oxford University Press, 1992.

Douglas, Davison M. *Jim Crow Moves North: The Battle over Northern School Segregation, 1865–1954.* New York: Cambridge University Press, 2005.

Du Bois, W. E. B. *Black Reconstruction in America.* New York: Free Press, 1998 [1935].

Duncan, Hannibal Gerald. "The Changing Relationship in the Border and Northern States." PhD diss., University of Pennsylvania, 1922.

Duster, Alfreda M., ed. *Crusade for Justice: The Autobiography of Ida B. Wells.* Chicago: University of Chicago Press, 1972.

Dyer, Stephanie. "Progress Plaza: Leon Sullivan, Zion Investment Associates, and Black Power in a Philadelphia Shopping Center." In *The Economic Civil Rights Movement: African Americans and the Struggle for Economic Power*, edited by Michael Ezra, 137–53. New York: Routledge, 2013.

Eastman, Herbert A. "Speaking Truth to Power: The Language of Civil Rights Litigators." *Yale Law Journal* 104, no. 4 (Jan. 1995): 869–72.

Eaton, John, and Ethel Osgood Mason. *Grant, Lincoln, and the Freedmen: Reminiscences of the Civil War, with Special Reference to the Work for the Contrabands and Freedmen of the Mississippi Valley.* New York: Negro Universities Press, 1969.

Ephemera Collection. Special Collections Research Center, Morris Library, Southern Illinois University Carbondale.

Etcheson, Nicole. *The Emerging Midwest: Upland Southerners and the Political Culture of the Old Northwest, 1787–1861.* Bloomington: Indiana University Press, 1996.

Ewing, Preston Jr., and Jan Peterson Roddy, eds. *Let My People Go: Cairo, Illinois, 1867–1973.* Carbondale: Southern Illinois University Press, 1996.

Executive Committee on Southern Illinois. *Southern Illinois: Resources and*

Potentials of the Sixteen Southernmost Counties. Urbana: University of Illinois Press, 1949.

Fairclough, Adam. "The Southern Christian Leadership Conference and the Second Reconstruction, 1957–1973." *South Atlantic Quarterly* 80 (1981): 177–94.

Fannin, Mark. *Labor's Promised Land: Radical Visions of Gender, Race, and Religion in the South.* Knoxville: University of Tennessee Press, 2003.

Fauset, Arthur Huff. *Black Gods of the Metropolis: Negro Religious Cults of the Urban North.* New York: Octagon Books, 1974 [1944].

FBI Freedom of Information Act File. Subject: Black United Front (Cairo, Illinois).

Federal Bureau of Investigation. *FBI Files on Black Extremist Organizations, Part 1: COINTELPRO Files on Black Hate Groups and Investigation of the Deacons for Defense and Justice.* Microfilm. http://cisupa.proquest.com/ksc_assets/catalog/101095_FBIBlackExtrOrgsPt1COINTELPRO.pdf.

Federal Writers' Project. *Cairo Guide.* Cairo, IL: Cairo Public Library, 1938.

Findlay James R. *Church People in the Struggle: The National Council of Churches and the Black Freedom Movement, 1950–1970.* New York: Oxford University Press, 1993.

Fine, Sidney. *Violence in the Model City: The Cavanagh Administration, Race Relations, and the Detroit Riot of 1967.* Ann Arbor: University of Michigan Press, 1988.

"The First Pulpit in Granville: The Story of the Village Age Post Office Mural," *Historical Times: Quarterly of the Granville, Ohio, Historical Society* 17, no. 2 (Spring 2003): 2–6.

Fogelson, Robert M. *Violence as Protest: A Study of Riots and Ghettos.* New York: Doubleday, 1971.

Foner, Philip S., ed. *Black Socialist Preacher.* San Francisco: Synthesis Publications, 1983.

Forman, James. *The Making of Black Revolutionaries.* Seattle: University of Washington Press, 2000 [1972].

Franklin, V. P. "'The Lion of Zion': Leon H. Sullivan and the Pursuit of Social and Economic Justice." *Journal of African American History* 96, no. 1 (Winter 2011): 39–43.

Fraser, Nancy. "Rethinking the Public Sphere: A Contribution to the Critique of Actually Existing Democracy." In *Habermas and the Public Sphere,* edited by Craig Calhoun, 109–42. Cambridge: MIT Press, 1989.

Frazier, Edward Franklin. *The Negro Church in America.* New York: Schocken Books, 1974.

———. *The Negro in the United States.* New York: Macmillan, 1957.

Frederickson, George M. *Black Liberation: A Comparative History of Black Ideologies.* New York: Oxford University Press, 1995.

Fukuyama, Yoshio. "Parishioners' Attitudes toward Issues in the Civil Rights Movement." *Sociological Analysis* 29, no. 2 (Summer 1968): 94–103.

Gallen, David. *Malcolm X: As They Knew Him.* New York: Ballantine Books, 1995.

Gamson, William A., and David S. Meyer. "The Framing of Political Opportunity." In *Comparative Perspectives on Social Movements,* edited by Doug McAdam, John D. McCarthy, and Mayer N. Zald, 275–90. New York: Cambridge University Press, 1996.

Garner, Roberta. *Contemporary Movements and Ideologies.* New York: McGraw-Hill, 1996.

Gellman, Erik S. *Death Blow to Jim Crow: The National Negro Congress and the Rise of Militant Civil Rights.* Chapel Hill: University of North Carolina Press, 2012.

Glaude, Eddie S. *Exodus! Religion, Race, and Nation in Early Nineteenth-Century Black America.* Chicago: University of Chicago Press, 2000.

———. *In a Shade of Blue: Pragmatism and the Politics of Black America.* Chicago: University of Chicago Press, 2008.

Gleeson, Ed. *Illinois Rebels: A Civil War Unit History of G Company, Fifteenth Tennessee Regiment, Volunteer Infantry: The Story of the Confederacy's Southern Illinois Company, Men from Marion and Carbondale.* Carmel, IN: Guild Press of Indiana, 1996.

Goelz, C. *General History of the Diocese of Belleville.* East St. Louis, IL: Messenger Press, 1939.

Goffman, Erving. *Frame Analysis: An Essay on the Organization of Experience.* New York: Harper and Row, 1974.

Good, Paul. *Cairo, Illinois: Racism at Floodtide.* Washington, DC: Commission on Civil Rights, 1973.

Grant, Jacquelyn. "Black Theology and the Black Woman." In *African American Religious Thought: An Anthology,* edited by Cornel West and Eddie S. Glaude Jr., 831–48. Louisville, KY: Westminster John Knox Press, 2003.

Greenberg, Cheryl Lynn. *A Circle of Trust: Remembering SNCC.* New Brunswick, NJ: Rutgers University Press, 1998.

Greene, C. P., Thomas H. Bacon, and Sidney J. Roy. *A Mirror of Hannibal.* Hannibal, MO: C. P. Greene, 1905.

Gregory, James N. *The Southern Diaspora: How the Great Migrations of Black and White Southerners Transformed America.* Chapel Hill: University of North Carolina Press, 2005.

Hadden, Jeffrey K. *The Gathering Storm in the Churches.* Garden City, NY: Doubleday, 1969.

Haviland, Laura S. *A Woman's Life-Work: Labors and Experiences of Laura S. Haviland.* Salem, NH: Ayer, 1984.

Hayes, Floyd W., III, and Francis A. Kiene III. "'All Power to the People': The

Political Thought of Huey P. Newton and the Black Panther Party." In *The Black Panther Party*, edited by Charles E. Jones, 157–76. Baltimore: Black Class Press, 1998.

Hays, Christopher K. "The African American Struggle for Equality and Justice in Cairo, Illinois, 1865–1900." *Illinois Historical Journal* 90, no. 4 (Winter 1997): 265–84.

———. "Way Down in Egypt Land: Conflict and Community in Cairo, Illinois, 1850–1910." PhD diss., University of Missouri–Columbia, 1996.

Henrik Clarke, John, ed. *Malcolm X: The Man and His Times*. Trenton, NJ: Africa World Press, 1990.

Herda, Ann Elizabeth. "Black Women's Inspirational Leadership in the Civil Rights Movement: A Case Study." Master's thesis, Southern Illinois University Carbondale, 1994.

Herda-Rapp, Ann. "The Power of Informal Leadership: Women Leaders in the Civil Rights Movement." *Sociological Focus* 31, no. 4 (Oct. 1998): 341–55.

Hicken, Victor. *Illinois in the Civil War*. Urbana: University of Illinois Press, 1991.

Higginbotham, Evelyn Brooks. *Righteous Discontent: The Women's Movement in the Black Baptist Church, 1880–1920*. Cambridge, MA: Harvard University Press, 1993.

Hogan, Wesley C. *Many Minds, One Heart: SNCC's Dream for a New America*. Chapel Hill: University of North Carolina Press, 2007.

Hopkins, Dwight N. *Shoes That Fit Our Feet: Sources for a Constructive Black Theology*. Maryknoll, NY: Orbis Books, 1993.

———. "A Transatlantic Comparison of a Black Theology of Liberation." In *Freedom's Distant Shores: American Protestants and Postcolonial Alliances with Africa*, edited by R. Drew Smith, 83–109. Waco, TX: Baylor University Press, 2006.

Horne, Gerald. *Black Liberation/Red Scare: Ben Davis and the Communist Party*. Cranbury, NJ: Associated University Presses, 1994.

Houston, Benjamin. *The Nashville Way: Racial Etiquette and the Struggle for Social Justice in a Southern City*. Athens: University of Georgia Press, 2012.

Howard, Ashley. "Prairie Fires: Urban Rebellions as Black Working Class Politics in Three Midwestern Cities." PhD diss., University of Illinois at Urbana-Champaign, 2012.

Hubbard, Mark, ed. *Illinois's War: The Civil War in Documents*. Athens: Ohio University Press, 2013.

Hunt, Darnell M., and Ana-Christina Ramon, eds. *Black Los Angeles: American Dreams and Racial Realities*. New York: New York University Press, 2010.

Illinois Advisory Committee to the US Commission on Civil Rights. *A Decade of Waiting in Cairo*. [Washington, DC]: [US Commission on Civil Rights], 1975.

Illinois Commission on Human Relations. *Sixth Report of Commission on Human Relations*. N.p., 1955.
——. *Seventh Biennial Report*. N.p., 1957.
Illinois Conference of Churches (ICC) Records (1880–1997). Abraham Lincoln Presidential Library, Springfield, Illinois.
Illinois Inter-Racial Commission. *First Annual Report of the Illinois Inter-Racial Commission*. N.p., 1944.
——. *Special Report on Employment Opportunities in Illinois*. Chicago: n.p., 1948.
——. *Third Report of Illinois Inter-Racial Commission*. N.p., 1949.
Illinois State Advisory Committee. Records Relating to Special Projects, 1960–1970. Office of the Staff Director, USCCR, Record Group 453. National Archives Building, Washington, DC.
Illinois Writers' Project. Negro in Illinois Papers. Vivian Harsh Research Collection of Afro-American History and Literature, Chicago Public Library.
Interreligious Foundation for Community Organization (IFCO) Papers. Schomburg Center of Research in Black Culture, New York Public Library.
James Forman Papers. Library of Congress, Washington, DC. http://rs5.loc.gov/service/mss/eadxmlmss/eadpdfmss/2010/ms010125.pdf.
Jeffries, Hasan Kwame. *Bloody Lowndes: Civil Rights and Black Power in Alabama's Black Belt*. New York: New York University Press, 2009.
Jeffries, J. L. *Black Power in the Belly of the Beast*. Urbana: University of Illinois Press, 2006.
Johnson, Cedric. *Revolutionaries to Race Leaders: Black Power and the Making of African American Politics*. Minneapolis: University of Minnesota Press, 2007.
Johnston, Hank. "Age Cohorts, Cognition, and Collective Violence." In *Violent Protest, Contentious Politics, and the Neoliberal State*, edited by Seraphim Seferiades and Hank Johnston, 39–53. Farnham, Surrey, UK: Ashgate Publishing, 2012.
Jolly, Kenneth. *Black Liberation in the Midwest: The Struggle in St. Louis, Missouri, 1964–1970*. New York: Routledge, 2006.
Jonas, Gilbert. *Freedom's Sword: The NAACP and the Struggle against Racism in America, 1909–1969*. New York: Routledge, 2005.
Jones, Charles E., ed. *The Black Panther Party Reconsidered*. Baltimore: Black Class Press, 1998.
Jones, James Pickett. *Black Jack: John A. Logan and Southern Illinois in the Civil War Era*. Tallahassee: Florida State University, 1967.
Jones, Patrick D. *Selma of the North: Civil Rights Insurgency in Milwaukee*. Cambridge, MA: Harvard University Press, 2009.
Joseph, Peniel E. "The Black Power Movement: A State of the Field." *Journal of American History* 96, no. 3 (2009): 751–76.
——. "Introduction: Towards a Historiography of the Black Power Move-

ment." In *The Black Power Movement: Rethinking the Civil Rights–Black Power Era,* edited by Peniel E. Joseph, 1–25. New York: Routledge, 2006.

———. "Perspectives on the New Black Power Scholarship." Paper presented at the 93rd Annual Meeting of the Association for the Study of African American Life and History, Birmingham, AL, October 2008.

———. *Stokely: A Life.* New York: Perseus Books, 2014.

———. "Waiting Till the Midnight Hour: Reconceptualizing the Heroic Period of the Civil Rights Movement, 1954–1965." *Souls* 2 (Spring 2000): 6–17.

———. *Waiting 'Til the Midnight Hour: A Narrative History of Black Power in America.* New York: Holt Paperbacks, 2006.

Justesen, Benjamin R. *Broken Brotherhood: The Rise and Fall of the National Afro-American Council.* Carbondale: Southern Illinois University Press, 2008.

Kelley, Dean. "Freedom of Religion." In *Papers from the Conference on American Freedom.* Washington, DC: n.p., 1973.

Kelley, Robin D. G. "'Comrades, Praise Gawd for Lenin and Them!': Ideology and Culture among Black Communists in Alabama, 1930–1935." *Science & Society* 52 (Spring 1988): 58–82.

———. *Freedom Dreams: The Black Radical Imagination.* Boston: Beacon Press, 2002.

———. *Hammer and Hoe: Alabama Communists during the Great Depression.* Chapel Hill: University of North Carolina Press, 1990.

———. "Stormy Weather: Reconsidering Black (Inter)Nationalism in the Cold War Era." In *Is It Nation Time? Contemporary Essays on Black Power and Black Nationalism,* edited by Eddie S. Glaude Jr., 67–90. Chicago: University of Chicago Press, 2002.

Kelley, Robin D. G., and Betsy Esch. "Black Like Mao: Red China and Black Revolution." In *Afro Asia: Revolutionary Political and Cultural Connections between African Americans and Asian Americans,* edited by Fred Ho and Bill V. Mullen, 97–154. Durham, NC: Duke University Press, 2008.

Kendrick-Brooks Family Papers (KBFP-LOC). Library of Congress, Washington, DC. http://findingaids.loc.gov/db/search/xq/searchMfer02.xq?_id=loc .mss.eadmss.ms006015&_faSection=overview&_faSubsection=did&_dmdid=.

King, Martin Luther Jr. *Strength to Love.* New York: Harper and Row, 1963.

Kionka, T. K. *Key Command: Ulysses S. Grant's District of Cairo.* Columbia: University of Missouri Press, 2006.

K'Meyer, Tracey E. *Civil Rights in the Gateway to the South: Louisville, Kentucky, 1945–1980.* Lexington: University Press of Kentucky, 2009.

Koen, Charles. *The Cairo Story: And the Round-Up of Black Leadership.* Cairo, IL: Koen Press, n.d.

———. *United Front Philosophy.* Cairo, IL: United Front, n.d. [Located at Memorial Library, University of Wisconsin–Madison.].

Kohn, Howard. "Civil War in Cairo, Ill.: A Dispatch from the Front," *Ramparts* 9, no. 9 (Apr. 1971): 46–51.

Lang, Clarence. *Grassroots at the Gateway: Class Politics and Black Freedom Struggle in St. Louis, 1936–75.* Ann Arbor: University of Michigan Press, 2009.

———. "Locating the Civil Rights Movement: An Essay on the Deep South, Midwest, and Border South in Black Freedom Studies." *Journal of Social History* 47, no. 3 (Winter 2013): 371–400.

Lansden, John McMurray. *A History of the City of Cairo, Illinois.* Carbondale: Southern Illinois University Press, 1976 [1910].

Lantz, Herman R. *A Community in Search of Itself: A Case History of Cairo, Illinois.* Carbondale: Southern Illinois University Press, 1972.

Lecky, Robert S., and Elliott Wright. *Black Manifesto: Religion, Racism, and Reparations.* New York: Sheed and Ward, 1969.

Levine, Lawrence W. *Black Culture and Black Consciousness: Afro-American Folk Thought from Slavery to Freedom.* Oxford, UK: Oxford University Press, 2007.

Levy, Peter B. *Civil War on Race Street: The Civil Rights Movement in Cambridge, Maryland.* Gainesville: University Press of Florida, 2003.

Lewis, John, and Michael D'Orso. *Walking with the Wind: A Memoir of the Movement.* New York: Simon and Schuster, 1998.

Lincoln, C. Eric, and Lawrence H. Mamiya. *The Black Church in the African American Experience.* Durham, NC: Duke University Press, 1990.

Logan, Rayford. *The Betrayal of the Negro.* New York: MacMillan, 1970 [1954].

———. *The Negro in American Life and Thought: The Nadir, 1877–1901.* New York: Dial Press, 1954.

Looker, Benjamin. *"Point from which creation begins": The Black Artists' Group of St. Louis.* Columbia: University of Missouri Press, 2004.

Makalani, Minkah. *In the Cause of Freedom: Radical Black Internationalism from Harlem to London, 1917–1939.* Chapel Hill: University of North Carolina Press, 2011.

Mao Tse-tung. *Quotations from Chairman Mao Tse-tung.* Peking: Foreign Languages Press, 1966.

———. *Selected Works of Mao Tse-tung.* 3rd ed. Peking: Foreign Languages Press, 1969.

Marable, Manning. *Malcolm X: A Life of Reinvention.* New York: Viking, 2011.

Marsh, Charles. *The Beloved Community: How Faith Shapes Social Justice, from the Civil Rights Movement to Today.* New York: Basic Books, 2005.

———. *God's Long Summer: Stories of Faith and Civil Rights.* Princeton, NJ: Princeton University Press, 1997.

Martin, William. *With God on Our Side: The Rise of the Religious Right in America.* New York: Broadway Books, 1996.

Maryadi. "The Roles of Black Churches in the Cairo Civil Rights Movement (1960s–1970s)." Master's thesis, Southern Illinois University Carbondale, 1995.

Matthews, Tracye. "'No One Ever Asks, What a Man's Place in the Revolution

Is': Gender and the Politics of the Black Panther Party, 1966–1971." In *The Black Panther Party Reconsidered,* edited by Charles E. Jones, 267–304. Baltimore: Black Classic Press, 2005.

Mays, Benjamin. *The Negro's Church.* New York: Institute of Social and Religious Research, 1933.

McAdam, Doug. "The Framing Function of Movement Tactics: Strategic Dramaturgy in the American Civil Rights Movement." In *Comparative Perspectives on Social Movements,* edited by Doug McAdam, John D. McCarthy, and Mayer N. Zald, 223–55. New York: Cambridge University Press, 1996.

———. *Freedom Summer.* New York: Oxford University Press, 1998.

———. *Political Process and the Development of Black Insurgency, 1930–1970.* Chicago: University of Chicago Press, 1982.

———. "Tactical Innovation and the Pace of Insurgency." *American Sociological Review* 48, no. 6 (Dec. 1983): 735–54.

McCutcheon, Steve, Judson L. Jeffries, and Omari L. Dyson. "The Black Panther Party and the Black Church." In *From Every Mountainside: Black Churches and the Broad Terrain of Civil Rights,* edited by R. Drew Smith, 127–44. Albany: State University of New York Press, 2013.

McDannell, Colleen. *Spirit of Vatican II: A History of Catholic Reform in America.* New York: Basic Books, 2011.

McDermott, Stacy Pratt. "'An Outrageous Proceeding': A Northern Lynching and the Enforcement of Anti-Lynching Legislation in Illinois, 1905–1910," *Journal of Negro History* 84, no. 1 (Winter 1999): 61–78.

McDuffie, Erik S. *Sojourning for Freedom: Black Women, American Communism, and the Making of Black Left Feminism.* Raleigh, NC: Duke University Press, 2011.

McGreevy, John T. *Parish Boundaries: The Catholic Encounter with Race in the Twentieth Century.* Chicago: University of Chicago Press, 1996.

McKendree University. *The McKendrean 1964 Yearbook.* Lebanon, IL: McKendree College, 1965.

———. *The McKendrean 1966 Yearbook.* Lebanon, IL: McKendree College, 1966.

McLaughlin, Malcolm. *The Long, Hot Summer of 1967: Urban Rebellion in America.* New York: Palgrave Macmillan, 2014.

Meier, August, and Elliott M. Rudwick. *CORE: A Study in the Civil Rights Movement, 1942–1968.* Urbana: University of Illinois Press, 1975.

Meier, August, and John T. Bracey Jr. "The NAACP as a Reform Movement, 1909–1965: 'To reach the conscience of America.'" *Journal of Southern History* 59, no. 1 (1993): 3–30.

Merrifield, Estelle, and Erma Bridgewater. "History of Bethel A.M.E. Church, Champaign, Ill." Champaign: n.p., 1991.

Moody, Anne. *Coming of Age in Mississippi.* New York: Laurel Press, 1968.

Morris, Aldon D. *The Origins of the Civil Rights Movement: Black Communities Organizing for Change*. New York: Free Press, 1984.

Mouser, Bruce L. *A Black Gambler's World of Liquor, Vice, and Presidential Politics: William Thomas Scott of Illinois, 1839–1917*. Madison: University of Wisconsin Press, 2014.

Mugambi, J. N. K. *Christian Theology and Social Reconstruction*. Nairobi: Action Publishers, 2003.

Mumford, Kevin. *Newark: A History of Race, Rights, and Riots in America*. New York: New York University Press, 2008.

Murch, Donna Jean. *Living for the City: Migration, Education, and the Rise of the Black Panther Party in Oakland, California*. Chapel Hill: University of North Carolina Press, 2010.

Murch, James DeForest. *The Protestant Revolt: The Road to Freedom for American Churches*. Arlington, VA: Crestwood Books, 1967.

Murray, Peter C. *Methodists and the Crucible of Race, 1930–1975*. Columbia: University of Missouri Press, 2004.

Myrdal, Gunnar. *An American Dilemma: The Negro Problem and Modern Democracy*. 2nd ed. New York: Harper and Brothers, 1944.

Naison, Mark. *Communists in Harlem during the Depression*. Urbana: University of Illinois Press, 1983.

National Advisory Commission on Civil Disorders. *Report of the National Advisory Commission on Civil Disorders*. New York: Bantam, 1968.

National Council of Churches. *Churches and Church Membership in the United States: An Enumeration and Analysis by Counties, States, and Regions, Series C, No. 14–15*. New York: n.p., 1957.

Negro City Directory of Cairo, Illinois. Cairo: n.p., 1936. Manuscript, Archives, and Rare Book Library, Emory University, Atlanta.

Nelson, Alondra. *Body and Soul: The Black Panther Party and the Fight against Medical Discrimination*. Minneapolis: University of Minnesota Press, 2011.

New Detroit Inc. Collection. Archives of Labor and Urban Affairs, Walter P. Reuther Library, Wayne State University, Detroit, MI.

Newton, Huey. *Revolutionary Suicide*. New York: Harcourt, 1973.

———. *To Die for the People: The Writings of Huey P. Newton*, edited by Toni Morrison. San Francisco: City Lights Books, 2009.

Nkrumah, Kwame. *Consciencism*. New York: Monthly Review Press, 1964.

———. *Handbook of Revolutionary Warfare: A Guide to the Armed Phase of the African Revolution*. New York: International Publishers, 1969.

Noyes, Edward. "The Contraband Camp at Cairo, Illinois." In *Selected Proceedings of the Sixth Northern Great Plains History Conference*, edited by Lysle E. Meyer, 203–17. Moorhead, MN: n.p., 1972.

Office of the Superintendent of Public Instruction (OSPI). *Directory of Illinois Schools, 1928–1929*. Springfield: OSPI, 1929.

———. *Illinois School Directory, 1946–47.* Springfield: OSPI, 1947.

———. *Illinois School Directory, 1966–67.* Springfield: OSPI, 1967.

———. *Illinois School Directory, 1967–68.* Springfield: OSPI, 1968.

Ogbar, Jeffrey O. G. *Black Power: Radical Politics and African American Identity.* Baltimore: John Hopkins University Press, 2004.

Oursler, Will. *Protestant Power and the Coming Revolution.* Garden City, NY: Doubleday, 1971.

Patillo-McCoy, Mary. "Church Culture as a Strategy of Action in the Black Community." *American Sociological Review* 63, no. 6 (Dec. 1998): 767–84.

Payne, Charles M. *I've Got the Light of Freedom: The Organizing Tradition and the Mississippi Freedom Struggle.* Berkeley: University of California Press, 1995.

Perrin, William Henry. *History of Alexander, Union, and Pulaski Counties, Illinois.* Chicago: O. L. Baskin, 1883.

Pfeifer, Michael J., ed. *Lynching beyond Dixie: American Mob Violence outside the South.* Urbana: University of Illinois Press, 2013.

Phillips, Christopher. *Missouri's Confederate: Clairborne Fox Jackson and the Creation of Southern Identity in the Border West.* Columbia: University of Missouri Press, 2000.

Phillips, Kimberley L. *Alabama North: African-American Migrants, Community, and Working-Class Activism in Cleveland, 1915–45.* Urbana: University of Illinois Press, 1999.

Pimblott, Kerry L. "Black Power and Black Theology in Cairo, Illinois." In *The Pew and the Picket Line: Christianity and the American Working Class,* edited by Christopher D. Cantwell, Heath W. Carter, and Janine Giordano Drake, 115–43. Urbana: University of Illinois Press, 2016.

Pinn, Anthony B. *The Black Church in the Post–Civil Rights Era.* Maryknoll, NY: Orbis Books, 2002.

Portwood, Shirley J. "African American Politics and Community in Cairo and Vicinity, 1863–1900." *Illinois History Teacher* 3 (1996): 13–21.

Raboteau, Albert J. "The Black Experience in American Evangelicalism: The Meaning of Slavery." In *The Evangelical Tradition in America,* edited by Leonard I. Sweet, 181–89. Macon, GA: Mercer University Press, 1997.

Reed, Adolph. *The Jesse Jackson Phenomenon: The Crisis of Purpose in Afro-American Politics.* New Haven, CT: Yale University Press, 1986.

Robinson, Armstead L. *Bitter Fruits of Bondage: The Demise of Slavery and the Collapse of the Confederacy, 1861–1865.* Charlottesville: University of Virginia Press, 2005.

Robnett, Belinda. *How Long? How Long? African-American Women in the Struggle for Civil Rights.* New York: Oxford University Press, 1997.

Roll, Jarod. *Spirit of Rebellion: Labor and Religion in the New Cotton South.* Urbana: University of Illinois Press, 2010.

Ross, Rosetta E. *Witnessing and Testifying: Black Women, Religion, and Civil Rights*. Minneapolis, MN: Fortress Press, 2003.

Sales, William J., Jr. *From Civil Rights to Black Liberation: Malcolm X and the Organization of Afro-American Unity*. Boston: South End Press, 1994.

Sanders, Cheryl J. *Saints in Exile: The Holiness-Pentecostal Experience in African-American Religion and Culture*. New York: Oxford University Press, 1996.

Savage, Barbara Dianne. *Your Spirits Walk beside Us: The Politics of Black Religion*. Cambridge, MA: Harvard University Press, 2008.

Sawyer, Mary R. *Black Ecumenism: Implementing the Demands of Justice*. Valley Forge, PA: Trinity Press International, 1994.

Schechter, Patricia A. *Ida B. Wells-Barnett and American Reform*. Chapel Hill: University of North Carolina Press, 2001.

Schwalm, Leslie A. *Emancipation's Diaspora: Race and Reconstruction in the Upper Midwest*. Chapel Hill: University of North Carolina Press, 2009.

———. "'Overrun with Free Negroes': Emancipation and Wartime Migration in the Upper Midwest." *Civil War History* 50, no. 2 (2004): 145–74.

Self, Robert O. *American Babylon: Race and the Struggle for Postwar Oakland*. Princeton, NJ: Princeton University Press, 2003.

———. "The Black Panther Party and the Long Civil Rights Era." In *In Search of the Black Panther Party: New Perspectives on a Revolutionary Movement*, edited by Jama Lazerow and Yohuru Williams, 15–59. Durham, NC: Duke University Press, 2006.

Sellers, Cleveland, and Robert L. Terrell. *The River of No Return: The Autobiography of a Black Militant and the Life and Death of SNCC*. New York: Morrow, 1973.

Seng, Michael P. "The Cairo Experience: Civil Rights Litigation in a Racial Powder Keg." *Oregon Law Review* (1982): 285–315.

Sernett, Milton G. "Black Religion and the Question of Evangelical Identity." In *The Variety of American Evangelicalism*, edited by Donald W. Dayton and Robert J. Johnston, 135–47. Knoxville: University of Tennessee Press, 1991.

———. *Bound for the Promised Land: African American Religion and the Great Migration*. Durham, NC: Duke University Press, 1997.

Shagaloff, June. "Progress Report on Northern Desegregation." *Equity and Excellence in Education* 4 (1966): 44–46.

Shagaloff, June, and Lester P. Bailey. "Cairo—Illinois Southern Exposure." *Crisis* 59 (Apr. 1952): 208–13.

Shattuck, Gardiner H., Jr. *Episcopalians and Race: Civil War to Civil Rights*. Lexington: University Press of Kentucky, 2000.

Skotnes, Andor. *A New Deal for All? Race and Class Struggles in Depression-Era Baltimore*. Durham, NC: Duke University Press, 2013.

Snow, David E., Burke Rochford Jr., Steven K. Worden, and Robert D. Benford.

"Frame Alignment Processes, Micromobilization, and Movement Participation." *American Sociological Review* 51, no. 4 (Aug. 1986): 464–81.

Soloman, Mark. *The Cry Was Unity: Communists and African Americans, 1917–1936.* Jackson: University Press of Mississippi, 1998.

Springer, Kimberly. *Living for the Revolution: Black Feminist Organizations, 1968–1980.* Raleigh, NC: Duke University Press, 2005.

Stalp, Marybeth C. "Comparative Responses to Activism: Catholic Religious in the Cairo Civil Rights Movement, 1967–1973." Master's thesis, Southern Illinois University Carbondale, 1996.

Strain, Christopher B. *Pure Fire: Self-Defense as Activism in the Civil Rights Era.* Athens: University of Georgia Press, 2005.

Student Nonviolent Coordinating Committee Papers, 1959–1972. Library and Archives of the Martin Luther King Jr. Center for Nonviolent Social Change Inc., Atlanta. Microfilming Corp. of America, 1982.

Sugrue, Thomas J. *The Origins of the Urban Crisis: Race and Inequality in Postwar Detroit.* Princeton, NJ: Princeton University Press, 1996.

———. *Sweet Land of Liberty: The Forgotten Struggle for Civil Rights in the North.* New York: Random House, 2008.

Superintendent of Public Instruction. Legal Department Correspondence, Colored Children File, Record Group 106.014. Illinois State Archives, Springfield.

Taylor, Clarence. *The Black Churches of Brooklyn.* New York: Columbia University Press, 1994.

Taylor, Henry Louis Jr. *Race and the City: Work, Community, and Protest in Cincinnati, 1820–1970.* Urbana: University of Illinois Press, 1993.

Taylor, James Lance. "The Reverend Benjamin Chavis-Muhammed: From Wilmington to Washington, from Chavis to Muhammed." In *Religious Leaders and Faith-Based Politics: Ten Profiles,* edited by Jo Renee Formicola and Hubert Morken, 115–40. Lanham, MD: Rowman & Littlefield, 2001.

Taylor, Verta, and Nancy Whittier. "Analytical Approaches to Social Movement Culture: The Culture of the Women's Movement." In *Social Movements and Culture,* edited by Hank Johnston and Bert Klandermans, 163–88. Minneapolis: University of Minnesota Press, 1995.

Teaford, Jon C. *Cities of the Heartland: The Rise and Fall of the Industrial Midwest.* Bloomington: Indiana University Press, 1993.

Theoharis, Jeanne F., and Komozi Woodard, eds. *Freedom North: Black Freedom Struggles outside the South, 1940–1980.* New York: Palgrave Macmillan, 2003.

Thompson, Heather Ann. *Whose Detroit? Politics, Labor, and Race in a Modern American City.* Ithaca, NY: Cornell University Press, 2004.

Townsend, Henry, and Bill Greensmith. *A Blues Life.* Urbana: University of Illinois Press, 1999.

Trotter, Joe William. *Black Milwaukee: The Making of an Industrial Proletariat, 1915–45.* 2nd ed. Urbana: University of Illinois Press, 2007.

———. *River Jordan: African American Urban Life in the Ohio Valley.* Lexington: University Press of Kentucky, 1998.

Turner, Ronny E. "The Black Minister: Uncle Tom or Abolitionist?" *Phylon* 34 (1973): 86–95.

Umoja, Akinyele Omowale. *We Will Shoot Back: Armed Resistance in the Mississippi Freedom Movement.* New York: New York University Press, 2013.

United Methodist Church (US) Southern Illinois Conference. *Official Journal and Yearbook of the 118th Session of the Southern Illinois Conference of the United Methodist Church.* Conference Committee on Journal Publications, 1969.

———. *Official Journal and Yearbook of the 119th Session of the Southern Illinois Conference of the United Methodist Church.* Conference Committee on Journal Publications, 1970.

United Presbyterian Church, USA. *Minutes of the General Assembly of the United Presbyterian Church in the U.S.A., Part 1.* Philadelphia: Office of the General Assembly, 1972.

———. *Minutes of the General Assembly of the United Presbyterian Church in the U.S.A., Part 1.* Philadelphia: Office of the General Assembly, 1973.

US Census Bureau. *Census of Population: 1860.* Washington, DC: GPO, 1864.

———. *Census of Population: 1870.* Vol. 1. Washington, DC: GPO, 1872.

———. *Census of Population: 1880.* Vol. 1. Washington, DC: GPO, 1883.

———. *Census of Population: 1890.* Vol. 1, pt. 1. Washington, DC: GPO, 1895.

———. *Census of Population: 1900.* Vol. 1, pt. 1. Washington, DC: GPO, 1901.

———. *Census of Population: 1910.* Vol. 2. Washington, DC: GPO, 1913.

———. *Census of Population: 1920.* Vol. 3. Washington, DC: GPO, 1922.

———. *Census of Population: 1930.* Vol. 3, pt. 1. Washington, DC: GPO, 1932.

———. *Census of Population: 1940.* Vol. 2, *Characteristics of the Population.* Washington, DC: GPO, 1943.

———. *Census of Population: 1950.* Vol. 2, *Characteristics of the Population.* Washington, DC: GPO, 1952.

———. *Census of Population: 1960.* Vol. 1, *Characteristics of the Population.* Washington, DC: GPO, 1963.

———. *Census of Population: 1970.* Vol. 1, pt. 15, *Characteristics of the Population.* Washington, DC: GPO, 1973.

US Commission on Civil Rights. *Cairo, Illinois: A Symbol of Racial Polarization.* Washington, DC: n.p., 1973.

———. *Hearing before the United States Commission on Civil Rights.* Cairo, IL, March 23–25, 1972.

US Commission on Human Relations. *Tenth Biennial Report.* Chicago: n.p., 1963.

US Congress, Senate Appropriations Committee. *Taxpayer Assistance and Com-*

pliance Programs: Hearings before the Subcommittee of the Department of the Treasury, U.S. Postal Service, and General Government Appropriations, 93rd Cong., 1st Sess. Washington, DC: GPO, 1973.

US Sanitary Commission. *The U.S. Sanitary Commission in the Valley of the Mississippi, during the War of the Rebellion, 1861–1866: Final Report of Dr. J. S. Newberry.* Cleveland, OH: Fairbanks, Benedict, 1871.

University of Illinois. *Transactions of the Board of Trustees.* Urbana: University of Illinois, 1958.

Van Deburg, William L. *New Day in Babylon: The Black Power Movement and American Culture, 1965–1975.* Chicago: University of Chicago Press, 1992.

Voegeli, Jacque. *Free but Not Equal: The Midwest and the Negro during the Civil War.* Chicago: University of Chicago Press, 1967.

Walker, Lucius. "IFCO and the Crisis of American Society." In *Black Manifesto: Religion, Racism, and Reparations,* edited by Robert S. Lecky and Elliott Wright, 133–39. New York: Sheed & Ward, 1969.

Ward, Stephen. "The Third World Women's Alliance: Black Feminist Radicalism and Black Power Politics." In *The Black Power Movement: Rethinking the Civil Rights–Black Power Era,* edited by Peniel E. Joseph, 119–44. New York: Routledge, 2006.

Washington, James Melvin. *Frustrated Fellowship: The Black Baptist Quest for Social Power.* Macon, GA: Mercer University Press, 1986.

Washington, Joseph R. *The Politics of God.* Boston: Beacon Cross, 1967.

Washington, Michael. "The Stirrings of the Modern Civil Rights Movement in Cincinnati, Ohio, 1943–1953." In *Groundwork: Local Black Freedom Movements in America,* edited by Jeanne Theoharis and Komozi Woodard, 215–34. New York: New York University Press, 2005.

Wells-Barnett, Ida B. "A Red Record: Tabulated Statistics and Alleged Causes of Lynchings in the United States, 1892, 1893, 1894." In *Selected Works of Ida B. Wells-Barnett,* comp. Trudier Harris. New York: Oxford University Press, 1991.

———. "How Enfranchisement Stops Lynchings." *Original Rights* magazine, June 1910.

Wendt, Simon. *The Spirit and the Shotgun: Armed Resistance and the Struggle for Civil Rights.* Gainesville: University Press of Florida, 2007.

West, Cornel. *Prophesy Deliverance! An Afro-American Revolutionary Christianity.* Louisville, KY: Westminster John Knox Press, 1982.

Wheeler, Joanne. "Together in Egypt: A Pattern of Race Relations in Cairo, Illinois, 1865–1915." In *Toward a New South? Studies in Post–Civil War Southern Communities,* edited by Orville Vernon Burton and Robert C. McMath, 103–34. Westport, CT: Greenwood Press, 1982.

White, E. Frances. "Africa on My Mind: Gender, Counter Discourse and African-American Nationalism." *Journal of Women's History* 2 (Spring 1990): 73–97.

Williams, Daniel K. *God's Own Party: The Making of the Christian Right.* New York: Oxford University Press, 2010.

Williams, Jakobi. *From the Bullet to the Ballot: The Illinois Chapter of the Black Panther Party and Racial Coalition Politics in Chicago.* Chapel Hill: University of North Carolina Press, 2013.

Williams, Johnny E. *African American Religion and the Civil Rights Movement in Arkansas.* Jackson: University Press of Mississippi, 2003.

———. "Linking Beliefs to Collective Action: Politicized Religious Beliefs and the Civil Rights Movement." *Sociological Forum* 17 (June 2002): 203–22.

———. "Vanguards of Hope: The Role of Culture in Mobilizing African American Women's Social Activism in Arkansas." *Sociological Spectrum* 24 (2004): 129–56.

Williams, Rhonda Y. "Black Women, Urban Politics, and Engendering Black Power." In *The Black Power Movement: Rethinking the Civil Rights–Black Power Era,* edited by Peniel E. Joseph, 79–104. New York: Routledge, 2006.

———. *The Politics of Public Housing: Black Women's Struggles against Urban Inequality.* New York: Oxford University Press, 2004.

Williams, Yohuru. *Black Politics/White Power: Civil Rights, Black Power, and the Black Panthers in New Haven.* St. James, NY: Brandywine Press, 2000.

Wilmore, Gayraud S., ed. *African American Religious Studies: An Interdisciplinary Anthology.* 4th ed. Durham: Duke University Press, 2000.

———. *Black Religion and Black Radicalism: An Interpretation of the Religious History of Afro-American People.* 2nd ed. Maryknoll, NY: Orbis Books, 1983.

———. *Pragmatic Spirituality: The Christian Faith through an Africentric Lens.* New York: New York University Press, 2004.

Wirt, Frederick M. "The Changing Social Bases of Regionalism: Peoples, Cultures, and Politics in Illinois." In *Diversity, Conflict, and State Politics: Regionalism in Illinois,* edited by Peter F. Nardulli. Urbana: University of Illinois Press, 1989.

Woodard, Komozi. "Amiri Baraka, the Congress of African People, and Black Power Politics from the 1961 United Nations Protest to the 1972 Gary Convention." In *The Black Power Movement: Rethinking the Civil Rights–Black Power Era,* edited by Peniel E. Joseph, 55–77. New York: Routledge, 2006.

———. *A Nation within a Nation: Amiri Baraka (LeRoi Jones) and Black Power Politics.* Chapel Hill: University of North Carolina Press, 1999.

———. "It's Nation Time in NewArk: Amiri Baraka and the Black Power Experiment in Newark, New Jersey." In *Freedom North: Black Freedom Struggles outside the South, 1940–1980,* edited by Jeanne Theoharis and Komozi Woodard, 287–313. New York: Palgrave Macmillan, 2003.

Woodson, Carter G. *The History of the Negro Church.* Washington, DC: Associated Publishers, 1945.

Wormer, Maxine E. *Alexander County, Illinois, 1850 Census.* Thomson, IL: Heritage House, n.d.

Wright, George C. *Life behind the Veil: Blacks in Louisville, Kentucky, 1865–1930.* Baton Rouge: Louisiana State University Press, 1985.

Wright, Terri K. "The Upper Circle: The History, Society and Architecture of Nineteenth-Century Cairo, Illinois." PhD diss., Southern Illinois University Carbondale, 1995.

Zinn, Howard. *SNCC: The New Abolitionists.* Boston: Beacon Press, 1964.

Index

Civil Rights and the Struggle for Black Equality
in the Twentieth Century

Series Editors
Steven F. Lawson, Rutgers University
Cynthia Griggs Fleming, University of Tennessee
Hasan Kwame Jeffries, Ohio State University

Freedom's Main Line: The Journey of Reconciliation and the Freedom Rides
Derek Charles Catsam

Gateway to Equality: Black Women and the Struggle for Economic Justice in St. Louis
Keona K. Ervin

*The Chicago Freedom Movement: Martin Luther King Jr. and Civil Rights Activism
in the North*
edited by Mary Lou Finley, Bernard LaFayette Jr., James R. Ralph Jr., and Pam Smith

The Struggle Is Eternal: Gloria Richardson and Black Liberation
Joseph R. Fitzgerald

*Subversive Southerner: Anne Braden and the Struggle for Racial Justice in the Cold
War South*
Catherine Fosl

Constructing Affirmative Action: The Struggle for Equal Employment Opportunity
David Hamilton Golland

An Unseen Light: Black Struggles for Freedom in Memphis, Tennessee
edited by Aram Goudsouzian and Charles W. McKinney Jr.

River of Hope: Black Politics and the Memphis Freedom Movement, 1865–1954
Elizabeth Gritter

The Dream Is Lost: Voting Rights and the Politics of Race in Richmond, Virginia
Julian Maxwell Hayter

Sidelined: How American Sports Challenged the Black Freedom Struggle
Simon Henderson

Becoming King: Martin Luther King Jr. and the Making of a National Leader
Troy Jackson

Civil Rights in the Gateway to the South: Louisville, Kentucky, 1945–1980
Tracy E. K'Meyer

In Peace and Freedom: My Journey in Selma
Bernard LaFayette Jr. and Kathryn Lee Johnson

Democracy Rising: South Carolina and the Fight for Black Equality since 1865
Peter F. Lau

Civil Rights Crossroads: Nation, Community, and the Black Freedom Struggle
Steven F. Lawson

Selma to Saigon: The Civil Rights Movement and the Vietnam War
Daniel S. Lucks

In Remembrance of Emmett Till: Regional Stories and Media Responses to the Black Freedom Struggle
Darryl Mace

Freedom Rights: New Perspectives on the Civil Rights Movement
edited by Danielle L. McGuire and John Dittmer

This Little Light of Mine: The Life of Fannie Lou Hamer
Kay Mills

After the Dream: Black and White Southerners since 1965
Timothy J. Minchin and John A. Salmond

Faith in Black Power: Religion, Race, and Resistance in Cairo, Illinois
Kerry Pimblott

Fighting Jim Crow in the County of Kings: The Congress of Racial Equality in Brooklyn
Brian Purnell

Roy Wilkins: The Quiet Revolutionary and the NAACP
Yvonne Ryan

James and Esther Cooper Jackson: Love and Courage in the Black Freedom Movement
Sara Rzeszutek

Thunder of Freedom: Black Leadership and the Transformation of 1960s Mississippi
Sue [Lorenzi] Sojourner with Cheryl Reitan

For a Voice and the Vote: My Journey with the Mississippi Freedom Democratic Party
Lisa Anderson Todd